Lost Levant

St Catherine's Monastery, Sinai

Lost Levant
A journey of ideas

Rupert de Borchgrave

23
ENVELOPEBOOKS

Published in the UK and the USA in 2025 by EnvelopeBooks

12 Wellfield Avenue, London N10 2EA, England
116 West 73rd Street, New York, NY 10023

www.envelopebooks.co.uk

© Rupert de Borchgrave

Rupert de Borchgrave asserts his right to be identified as the Author of the Work in accordance with the Copyright, Designs and Patents Act 1988.

Stephen Games asserts his right to be identified as the Editor and Designer of the Work in accordance with the Copyright, Designs and Patents Act 1988.

Cover design by Stephen Games | Booklaunch

Main text set in Quadraat 10.1/12.4

All rights reserved. No part of this book may be reproduced, stored or transmitted in any form or by any means, electronic or mechanical, including photocopying, recording or by any information storage-and-retrieval system, without the written permission of the publisher, nor be otherwise circulated in any form of binding or cover other than that in which it is published and without a similar condition being imposed on any subsequent purchaser.

A CIP catalogue record for this title is available from the British Library and the Library of Congress Cataloging in Publication Data.

EnvelopeBooks 23
ISBN 9781915023513

For Mariam

Acknowledgements

Alex Paseau, Avi Shlaim, Charlie Gammell, Christopher de Bellaigue, Dominic Jacquesson, Eugene Rogan, Gagik Stepan-Sarkissian, Hossam Shobokshi, James Howard-Johnston, Jason Pack, Jeffrey A. Gray, Jen Hornsby, John A. White, John Feehan, Justin Butcher, Justin Priestmonk, Marius Kociejowski, Martin Brons, Michael Gabbay, Moshé Machover, Mungo McCosh, Nicholas Shakespeare, Paul Laikin, Pavlos Eleftheriadis, Richard Dumbrill, Snjezana Lelas, Stephen Games, Stipo Androvic, Thomas Cull, Tom Burgis, Tom Sinclair, Vicky Rangeley-Wilson and Victor Garrabou von Trotha.

Peregrinations

Avignon
Rome
Naples
Trinacria
Trapani
Agrigento
Tripolitania
Cyrenaica
Siwa
Alexandria
Cairo
Sinai
Jordan
Damascus
Southern Syria
Deir Mar Musa
Aleppo
Northern Syria
Antioch
Edessa
Diyarbakir
Ararat
Anatolia
Aegean

Essays

Avignon	1
Origins of a journey	3
Makropoulos	5
Dulce et decorum est	7
Flow	8
The riddle of the mechanism	11
The ecstasy of St Teresa	15
Rome	17
The silence of the transcendent	21
Why do people pray?	25
The quest for perfect love	27
Naples	29
Love as the supreme categorical activity	30
Ama et fac quod vis	31
The mystery of the present instant	36
The insufficiency of Epicureanism	40
Trinacria	44
Archimedes and infinity	45
The death of Archimedes	48
The transcendence of nature	52
Trapani	63
Existential freedom	66
The wisdom of Father Gregory	68
Agrigento	75
Solitude	76
Eros	77
Fidelity	78
The charm of Albert Camus	81
Tripolitania	87

Cyrenaica	102
The Green Book	107
The Green Book continued	109
Siwa	117
The eternal contingencies	123
Alexandria	131
The wisdom of Martin Savage	132
Chatwinism	133
Logos	144
The desert a city	149
Cairo	153
Demography and development	162
Anscombe versus Azhar	173
Oriental Weavers versus Axminster	176
The insufficiency of materialism	179
Sinai	186
Heterodoxy	191
Particularity	196
Platonism	198
St Thomas revisited	202
Mystical Epicureanism	203
Jordan	205
From hijra to crusade	211
Maimonides and Israel	222
A Common Word	231
Damascus	236
Consumption versus craftsmanship	241
Economic haecceity	244
The paradox of Zeno's gadget	249
Time and freedom	256
Debt and interest	262
Efficiency versus distribution	264
Holy Mother Earth	268
Political values and international capital flows	270
Thieves of State	274
Southern Syria	280
Dream, death and the soul	288

Deir Mar Musa	292
The wisdom of Father Paolo	294
Babylon and Greece	302
Aleppo	307
Northern Syria	319
Syrian Civil War	334
Antioch	339
Pagans and Christians	349
Ketman and the Pill of Murti-Bing	356
Edessa	360
Annihilation of the Ottoman Armenians	361
Diyarbakir	385
Ararat	398
First Armenian Republic	415
Anatolia	421
Kemalism and modernism	432
Aegean	436
Parousia	441
Afterword	447
Bibliography	451
Index	457

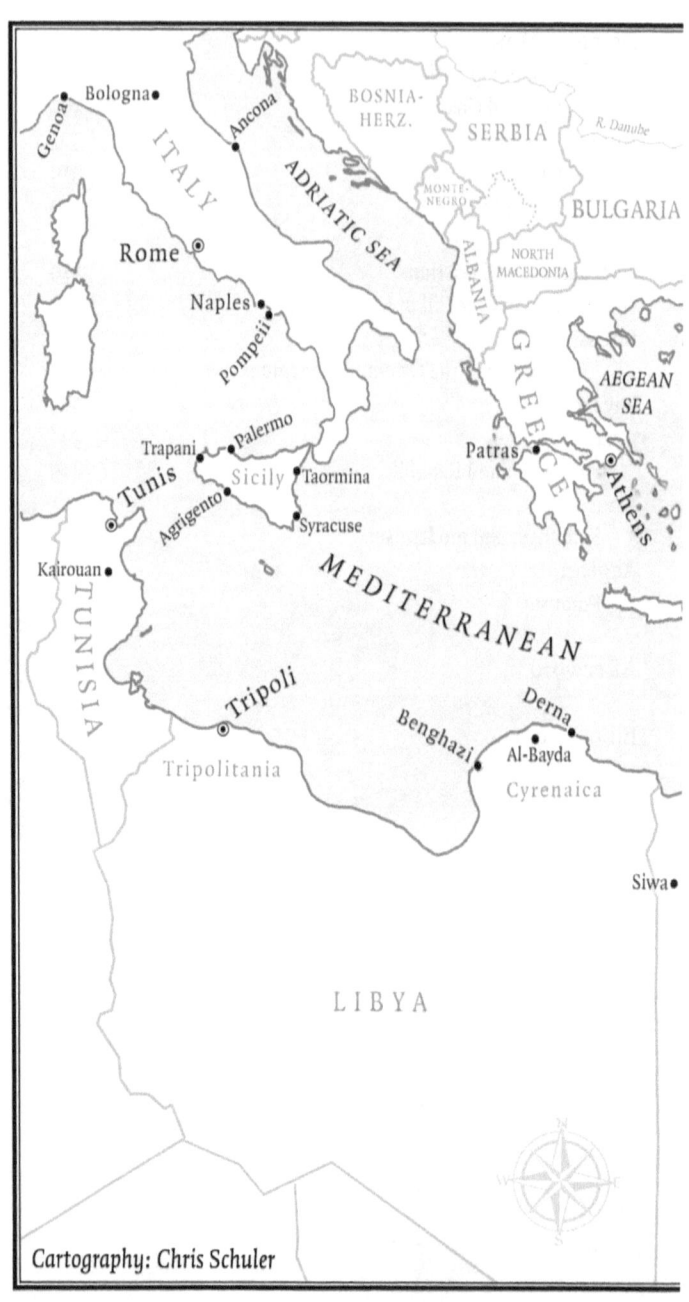
Cartography: Chris Schuler

Avignon

MONDAY 17 MARCH 2003 | PARIS
'Farewell, Sweetpea,' I say, kissing my tearful girlfriend goodbye as she leaves for work. Pyrrha is going to hold the fort, tiny as it is: water the plants, collect the post and be at the end of the telephone in case of disaster. After attending to some last-minute necessities, and deciding on the right amount of cash for emergencies (I follow a friend's sage advice and take very little), I post books to Father Justin in Sinai and James Mackay in Hatay to cover that other more serious hazard, namely running out of reading material.

At eleven o'clock I turn the key in the door of my Pimlico flat and walk over Vauxhall Bridge. I am carrying a green rucksack, a yoga mat and, slung over my shoulder, a large stripy canvas bag full of books. Despite trying to keep to eight kilograms—Roman soldiers on the march never carried more than ten per cent of their bodyweight—my bags are too heavy. But the first steps of a long solitary journey are bound to be tremulous and there is no time now to repack. Setting off for Mount Ararat via Sicily and Tunis, I take the train to Waterloo. By the Eurostar terminal I buy *The Independent* and browse the articles discussing weapons inspectors, international law and the British government's support for the planned American invasion of Iraq.

The Eurostar is wonderful. Only the briefest of torments and you cross to the continent at speed. Soon the train is ascending from the depths of the bedrock and you know your chances are good. No Bernoulli Effect. No circling in a spacecraft above crowded cities. No faith in the rivets of an unknown welder. I think of the family who escaped boarding doomed flight TWA 800 because there was no space in the hold for the coffins of their recently departed relatives: saved from death by the dead.

Arriving in Paris on a spring afternoon, I walk down the hill to Opéra wondering how I am going to carry this deadweight all the way to Ararat. I take the metro to Pereire and find a bar on the square. As I watch the world go by, the Cabinet in London is deciding that owing to France's statement that 'there are no grounds for waging war to ... disarm Iraq' the diplomatic process is over and Parliament will be asked to endorse military action. As I observe the busy streets in the evening light, I am unsure whether to feel liberated or fearful about embarking on a six-month pilgrimage. But there is nothing like the pleasure of simple French indulgence: croque and bière blonde. As the alcohol takes effect, it occurs to me how strange it seems: all these people rushing pensively home, not knowing quite what day it is, or even possibly which year they are in, only to set off again in the opposite direction in the morning. I sit on the brink of total freedom with no greater obligation hanging over me than to find a place to sleep and decide where to go next.

I buy flowers for my hosts, Giles and Anna, student friends and now career diplomats. After cooing over their newly born son, we launch into a furious discussion about the legitimacy of the imminent invasion of Iraq. Giles is loyal to the government he serves and advocates for the official British position. Having participated in street protests against the war, which culminated in the million-strong 'Stop the War Coalition' demonstration in London on 15 February, my views are sharply opposed to his. Giles says that Iraq is believed to have stockpiles of anthrax and refers to the arguments about democracies not going to war against each other. I argue that an illegal war is state-sanctioned murder: there is no firm evidence that Iraq possesses weapons of mass destruction, nor that the Iraqi government has links to Islamic terror groups. Can a diplomatic solution not be found to remove Saddam through some sort of plea bargain without killing tens of thousands of innocent Iraqis? Is this invasion not going to destabilise the country and lead to many more years of conflict?

Origins of a journey
What is the purpose of this 'Grand Tour'? To escape the domestic project on a shoestring? To cling to youth and slow the years as they cascade over each other at an ever-accelerating rate? To satisfy wanderlust and the restless urge to see the world? Certainly all of these. Weary of putting numbers in boxes in drab provincial towns, baulking at the prospect of shackled domesticity and never having had the chance to escape the taut bonds of our damp, cramped northern isle, I decided to slip the noose. It was my thirty-second year. 'You want to find yourself?' a colleague asked. He pulled me in front of a mirror and jibbed: 'There you are! Now get back to work!' But it was inspiration and enchantment I sought, not just escape. The quest was more for Calypso than Penelope; the spirit of it more Gilgamesh than Odysseus.

Friends sent me farewell greetings. 'There is something deep and certainly historic about our need to wander. By travelling, we establish contact with parts of ourselves that get lost in the passage of ordinary stationary life,' wrote one. 'How envious I am of you, to make a journey across the 'Levant'. Ah that term conjures up a long past era, when European gentlemen explored the 'mysterious Orient'. I hope you record your impressions, for gone are them days!' said another. Surely, I thought, they always were?

Taking local public transport, I set off to explore the eastern Mediterranean and its hinterland, from Sicily to Cyrenaica, from Siwa to Syria, from Aleppo to Ararat. There may be nothing mysterious about 'the Orient'. But travelling allows one to see life and society from a different vantage point. Where better than the lands of the source of our civilisation to imagine the distant past and gain perspective on the follies of the moderns? Where better than the Levant to discover secret places whose pre-modern spirit is preserved? I planned of course to report my impressions, like Darwin collecting specimens on the Beagle.

Woven into the diary of a physical voyage, recording places visited, people encountered and friendships made, this book relates a journey of ideas through a series of essays. About what? Love and money, since these are the most enduring of human motivations. Then there is philosophy and history too —between the dialogues, the landscapes and the ruins. This book is a book of books that represents a quest for universal humanism: Western cultural history is reinterpreted as a philosophy of liberation that finds its expression in a theory of political economy called 'Epicurean economics'. But it is not an easy task to integrate a total worldview. For in all the currents of human thought, there are no complete systems that make sense of all experience. That is why people are fond of slogans and pre-packaged ideologies, not to mention all the distractions the modern world provides in 'getting on with life': it stops them from having to think.

TUESDAY 18 MARCH | AVIGNON
During the night, the American President has delivered the final ultimatum to Saddam Hussein to leave Iraq within forty-eight hours. But the war is forgotten in the morning and we talk about my travel plans over breakfast. After bidding farewell, I take the metro to Gare de Lyon. Paris goes about its business but there is a distinct feeling of abnormality in the air. The train to Avignon is delayed. So I find a brasserie in the shopping mall over the walkway and order steak tartare. Looking through the window at a solitary plane tree as it catches the light, I begin to read one of the books of heterodox economics I have brought with me.

As the TGV speeds south, the House of Commons debates Iraq while the United Nations and International Atomic Energy Agency inspection teams complete their evacuation from that tragic country. Inside the city walls of Avignon, I take a room at the Hôtel des Arts and experience for the first time on this journey that sense of relief which comes from having a quiet, comfortable and inexpensive haven in which to lie down and rest. The warm air and the soft stone buildings and the birds chattering in the evening sunshine tell me that I have already escaped the darkness and frigid anxiety of the North. Walking around the city's cobbled streets and squares, I think of Youssef Chahine's film *Destiny* about the world of

Averroes and Maimonides, advocates for individual freedom and humanism, and imagine myself transported to mediaeval Cordoba. In place of the Andalucian Mezquita, I admire the carved portals of the Palais des Papes and look over the grey-green Rhône from the hanging gardens of the Rocher des Doms.

In the absence of any troubadours, I find a theatre venue, Salle Benoit XII, and listen to a rendition of Shakespeare's sonnets sung by one Norah Krief. Surely no better source for musical invention than the lines of the bard? What does it say about England that, despite the achievements of our poets, we never developed a tradition of lieder, not to mention the sonata or the other classical forms? Has the continuous banging of those dark satanic mills drowned out the still small voice? In a side street near the waters of the Sorgue, I find a bistro. Thinking of the poems, I lament the shackles our world machine seems to place on the full expression of our innate gifts. Yet as I sip my digestif, the House of Commons votes that the United Kingdom should use 'all means necessary' to ensure the disarmament of Iraq, citing that 'Iraq's weapons of mass destruction and ... non-compliance with Security Council Resolutions pose a threat to international peace and security'. Is not the legitimacy of Parliamentary approval still bogus in the case of an unjust war?

Makropoulos
We should not ask whether 'to be or not to be', as the return to empty nothingness cannot be avoided. Nor can we expect to achieve a perfect state of subjective experience: ecstasy can only ever be fleeting. The question is what to *do* with the narrow window of incarnation the cosmos grants us between two states of annihilation. What is worth doing and why? In the 1930s it was discovered that animals would work to stimulate the pleasure centres of the brain. But until now, neuroscientists have failed to provide a non-circular explanation of this phenomenon. The pursuit of the pleasure state as a goal in itself is a dead end, for inactivity is impossible. The conclusion is that only actions not states can be meaningful.

In *The Makropoulos Case*, the philosopher Bernard Williams suggests that the challenge for every human being is to find activities worth engaging in entirely for their own sake. Following Immanuel Kant, he calls these activities *categorical actions* to distinguish them from actions whose value derives only from some end they are the means of achieving. Inspired by Janacek's opera *Elina Makropoulos*, and in opposition to Miguel de Unamuno, Williams discusses the inherent desirability of mortality. Born in the sixteenth century, Makropoulos has taken the elixir of life and continues to live as though she were forty-two years old, the age at which she drank the potion. The opera is set in the 1920s, by which time Makropoulos is over 300 years old. Having seen generations of friends age and die and having experienced everything to the point of repetition and ennui, and despite being healthy and not in any physical pain, Makropoulos decides that she wants to die—even *needs intensely* to die—and takes her own life. Yet it is the infinitude of annihilation that makes life so precious.

People talk about reaching the end of their useful lives. But is being alive not sufficiently useful unto itself? Why could Makropoulos not have continued to engage in categorical activities that gave her life meaning? Could it be that continuing to find meaningfulness takes a strength of *will*, of which we are only born with a finite quantity? Could it be the loss of that will that gets us in the end? Or is that will rooted in the body, its loss the inevitable accompaniment to the body's physical decay? If we are to survive our deaths, then paradise must come equipped with sufficient categorical activities to maintain this will for eternity. On retiring, Williams took up piano playing: sadly for him his body expired before his will. But if Makropoulos had been a pianist, could she not have always found another piece to master? Had Johann Sebastian Bach lived 300 years, would he not have had the skill and imagination to continue creating masterworks?

Wednesday 19 March | Avignon
It is delightful to wake up in the southern sunshine. I buy *The Guardian Europe* on Place de l'Horloge and follow the latest

developments. The Foreign Secretary has resigned in protest over the war. There is much speculation about the horrors of a siege of Baghdad. The supplement contains email transcripts of the peace activist Rachel Corrie, killed by an Israeli bulldozer while protesting against the destruction of Palestinian houses. Restless, I explore the gothic mass of the Palais des Papes, where popes kept nightingales in vast bedrooms during the period of the Avignon papacy. The spaces and fine masonry are impressive. But it feels bare and unlived in, which it has not really been since the end of the Western Schism in 1417.

I visit the Petit Palais with its mediaeval paintings and Botticellis and walk along the ramparts. Outside the museum is a stone ramp that makes the perfect place to lie on one's back in the warmth, freed from any duties or the tedious obligations of money making and object accumulation. The 'great world machine', the pressure to conform, is left behind and the feeling is intoxicating. The evening sun radiates in perfect silence, with birds singing and small gusts of wind blowing around the leaves, high above the madding crowd in the dressed stone of a vanished mediaeval world. After some time, I walk down to the famous Pont d'Avignon to watch the scullers gliding past and explore the streets in search of fondue.

Dulce et decorum est
How tragic that a well-meaning young woman such as Rachel Corrie should have her life pointlessly terminated. Of the merits of the Palestinian cause, equal rights for the Jewish and non-Jewish inhabitants of former Mandatory Palestine, there can surely be no doubt. But how could such a cause be worth the sacrifice of one's own life? Why die for the sake of an abstract and uncertain re-equilibration of political forces? During the First World War, as in the Napoleonic wars, Britain required that every man do his duty: *Dulce et decorum est, pro patria mori*. A century later, the inexplicable insanity of that slaughter still stands over us, the watershed of the idea of progress, the death of European civilisation, the benchmark of follies.

In the New Testament we are told that 'a man can have no

greater love than to lay down his life for his friends'. But extreme altruism runs against our instincts. In the absence of any firm proof of life after death, can that ever be rational? If our ethical framework is based on virtue, on what is good for us, can there ever be a moral justification for paying the price —even the ultimate price—for someone else's folly? Should we not aim to live quiet, self-contained lives, keeping our heads below the parapet, firmly out of trouble? And if we all did so, would we not minimise the total amount of circulating folly and hence the likelihood of causing trouble to someone else? Is there not something noble and also naturally rational in the instinct for private self-preservation? Must the quest for perfect love require communitarian self-sacrifice?

Thursday 20 March | Villeneuve

I walk over the bridge to Villeneuve and buy a box of strawberries at the street market below the tower of Philippe le Bel. If Avignon is grand and bustling, Villeneuve is serene and tranquil. The town has winding lanes with stone houses whose pale green doors and shutters sit easily with the lavenders and perennials of Provence. Up on the hill is the Fort Saint-André, built to protect the Kingdom of France from the Holy Roman Empire. Part of the fort is preserved as a house with a charming garden, while the outer walls encircle a wild ruin with views across the Rhône and the Carthusian abbey below.

After eating steak on the square, I continue south to Nice while 'shock and awe' is unleashed on Iraq. I find the apartment of some other friends, former colleagues, and climb the Colline du Château before joining them for fish soup on the Rue d'Angleterre. There has long been a resident English community along the Riviera. Graham Greene travelled the world and chose to live in Antibes. Nowadays however, the Côte d'Azur has become unaffordable as the locals compete for space with the international kleptocracy.

Flow

In his book *Beyond Boredom and Anxiety*, a riposte to Skinner's deterministic polemic *Beyond Freedom and Dignity*, the psychologist Mihály Csíkszentmihályi argues that happiness lies in a mental state he calls 'flow'. If one is completely absorbed in a focused activity, mind and body are seamlessly joined in a state of high awareness: the self is transcended while time is suspended. When fully engaged in an activity such as playing the piano, the person is calm, yet alert and energetically inspired. Performers at peak flow embody the music spontaneously flowing through their instrument, while experiencing an ecstatic state of integration and internal peace.

Flow theory contrasts with the hedonistic theory of mechanistic psychology that focuses on how reward and pleasure determine the value of outcomes and motivate behaviour. Mihály believes that self-actualisation through active flow is more conducive to happiness than hedonistic stimulation. In flow, the activity is an end in itself rather than an instrumental means to obtain valued goals.

Paradoxically, the essence of hedonism is not so much 'thrills' but something more akin to 'abandonment' or Baudelairean oblivion, which is perhaps not so different from the detachment from the self that one experiences in flow. Hedonists think they can find what they are looking for in a pleasure object when what they really need is a flow activity. Or perhaps another way of describing it is that the peak flow experience is what our motivational system has been designed for, while hedonism is the short circuit: apples versus sugary sweets; playing a Beethoven sonata versus chemically induced intoxication. Perhaps it is a fact of our construction that not to be engaged in a flow-generating categorical activity is the root of all our ills?

Flow theory can be traced back to the writings of Epicurus. These ideas matter because our understanding of human motivation lies at the root of our economic and political structures. Flow theory and its historical antecedents are not so much psychological theories as a political programme. The utilitarian theories that underpin our social institutions are as flawed as the psychological theory that spawned them. Economic theory is based on consumer choice, the assumption that creating more choices must expand freedoms. But the notion of consumption is rooted in the hedonistic model of the subject as recipient rather than as a person engaged in an activity for its own sake. The lacuna in the utilitarian calculus of *homo economicus* is that the cost of non-existence is infinite. Imagine if our economic and political structures were redesigned to maximise total peak flow instead of the slippery notion of utility: what would they look like?

Friday 21 March | Roquebrune

After yoga at dawn, I walk to the train station and think of the working world I have left behind. To alleviate the boredom of manipulating the symbols of a programming language on a screen, I used to write poems. I wonder if the joy experienced by those people capable of generating original ideas is not greater than the ecstasies of Parnassus and St Teresa. Alas it is so difficult to tap the veins of creativity! To write a sonnet requires a procedure: one idea per quatrain, finding the scan with the rhymes as hooks. Musical forms are the same: the computer can write a fugue or sonata or symphony in any given style. But procedures that ape traditional forms are empty of artistic content: the computer can neither invent a form nor find the zest of deviation that brings forms to life and distinguishes the works of the masters.

Perhaps there is more art in the Côte d'Azur railway, as it passes through tunnels from one aloe clad beach to the next? Once the fortress of a Genoese pirate, Monaco is now a refuge for tax exiles and gamblers, though it is still beautiful on its rock. In the village of Beausoleil above Monte Carlo, the old paths remain, tracing the lines of the streams off the hills. I climb up the Chemin du Tenao and listen to the spring chorus of the frogs in the meadow before walking down towards Roquebrune. At a certain moment on the footpath, you leave behind the world of cars and offices and apartment blocks, and suddenly taste *merazea* in your nostrils—the smell of seaweed and salty waves breaking over the rocks. I sit in the sunshine eating Moroccan merguez sausages from the beach restaurant on the Golfe Bleu and examine my volumes of heterodox economics, from J.K. Galbraith to Robert Heilbroner and Amartya Sen.

As Baghdad is pounded into submission by the self-proclaimed 'defender of liberty', the high priest of Mammon, guardian of the world machine, I imagine the world of colonial Oran that Albert Camus conveys in his direct prose, with sun, sea and carefree women. At that time endemic pessimism was the legacy of world wars and privation. Nowadays, the fruits of economic progress have eliminated material discomforts in the developed world. But our existential freedoms remain just as elusive, and pessimism has been replaced by distraction. When the light fades and the cold air chills my fingers, I take the train back to Nice.

The riddle of the mechanism
On the face of it, the liberal economic system promotes individual freedom through innovation and the maximisation of productive efficiency. Allocating capital to maximise returns, continuously upgrading the capital stock, globalising supply chains to integrate low wage labour pools, and developing new products—from the high-speed train to the digital camera—have created an elaborate profusion of globally competitive goods markets. But as productivity has increased in the West, working hours have increased too, while access to well compensated work has diminished. The average American need only work five hours per week to enjoy the same economic value of consumption as in the 1950s. But having a job or a business requires working ever longer hours to remain competitive. Median wage stagnation since the 1980s implies that most people only see the gains of growth in the availability of cheap goods.

Despite the efficiency of the liberal economy, we seem to be locked into a mechanism of ever-accelerating consumption that prevents us from enjoying the time dividend of increased productivity, while also increasing the intensity of the competitive struggle to gain assets or grow household equity. This *mechanism* is the forced Faustian trade of each person's time for wealth, objects, security and social position. Everywhere intelligent people graduate from universities and rush to *get on*, to work for an unknown purpose, because the cultural ley lines of their environment require them to. Yet increasingly they find that they are running to stand still, that they cannot reach a point of financial independence.

Economic coggery—envelopment by the mechanism—cannot easily be escaped. Freedom lies in economic self-sufficiency. But the freedom to stand above the bonds of coggery requires wealth, and where does such wealth come from but the competitive struggle and the domination of others? The forces that make us the servants of capital in this battle are the same natural processes that perpetuate our genes and make our individuality irrelevant. The mechanism is the translation of the biological forces of natural selection into the context of a modern industrialised society. In *The Hidden Dimension*, Edward Hall discusses behavioural experiments relating to the allocation of space. Put a hundred rats in a box, and after a period of time, the space will divide into one third for the ninety servants, one third for nine barons, and one third for the king. Under the guise of market efficiency, King Rat commands capital that commands labour.

Economic freedom for the individual requires ownership of some assets. But as globalism proceeds, capital concentrates and the majority who lack assets lose their freedom. Capital needs people who sell their labour to the market and want to consume; who wish to be distracted by the adoption of new needs and whose tastes can be shaped by marketing like iron filings by a magnet; in short, who accept to become expendable cogs. The masses cooperate because they have no choice. But in the absence of owning assets, the need to earn a living means there is no escape from the mechanism. Its reach is everywhere.

Even the academy has been swallowed up: thoughts must be quantified, packaged and sold in the marketplace for ideas. The mechanism has no time for non-commercial thought or reflection-for-its-own-sake. But life is too short and too precious to allow the full elaboration of its meanings to be compromised by the reach of the mechanism. Is it not better to understand the universe in the beauty of a painting or a fugue or the frogs of Tenao?

SATURDAY 22 MARCH | GENOA

After visiting the Lascaris Palace, with its baroque painted ceilings and Flemish tapestries, I proceed to Ventimiglia. From the station I walk across the Squarciafichi pedestrian bridge past the swans and fishermen wading in the Roya. At the beach the river is cut off from the sea by a bank of gravel, except for a narrow turbulent channel, the junction of sea and sky, mountain and river. There you can lie on the parapet and feel the sun on your face and the warmth of the stones underneath. The ancient hill town above is reached by a series of brick-paved paths. At its centre lies the cathedral whose thick walls date back to the seventh century. Opposite is another Lascaris Palace. The Genoese Balbi, Counts of Ventimiglia, took the name Lascaris after Guglielmo Balbi married the daughter of the Byzantine emperor in 1269. Their domains were absorbed into Savoia through a further dynastic marriage in 1501. But the link to Byzantium remained. For Genoa became one of the conduits by which the eastern culture of Rum arrived in Italy after the Ottoman conquest, contributing to the acceleration of ideas that we call the Renaissance.

Like most Ligurian towns, Ventimiglia is a warren of alleys and staircases, protection against Barbary corsairs from North Africa. At the top of the hill, next to the twelfth-century church of San Michele, is the convivial communisti bar, identifiable by the imprint of interlocking hands and sleeves beside the entrance. Sitting under the lemon tree on the terrace, I gaze over the Roya valley, at the greenhouses on the hillsides and the shimmering sea beyond. The friendly barman serves potent, aromatic coffee in porcelain cups: there could be no better place to read, write, think and converse. In this era of shallow breathing and speed reading on electronic devices, it is good to open a book in natural light and take notes with pen and paper.

The train passes the fields and shingle beaches of Liguria to Genoa, where I take a room in the Hotel Balbi. At the end of

Via Garibaldi, the street of the baroque palaces, I find Mario Rivaro's restaurant where Severino Maragno has been serving Ligurian cuisine for decades. When you ask Severino for a glass of wine he brings a bottle. When you explain that you only want a glass, he replies that he only charges for what you drink. I order fish soup and goulash, and wonder if I should not stay in Genoa for a month to try everything on the menu. At least that would be one solution to his impenetrable cramped handwriting.

Genoa seems dilapidated compared to her former rival Venice. In the seventeenth century, the wealthy families moved away from the mediaeval city to Via Garibaldi, then with industrialisation into villas on the hillsides with views over the sea. Now Genoa's ancient districts are cut off from the sea by a raised flyover and have become the haunts of prostitutes and touts. Instead of haute mode and culture vultures, you find shops selling halal meat and phone calls to Senegal. Below Piazza Principe is the Ospitale di San Giovanni di Prè, operated by the Hospitallers for the Crusaders. I sit in the bright church and imagine Latin knights pondering their journey to the Levant and planning intrigues with Saracens and Byzantines.

SUNDAY 23 MARCH | ROME

The Rome Express is noisy and close. But the train gives one the feeling of getting something for nothing—of making progress without having to do anything. From Termini I hail a taxi, which passes below the Campidoglio and up the Aventino to the Piazza dei Cavalieri di Malta. Knocking at the entrance of the Benedictine College of Sant'Anselmo, I am warmly greeted by my host Dietrich. The son of a Lutheran pastor, Dietrich is a German scholar-theologian with a broad interest in the history and philosophical interpretation of Christianity. We had met at the Lutheran Hospice in Jerusalem in the year of the Jubilee and become fast friends. Now Dietrich is studying in Rome and has invited me to stay in the seminary guest house. Dietrich shows me the keyhole on the square through which one can see three nations at once—Malta, Italy and the Vatican—with the dome of St Peter's perfectly framed by the open barrel of the lock. The seminary buildings were formerly the Roman lodgings of the Sovereign Military and Hospitaller Order of St John of Jerusalem, more commonly known as the Knights of Malta.

Dietrich is researching Patristics and Coptic Studies at the College, which receives students from all over the world, and especially from Lebanon, Syria and Iraq. Dietrich introduces me to the administrator, Father Roberto, who takes me to one of the guest rooms above the nearby Chiesa Sant' Alessio. After lunch in the refectory, we speak with some visiting Lebanese Maronites who laugh about the apparent 'uselessness' of their theological studies but explain how important it is to their cultural identity. I reply that I am envious of their opportunity to immerse themselves in the mind worlds of the ancients. Dietrich tells me how much he enjoys talking with his fellow students. But most of all he likes to walk through the streets of the eternal city. 'You will see how "inutile" it all is,' he says. But what does utility mean when for millennia the Roman mentality has been to frame the petty concerns of daily life against grand ruins and decay? Dietrich leaves me to walk around Rome. From the Aventino I retrace the ancient path through to the Campidoglio, then to the Quirinale and along to the Piazza San Bernardo.

The ecstasy of St Teresa

In the Cornaro Chapel of Maderno's 1620 Church of Santa Maria della Vittoria stands Bernini's sculpture of St Teresa of Avila impaled by an angel. In her own words: 'Beside me on the left appeared an angel in bodily form, and his face was so aflame that he appeared to be one of the highest ranks of angels. In his hands I saw a great golden spear, and at the iron tip there appeared to be a point of fire. This he plunged into my heart several times. ... When he pulled it out, I felt ... utterly consumed by the great love of God. The pain was so severe that it made me scream aloud. But simultaneously the infinite sweetness caused by this intense pain was so extreme that I wished the pain to last eternally.'

In this state of ecstasy, of maximum peak flow, time is

suspended and non-existence is deferred. Like opium, erotic-romantic love can transform the prosaic into rapturous enchantment; like opium it can destroy a man's soul. But whereas opium taps into the system illicitly, short-circuiting the brain, erotic-romantic love is what the system was put there for: it is the real thing. Physical acts on their own are inert: the mystery of erotic ecstasy is that it requires love to be fulfilled. But that love is elusive, fleeting and inscrutable: perhaps it is only given to a very few? Perhaps that is why erotic love is such a potent force?

If the fulfilment of earthly love is so rare, dependent as it is on the vagaries and mutually incompatible expectations of weak-willed human beings, it is not surprising that throughout the ages people have sought a higher and more dependable power. So the ecstasy of eros has often been linked with mysticism. St John of the Ladder, seventh-century abbot of Sinai, wrote that the fullest love of God should have all the passion of eros. From Dionysian midwinter festivals of sensory indulgence on Mount Parnassus to the mediaeval mystics and renaissance St Teresa, the intensity of divine love has served as a substitute for the embodied human version.

Doubtless Teresa and the mystics had colourful imaginations which they channelled into the intimate knowledge of their own bodies. But you cannot experience the ecstasy of religious feeling with the intensity of St Teresa unless you have the same intensity of religious *belief*. In the absence of that belief, one cannot experience the ecstasy. And what does it mean to believe? People of faith talk about belief as something given to them. Yet it is elementary logic that holding a belief does not make its contents true. As Father Daniel, a Coptic monk from the monastery of al-Suriani in the Wadi Natrun, expressed it, faith is like a fly in a bottle: once released it is gone. The enlightened rational mind cannot return to the bliss of blind faith, and can therefore never experience the ecstasy of St Teresa, however much it would like to.

Rome

MONDAY 24 MARCH TO THURSDAY 27 MARCH

When travelling for an extended period it is natural to alternate between modes. In one, you remain on the move, seeing places quickly, staying in a different bed each night. This is liberating and exhilarating, with its continuous stream of new discoveries, although the perpetual search for good food and a comfortable bed can sometimes become wearying. In the other mode, you decamp, unpack, establish a routine and remain in one place so that, temporarily at least, it feels as though you live there.

The seminary guest house has another visitor. Isabelle is vivacious and entertaining and for these charmed spring days we fall into a routine: coffee on Via Marmorata, lunch in the refectory, and evening discussions with Dietrich and his fellow seminarians. At lunch we sit in silence in the spacious hall while the teacher-monks read the grace in Latin. When the signal is given, we launch into our food at breakneck speed before the plates are cleared away. At least there is time to drink the wine. In the afternoons we explore the eternal city.

From the Colosseum we walk along the Via Sacra to the Curia. On the Palatine Hill we explore the Farnese Gardens—laid out over the remains of the House of Tiberius—and imagine the intrigue of the first-century Principate where Augustus ruled Rome and Livia ruled Augustus. The most astonishing object in the Palatine Museum is the luminous marble Aphrodite whose flowing garments leave one in no less awe than the Renaissance masters these classical works inspired. From the Hill of Palaces we walk past the Theatro di Marcello and Piazza Mattei with its distinctive turtle fountain, to the Pantheon, likewise a reminder of the technical facility and creative inspiration of imperial Rome at the long zenith of its power and prosperity.

From the Spanish Steps we walk down Via delle Quattro Fontane to Santa Maria Maggiore and on to the Chiesa di San Giovanni in Laterano where we pace laps around the cloisters. The Lateran Palace was the seat of the Roman Patriarchate until the fire of 1308 and its evacuation to Avignon. On returning to Rome in 1376, papal government was transferred to the well-fortified Vatican. Yet it was at the Lateran that the Patriarch of Rome assumed the pagan office of Pontifex Maximus, which had itself been adopted by the emperors. After the conversion of Constantine, the Church became exempt from certain taxes and enjoyed sinecures. Later the Papacy stepped into the shoes of the Principate and took over the administration of the Western Roman Empire: Peter and Paul became the new Romulus and Remus.

On another bright spring morning we cross the ancient Ponte Fabricio whose double span has lasted for two millennia. In the streets of Trastevere we fall in with a demonstration organised by the Italian teachers' union against the war in Iraq. We walk up to the Vatican Palace and study the figures in Raphael's fresco, *The School of Athens*. In St Peter's Basilica, we admire Michelangelo's *Pièta* and Bernini's tomb of Pope Alexander VII, who more than anyone else shaped the appearance of the baroque city during his Pontificate from 1655–67. Beneath the bronze canopy of the Baldocchino we peer down at the crypt: the ancient cemetery under the basilica contains bones dated to the first century and venerated since the time of Constantine as the relics of St Peter.

Living in the eternal city would certainly make one susceptible to Roman Catholicism. Yet for all its grandeur, the new basilica of St Peter's is a temple of state power—the successor to Jupiter Capitolinus. Despite the splendour, the Vatican feels no more sacred than Versailles or the Louvre. One cannot help but feel sympathy for the Protestants, confronted with the Borgias, Tetzel and indulgences, so wholly against the teachings of the Master. For the first reformation began in the 1200s with the Fourth Lateran Council when Pope Innocent III dreamed that the mendicant monk Francis would repair the Church, and approved the Franciscan Order. It is a shame that reform could not have been sustained: or perhaps enforced celibacy of the clergy and their professionalisation into an economic class doomed the Papacy from much earlier?

The greater tragedy is that after his German Landesknechte sacked Rome in 1527, the most destructive pillage in the city's history, Charles V failed to put Luther on the papal throne. For if Luther had reformed the Roman church from within, the Latin West could have remained whole and there would have been no wars of religion in the early modern period. Europe would have retained its unity as an integrated bloc, capitalism would have taken a different course, guided perhaps by the precepts of Christian ethics, and English country churches would still carry colourful mediaeval frescos.

FRIDAY 28 MARCH | VIA APPIA ANTICA
On Isabelle's final day in Rome, Dietrich takes us pillion on his motorino past the Baths of Caracalla to visit the Catacombs. For centuries these quarries had been the location of extramural burial sites. During the persecution of Nero the Christian community used the tombs and quarries as refuges. As they believed in the physical resurrection of the body in the afterlife, they dug cavernous subterranean chambers out of the tufa rock to preserve the corpses of the martyrs. The Christians also carved symbols into the soft stone such as CHI RHO and ICHTHOS. Later these underground tombs became pilgrimage sites, and images of the early martyrs were painted on the walls. We descend into the subterranean necropolis from the entrance to the Catacombs of St Sebastian, a Roman soldier executed for defending the Christians.

At the Catacomb of Callixtus, we wander through the passages between the three-layered narrow tombs of the martyrs. All this blood spilled for an idea: nothing changes down the millennia. The persecution of the early church seems to have stiffened Christian resistance to the assimilation of worshiping pagan gods and strengthened their willingness to die for their faith. I think of the soldiers on the Somme waiting to go over the top and wonder if these Christian martyrs experienced the same intensity of terror, or whether the strength of their belief in the afterlife overcame that fear, the psychological mirror to St Teresa.

Dietrich returns to Rome on his motorino while Isabelle and I walk back along the Via Appia Antica. Lined with marble scree and traces of its original polygonal basaltic paving, this was the primary highway of the ancient world that connected Rome to Brindisi and across the Adriatic to the Via Egnatia and Byzantium. The narrow straight route passes classical patrician tombs, shaded by ilex, cedars and pines, and some stretches are far enough away from modern road noise to imagine walking in the footsteps of the ancients.

The road stops at the church of Domine Quo Vadis. By tradition Peter was walking towards Brindisi when at this spot he saw an apparition of Jesus carrying the cross. Peter asks, 'Lord, where are you going?' Jesus tells him that he is travelling to Rome to be crucified again, and thus Peter returned to Rome and to his martyr's death. Scholars agree that if Peter came to Rome, it is unlikely that he arrived before the time of the Neronian Persecution (64–68). So Peter as the founder of the Roman Church must have been honorific or in absentia. In contrast to the ample description of Paul's journeys, there is no textual evidence that Peter ever went to Rome. The Roman Patriarchate appropriated Peter as its founder on the basis of the gospel text that: 'on this rock I will build my church'. The Primacy of Peter was asserted by the second-century writers Irenaeus and Tertullian and was affirmed at the Council of Ephesus in 431. Since Rome was the imperial capital it was natural that the Roman Patriarchate would seek primacy among the original five.

Sad to part after these happy few days, we sit for a while in the church of Santa Maria della Consolazione. Isabelle departs for her flight and I wander back to Sant' Alessio via the Campidoglio, admiring the bronze statue of Marcus Aurelius and the beauty of Michelangelo's conception with its multiple levels and steps. Dietrich invites me to join him with Father Gregory, an Irish Benedictine from Limerick. We pass the evening at the seminary and engage in a well lubricated disquisition on faith, philosophy and monasticism.

The silence of the transcendent

The greatest weapon in the intellectual armoury of Roman Catholicism is the aesthetic. Sitting in the church of Santa Maria della Consolazione at the heart of ancient Rome, one could be forgiven for concluding that beauty entails truth. This plain basilica of sorrows was built next to a plague hospital in the 1590s at the height of the Counter-Reformation. It is overlooked by most visitors to the eternal city where there are so many more important architectural treasures. But it is unusual in having windows behind the altar that flood the chancel with light, symbolic perhaps, of the Christian message that beyond the grave there is light instead of darkness. In this atmosphere of thoughtful consolation, it is tempting to be seduced by that hope.

But God remains silent and beauty does not imply truth. For the fundamental solecism of Christianity has remained unchanged through the centuries: it was there from the start. It is there in the Gospels. Stripped to its essence, Christian doctrine takes the form of a proposition: believe in the Resurrection and you will be saved from annihilation, survive your death and live in a state of eternal blessedness. Christianity is about salvation through faith, and as Paul explains, faith is being certain of what we do not see. To an educated Roman, trained in Greek mathematics and the precepts of rational enquiry, testing hypotheses about nature against the evidence of the senses, this proposition must have seemed absurd.

Did the Resurrection occur? Let us assume that contemporary witnesses believed they saw the risen Jesus. Either the Resurrection occurred and their observations were true; or the witnesses were deceived for whatever cause such as a state of emotional disturbance or other mental predisposition. Given the evidence of our senses today and the available sources of data, we can never have direct knowledge of these distant events. So we can only assign credence to the logical possibilities based on a balance of probabilities. Those who have direct experience of paranormal or supernatural phenomena are more inclined to give the first-century witnesses the benefit of the doubt; while those who do not will conclude that the witnesses were deceived. Personally I have no experience of paranormal or supernatural phenomena. So on the balance of probabilities, I cannot believe that Jesus—or indeed anyone else—came back from the dead.

As David Hume expressed it seventeen centuries later, stating the epistemologically obvious: when presented with what purports to be a miracle—that is, an event that is extremely unlikely to have happened given everything else that one knows about the cosmos: what physicists call a 'seven sigma' event—then one must either revise one's understanding of the cosmos to incorporate that new fact or conclude that there is an alternative explanation that is consistent with the prior understanding of the cosmos. Whether we are talking about muons or the raising of Lazarus, our process of gaining knowledge about the cosmos is the same: there is something fishy about the very concept of so-called miracles.

St Thomas thought as Hume did. Thomas did not accept the proposition of salvation through faith. However much he trusted the testimony of the other apostles he knew that dead men do not walk. According to the Gospel of John, Thomas tells the other disciples that unless he sees the nail marks and imprint of the spear, he will not believe. One week later he is given the evidence of his senses. Jesus says: 'you have believed because you have seen, but how much more blessed are those who believe and have not seen.' Thomas receives special treatment for he gains salvation without having to compromise his rationality. Despite asking for the evidence before revising his theory of the cosmos to incorporate the new datum of the Resurrection, Thomas is saved nonetheless. But the rest of us must take it all on trust. Why should Thomas be privileged in this way? If Thomas was given firm evidence, why should not you or I?

Then there is the retrospective belief problem which troubled the pagan philosophers who analysed Christian doctrine: if salvation and the kingdom of heaven require belief in the Resurrection, what happens to those who died before the events of Calvary? If Christ died to redeem all mankind, are those preceding souls not saved or are they spared the need to believe in order to achieve salvation? Perhaps it is all just mysterious. But there are endless improbable or internally inconsistent ideologies that one could subscribe to. Why Christianity? In logic, any proposition follows from a contradiction.

Saturday 29 March | Colli Albani
Dietrich has another guest for the weekend, Anata, and we set off to explore the Christian sites of Lazio. The Basilica of St Paul's Outside the Walls was constructed by Constantine over the traditional burial place of St Paul. It is the second of the four Major Basilicas that became associated with plenary indulgence in the fourteenth century. Unprotected by the third-century Aurelian walls, the original church was sacked in the Saracen raid of 846 and later destroyed by fire. So the present building is an elaborate nineteenth-century reconstruction, with an elegant cloister before a portico of Corinthian columns and lavish pediment. The interior resembles Sant' Apollinare in Ravenna, whose geometric colonnade culminates in a grand apse mosaic, although rather less airy. The mosaics are beautifully executed. But the church lacks that sense of continuity and contact with the distant past that one experiences in Ravenna or Santa Maria Maggiore.

Strikingly, the enormous basilica is completely empty. Far from the throngs of the Vatican, there is literally not a soul. Yet more than anyone else, Paul shaped the mind world and practice of the early church: without Paul, apostle to the gentiles, the Nazarenes would have remained an obscure Jewish sect like the Essenes or the Zealots and would probably have vanished along with them. Tentmaker from Tarsus, jurist and convert, Paul spread the 'good news' of the Nazarene revelation through the cities of Asia Minor, back and forth along the Via Egnatia and eventually across the sea to Sicily and Rome. Most likely written in the 50s, Paul's letters are the oldest surviving Christian texts.

The world of Paul's Epistles is distinctly the drama of the End Time: of the impending kingdom of God, meaning the Second Coming and the turning of all nations to worship Yahweh the god of Israel. Paul's world is one of supernatural agencies, of powers and principalities, of the struggle of the spirit against the flesh, of the call to repent and live pure lives in anticipation of the coming of the Lord. But instead of Messiah it was Antichrist who came: the Emperor Nero blamed the Christians for the Great Fire of Rome and initiated the first persecution. According to tradition, Paul was executed by decapitation not crucifixion and buried as a Roman citizen outside the Servian wall.

The heavy polished marble of the church feels remote from the character of its charismatic dedicatee. Even so, we walk down the steps to the crypt, where there is a grille and a glass covering the edge of the rough sarcophagus, and stand in front of the tomb. The Roman Patriarchate emphasised the primacy of the Petrine donation. Yet it was Paul, the Greek-speaking literary Jew who through his mastery of epistolary rhetoric took the new faith into the world of the Graeco-Roman city and in his journeys carried the promises of Israelitic redemption from Jerusalem to Rome. If Jesus was the Messiah, then Paul the apostle was the founding prophet of Christianity as a world religion. In light of all this, Paul Outside the Walls feels oddly neglected, even though archaeological analysis suggests that this spot could very likely be his burial site.

Dietrich, Anata and I take the metro to Anagnina and a bus into the Alban Hills south-east of Rome. At Albano Laziale we visit the cavernous Severan cistern and examine the catacomb frescos of Jesus, Peter and Paul. We walk along the quiet roads to Castel Gandolfo, the summer residence of the popes, and look over the volcanic crater lake of Albano. In the town of Grottaferrata we explore the Uniate Orthodox monastery church of St Nilo. Dietrich explains that after the Great Schism of 1054, some churches in the West retained the Orthodox creed and liturgy despite being nominally under the authority of Rome. St Nilo was one of these churches and has preserved the Byzantine rite unchanged since its foundation in 1004.

It is one of the conundrums of papal authority that the Roman Catholic Church can absorb Uniate Orthodox married priests without showing any sign of relenting on the question of married priests in the Western Church. Perhaps the Curia is afraid of how the dominos would fall: after celibacy of the clergy, what would be next? Still, Grottaferrata has delicious porchetta, which more than makes up for the arbitrariness of Vatican authority. We take the bus to Rome in the bright evening sun and I prepare for my departure in the morning. Dietrich returns my laundry that he hung up to dry on the seminary terrace (ah for the joy of clean clothes) and I pay Father Roberto for the room. Dietrich takes me on the back of his motorino to a farewell party with some German students in Rome, one of whom knows a lot about Nietzsche.

Why do people pray?
Even those with no religious upbringing sometimes pray—perhaps when they experience turbulence on a flight. But why would the creator god, so rarely called upon, pay attention because that person is suddenly aware of mortality? At the other extreme there are those who pray all the time, and one imagines that the divinity would rather be left alone than bothered with their trivial concerns. Is it not preposterous vanity to think that the creator of the cosmos cares any more for humans than for cockroaches and lobsters? Is it not anthropocentric arrogance to make God in our image and think that we are made in His?

Perhaps prayer can be traced back to the tendency of the ancients to propitiate the gods in the hope of affecting those impersonal external forces over which they had no control? We are distinguished from animals by our consciousness of death, by our deep wish to avoid it, and by the awareness of our powerlessness in the face of nature. The ancients thought they could communicate with the gods, perhaps even strike bargains with them, and Christianity adopted the idea of a personal god with human psychology. But to the rational mind, the notion of two-way communication with the creator seems as improbable as the Resurrection itself. Would it not be plausible to rationalise any direct personal experience of that communication as simply losing one's marbles? That does not mean that the cosmos is not infinitely mysterious. If God is what lies beyond the limits of our possible comprehension, then what we know and what we can ever know will always be a tiny proportion of all that there is.

Praying is a metaphor for speaking to oneself—to parts of one's own mind that murmur softly as a distant fountain and are ignored in the torrent of daily life. Tibetan monks say that the only real miracles are the elimination of negative emotions. In that vein, faith is not the rational deduction of articles of doctrine from some datum. Neither is faith an emotional attitude of confidence in the goodness of things, or an expression of longing for the cosmos to be different from how it is. Rather faith is the desire to understand and experience the mysteriousness of things with the whole of one's being. The most important aspect of prayer is to open one's consciousness, whether to the transcendent being or to the voice in our own subconscious. At least the silence helps us to see everything more clearly, and perhaps then we do less foolish things?

Sunday 30 March | Mergellina
The company is charming and the diversions of Rome are limitless but it is time to continue my journey. After sending emails on Dietrich's computer, I bid him farewell and set off with my bags to Termini. Despite being stitched with super strength twine my stripy canvas bag splits open as I board the train: I am obsessively seeking to travel light and am already thinking of what ballast I can shed. But the journey to Naples is fast and the train stops at Mergellina near to the Ostello della Gioventu. It is a warm afternoon and Naples is in a relaxed mood. After leaving my things, I walk along the sea front to the city centre, enjoying the salty air, parading couples and hawkers. The embankment stretches unbroken from Mergellina along the bay, and I reflect on my recent experiences, happy to be once again resuming my solitary wanderings.

Dialogues
Dear Rupert, the war is horrifying. Listening to Radio Four today, the Syrian press is jubilant about American and British casualties and claim that captured American pilots are Israelis who have been given American passports. Everyone here is in a bizarre mood. The shock and awe being unleashed in our names seems all the more remote and unreal while we are blessed with gentle sunny weather. It is impossible not to feel positive in such a spring. Over the past week it has been warm enough to sunbathe. People are watching the war unfold while sitting out in their gardens as if they are watching the cricket! I almost wish it would rain so I could feel suitably gloomy. Practising the piano seems to be the only thing that blocks out the sense of unease. I have spring-cleaned the flat and it looks beautiful. I bought some tulips. Pyrrha.

The quest for perfect love
It may be the categorical activities we find that keep us going, that deeply underpin our will to live. But in the end there is nothing quite like being in love! That is why we are all little Don Quixotes, knights-errant on a chivalrous quest, searching for passion and intensity of experience to conquer the drabness of daily life. But like the knights and their grail, we never find perfect love. Nothing reaches deeper into the soul than the ecstasy of the mutual erotic adoration of another. But like the finest works of music, that give only fleeting glimpses of ecstasy, no sooner do we discover the joy of passion than we are shocked back into reality. For it is impossible to reconcile erotic love with the demands of living in a society, with the world of labour and capital—of cowards and bastards, as some existentialist philosophers have expressed it.

So too thought the Desert Fathers who fled that world. In his 1890 novel *Thaïs*, Anatole France revived the story of Paphnutius and Thaïs. Paphnutius was a fourth-century philosopher turned monk who fell in love with the beautiful courtesan Thaïs. Seduced by the metaphysical promises of abstinence from worldly pleasures, Paphnutius abandoned the cultural and sensual glories of Alexandria, and went into the desert, keeping only sand flies and scorpions for company. Driven by his passion for Thaïs, Paphnutius returned to Alexandria and converted her to Christianity. Had the lyre become repetitive, and the joy of men's hands begun to cloy? Thaïs followed him into the desert and for decades they lived in separate cells in a state of unfulfilled love. One day Paphnutius was called upon to give the last rites to Thaïs who died in his arms. So they discovered the depth of their love for each other, but too late to elaborate and explore it.

The most enduring quest is for perfect erotic love. In Platonic tradition this is unleashed by the discovery of one's metaphysically given other half. But in reality there always seems to be a countervailing force that stands in the way of its realisation and turns the joy to bitterness. Apart from anything else, marriage forces people to give up their freedom and submit to the authority of the market to provide economically for the progeny. What happens to the ecstasy amid the bickering conflicts and tedious compromises of day-to-day domestic life, or when the enchantment of its object fades, as inevitably it must? What does it take to make the pursuit of love compatible with practical freedom—to pursue the ecstasy and yet be neither a bastard nor a coward in this world? Where does nature end and human will begin?

Naples

MONDAY 31 MARCH | POMPEII

I decamp to the Casanova Hotel by the blank expanse of Piazza Garibaldi in the centre of Naples. In the surrounding streets there are shops selling produce from across the Mediterranean, and I take the train to Pompeii with a large bottle of Egyptian guava juice. I tag on to a tour group and am joined by an American film-making couple. We walk around the ancient city and see the temples of Jove and Apollo in the forum, the baths, the houses of the wine merchants Cassius and Vittei, Pompeii's official brothel the Lupanare and the Villa of the Mysteries with its remarkable murals. Over lunch we chat about the Pompeiians, how impressive their craftsmanship is and how close to us they feel.

Quite apart from its setting under Vesuvius and the beauty of the ruins rising out of the vegetation, Pompeii feels vividly contemporary, a clear demonstration that the essentials of life remain unchanged. Many quotidian details are visible, from the slots in the counters of the wine bar to cool the amphorae, to the 'pizza oven' with mill stones for grinding corn, to the baths (caldarium, tepidarium and frigidarium), chambers of commerce, private houses, gymnasia and theatres. Most revealing in its freshness is the brothel, situated above a wine bar. On the walls above the doorways are pornographic frescos indicating the activities that clients might expect to find in the various rooms: it is all on display at Pompeii.

Pliny and others report that when Vesuvius erupted in the night of 24 August 79 AD, clouds of ash and gas killed more than 20,000 people. Pliny the Elder watched the eruption from a boat on the coast and is thought to have succumbed to the gas while attempting to rescue his friends from Stabiae. The lucky victims were incinerated at 400 degrees. When Pompeii was excavated in the nineteenth century, many of the bodies—having decomposed inside the pumice—were turned into plaster cast models by pumping plaster into the cavities in the lava. One can see the positions of their bodies as they fell down with their arms outstretched, choking from the gas, and even the expressions of panic and pain on their faces as they died.

Love as the supreme categorical activity
For the Pompeiians, erotic activity was as much a part of healthy daily life as visiting the baths and transacting business: an appetite to be satisfied and appreciated, much like a bottle of fine wine. But the early Christians seized on the destruction of Pompeii to champion the repressive Pauline view of sexual ethics that spread around the empire with the new religion. From millennarians to the Black Death to contemporary outbreaks of venereal disease, the same notion of divine retribution has made periodic appearances down the centuries. This prurient ethical stance of salvation through behaviour is the mirror to the primitive notion of propitiation. But the essence of Christianity is the idea that love transcends death.

In *The Art of Loving*, Erich Fromm gives a psychoanalytic interpretation of the same idea. Fromm argues that our society is obsessed with falling in love, rather than standing in love, and that the state of infatuation demonstrates not so much the intensity of two peoples' love as the degree of their preceding loneliness. In our culture we seek partners on the personality market hoping for a good bargain. We run algorithms to evaluate the attractiveness of our present or potential partner in the light of our imagined self-worth. The biological process of sexual selection instantiated in the modern economy means that people see the problem as one of being loved, not one of loving. This particularly affects women from their mid-twenties to their forties as they seek a man to give them children before their biological clock stops ticking.

Fromm argues that the desire for love is the most powerful of human strivings. We have come from nature but have transcended it by acquiring rationality. The corollary of rationality is the awareness of isolation and mortality which in the absence of love results in anxiety. Perfect love is interdependence with another that preserves one's integrity and individuality. The ecstasy of mere orgiastic fusion on the other hand is transitory and unsatisfying: sexual desire reflects the need for love and not vice versa. Loving presupposes the attainment of a productive orientation, overcoming dependency and the wish to exploit others. Equally, since love for one person implies love for all people, two people in love with each other but without love for anyone else, *egoism à deux*, have merely expanded the individual and have not achieved union.

Call me as corrupted as the Pompeiians, but is not Fromm, so terribly sober and public spirited in his ideal, as repressive as St Paul? He constructs loving as the most important thing in the universe and makes it as exciting as filling in a tax return. Is love really a question of social duty and obligation? Is that the essence of wisdom: to drive out simple joy and ecstasy from our mental worlds and replace it with communitarian service? What happened to innocent desire, idly settling on its object like a bee on a tender flower? What happened to the free enjoyment of our embodied physicality for its own sake? What happened to wine, women and song, to carefree fauns and nymphs frolicking in an Arcadian landscape?

Tuesday 1 April | Vesuvius

Herculaneum has grand baths beside the sea. But it is disappointing after Pompeii and could be a tannery or an artisanal mine with just so many mud holes and planks. The journey to the summit of Vesuvius though is gorgeous: the road winds up the mountainside, becoming gradually more desolate. At the top you can peer over the side of the cone and see the frozen molten rock. On descending, I take the train to Sorrento and explore the charming clifftop gardens with their canoodling couples and views of Capri.

Ama et fac quod vis

When Vesuvius engulfed Pompeii, the Christians argued that this event was divine punishment for the Pompeiians' sins of sexual excess, similar to televangelists fulminating today about the scourge of 'liberalism'. As an empirical statement concerning the target of Acts of God, history would argue to the contrary: there have been innumerable calamities that have killed the virtuous in equal if not greater number than the sinful, such as the interminable wars of religion and the Black Death. A better argument might be that the wages of sin are venereal diseases. But with investment in public health campaigns, these afflictions are more the fruit of carelessness and ignorance than the indulgence of sinful pleasure per se.

Even if Pompeii was a wealthy resort town whose citizens had plenty of time to indulge in the pursuit of pleasure, their mores were not very different from those of Roman society generally. The evidence we have concerning the attitude of the ancients to sexuality demonstrates the revolution in sexual ethics that Christianity brought about. For the Romans sex was an appetite to be stimulated and satisfied: the only difference perhaps, between a banquet and an orgy, is that in the fornicatorium, pleasure can be continued indefinitely without having to make a visit to the vomitorium. Just as hunger makes food tastier and more attractive, sexual desire paints its objects in a golden hue. Far from being an itch best left unscratched, desire is the path to pleasure. To be sure, familial duty, marriage and the hearth were central to Roman life and civic virtue. But the pursuit of sexual pleasure entirely for its own sake, both before and outside marriage, was accepted: 'love and do as you wish' seems to have been the order of the day. Or was it?

To St Paul, sexual desire is an obstacle to the true purpose of life, which is to follow Christ. Instead of considering desire as a natural force given to electrify pleasure, Paul writes in his *Letter to the Romans* that sexual desire is in fact a punishment that expresses divine anger towards the ungodly. In his *First Epistle to the Corinthians*, Paul argues that celibacy is the optimal state and that a man should only marry if his desires distract him from purity. To St Augustine however, who before his conversion was no celibate, *Ama et fac quod vis* meant that the love of God should overwhelm all other motivations. Did St

Augustine redirect his thwarted love for his mistress into a divine love? Or could loving God mean loving creation, of which the erotic is a part? Pauline repression remains in the subconscious of the Western mind, and perhaps this has been one cause of the post-enlightenment disenchantment with Christianity.

Wednesday 2 April | Naples

Old Naples is underappreciated: the Duomo, baroque churches and the city's seventeenth-century charitable foundations with their distinctive courtyards and staircases are monumental. But most magnificent is the collection of ancient artefacts in the National Museum. Here on a dramatic mosaic representing his triumph over the Persian King Darius at the Battle of Issus, you can see the face of Alexander, the man who spread Hellenism around the Levant and even as far as the Indus. This image is thought to have been copied from a portrait made in his lifetime, so it is possible that the flowing red hair and large intelligent eyes are close to his actual features. Without Alexander's conquests, the New Testament would not have been written in Greek, or indeed at all, and Christianity could not have spread from the writings of a tiny sect into the minds of the educated classes over a large part of the ancient world.

Even more extraordinary than Alexander is the collection of ancient erotica in the museum's secret room. When they were discovered in the eighteenth century, these objects were thought to be against the educational spirit of the museum's foundation. So they were hidden away by a succession of cardinals and secular authorities, and only put on public display in 2001. Most of the objects are fairly mundane, such as small terracotta statues of laughing men with outsized phalluses and other priapic symbols linked to the fertility cult. But other items in the collection suggest that these ancients had an eclectic erotic palette.

It seems that the Romans were fascinated by Hermaphrodite, who makes a regular appearance as a beautiful woman with flowing hair, voluptuous breasts and a penis. Several of the frescos in the museum depict the moment when the male in the scenario discovers that all is not quite what it seems with the object of his affections. But far from being horrified, after his initial surprise, he carries on regardless. Even more startling than the frescos of Hermaphrodite is a beautifully and intricately carved sculpture of a man making love to a goat. The piece is about two feet high, with the man standing and the goat lying on its back. The participants in this act are captured with their eyes locked on each other in a fierce gaze of mutual adoration. Could the sculpture be an allegorical representation of the liberation of the subconscious mind?

On leaving the museum I visit the gothic church of Santa Chiara and climb the broad winding staircase up the hill that divides the city to the Certoso di San Martino. After exploring the cloister with its lovely trellis garden, I sit on the parapet eating a picnic, looking over the city and its bay. As the light fades, I am accompanied in the piazza by a stream of small cars whose occupants watch the sunset from inside without getting out. After some time, I notice that the cars start rocking gently from side to side as couples romp together in a strange form of shared private intimacy. It occurs to me that perhaps the Neapolitans are more in tune with the mores of the ancient Pompeiians than the prudish curators of the National Museum. Or might it just be that the young live at home and have nowhere else to go?

Thursday 3 April | Taormina

The train to Villa San Giovanni glides past the olive groves and beaches of Calabria. Soon I am on the ferry for Messina. The deep blue water foams behind the ferry into white spuming eddies that make me think of Homer's Charybdis, the whirlpool associated with this channel. The strait is noticeably turbulent as it narrows towards the northern end. But it is a short journey across to the island of Trinacria, whose hills beckon me as they did the ancients, and I see neither Scylla nor Charybdis. Messina, which was destroyed in an earthquake in 1908, is as grey as the weather, and I continue south.

Taormina is famous for its theatre, adulated by Goethe,

with views over Mount Etna and its intermittent plume of ash. Today it is raining and the only view is mist. Even so, every detail of Taormina is beautiful, from the black and white marble paving of the main square to the colourful neo-Moorish tile work in the train station to the terraced botanical garden with bougainvillea and cypresses looking over the sea. Well known as a stop on the eighteenth-century Grand Tour, Taormina remains a popular destination for honeymooning couples. The hotels are expensive but I find a berth in the delightful Ostello Ulisse.

After smoking Toscano Extra Vecchio cigars on the tiled parapet of the gardens, made more delicious by the smell of the wet box hedges and the humid air rising up from the Ionian Sea, I buy the *International Herald Tribune*. But looking at the newsprint photos of all these dead Iraqi children, I am overwhelmed by an intense solitude. There are no weapons of mass destruction in Iraq and the war is going to unleash a massive wave of violence. Looking about me I see that in Taormina two is company and three is a crowd. For the path of freedom requires the courage to be alone, depending as it does on chance encounters, without the reliable but perhaps not so exciting companionship of a life partner. I find a seat at a table in the corner of La Bougainville restaurant, and read the newspaper with its accounts of all that unnecessary slaughter, the brutality of Leviathan that none of us could stop. Hiding behind the paper, I burst into tears, crying into my *cozze*. I feel as if I have taken on the sorrows of all the world. But I see that the waiter looks agitated. So I recover myself and am consoled with a bottle of Etna Rosso Donnafugata.

Friday 4 April | Taormina
Can one be impressed by the beauty of a place and still feel gloomy to be there? Is it the solitude, the effect of too much wine or the weather? The rain pours down and since I have the dormitory to myself, I spend the morning in bed. The Ostello is by some trees at the edge of the town, and with the windows open it is lovely to listen to the drumming of the falling rain on the trees and smell the soft damp earth. It is amazing how

quickly and easily a whole day can pass when there is nothing that needs to be done.

At Wunderbar on the main square I play some lines of Bach on the upright piano. But I am driven away by the waiters, whose white shirts and black waistcoats match the flagstones, and retreat to the corner to read Herbert Marcuse's *One-Dimensional Man*. The rain stops and I climb the stone path past the chapel of S. Madonna di Rocca to the Saracenic Castello. The castle has been closed for restoration for as long as anyone can remember. But the winding lane is elemental in the evening mist, and from the top the outlines of Etna and Monti Nebrodi are visible against the sky. I descend in the dark for dinner at La Bougainville.

The mystery of the present instant

To a child, time is a vast ocean whose distant shore is out of reach. Yet once the ocean is crossed, there is nothing: we fall off the edge like mediaeval ships into the void of annihilation. Why then do we ever long for time to pass? Why do we not seek to master time? How can open weeks or months of indolence and inactivity be anything but pure delight? Where springs the need to *do*, to *consume* time, to maximise the *use* of time? When time is short, we fit a thousand tasks into the briefest interval. Yet when time is long, we feel suspended, hanging or adrift. If happiness is an empty to-do-list, then who is afraid of empty time? Waiting at a bus stop, not knowing when or if the bus will come, time comes to an abrupt halt. If your belly is full and your bladder is empty; if it is breezy and the road is quiet, then you could sit and wait for hours. This time is a gift. But if it is hot and polluted, noisy and crowded, then each instant of waiting is a torment.

So that is what time is for us: not a circle or a spiral or an arrow; rather being present and alive, the mind idling calmly without a care in the world. But when something needs to be done, an appetite relieved, or a place evacuated, or disaster averted, then we cease to be, and time takes its fearsome form devouring all. There are people who are waiting to die, tired of living and yet afraid to leave; and there are others facing death who cling to each moment, desperate to make them last as long as possible. Our minds are always *about* something: planning, asking and remembering. Sometimes when we look obliquely away from an objective, it can be seen more clearly, as in night vision. Equally, when we strain to think of something, nothing comes; but when we are distracted, dreaming or absorbed in something else, inspiration becomes a steady flow. So the challenge of being is to delight in each moment purely for its own sake. We cannot win the fight against decay but only seek consolation in time's suspension. For a joyful moment in subjective time has no duration and only then is time vanquished.

SATURDAY 5 APRIL | CATANIA

It is sunny at last. Now I see the splendour of Taormina's theatre high up on its spur, with dramatic views over Etna and the coast. Goethe was not mistaken. The Romans rebuilt the theatre in terracotta brick, enclosing the space with thick walls and barrel vaults, punctuated with arches and columns behind the stage. But this elaborate mass paved over the Greek conception which was designed to inspire the audience with an open vista and the light of Eos rising over the sea. The Greeks chose the site for its transcendence at dawn, while the Romans converted it into a simulacrum of the functionalism of their capital. Fortunately, the heavy screen has mostly disintegrated over the centuries, and sitting at the top of the semicircle one can still see across the landscape from Etna to the glittering waters below. I descend the steep path to the station past the church of Madonna della Grazie. The train to Syracuse is delayed. But waiting on the platform in the sunshine, with the desaturated Mediterranean colours and the sound of the waves, time stands still. The train could be delayed all day and it would not matter in the least.

At the station bar I meet an opera singer, Ferdinando Musamerchi, who sings Donizetti bass parts. Ferdi tells me that he is working on *Lucia di Lammermoor* but is coy to sing in the station. Ferdi is from Gela, the earliest Greek colony on the southern side of the island. Now Gela is ruined by industrial development, and although Taormina is full of small-minded twits and drunks, he likes living here all the same. It is ironic that in these retreats of simplicity we metropolitans seek out for rest and recalibration, the locals, lacking the distractions and stimulation of urban life, pass away their lives in sustained inebriation. But holding an impromptu conversation on the train platform with the wit of erudition is surely the mark of civilisation. We speak about ancient history and the Iraq war. Ferdi tells me that I will love Syracuse, for if I am interested in Hellenism, it is the Sicilians who are the true inheritors of ancient Greece. Continuing south, gusts of sea air come in through the open windows of the carriage, bringing with them echoes of mythology as the train passes Acireale and the Scogli dei Ciclopi, volcanic discharges of Polyphemic Etna.

After changing trains under grey skies at Catania, I arrive at Syracuse, the capital of western Magna Grecia and have reached the north-west corner of the Levant. I take a macchiato in the square outside the station and book into a room in the Hotel Centrale on Corso Umberto. On the fondo of Ortygia, the city's original island district, I find a sunspot beside the water and read the letters of Epicurus. The sun beams across the Great Harbour and reminds me of Claude's embarkation of the Queen of Sheba at an antique seaport, and of Blake's engravings of the sun over an ancient sea, suffused with a timeless optimism. Following the embankment, I imagine life in ancient Syracuse. The city's location was chosen by colonists from Corinth for its geographic features: a defensible island, a large natural harbour and most propitiously, a freshwater spring that would make Ortygia unassailable in a siege. During the Peloponnesian War, Syracuse defeated Athens and would remain the most powerful Hellenic state west of Alexandria until the Roman conquest.

Along the fondo, separated from the sea by just a few feet of stone, the Fonte d'Arethusa provided the island with drinking water in ancient times. Now embanked and overshadowed by a ficus, the spring has turned salty and has ducks and swans swimming in a bed of reeds. I drink wine in a bar nearby and watch the sun set over the Great Harbour where, as

Thucydides relates, the Athenian fleet was destroyed at the end of its ill-fated Sicilian Expedition. Suddenly I am seduced by Hellenism in a way that never quite happens in Greece itself: seduced by the ideals of beautification, rationalism and discovery, the free testing of ideas and the quest for the transcendent. On one of the diagonal streets off Piazza Archimede I find a trattoria serving fritto misto and read Robert Fisk's newspaper reports from Baghdad.

Sunday 6 April | Ortygia

The room is small and noisy from the shipyard behind the hotel. But the balcony gives a fine view of the Great Harbour above the cranes and the boats. I wander past the rough Doric columns of the Temple of Apollo, and follow the alleyways down the eastern, exposed side of the island of Ortygia, whose houses are set back from the sea by a raised promenade. In the semi-circular piazza, laid out by the bishops in the seventeenth century, stands the Duomo, with its elaborate baroque façade and statues of the apostles either side of its wide steps. By tradition the church in Syracuse was founded by St Peter. But according to *Acts of the Apostles*, St Paul passed three days in the city on his way to Rome and would have preached to the Jewish community as well as to pagan philosophers in the forum or by the temples of Athena and Apollo.

The Temple of Athena was constructed by the tyrant Gelon to celebrate victory over Carthage at the Battle of Himera in 480 BC. In the seventh century, it was converted into the present cathedral: the Christians punched holes in the cella walls and used the material to block up the gaps between the columns in the outer porticos which remain otherwise unchanged along the outer wall. Inside the building, one has a rare sense of what the space inside the pagan cella might have felt like. It is astonishing to see the continuity of religion in the same building that St Paul would have seen, with the adapted cella resembling the structure of a basilica and the original Doric columns preserved either side of the main door. The Duomo is reflective of Ortygia as a whole, which preserves its ancient spirit, languid with the sea on all sides.

Sitting on the fondo with the sun setting over the Great Harbour, I drink wine with mozzarella di bufala and read John Osborne's *Luther*. In the play the monks complain about their tedious daily duties, about having to share everything and arrive in time for the offices. The bitterness of a monk's life, foreseen by St Benedict, lies in refining the daily labours of life to their starkest core while finding their burden the same. But here in Syracuse, as the low orb shines across the ancient harbour over the baroque city, the sun, sea and warm stones suspend the weight of the quotidian. There is some local vitality—the usual cacophony. Otherwise nothing changes but the colours and the angle of the sun on the stones.

The insufficiency of Epicureanism

According to *Acts of the Apostles* St Paul preached to Epicureans and Stoics at the Areopagus in Athens: for, by the first century, Epicureanism had become widespread throughout the Roman Empire. Epicurus lived in Athens from 341–270 BC and established his own school in a garden outside the city walls. He had been trained in atomism, the theory of the finite divisibility of nature, by a pupil of Democritus. Democritus argued that if matter is infinitely divisible, the elements would be points without extension that cannot be combined into material with extended dimension. Hence the elements of matter must be indivisible units that Democritus called atoms. Modern physics would relate these conceptual atoms to Planck lengths, the minimum theoretical possible distance in nature. As a result of the intellectual purges of the Theodosian era, almost nothing survives from Democritus's own hand. But Lucretius summarised his arguments in *De Rerum Natura*, and related atomist physics to Epicurus's philosophical worldview that the gods are indifferent to the human sphere and do not intervene in the operations of nature.

Epicurus was known to be of insuperable kindness and humility. He lived an exemplary life, received visitors, sought no honour or public office but was venerated with bronze statues by his many disciples, friends and admirers. Like Democritus he wrote on all areas of enquiry from logic to atomism, biology and ethics. In his Letter to Menoeceus, *How to Live a Happy Life*, Epicurus explains that 'pleasure is the beginning and end of the happy life', that 'all joy of the soul supervenes on the prior experiences of the body' and that 'everything we do is for the sake of freedom from pain and anxiety'. Present experience is the ultimate source of value to which all actions and decisions should be referred. Epicurus distinguished between *katastematic* pleasures (the relief that comes from the absence of disturbance and suffering) and *kinetic* pleasures (joy and delight). 'It is when we feel pain that we must seek relief, which is pleasure. And when we no longer feel pain, we have all the pleasure we need.'

Today Epicurus is associated with a comfortable sybarism. But far from advocating hedonism—the blind pursuit of sensation regardless of the consequences—Epicurus argued for an ancient version of the utilitarian calculus, whereby courses of action are chosen that maximise the overall value of their results, considering both the benefits and the costs. 'It is not continuous drinking and revelry, the sexual enjoyment of women and boys, or feasting upon luxurious cuisine which result in a happy life. Sober reasoning is what is needed, which decides every choice ... and liberates us from the false beliefs which are the greatest source of anxiety. Despite what may be said by those who misunderstand, disagree with or deliberately slander our teachings, the goal we seek is freedom from pain in the body and freedom from turmoil in the soul.' So the primary obstacle to living a happy life is anxiety, whether caused by the fear of adverse events or by the unsatisfied desire for unnecessary luxuries. Epicurus was known for his four-part cure, an inscription of which was uncovered in Pompeii, and which runs as follows:

> Do not fear God who exists in a state of perfect blessedness and cannot harm us. People embellish their notions of God with false beliefs: they credit the divine for delivering rewards and punishments. But preaching popular superstitions about propitiating the divine is impious.
>
> Do not fear death, for when we exist, we do not experience death, and when death is present we do not exist. All good and

bad consists in sense experience and death is the purification of sense experience. So there is nothing fearful in life for one who has grasped that there is nothing fearful in the absence of life. Since the continuity of our experience is the root of our being and is severed by death, death is final. Life is not improved by adding infinite time: removing the desire for immortality is what is required. There is nothing bad about non-existence. So mortality anxiety is a form of ingratitude, like a greedy dinner guest who expects an infinite number of courses and refuses to leave the table at the end.

Do not fear want, for everything that is good is easy to obtain from nature's riches. Our bodies need food, water and safety, while our souls need friendship. Luxuries should be enjoyed if they happen to be easily available, but doing without them keeps us fearless against changes of fortune.

Do not fear pain, for sickness is either brief and intense or chronic and mild and therefore can be endured. Fate has no power over us because dignity lies in making good decisions regardless of the circumstances. It is better to suffer setbacks while acting wisely than to have miraculous luck while acting foolishly.

Epicurus disagreed with the Cynics, who praised self-sufficiency but despised social convention, teaching that it is not possible to live pleasurably unless one also lives virtuously. Epicurus also disagreed with the Cyrenaics who argued that pains of the body are worse than troubles of the mind. To Epicurus, the troubles of the mind are the most painful, while the pleasures of the mind are greater than those of the body. The wise man will never be passionately in love, for erotic love enslaves the lover in unnecessary vulnerabilities, while nothing contributes more to a blessed life than friendship. The Epicureans connected eros with divine love but rejected both, reasoning that the most tranquil course is also the most virtuous.

By the time Paul preached Christianity to Epicureans in Athens in the 40s AD, the rationalism and moderation of Epicurean thought had been embedded in Hellenic culture for three centuries. Yet the new oriental mystery religion spread around the Levant like wildfire. Something of vital importance to human experience was missing from the Epicurean worldview. Christians would say that rationalism left the ancient Greeks thirsting for the water of life: we are not atoms in the void and cannot live by reason alone.

Whereas the goal of the Epicurean life was the freedom of the soul from disturbance through prudence and virtue, Christianity offered something less anodyne, namely the *passion* of Christ and the *ecstasy* of divine love. One imagines Paul's audience at Syracuse, feeling that there must be more to life than Epicurean rationalism, captured by the charismatic message of the apostle. But one also wonders how they suspended their reason to make the leap to belief in the Resurrection. In *Fides et Ratio* Pope John Paul II wrote that faith without reason leads to superstition while reason without faith leads to nihilism. Yet Thomas was granted revelation as a datum and all the charisma of the preacher cannot make dead men walk. So we are back to the riddles of St Thomas and St Teresa: the Pauline worldview unleashes our natural passion and focusses it on a divine object through faith. But in the absence of belief in those articles of faith, we are caught between the Scylla of dry rationalism and the Charybdis of Pauline repression.

Trinacria

Monday 7 April | Syracuse

I discover the Numismatico Museum hiding away above municipal offices in the corner of the Piazza del Duomo. There are coins from all over Magna Grecia, laid out as a spatio-temporal map of the Hellenic world from the Archaic to the Roman periods. Each polity, from Syracuse to Cyrene, from Alexandria to Antioch, articulated their identity through coinage. To begin with, the display seems as chaotic as those collections of bank notes one sees in the counters of hotels, bearing hagiographic portraits of independence leaders and other national heroes. But with some attention the coins tell stories. The plurality of political regime is reflected in the variety of the designs, from monarchs' heads crowned with laurels to the emblems of the different city states. Syracuse is represented by the nymph Arethusa, with dolphins swimming around her head, in recognition of the source of the city's resilience and independence.

From the museum, I explore the other districts of Syracuse, passing the arcades of the ruined San Giovanni in Achradina to Neapolis. At the Archaeological Park I wander around the theatre and Dionysius's Ear, the limestone quarry where the 7,000 Athenian prisoners were set to work, and clamber over the vast altar of Hieron. On feast days the Syracusans would slaughter hundreds of bulls and burn them on this enormous slab to propitiate the gods. But it did not save them from *Realpolitik* and the brutality and venality of Rome. For while the Romans developed a taste for Hellenic art and thought, linking their foundation myth to Troy and adorning their villas with Greek sculpture and their conversation with Greek philosophy, their mind world was functional, their mathematics merely applied engineering and their rule extractive.

Absorbing the spirit of Greek Sicily, I walk the full length of the ancient city to the outer walls and the citadel of Euryalos. The walls and the fortress were built by the Archon Dionysius the Great after the defeat of the Athenians around 400 BC to defend Syracuse from the higher ground on the landward side. Later the fortifications were strengthened by Archimedes at the time of the Roman invasion of Sicily in 214 BC. As I reach Euryalos the mist turns into a downpour and there is not much to appreciate in the rain. So I find a bar for old men at Belvedere and reflect on what I have seen. When the world was young and fresh and had not yet been covered in layers of refuse by the detritus of industrialised humanity, it must have been easier to apply reason to nature and experience the joy of conquering it with thought.

Archimedes and infinity
Even today the Syracusans are proud of their most lauded son, Archimedes, and there has emerged a quasi-official portrait of the great man, looking ruggedly intellectual with a short grey beard and curly hair, sitting on a finely carved desk chair with a pile of scrolls at his feet. We know him for 'Eureka'—for leaping out of his bath and running naked through the streets: the model for other legendary moments of inspiration from Newton's apple to Kekule's snake eating its tail. But his greatest contribution to mathematics was to devise a 'method of exhaustion' that allowed the successively finer measurement of π. The ancient Greeks knew that π was constant but could not find a means of constructing a straight line of *exactly* that length.

Archimedes inscribed and circumscribed successively finer regular polygons around a circle. The points of the smaller polygon touch the inside of the circle and the sides of the larger polygon touch the outside: if the diameter has unit length, then the length of the circumference is π, and lies between the lengths of the two polygons. As the number of sides of the polygons increases, the approximation comes closer to the true value of π. This method is the forerunner of differentiating a function with successively smaller increments, as well as finding the area under a curve by numerical integration, developed by Newton and Leibnitz eighteen centuries later. Archimedes understood that his method worked by tending towards a limit without reference to the infinite as a completed totality: all that is needed is an ever larger (or smaller) number.

Much of Greek mathematics had the same objective: to gain access to a non-material, transcendent reality by devising a sequence of well-defined steps over basic elements drawn from the natural world. The geometric method of exhaustion could give an ever-finer approximation to the quantity in question but could never reach a definite limit. Since the time of the Pythagoreans and possibly the Babylonians before them, mathematical abstraction has been linked to the infinite and hence the theological. The Pythagoreans believed that reality consisted of order (*peras*) set against the boundless void (*apeiron*). Numbers result from the imposition of order onto that void.

The ancient Greeks had two concepts of the infinite: the metaphysical idea of the absolute unity of everything that exists; and the mathematical idea of a quantity continuing endlessly without limit. Metaphysical infinity relates to questions such as why is there something rather than nothing, and how does the totality of everything relate to the nothingness beyond its limit? Archytas reasoned that if there was an edge to the universe, extension beyond the edge would either show more space beyond, or that something was preventing extension beyond the supposed edge, in which case there would be something beyond. So there cannot be an edge and the physical universe must be infinite. Democritus and Archytas used similar forms of reasoning to reach apparently opposite conclusions: one to support the finite divisibility of matter into irreducible atoms and the other the infinite extension of space.

Mathematical infinity gave rise to Zeno's paradoxes of the infinitesimal. For example, if Achilles runs halfway to his target and then halfway again and so on, he gets infinitesimally close to his destination but never arrives. Zeno argued that if reality were divisible into parts, it would have infinitely many parts. But there cannot be infinitely many of anything in nature. There may be no limit to the sub-divisions that can recognised within the trajectory of an arrow's flight. But the time it takes for an arrow to fly through the air is not composed of infinitely many parts. So reality must be an indivisible or continuous unity.

Zeno's paradoxes suggest that if reality is infinitely divisible, the elemental unit of physical reality must keep on getting smaller without limit. There could be no least space-time interval. But if reality is finitely divisible then there must be a smallest spatio-temporal unit or interval such as an atom in the sense of Democritus, or fundamental particles and Planck lengths in contemporary physics. Concepts of mathematical infinity—for example of continuing to count whole numbers without limit—do not need physical extension, and paradoxes of mathematical infinity have proven to be misleading in physics. But the ancients intuited a tension that remains unresolved today in quantum gravity and the frontiers of physics.

The same concepts can be applied to our subjective experience. Immanuel Kant thought that the *noumenal* world, the ultimate physical reality that exists independently of any mind, is metaphysically infinite, while the *phenomenal* world of appearances or subjective experience is mathematically infinite. The idea of the infinite suggests something paradoxical but at the same time meaningful and substantial to the rational intellect. In dealing with the infinite one has the impression of expanding the mind into a higher level of consciousness without dabbling in alchemical nonsense. Or perhaps it is the hope that the finite nuisance of the quotidian becomes irrelevant when set against the broader canvas of the transcendent?

Tuesday 8 April | Euryalos

I explore the expansive and well laid out Archaeological Museum of Paolo Orsi with its figures of Venus, male torsos, and Greek vases decorated with scenes of fighting and banqueting. The recurring forms of ancient Greek pottery—the krater and kylix, amphora and lekythos—are as elaborate in their artistic conception as the sculpture and the friezes and the temples themselves. Now with a sense of the extent and scale of Greek Syracuse, I take the bus back to Euryalos and wander through the broken blocks of masonry, solitary but for the wind and the grass snakes. Standing on the highest point of the fortress you can see over the whole area of ancient Syracuse that once contained a quarter of a million people. I sit in the bar at Belvedere looking through Hegel's lectures on history and return to Ortygia for fritto misto.

The death of Archimedes
Hellenism is the spirit of beautification, rationalism and discovery, set against the countervailing forces of destruction, dogmatism and plutophilia. For this spirit can show itself in different societies at different times and places. In his *Lectures on the Philosophy of World History* Georg Hegel interprets the history of the world as a 'sceptre of domination' that passed in a succession from one world historical people to another. Divine wisdom, *hagia sophia*, is reason or *Geist* endowed with power to achieve the absolute rational design of the world. The destiny and spirit of reason, driven by its own force, is the consciousness and ever greater realisation of human freedom. This world spirit realises the idea of freedom through the activity of rational individuals. The essence of religious truth is that divine providence guides and intervenes in the world through the power of reason: the physical world is the embodiment of reason subject to natural laws.

For Hegel the Hellenic world was the era of the youthful optimism of humanity. Hellas is the adolescent of history, drawing itself to perfection and anticipating its destiny, but immature and vulnerable. The Greeks gave a freshness and vitality to the spirit, expressing its beauty in sculpture, pottery and architecture, in philosophy, music and mathematics. The Greek era formed under the protection of the Delphic Oracle, whose precepts were 'know thyself' and 'nothing in excess'; achieved victory and dissemination with Alexander; and declined due to internal dissension and defeat at the hands of the higher power of Rome. Polybius expressed the anguish: 'In Greece, a noble nature has nothing left but to despair at the state of affairs and retreat into philosophy. If it attempts to act, it can only die in the struggle.'

The Romans besieged and sacked Syracuse in 212 BC. At the Battle of Magnesia in 190 BC, they broke Hellenic power in Asia. Then Corinth was sacked in 146 BC, leading to the domination of the Delian League, and in 64 BC Rome absorbed the remnants of the Seleucid Empire. As Hegel observed, Rome the plunderer had no respect for other nations and gave them no recognition of equal existence. Exceptionalist Rome exercised her brute will, crushing destinies. Under the inexorable persistence of the all-conquering Jupiter Capitolinus, all states and individuals had to submit to the inescapable power of circumstances.

It is obvious that odious though Saddam may be, he poses no military threat to the West. But by launching its invasion of Iraq without the UN Security Council Resolutions that would legalise it, the United States has emasculated the Charter, exposing it as merely a fig leaf to force. By proclaiming its exceptionalist right to act unilaterally, the US government has demolished the idea of the equality of Sovereign States before a common legal principle and has taken the world back to the dynamic of great power politics. Or perhaps it never went away? Perhaps the UN was never more than a velvet glove over the iron fist of the Great Powers? It is possible that as Hegel prophesied, America will remain the dominant power in perpetuity. But what if Hegel was mistaken? What then will protect the West against a hostile coalition that becomes more powerful than the United States and her allies?

If Hegel was right and America is the final hegemon, then history will only end when all great powers have been democratised. Perpetual peace requires the perpetual hegemon. If we really believe that our basic values of freedom of the individual, equality before the law, representative government and regulated competitive markets are universal, then the West cannot tolerate challenger powers that reject those values. The Thucydides trap is a false analogy: neither Sparta nor Athens was a hegemon resisting a challenge from a rising power. The two city states alternated between squabbling and cooperating against the external Persian threat. A better analogy would be Rome who systematically eliminated her challengers one after the next. But Rome collapsed from within as the power of the original patrician and equestrian classes was displaced by the non-Italian Army from around the empire.

Sitting on the fine hewn blocks of the Castello Euryalos at Epipolae, I imagine the death of Archimedes. The action begins at the funeral of Hieron II. For fifty years Hieron has kept the growing power of Rome at bay through subtle acquiescence to Rome's excise demands, by assisting in the wars against Carthage and by maintaining a network of friendships with former consuls. Now Carthage is weaker and Rome wants the Hellenic states as dominions, not as autonomous allies. Hieron's successor Hippocrates rejects Rome's demands and forms an alliance with Carthage. Archimedes is the pre-eminent mind of his generation and advised the old king. His has been the hand behind policy for decades, creating at Syracuse the model of a rational society promoting prosperity and individual freedom. His inventions have reduced toil and increased the people's time for the arts and philosophy, for social service and worshipping the gods. Syracuse has been at peace for 200 years since the defeat of the Athenian expedition. At the bicentenary celebrations in the Temple of Athena, Hippocrates decides that a unified Trinacria has the power to confront Rome, and he is encouraged in this by devotees of the cult of the healer-serpent Asclepius.

In Rome the Senate debates the refusal of Syracuse to accept its demands for free trade over the whole island. It is Rome's destiny to be the master of all men's fortunes. All her rivals will be destroyed. The perfidious Greeks must be shown their place. The gods have spoken unequivocally: the augurs, eagles and entrails are aligned. The Sybil has confirmed it. Rome is the conduit for the gods to determine human history. Marcellus is tasked to capture the city and to protect it from the Carthaginians. But the Senate orders that Marcellus must not kill or enslave any free Syracusans. At Epipolae, Archimedes is directing the expansion of the fortifications and preparing his catapults and scorpion archers when the Romans arrive.

The siege begins: the Greeks propitiate the gods and celebrate a feast to Artemis. Archimedes does not participate and explains that the same god cannot be partisan to both sides. The fighting is bitter on the walls of Euryalos and at Hexapyli on the seaward side. But the master's inventions are effective and the Romans cannot break the defences. 'What happened?' I ask the long black grass snakes as they slither past my feet. 'Polybius's account makes no sense. Was it treachery?' 'Destiny,' they hiss, 'destiny,' and a soldier struck down the sage with his gladius. In Rome, humans are resources to be exploited for expansion, conquest and enslavement. The populus is obsessed with the games and violence. Tragedy bores them: they lack the attention span. Roman laws enrich Roman lawyers: they do not protect justice as Solon's laws did. They threw out their tyrant Tarquin some centuries ago: he was mad. 'No taxation without representation,' they said. But the plutocrats lost their sense of civic virtue and eventually the war machine collapsed.

WEDNESDAY 9 APRIL | NOTO

It is another day of warm drizzle in Syracuse, so I run errands and find a *lavanderia* along the Corso beside a drab café with plastic chairs. While my clothes spin in the machines I exchange emails at the internet point across the road. After ten days of solitude since leaving Rome, I am beginning to pine for company. But the only English speaker in Syracuse is a sinister German called Manfred who seems to be following me around. Bad company can never be preferable to solitude. I see on the television that Baghdad has fallen to coalition forces: American tanks have rolled into Firdos Square and toppled the giant statue of Saddam. So it seems the war has finished and I can think about crossing the Mediterranean into the Arab lands.

After posting some cards I set off for Noto, thirty minutes from Syracuse. Following the earthquake that shattered Sicily in 1693, Noto and the nearby towns of Ragusa and Modica were rebuilt according to baroque principles of town planning and design. Although Sicily was under the rule of the Bourbon monarchy in Naples, construction was overseen by the bishops, as the Church was the leading social institution at that time. In effect Sicily operated an ecclesiastical command economy supported by the aristocracy. The grandeur of imagination and quality of construction reflect the tastes and culture of the ruling class. During the Risorgimento it was at Noto that Garibaldi signed the first constitution of the Unified Kingdom of Italy, a symbol perhaps of the continuation of the same ideal? Back in Syracuse I eat fritto misto under the portrait of Archimedes, and take a final walk around Ortygia, crumbling but in the process of gentrification as Romans and Milanese buy up the town.

The transcendence of nature
Possibly from surveying fields, the ancient Greeks discovered an incommensurability in the measurement of the length of the diagonal of a square. If the length of the side of the square is taken as the unit length, the diagonal has length equal to the square root of two and cannot be expressed as the exact ratio of whole numbers of unit lengths. No matter how small the units of one's measuring rod, there will always be something left over. Hence $\sqrt{2}$ cannot be expressed as the ratio of two whole numbers (integers or naturals). Such 'irrational numbers' can be represented as the ratio of integers to an arbitrary limit of accuracy. But they can never be expressed exactly by the decimal expansion of integers with a finite number of terms.

Some irrational numbers such as $\sqrt{2}$ can however be expressed as the solution to polynomial equations with integer powers, and hence are called algebraic. What about π? Alas this algebraic method of representation does not work for π. Nor does it work for *e*, that strange number which when expressed as a function to the power of its input, has a rate of change equal to itself. Perhaps these non-algebraic numbers such as π and *e* can be expressed as other yet more complicated finite sequences of elementary operations on the integers? Again, alas no! Mathematicians call the set of algebraics and non-algebraics together the real numbers.

Using a method of one-to-one correspondence by which different sets of numbers are paired off in an ordered sequence, Georg Cantor showed in the nineteenth century that there are as many rational and as many algebraic numbers as there are whole or natural numbers. Using his famous diagonalisation argument Cantor then showed that the real numbers cannot be paired off with the naturals in this way: nor can the irrational or non-algebraic numbers on their own. Considering these numbers as whole sets or completed totalities, Cantor's Theorem implies that the *continuous* reals and *discrete* naturals are infinite sets of different sizes. Cantor also proved that although we do not know very many of them (apart from π and *e*), there are exactly as many non-algebraic (transcendental) numbers as there are real numbers.

Like Archimedes' method of exhaustion, Newtonian calculus works by approaching limits as closely as desired: π and *e* are idealised abstractions that can be used to approximate calculation to any arbitrary level of accuracy. But many mathematicians dismissed the notion of whole infinite sets or completed totalities as merely a *façon de parler*: a useful device to analyse calculus but with no existence in reality. According to this view, so-called 'theorems' of axiomatic set theory are elaborate fictions, like the constructions of the mediaeval schools of metaphysics, providing employment but having no greater claim to describe reality than 'theorems' about unicorns. As Kronecker expressed it, 'God created the integers, all else is the work of man.' Likewise arithmetic operations have no meaning when applied to transfinite quantities.

Discrete mathematics refers to theories or mathematical statements defined over discrete elements that can be counted —much like numerical summation works as an approximation to integrating the area under a curve. Continuous mathematics defines operations over the continuum, as functions operating over fields of real numbers that cannot be translated into finite sequences of operations on whole numbers. Irrational numbers can be represented in terms of discrete whole numbers to an arbitrary degree of accuracy by summing the successive terms of their series expansions. But they cannot be represented exactly without apprehending the series expansion as a completed totality of all its elements that continue without limit.

Number theorists have discovered that if one tries to replicate the endless decimal expansions of irrational numbers using functions derived from discrete mathematics, in other words using finite sequences of elementary operations defined solely on the integers, then even the first surds, √2, √3 and √5, have an internal structure quite different from one other. √5, the source of the golden ratio that runs through sacred geometry, is particularly elaborate. If even the simplest irrational algebraic numbers have such characteristic nature inherent to themselves, how can they be merely the 'work of man'?

The ultimate nature of physical reality must be objectively mind-independent—otherwise it would be impossible to test theories about nature through experiment. Metaphysical realism in this sense is foundational to the scientific enterprise: all significant breakthroughs in physics have occurred by formulating testable hypotheses and letting nature speak. But the twentieth century quantum revolution showed that the measurability of reality-in-itself is constrained by the interaction between the measuring instrument and the system being measured. Hence there are limits to the knowability of ultimate reality.

Quantum physics suggests that at its most fine-grained, objective reality consists of discrete entities such as the most basic units within the Standard Model of particle physics or Planck lengths in the finest possible resolution of the fabric of space-time. Yet space-time as described by Einstein's theory of general relativity is treated as continuous. Transcendental numbers such as π and e appear throughout the mathematical models used in contemporary physics to describe reality. Is the use of continuous mathematics merely a device for convenience of calculation: could theories in physics be translated into a set of statements consisting entirely of numerical recipes of addition and multiplication?

Some physicists believe that a theory of quantum gravity that unifies general relativity with quantum theory will require that space-time is discrete down to the level of the resolution of Planck lengths. If the ultimate elements of physical reality are discrete and finite, then a complete mathematical description of the physical universe would be computable using only a finite sequence of elementary operations defined on the natural numbers. As of now this is speculation: it may also be discovered that the discrete nature of subatomic physics is the result of some filtering operation on the underlying continuum of space-time. Something about the tension between the discreteness of the natural numbers and the continuity of the real numbers lies at the root of the present cosmic riddles that physicists have been unable to solve.

This paradox connects with the question about why mathematics, apparently the product of the human mind, fits the independently existing reality of physics. If π and *e* are merely ratios of coincidence that have no mind-independent existence, why would we project these numbers onto a discrete world or see them at all? Some have followed Immanuel Kant in suggesting that mathematics is hardwired into us by evolution as a reflection of the structure of the natural world in which we evolved. By this line of thought, the very descriptive power of continuous mathematics reflects the continuous nature of physical reality.

This puzzle of meta-mathematics, about the *fit* between mathematics and nature, is not only relevant to physics. With the rise of artificial intelligence, the entire Hegelian Geist of freedom is at stake. Enthusiasts of strong artificial intelligence believe that given enough computing power, machines performing finite sequences of operations on strings of ones and zeros, i.e. discrete natural numbers, will ultimately provide a complete representation of human mental function and experience, including motivation, meaning, aesthetic judgement and inspiration—indeed all the things that make us human.

Practitioners of artificial intelligence create algorithms to simulate the intuitive solutions that minds find to non-algorithmically defined problems. But our brain processing has qualitatively different modes of operation from programmed algorithms performing operations on a discrete machine. As biological organisms, humans do not live in a discrete, quantised world: at the level of resolution at which we experience and act upon reality, the natural world is continuous. If our brains process continuous data, then even trying to represent the retina with a binary machine is doomed to fail.

Suppose physical reality is discrete and completely describable by a future theory constructed using finite sequences of operations defined on natural numbers. Even with complete discrete physics there may be no limit to computational complexity such that artificial intelligence will only ever operate in the tiniest speck of the vast space of mathematical combinatorial possibility. Like Archimedes' method of exhaustion, artificial intelligence using binary machines will never measure us exactly as we are. For we are like π: we remain free!

Thursday 10 April | Catania

At Catania I run into Ferdi who recommends that I read Diodorus Siculus on the fall of Syracuse. Leaving my belongings at the station I have two hours to walk around. Passing through earlier in the rain, the grey cloud enveloped the grey stone of the town giving an impression of irredeemable drabness. But now the sky is cloudless blue, revealing the cleft peak of Mount Etna. After several eruptions and an earthquake in 1693, Catania was reconstructed out of the soft volcanic tufa rock. The city's monuments look superb in the spring sunlight, from the cavernous church of San Nicolo to the octagonal arcades of Piazza Mazzini. I eat an excellent pizza in a friendly place popular with students who seem to live the quest for youth perpetual.

The train to Palermo passes through the open landscapes and green hills at the centre of the island. The single carriage ambles down to Caltanissetta with wild spring flowers beside the tracks and gusts of pollen coming through the open windows. Arriving at the island's capital I take a room in the Albergo Orientale on Via Maqueda. The hotel is on the first floor of a baroque palace with arcaded courtyard and grand staircase, built in 1760 according to 'the idea and the design of the Principe di Cuto'. Like much of Palermo, the building survived the bombing of the Second World War but suffered from the subsequent stranglehold of the Mafia. The elderly owner, Cuti, is from the original family and is restoring the palace. In the ceiling of the reception room is a recently cleaned fresco of a flying nymph that beams down in bright colours. My room is above an archway over the street, and I observe the evening activity from the balcony.

FRIDAY 11 APRIL | PALERMO
From the albergo I walk through the Mercato di Ballarò, which still bears the imprint of the Arab presence on the island, with its cacophony of street sellers, severed cows' heads and spices, and find my way up the hill to the Palazzo Reale. Under its Norman adventurer kings, Palermo flourished from 1072 to 1250 as a vibrant fusion of the Frankish and Arab cultures, absorbing the strongest elements of each in a model of pluralist tolerance, parallel to its contemporary: Cordoba. The palace is now the seat of the regional parliament. Walking through its courtyards and up the monumental staircase to the Cappella Palatina, one can imagine the magnificence of the Courts of Roger II and his grandson Frederick II. Anyone with interesting ideas would have had the ear of these rulers, whose aims beyond conquest seem to have been to build grandly, administer fairly and allow the intellect to flourish.

The Byzantine-Saracenic chapel itself is the city's finest gem, with cycles of mosaics from the Genesis stories to Christ Pantocrator and the lives of Peter and Paul. The light from the dome picks out the figures against their gold background. To the mediaeval mind it must have seemed a glittering vision of angels and saints. Down the Corso from the Palazzo Reale, the Duomo has an eclectic array of styles, but does not compare with the Cappella Palatina. Its most striking feature is the large red sarcophagus of the Emperor Frederick II 'Stupor Mundi', the last ruler of an independent Sicily and on whose tomb the Palermitans lay red roses out of longing. Further along is La Martorana, Santa Maria dell'Ammiraglio, founded by Roger II's admiral, George of Antioch, another church with dazzling mosaics including of Roger II himself.

The Archaeological Museum has an impressive collection arranged around two courtyards. The museum is known for its high relief metopes from Selinunte, as well as a contemporary head of Socrates that expresses his irrepressible talent to irritate the mighty with the force of his logic. But what catches my eye is the Palermo Stone of Sofis, dating from the twenty-seventh century BC, and possibly the oldest surviving text from ancient Egypt. Inscribed on black basalt, the hieroglyphics depict the Royal Annals of the Old Kingdom up to the fifth dynasty. The deciphering of the Rosetta Stone enabled the translation of stele such as these, as the Behistun Inscription did for Mesopotamian cuneiforms. The discovery of Ashurbanipal's library at Nineveh by Layard and Rassam in the 1850s led to the recovery of more than 30,000 cuneiform tablets. Ironically these tablets were glazed in the fire that destroyed the library in 612 BC, thereby preserving for posterity these records of ancient Iraqi civilisation including *The Epic of Gilgamesh*. What else lies buried under the sands? Leaving the museum, I find an internet point nearby.

Dialogues
The irony of these two press releases on the same page cannot be lost on anyone. Anne Yasmine Rassam.

BUSH THANKS UZBEKISTAN'S PRESIDENT FOR SUPPORT AGAINST TERRORISM
Uzbekistan's presidential press service announced on 18 March that President Bush sent a letter to President Karimov thanking him and his government for Uzbekistan's contribution to the fight against international terrorism. The letter mentioned Uzbeki-

stan's decision to allow the international coalition to use the military airbase at Khanabad to support its actions in Afghanistan and went on to assert that the world is facing the challenge of a combination of weapons of mass destruction, terrorism, and countries sponsoring terrorism. Bush's letter said that to succeed in this challenge depends on the broad involvement of the international community. Uzbek officials have fully supported the United States in its handling of the Iraq crisis.

UN COMMISSION CONCERNED AT USE OF TORTURE IN UZBEKISTAN

The session of the UN Commission on Human Rights that began on 17 March is focusing on Central Asia. One of the problems under examination is the continued use of torture by law enforcement agencies in Uzbekistan. A special report on the subject was drawn up at the end of 2002. The report notes that a large number of civil society activists and journalists have been harassed, arrested and mistreated by the authorities. The practice of forced incarceration in mental institutions still exists. Recommendations made in the report include the closure of the notorious prison camp at Jaslyk in the Karakalpakstan desert where many inmates have died. The report calls for the authorities to take a stronger line against torture and for Uzbek legislation to be brought into line with international standards.

Dear Yasmine: what do you think about the situation in Iraq? Baghdad has fallen to the so-called 'coalition of the willing'. But is this not just the end of the beginning? When 'liberation' becomes 'occupation', will the conflict not turn into a new Vietnam? Your father obviously thinks differently. Rupert.

Rupert, the case for intervention in Iraq is not as black and white as portrayed by the media. My father was tortured in Saddam's death camps for a year, along with many of the opposition who saw their families killed one by one until they agreed to collaborate. Saddam destroyed the culture of the marsh Arabs that goes back to the Sumerians, gassed the Kurds with chemicals, slaughtered the Shi'a and sent one million Iraqis to their deaths in the war with Iran. Under the oil-for-food programme, Saddam stole billions of dollars and built seventy palaces. Of course American goals in this war are not for humanitarian intervention. But the man has flouted twelve Security Council Resolutions! When do you use force? The French let 500,000 Rwandans die by pulling out UN peacekeepers. It took unilateral action by NATO to stop the war in Bosnia; it took the Australians to go into East Timor to stop that genocide. Yasmine.

Dear Yasmine, the war is over, and the Bush administration has backed down on Syria. But the cultural losses in Baghdad are irreparable. Fossil fuels will either be depleted or become obsolete. The cultural heritage of ancient Iraq is the patrimony of all mankind. Even in strict accounting terms, the pecuniary value of the looted artefacts in Baghdad is greater than the worth of the oil. The US government should be booked for those crimes: the warnings were clear and they did nothing. Why were the museums not secured? Your rulers do not care about such things: there is little short-term profit in state antiquities after all. What will there be to show for the wealth and power of America in eighteen centuries' time? Perhaps the problem with the Americans is their lack of understanding or interest in other cultures? The war may be over, but they will soon find themselves suppressing a hostile population. Rupert.

Dear Rupert, I agree with you on the antiquities and the toppling of the Ba'ath party. The US government is propelled by Cold War warriors flanked by Christian soldiers. The turn on Syria is proof of everyone's greatest fears. Of course poor Iraqis are going to loot government buildings and museums. Yasmine.

SATURDAY 12 APRIL | MONTE PELLEGRINO
I visit the Norman-Saracenic church of St Giovanni degli Eremiti with its hammam-style terracotta domes and charming cloister garden of palms and cacti. In the public library on the Corso I retrieve a copy of Diodorus Siculus and browse through the sections about Greek Sicily. Further along

the Corso near the Quattro Canti, the monumental crossroads decorated with baroque fountains of the seasons, I find a barber's shop. Waiting for the cut, I listen to the barber discussing Palermo life, and examine the pictures on the wall of two young kneeling girls, models of romantic desire, and the intended audience for all this immaculate grooming. Where better to gain an insight into contemporary Sicilian society than a barber's shop? On this island of five million people traditional family life and children remain paramount.

I catch the bus to the grotto of Santa Rosalia on the promontory of Monte Pellegrino that conveys a message of god in nature. The stone path back down the hill to Palermo is extremely charming, with pines, prickly pears and spring flowers, as well as fine views over the bay and the Conca d'Oro. I continue to La Cala, the one part of the city that gives contact with the sea, and take pizza in a jolly family restaurant. At the Orientale Cuti offers limoncello and asks me if I like Palermo. 'Wonderful,' I tell him. 'But it is a shame so much of the city centre feels like a wasteland, still damaged from the Second World War.'

As we sit under his restored eighteenth-century ceiling fresco, Cuti recounts a tortuous narrative involving a complicated cast of characters from Mussolini to Andreotti. When Allied Forces invaded Sicily in July 1943, the Americans advanced quickly from Licata on the south coast to Palermo, having already made arrangements with the Mafia, leaving British troops to fight inch by inch up the east side of the island. The Americans released criminal bosses from the Ucciardone prison, undoing earlier attempts to eliminate the Cosa Nostra. As a goodwill gesture towards Italy, aimed to undermine Soviet influence in the late 1940s, the British Parliament voted £30 million to reconstruct Palermo after its aerial bombardment prior to the invasion. But the money was stolen by the Mafia and the city remained in ruins for decades.

Sunday 13 April | Monreale
What a change from all that solitude: to have light and attractive company. While hanging out my wet socks to dry on

the balcony in the nude, two girls giggle at me from the room opposite. Jovanna and Claudia are exchange students from overseas studying in Malta and are now taking their Easter holiday to travel around Sicily. Over breakfast in the albergo we fall in like fellow pilgrims and I offer to be their guide. We visit La Martorana and attend the bright and uplifting Palm Sunday mass in the Cappella Palatina.

We walk up the hill to Monreale in the spring sunshine, stopping for water at the baroque fountain along the road, and eat pasta at the Trattoria Peppino. Suitably energised, we absorb the narrative of the twelfth-century cathedral, reading the bible stories as they are related in the well-preserved mosaics that cover every inch of the church from floor to ceiling, from Genesis to the Gospels. Two hours is a blink in Monreale, where not a tessera is out of place, and the splendour of the gilded shimmering whole is surely the Christian encapsulation of Platonic forms—the material instantiation of heaven on earth. Perfect in its conception and execution, Monreale is the peer of St Peter's and Hagia Sofia. Alas the cloisters are closed, and we take the bus back to Palermo where we laugh and drink limoncello.

Trapani

MONDAY 14 APRIL | SEGESTA

Dopey from the evening's excess we catch the train to Segesta and take the path behind the station to the incomplete Doric temple. Jovanna's guidebook explains that the temple had no cella or roof and its dedication is unknown. We continue up the hill to the theatre of Segesta with its views across the landscape to Monte Sparagio and the Golfo di Castellammare. Clambering over the blocks, I imagine the ancient players stretching the muscles on their faces before dawn in preparation for the performance. This is truly an idyllic place, with its views and wild flowers and soft breaths of wind. If the Globe Theatre can be reconstructed on the banks of the Thames, why should not Greek drama be performed here at dawn?

Naked was the earth when the ancients chose the locations for their temples and theatres, not yet drawn by the accumulated clutter of decay. That is the magic of these sites, built in the best natural positions when everywhere else was still wilderness: to visit them is to connect with an earlier world, de-toxified of its motorways, industrial facilities and urban sprawl. In their construction, the Greeks were inspired by geometry: to generalise from the natural to the ideal requires abstraction and imagination. That was how they used geometric forms and ratios in their architecture. Something has been lost in the interim as our economic and cultural structures have become ever more functional and utilitarian. Could the Hellenic spirit of sacred geometry ever be recovered in the operating mechanics of a modern economy?

At Castellammare we walk along the beach discussing love in the sunset, drinking inky local red wine from plastic bottles. We eat scallopine in Palermo station and canoodle in the albergo: the most poignant and delightful pleasures in life depend on chance meetings quite beyond one's control. But Jovanna does not want to spoil the companionship of these days together. 'The devil is in your trousers,' she says.

Tuesday 15 April | Cefalù

A happy third day with my new friends, such enormously cheerful and good company. Yet there is no entanglement. Perhaps it is good to have two female companions, as then one can be sure that nothing complicated will happen, like Buridan's Ass or a dog with two bones? There is not much romantic spark, but we have an excellent camaraderie: a Platonic ideal with no quarrels of expectation. While Jovanna and Claudia pass the morning together, I return to the public library, taking notes from Diodorus Siculus.

We take the train to Cefalù and amble around the town, admiring the Norman cathedral with its impressive apse mosaic of Christ Pantocrator. What is the meaning of this divine omnipotence, the Byzantine tendency to show Christ victorious, the opposite representation from the Latin focus on the crucifixion? Does it reflect the desire for order, the consoling thought that someone competent is in charge? And yet no one is: there are no grown-ups. We climb up the hill to see the views from above the Duomo and pass the afternoon on a restaurant terrace beside the bay. What a shame to break the trio: we are a little sad, knowing we may never meet again. We drink two bottles of wine, talking about our different worlds, until we understand there can be no life of youth perpetual, and return to Palermo in the dark, silent and reflective.

Dialogues

Ciao Rupert! Thanks for your card that arrived today—I will do my trip in your footsteps. I found a flight to Palermo and will arrive Easter Day in the evening. My first days will be spent in Palermo and the surrounding area—if there remains any time, I will go to Syracuse. Cordialmente, Dietrich.

Dear Dietrich, you will love Sicily, which shows the continuity of Hellenism from the classical period into late antiquity. How can we trace the thread of the philosophers from Hesiod to Epicurus into all that plagues us today? By the time you reach Sicily I will be en route to North Africa. The war in Iraq is officially over. But now we read in the press that the Iraq National Museum in Baghdad has been looted, and invaluable antiquities stolen or destroyed, including the recently excavated Sippar Tablets. Meanwhile the Iraq National Library has been burned, vaporising the Sharif Hussein correspondence and 400 years of official Ottoman documents. It is the most significant event of cultural destruction in Iraq since the Mongols sacked Baghdad in 1258. What else is being destroyed in that country, the first source of all our civilisation? At least spring feels like a dream on this magical island of Trinacria. Rupert.

Wednesday 16 April | Trapani

Farewell sweet friends: I had wanted to be a solitary wanderer, free as a bird. Yet now I am alone and anxious again. What can be done? Only to return to my journey and resume my reflections. So to Trapani, passing Segesta and arriving at the port city at the end of Italy, almost within sight of North Africa. Trapani is breezy and fresh on its sun-drenched tongue of land, and like Syracuse, carries something of the spirit of the ancient Mediterranean. But it is lunch time and the hotels are closed.

So I find a café by the fish market and wait to see if any rooms become available. Absorbing the indolence of Trapani's siesta, I take notes from Mary Warnock's *Existentialism* with coffee and Toscano Extra Vecchio. These cigars are remarkably good for the price: just a few euros for a pack of five finger length cheroots, and the tobacco comes alive in the salty humidity of the sea air, stimulating the mind. As Warnock explains, the essence of experience lies in the active use of the imagination. Beautiful places must be sought out and well savoured when they are discovered. But the real power is to transform the ugly.

In due course I am offered a double room at the Albergo Moderno with a first floor balcony on the street, the perfect vantage point to observe the town's Holy Week activities. I walk down the Corso past the cathedral to the end of the peninsula and sit beside the Torre di Ligny reading about Syria in the *International Herald Tribune*. Walking along the walled promenade embanking the houses to the north, I have the feeling again of falling in love with a place, an ancient city surrounded on three sides by the sea. Between the Albergo Moderno and the port terminal I find the cosy Trattoria Zichichi and drink local red wine with the restaurant's talkative parrot.

Existential freedom
Philosophers from Kierkegaard to Sartre have written at length on freedom. From a twenty-first century liberal perspective, much of what they say seems obvious. Statements of existentialist thought might go as follows: humans are unique in having the practical freedom to choose their own courses of action, what to value and how to live. Existence precedes essence: we do not have fixed pre-existing selves that organise our behaviour. Rather the self is the outcome of experience and actions that can be chosen. Therefore we can create the future person we want to become by shaping ourselves and determining our life. Although our freedom rests against a background of unchosen elements, we are free in the way in which we experience them. We can learn to control our emotional reactions, putting aside sadness to greet a friend in the street with a smile, or deliberately eliminating negative emotions such as anxiety and frustration.

Exercising the freedom to shape ourselves requires effort. It takes self-control to break bad habits and control negative emotions. Like muscles that become flaccid from underuse in the unnatural environments we inhabit, using our independence of thought requires us to fight every day against countervailing laziness. The alternative to actively choosing the person we want to become is to passively renounce our freedom and relapse into cowardice or bastardy. Cowards accept the values of the prevailing social institutions and conventions around them; or they adopt deterministic ideologies such as psychoanalysis, Marxism and religious fundamentalism. Bastards on the other hand impose those values and frameworks on others. Our scope to wield freewill is constrained by those aspects of ourselves that cannot be changed: our age, genes, life history and deeply rooted dispositions. These constraints are basic facts—inexplicable and absurd. But however pressing their limits, we must exercise our will and avoid succumbing to ennui.

Although existentialism has been associated with phenomenology, the systematic scrutiny of the subjective contents of the mind, its principles form the axioms of an economic theory. To exist rather than subsist, we must be capable of *choosing* our lives. Yet economic reality is such that few people —perhaps only a tiny proportion of all those that have lived— have the opportunity to fully exercise their existential freedom. And perhaps human nature is such that an even smaller fraction would want such freedom if they were offered it? For absolute freedom is also a heavy weight: disconnected from established routines and familiar patterns of life, it is usually easier to follow the tram tracks as they already exist than to strike out and find new ones. The vast canvas of open empty time can seem like an overwhelming void. But in a small way, in every moment of our experience, we can still seek to choose our own unique path.

While the discipline required to quash negative thoughts and be good is independent of wealth, in practice owning property gives one the elbow room to explore different kinds of life path. Necessity may be the mother of invention. But there is nothing like economic security to enable the pursuit of ideas, experience and learning for their own sake. Exercising freedom requires access to empty time which in turn requires solvency. For a debt is a bond and if a man is bound he is not free. The same thought can be reversed: what kind of economic structure would maximise empty time and hence the scope for people to exercise their existential freedom and become the individuals they most wish to be? This is a different question from how to maximise existential freedom given the prevailing economic system. What would existentialist economics look like? Would such an economic revolution be feasible? Would people want those freedoms if they had them? Perhaps our economic structures are the way they are because at root people fear empty time: deep down they dread existential freedom and seek any available distraction to avoid it?

THURSDAY 17 APRIL | MARSALA

The weather is dismal and I am feeling lonesome after three happy days with Jovanna and Claudia. So I resolve to put these principles into effect and distract myself with errands. I post books home and buy a ticket at the ferry terminal for the Saturday night sailing to Tunis. Having originally planned to cross to North Africa the previous Saturday, I am now a week behind schedule. But as long as I reach the Libyan frontier before my visa expires at midnight on Sunday 27 April, I can recover the days. The delay means that the Iraq war will be finished by the time I arrive in Arab lands and gives me the chance to follow the Good Friday Procession of the Mysteries in Trapani. Since arriving in the town, I have heard intermittent fragments of bands and singers practising for the most important local event of the year.

The train to Marsala at the western tip of Trinacria passes the Stagnone salt pans whose windmills rise out from the lagoons. Arriving at the town, best known for its fortified wine, I join the Holy Thursday procession in the pouring rain. Cold and wet, longing for the warmth of the sun on the stones, I pace though the pretty streets of the town and buy two large packets of Amphora tobacco that will keep me in smokes until Egypt. The museum is closed but I find an ornate, cramped bar, with a crowd of heavily made-up local duchesses, damp from the procession, rowdy and already well watered. The Marsala wine is delicious. But sometimes hell really is other people and I retreat to the corner with my notebook.

The wisdom of Father Gregory

'Do you have faith?' asked Father Gregory at the seminary in Rome. I replied with an image of infinitude. The interior of the

Roman Catholic cathedral at Westminster was originally intended to be covered with marble tiles and mosaics. But the project faltered, and the decoration remained incomplete. Human concepts, rationalisations and explanations are like the tesserae that cover the floor and lower parts of the walls. But beyond the countable elements of finitude lies the limitless void of ultimate reality. As the ceiling disappears into unadorned darkness, so the void is infinite and there must be a dividing line—a limit. The tiles can never cover the whole void and knowledge can never be complete. Father Gregory believes that the modern scientific worldview has undermined belief in Christian metaphysics. 'Humean considerations of observation and deduction as the sources of reliable knowledge stand to philosophy as grammar does to poetry: on their own they have no content. The experience of God is the central focus of theology.'

'Is Orthodoxy any different, with its reverence for mysticism?' I ask. Father Gregory explains that Orthodox theology has elaborated its own system to rationalise the doctrine of salvation through faith. Orthodoxy's position does not delegate apprehension of these beliefs to the passive acceptance of mystery, as that would be compatible with any doctrine and would undermine Christian ones. The Orthodox churches may provide a refuge to musical converts like John Tavener with their liturgy and chanting. But the grass is always greener: where Orthodoxy diverges from the West is that their theology has hardly changed in five hundred years, which is why the Russians and Serbs and Greeks are susceptible to a militant mediaeval nationalism.

On the other hand, the problems of the Roman Catholics revolve around dogmatic insistence on the primacy of Peter as well as issues related to sexuality: child abuse, family planning, sexual orientation and divorce. In Father Gregory's opinion, the Anglicans have the best combination of maturity, tolerance and, above all, humour. Anglicans are strong on ecumenical dialogue, seeing Christianity as one source of religious interpretation of the world: thousands of years of Hindu devotional practices cannot just be wrong. The experience of god occurs in different ways in different cultural traditions, all of which must learn to communicate with each other and peaceably coexist.

How then did the expectation of an imminent Second Coming in the Apostolic Age shape Pauline sexual ethics? If the early Christians had to keep themselves pure for the Second Coming, what difference does it make that they thought it would come in their lifetimes? Should we not strive to do the same? What lets us off the hook? Whether we agree on the cosmic insolence of supposing that one can *communicate* with god, how can we ever know that we are experiencing god? If god is everywhere, what distinguishes the 'spiritual' experience of god, which might occur in the process of meditation or reflection, from the passive experience of the transcendence of nature? Seeking to reconcile Christian doctrine with science is futile. But religious understanding provides an experiential reception to the void. For since the time of Gilgamesh, awareness of our mortality has been the greatest challenge we face as individuals.

Dialogues
Dear Rupert, to update you on the security situation in Iraq: arsonists are burning ministries, libraries and archives. Some people are saying that an insurgency is already beginning as the 'army of liberation' becomes an 'army of occupation' and there are outbreaks of Sunni–Shi'a violence. Fisk wrote that 'People in Baghdad do not believe Saddam's former supporters are starting these fires. So who are they, this army of arsonists carrying Kalashnikovs? In whose interest is it to destroy the entire physical infrastructure of the state along with its cultural heritage? Why does the US Defence Minister say that there is no widespread looting or destruction in Baghdad and then claim there are insufficient US troops to control the fires when US servicemen sit idle in the gardens of the presidential palace?' Meanwhile there is now a petition going around entitled 'Reject the Nomination of Bush and Blair for the Nobel Peace Prize'. Keep well. Pyrrha.

Friday 18 April | Trapani

Good Friday: the long-awaited Procession of the Mysteries is about to begin. All over Sicily these theatrically captivating processions are the most lavish and dramatic events of the ecclesiastical year. A legacy of the Counter-Reformation and Spanish rule over the island, they have been elaborated and made quintessentially Sicilian in their emotional power, cathartically venting the sorrows of the preceding year in the passion of the Christ. By constructing a lament focussed on the intensity of another's suffering, our own griefs are somehow framed and contained. The Trapani procession is less well known than Enna's, with its sinister ku klux robes. But Trapani pools the efforts of the villages in the north-west corner of the island and is the largest procession in Sicily. There are twenty biers of wooden sculptures, the *Misteri*, that illustrate the episodes of the Passion. These elaborate sculptural groups were mostly carved in the 1620s and are kept in the Chiesa delle Anime del Purgatorio by the port. During the settimana santa, the statues are dressed in silver regalia and decorated with flower displays by the local guilds that maintain the biers.

Each bier is shouldered by eight or ten men dressed in black suits, with starched white shirts, black ties and dark glasses: for the procession is the central public performance of the Mafiosi. In front is a cohort of uniformed young women bearing the flags of their respective guild. Behind pass sixty strong brass and wind bands, their instruments affixed with miniature music stands. In total more than a thousand musicians play haunting dolorous laments, mixing Spanish tunes, melodies of the local composers, some polyphonic, and excerpts of funeral marches from Beethoven and Chopin. The music is passionately heart wrenching and somehow made more solemn by the slight desynchronisation of the parts.

At two o'clock the first bier emerges from the Chiesa del Purgatorio and the day-long procession begins. As they process down the streets, the men sway from side to side, periodically tilting the biers, crouching to kiss the ground at churches and chapels as they pass. Walking the Via Dolorosa itself could not give a stronger feeling of sensuously lugubrious passion than watching these Trapanesi process under the burden of the heavy statues while the musicians pipe their way through the laments. I follow the groups as they make a circuit through the old town to the end of the peninsula and back along the Corso. After several hours the solemn procession arrives in the city gardens and the road up the hill towards Erice becomes a fairground. Tuning in and out, meandering along the route, I become a *penitente* for one night.

SATURDAY 19 APRIL | TRAPANI
While the procession rests in the city gardens I retire to sleep for a few hours. In the morning I take coffee beside the Corso and read about mythical cyclical time versus historical spiral time while the procession continues. What a place to discover! I savour the last moments of the Misteri as the statues find their places in the Chiesa del Purgatorio and the biers are relieved of their silver adornments. And there is Illiana across the street, blushing coyly in my direction, also captivated by the end of the procession—for which she came expressly to Trapani—and I catch her as she walks away. We sit in the sun by the port drinking coffee and talk about everything we have seen. Later Illiana moves her things to the hotel and I sit on the steps of the Duomo opposite, wondering about the abandonment of my boat to Tunis, and laughing at the bemusement of the Albergo Moderno that I should stay longer. Slight and elegant, with chestnut hair, blues eyes and an aquiline nose, Illiana is Swiss-German-Jewish, a little older than me.

We talk about Israel and her ethnology studies in Zurich, agreeing on important distinctions as we eat our insalata di mare by the port. Then Illiana speaks of her astonishing misfortunes: childhood abuse by a teacher, the ensuing years of dumbness, a train crash that restricted her ability to walk for five years, the death of one lover on a mountainside, the paralysis of another by a stroke, and her father's suicide. Illiana tells me to read Martin Buber and Frank Rosenzweig—Jewish existentialists and Zionists who wanted full integration and equality with the Palestinians. Illiana is fragile but strong, with a sense of adventure and full of insight. After resting from the nocturnal procession of the sacred mysteries, we sip Marsala wine and smoke Toscano cigars by the port. I am supposed to be on the boat to Tunis. But Trinacria has hooked me: the next crossing is not until the following Saturday, and I am happy to lose my planned week in Tunisia to spend these days with Illiana.

SUNDAY 20 APRIL | ERICE

Easter Day: it is pouring down and there is no bus up the hill to the village of Erice, so we sit at the train station with spinaci (spinach feta pastry) and milky coffee, waiting to see who turns up. In the end we share a taxi with a thoughtful young Norwegian who talks about political economy and infrastructuralised poverty. 'It is extraordinary,' he says, 'that in London, the parks and garden squares are surrounded by railings. In Norway, it would be unthinkable to enclose land in that way.' 'Would that Britain were like Norway, with its high standard of housing, education and welfare,' I reply. Alas nations are carried by their particular historical paths and the endowments are different between the two countries. Norway has a small, homogenous population and strong external balance from its hydrocarbon resources, while Britain has a legacy of weak public education and struggles to maintain current account surpluses.

None of this matters once we reach Erice, high on its rock looking over Trapani and commanding views across the Mediterranean. On a clear day one can see the coasts of Sardinia and Tunisia, which is perhaps why the ancients revered this spot as the watchtower of the passage between Sicily and Africa. At the highest point above the village, an acropolis to the whole island presently contained within the ruins of an Arab fortress, lay the sanctuary of Aphrodite. According to Diodorus, the quasi-mythical Minoan Daedalus presented a golden honeycomb to the pre-Hellenic sanctuary at Erice, a symbolic representation of the sweetness of Greek colonisation of the island.

The Castello di Venere is closed and we cannot see the

remains of the sanctuary. So Illiana and I wander through the streets of the mediaeval village and talk of her travels to the Mozarabic towns of Algeria and in Türkiye where she works on Kurdish rights with a friend called Uli. We make plans to connect at a later point on my journey and walk down the hill towards Trapani in the wind and the rain. Illiana loves the mountains: after walking across the hillsides deep in thought, we hitch a lift with some young locals back to Trapani. At Trattoria Zichichi, we eat fish with local wine and discuss university life, accompanied by commentary from Signor Zichichi's parrot; and wandering the wet streets to the Torre di Ligny, talking and talking, we catch the sounds of 'popolo!' that linger from the procession on the tongues of the townspeople.

Agrigento

MONDAY 21 APRIL | TRAPANI
It is raining hard. So there is nothing to do except spend the day in bed. Eventually we rise for coffee and spinaci at the station. Everywhere else is closed. With no boat to Tunis until the overnight crossing on Saturday, I worry about my visa which expires on the Sunday, leaving me with just one day to get from the port in Tunis to the Libyan frontier. At the Libyan Embassy in London, Naziha had explained that I must arrange a rendezvous at the border, advising them in advance of my arrival time, so that I can be appointed a guide (for 100 dollars per day) who will 'look after me' during my visit. So I try to call the embassy. Do I really need a guide? But I have no luck: no one answers. Illiana and I return to the Torre di Ligny, sitting on the stone blocks with the waves lapping at our feet, talking of philosophy and language in the encircling gloom, explaining it all again with our wine to the parrot at Zichichi's.

TUESDAY 22 APRIL | AGRIGENTO
We are reluctant to bid farewell. But we walk to the station bar and take our coffee and spinaci. A man sits on a bench in the square. Next to him, a couple of feet away on the bench, is a large muscular dog looking in the opposite direction. They seem like a married couple, mutually needy, each a little forlorn and mildly irritated by the other. We laugh and understand something. We talk until the taxi arrives to take her to the airport and suddenly the fierce presence of Illiana has become an email address. Worrying again that the expiry of my Libyan visa could frustrate the entire plan of my journey, I return to the ferry terminal and explore the possibility of alternative routes to Tunis via Malta or Cagliari. But they are too uncertain, and I have to trust that my Tunisian friend

Karim can find a way for me to reach the frontier by midnight on the Sunday. Suddenly time hangs. I am not unhappy to be alone again, but a little dazed. So I take the train back to Palermo and continue on to Agrigento. I tramp up and down the hills of the town, and after finding a room at the Bella Napoli, begin reading Olivier Todd's *Albert Camus: A Life*.

Solitude
Here is the conundrum: humans are social animals but we must each face death alone. We can retreat from the complexities of living with other people but to be isolated is to be incomplete. When confronted by the joy of intimacy, even the most disciplined hermit such as Paphnutius will see himself as only having grown used to his solitude—to having made the best of a bad lot—not to having chosen it as the most perfect form of being. How then can 'love be the solution to the problem of human existence' as Erich Fromm claims? We all need to love and to be loved. But in the end it cannot solve the existential problem of solitude. Love is a distraction, an absorption, a means of passing the time, of diminishing the weight of the present. Lovers die, change or move on; and when the trance of distraction is lifted, how much more alone do we feel than if we had been in solitude all along?

Here is another fact of being: our state of physical comfort cannot always be good. Desensitised moderns are supposed to perform well regardless of their state of discomfort. Does a man bent over a lathe for fifty years ever get used to the contortions of his spine? Nowadays technology is supposed to have eased the physical burden of work. Instead of pulling a plough through sun-baked earth, we sit at computer terminals. Dare it be said that the peasant can stop and look up at the sky, while over-caffeinated software developers and call centre assistants are chained to their desks? With our street lights and nocturnal living, we miss the dawn. No wonder our days begin with the foggy gloom of partial sleep. The perfect sleeper arises without anxiety and takes the stimulant to coax the fertile flow of the already exuberant rested mind. In contrast, modern office workers grasp their coffee to mask their slumber, which was not a natural repose, an incubation of creation, but a refuge from exhaustion in the solitude of the alienation of labour.

Wednesday 23 April | Agrigento
From the station bar I walk down the hill to the Valley of the Temples, stopping at the outstanding museum of ancient Akragas. As at Syracuse, there is a substantial collection of Greek vases, some with scenes so perfectly represented that they come alive off the terracotta. The reconstruction of the vast, hubristic, Temple of Zeus is also fascinating. In the valley the abandoned ancient city is beautiful, with wild flowers scattered through the fields between the olives and the almond trees, and the temples themselves are mysterious and striking. Once again I am entirely enchanted by Hellenism.

At the Hotel Villa Athena I stop to drink water and am joined by a tall, playful Italian woman who tells me stories about the temples. The best preserved is the Temple of Concord, which has all its columns, most of the cella and both entablatures completely intact. Lacking the energy to explore the site fully, I lie in the meadows with my back against an olive tree, writing in my notebook. By now the afternoon sun is beginning to scorch the valley, and I return to the town, drinking sweet fresh orange juice on the way. Finally I get through to Naziha at the Libyan Consulate in London, and send an email to her contact in Libya stating my estimated arrival time at the frontier on Sunday. After dinner at the Trattoria di Paris, I wander the streets of Agrigento and call Illiana from a public telephone box in the city gardens.

Eros
Each new lover is proof that the previous one is not the only source of love, sweetness and affection. The opposite of that thought is often the reason why we stay with someone, afraid that once they are gone, the world will be hostile and dark. There may be other fish in the sea, but the good ones have either been caught or swim too deep for the nets. Far from a sense of meaningless repetition when we find a new lover, of

feeling that the same old habits and patterns will of necessity recur, there is in fact wonderment at the discovery of another person and joy at the variety of human individuality and experience. There are those who say that sex is simply about reproduction, and that passion and desire are the functional means of continuing the species—some go so far as to call it a human duty to the collection of all the faithful.

They are fools. Sex has no more to do with reproduction than playing chess has to do with slaying a woolly mammoth. For erotic love is the most perfect way of being with another person. This faculty is no more functional than conversation, art, music, literature, philosophy and mathematics have to do with the finding of food or the avoidance of predators. Our libido stands to the erotic as our innate curiosity stands to the intellectual: it is vital, but nothing more than fuel. The rest is down to exploration and discovery, courage and imagination. Erich Fromm considers 'the awareness of human separation' to be the source of shame and anxiety. But in the sense in which we are separate, isolated or alone—namely the metaphysical one—love is no solution. Acceptance of oneself is the only option. What is more, to love well, one must first be content in oneself. Only then can the other be appreciated, understood and loved.

Thursday 24 April | Agrigento
I write in the coffee bar at the station, entertained by the chatter of the hyperactive waiters, smart in their black suits and pressed white shirts. I walk to the Valley before it becomes too hot, exploring the temples of Hera Licinia, Olympian Zeus and Concord, as well as the Sanctuary of the Chthonic Divinities.

Fidelity
How did the Greeks use these temples? For the oracles and altars for offering sacrifices were elsewhere. Inside there was a flame, a statue of the deity and furniture for the priests and priestesses. At Akragas, Zeus and Hera lived at opposite ends of the city with the Temple of Concord halfway between them.

Hera had the better position up the hill while Zeus lived closer to the sea. What does this suggest about Hellenistic domestic life? Hera was the goddess of the nagging housewife, past her prime and hostage to Zeus's roving eye. When women from Akragas discovered their husbands' infidelities, they would sit in the Temple of Hera to console with other women in the same situation.

Ironically, the temple was also used for marriage ceremonies. One wonders what went through the mind of a young bride as the temple was cleared of distressed neglected wives before the wedding. If male infidelity was so widespread, why were these women surprised or saddened when it happened? Surely Akragan women were not so passive? Perhaps they sought erotic comfort in each other while their husbands chased young girls or boys as swans or showers of rain? Perhaps young men without the material resources to support a family and acquire a wife also came to the Temple of Hera in search of encounters with older women? What did the men do whose wives had been unfaithful?

Were grounds for divorce asymmetric in those days? If marriage is truly based on the love between two equal and interdependent people and the wish for each to be free to fully develop and experience life—why should one person not rejoice in the erotic adventures of the other and vice versa? What happened to *Ama et fac quod vis*? When we look at the divorce rate in Western society, freed from the fetters and constraints of traditional sexual ethics, does it not suggest that there is something wrong with what people might reasonably expect from marriage in a liberal society? Marriage is marriage and love is love. Marriage has always been an economic institution designed to create a secure environment in which to raise children, the cultural instantiation of a biological process of pairing contractualised as a business relationship.

Lampedusa's novel *The Leopard* opens with the old prince travelling from his palace to the brothel in Palermo, accompanied by his young sons and the padre: the sons to be educated and the padre to give them confession. And the principessa is furious. If these enduring conflicts of domestic life have been present since ancient times, and the same dynamics, rooted in human nature, persist, why can a civilised, liberal society not find an honest solution that keeps everyone happy? It is hard to be romantic these days, when check lists are so engrained in our subconscious. But it is dangerous to fall in love, and perhaps we should be grateful that Cupid strikes so infrequently. We cannot choose who we fall in love with: it creeps up on us from behind, infiltrating our defences, and the entire prior edifice of a self-contained life crumbles to dust. The lover passes his lovee a loaded revolver on a silver platter and instructs her to fire.

Despite the feminist complaint about male domination down the centuries, and the alleged objectification of women to serve the needs of male sexuality, people are people, and female sexuality is as potent a force as the male equivalent. Many women see marriage as a form of security because it raises the cost of infidelity and forces the man to commit to them. But does it not work both ways? Marriage seems to be a land of conflict. Either there is democratic expression, in which case each person must pursue their interest within the institution; or one party submits to the will of the other. In some cultures such as Lampedusa's, the patriarch is dominant. In England, the working man is slave as much to 'she who must be obeyed' as to his employer. For these women, any man will do, so long as he is well behaved and puts bacon on the table. But the minute economic transaction enters the equation, the joy of erotic love is irredeemably corrupted.

Friday 25 April | Monreale

I make my way back to Palermo, deposit my bags at the station, and take the bus up the hill to Monreale. Once again I am delighted to read this book of floor to ceiling mosaics telling stories of the Old and New Testaments. The tower is open but for the second time the cloisters are closed. I return for lunch at Peppino's and absorb the streetscape of well-dressed locals promenading in the Italian way. To be alone is sombre. But I am less distracted by the chatter of the charming company I had enjoyed in Monreale earlier and see that my powers of observation are somehow more vivid. Returning to Trapani, I am struck afresh by the natural beauty and tranquility of the town. Zichichi's is closed, so I smoke Amphora roll-up cigarettes and read Todd's biography of Camus under the ficus trees of the Villa Regina Margherita.

The charm of Albert Camus

In L'Étranger Camus delineates the phenomenology of moral action in the shimmering transience of the protagonist killing a man on the sun-judged beach of Algiers. As Gilgamesh discovered, awareness of mortality gives us the sense of powerlessness against external forces over which we have no control: fate rules our destiny. Can it be changed? Through propitiation, intercession, sacrifice, good behaviour or naïve optimism? Or can we do nothing more than look inside, to divine and accept our fate? Camus praised solitude as a means to shake off distraction and confront the elemental rawness of existence. But he did not see any value in the religious impulse, concluding that if nothing exists except atoms in the void, life has no intrinsic meaning beyond the struggle to survive and the value we create for ourselves.

Camus was a devotee of sexual pleasure and champion of individual freedom against the repressive bonds of tradition; although even Camus advocated periodic abstinence as a spur to creativity. In The Myth of Sisyphus, Camus discusses the absurd as the contradiction between the irrational character of the world and every person's desire for clarity, happiness and reason. The absurd is the confrontation between the human cry of defiance and the world's unreasoning silence, like a man attacking a machine gun with a bayonet. The consequences are revolt, freedom and passion. The absurdity of our metaphysical situation means that we must create meaning to value life and that, like Sisyphus, we must find meaning in futile work.

There was nothing absurd about Camus's personal life: he kept his wife happy, while passing through a succession of interesting and beautiful mistresses. One wonders what his girlfriends thought of each other, or if they went off to the

Temple of Hera to commiserate. Anglo-Saxony considers that attractiveness is a function of material success, that a man's money is the equivalent of a woman's beauty. In this mind world, the currency of value, the ultimate validation of a man's worth, is female affirmation: the greatest pleasure for any man is to see other more 'successful' men desire his woman and know that she loves him. Camus never had much money, so his attractiveness to women must have been due to his art, his manner and his voice. In Cromwellian England the wallet is mightier than the pen. But those French existentialists impaled their women with words.

SATURDAY 26 APRIL | TRAPANI
Anxious at the prospect of leaving the fastness of Sicily, I prepare for my departure to North Africa. I call Karim in Tunis and he confirms that he will meet me off the boat. On leaving the Albergo Moderno, I hide my yoga mat under the staircase, loathe to lose it, but keen to minimise weight. The Stazione Marittima lies across from the glazed green dome of the Chiesa del Purgatorio. I enter the church and look again at the undressed processional biers, before confronting the paperwork at the stazione. In the queue of foot passengers for the ferry, three Polish boys express their anxiety at the Tunisians standing beside them. 'We thought there were black people in Africa and we are afraid of the dark people,' they say. Perhaps it is normal that the untravelled mind should fall prey to prejudice born of ignorance? 'Don't worry,' I explain. 'Aside from the odd hawker, Tunisians are among the kindest and most hospitable people you could meet.'

I climb up to the sundeck and light an Amphora roll-up cigarette. Looking over the town I feel sad to leave the magical island of Trinacria, whose acquaintance I had scheduled for one week on this journey, but which for one reason or another has absorbed me for three. The crossing is long and the seas are rough. I pass the time reading Lawrence Durrell's novel *Justine*, whose nymphomaniac heroine breaks the hearts of all the men who love her, and eventually leaves Alexandria to become a kibbutznik, finding peace through labour. What is

Durrell's message, I wonder, from his fastness at Bellapais on Cyprus, far from the drabness of post-war Britain? That indeed *Arbeit macht frei*? That the curse of Cain cannot be escaped, and that the path of hedonistic sensualism leads only to toil and servitude? Or that the intellectual edifice of utilitarianism on which our economic system rests is directly self-defeating?

Sunday 27 April | Tunisia

Cap Bon appears on the horizon at dawn, and there is Africa across the blue-green waters of the Gulf of Tunis. We round a small desert island in the gulf and speed towards the port. On the right are the remains of ancient Carthage on its hill, the village of Sidi Bou Said and the seaside town of La Marsa; on the left the sun picks out the white houses of the southern suburbs of Tunis under the twin peaked Jebel Boukornine, scattered like granules of stardust over the hillside. After walking on to the concrete with the Tunisians clutching their Sicilian shopping, and passing up and down a series of ramps and staircases, there is my charming friend, chicken farmer turned landscape gardener, Karim Akrout, to welcome me. Karim drives me from the port to a seaside café at La Goulette where young boys serve strong coffee and croissants.

We speak about religion and politics, and Karim loses no time to convince me of the virtues of Islam. What an evangelist! 'Islam is the biggest religion in France now, so it must be the one true faith. You can't fight against the truth of Islam for ever!' Karim is recently married and says I must find a bride and return to Tunis for my honeymoon. 'Marriage is the answer to all men's quests.' 'Perhaps,' I reply, 'but only if you find the right one.' Is not the decision of who to marry the most important one in a person's life? In this sense, the metaphysical view of marriage has some foundation: what God has joined together let no one break apart. Marriage is not so much a gilded cage as a diamond shackle. In parts of India the prospective couple are literally shackled for two weeks to see if they can tolerate one another before the wedding goes ahead. 'Better be bound to the right one,' I say.

Given all the fish in the sea, how do you know whether to

eat the catch or throw it back? Which way to go in the perennial dilemma of human decision-making: to explore or to exploit? The answer is that love is simple but also improbable. First there must be the original *coup du coeur*—the undeserved thrill of triumph, like holding the winning lottery ticket—and it must be reciprocated. Then the enchantment should continue as a *chantilleuse du coeur* that is certain and symmetric, that transfigures the tedium and the toil; that makes being with the other categorical and sufficient. The tiniest suspicion that there could be someone better means there probably is: the slightest thought of 'stick or twist' means twist!

In any case, I argue, is not marriage an economic institution rather than a metaphysical one? Is there not always one side that benefits at the expense of the other? Today, in Western societies there is little rational incentive for a man to marry. Karim agrees that the cost of marrying the wrong one is high. But he explains that he willingly entered the gilded cage of marriage with all its necessary sacrifices. 'Why complicate something so simple?' he says. 'Just meet someone you like, fall in love and raise a family.' For him things are simple, and I wonder why the fly of faith never left his bottle.

I remind Karim that I must reach the Libyan frontier by midnight when my visa expires. He tells me not to worry and drives me across the Lac de Tunis to the taxi station on the western edge of the Medina. Karim negotiates a seat for me in the *louage* (shared taxi) to Tripoli and we wait for it to fill up. My companions for the nine-hour journey are an elderly English-speaking Libyan called Mu'ammar, his son Hani, and another quiet man who keeps himself to himself. Karim warmly embraces me and the louage departs.

Mu'ammar is in the front and I sit behind him, trying to hear what he is saying in the breeze. Mu'ammar was formerly a senior official in the Libyan finance ministry and has been in Tunis for cancer treatment. Despite being in pain he is remarkably good humoured. I ask him why he had to travel all the way to Tunis to get this treatment, when one imagines that Libya ought to have the resources to develop these facilities herself. Mu'ammar demurs and explains that his country is not ready, but that in time these things will come to Libya. The journey is difficult for him. But the roads are straight and clear, and the taxi is a comfortable 1970s Mercedes whose engine softly purrs away as we head south at speed.

The route ascends to a low plateau of wheat fields and olive groves ringed by distant hills glowing in the morning light. Far away to the right is the Dorsale range while to the left is the small mountain of the Jebel Zaghouan that watches over the plain whose ancient cities it watered. For some distance, the road passes beside the remains of the ancient aqueduct that carried water from the hills to Roman Carthage. We pass several brown signposts to Roman sites in this eastern part of the Tell, but as we descend to Kairouan, the land becomes drier and more yellow. Barely three hours from Tunis, we have passed from the Mediterranean to the Sahel. At my request we take a short detour to see the famous mosque. They are anxious about delaying in case we get held up at the border, but we have a short time to wander around.

For an infidel, the Holy City of Kairouan is the nearest one can get to the experience of being a Muslim pilgrim. For the holy places of the Hijaz and al-Quds are closed to non-Muslims. So Kairouan is special, and indeed four pilgrimages to Kairouan are considered equivalent to one full Hajj to Mecca. The town has dusty boulevards with spacious low buildings that would not feel out of place on the Euphrates. Surrounded by the walled town rising out of its sun-baked plain, the ninth-century Great Mosque is the historical epicentre of Maghrebi Islam. Entering the marble paved courtyard, one sees a contained expanse, timeless in its barren emptiness. The façade of the central entrance of the hypostyle prayer hall, with its dome and stone arcades, summons one to a geometric nothingness inside, the austere abstract Islamic interpretation of transcendence. The contrast with Monreale could not be more stark.

We continue south and stop for spicy chicken and rice at a road-side canteen. The expanse of desert and the road stretching into the distance are astonishingly beautiful, and as I clutch my seat squeezed into the back of the taxi, I am full of ideas. We reach the border at six o'clock, three hours before the 'tourist guide' expects me, and with six hours to spare before my visa expires. My passport is examined and date stamped, together with the others. Under the gaze of giant pictures of Qadhafi in his officer's uniform and African outfits, we make it straight through with only the briefest of questions. Thanks to the presence of Mu'ammar in the taxi, I have entered Libya clandestinely and can wander freely in what is essentially a closed country. I am also 1,400 dollars richer, as that is what I would have had to pay my handler for the privilege of his services. On reaching the outskirts of Tripoli, Mu'ammar and Hani alight and ask the louage to drop me at the comfortable Qasr Libya Hotel on the eastern side of the Medina, which is popular with Tunisians.

Tripolitania

MONDAY 28 APRIL | TRIPOLI

My room is on the fourth floor on the seaward side with views of the harbour. Descending the stairs, I study the full-length portraits of the Great Leader that adorn each landing: Qadhafi the freedom fighter in khakis; Qadhafi the Generalissimo with epaulettes and sunglasses; Qadhafi the Arab sheikh; Qadhafi the pan-Africanist with camel coloured robes and cap—each incarnation expressing a different aspect of the deity, recounting a different episode of his story. After breakfast, I chat with the money changers at reception, and realise that while the Qasr is reasonable, the bureau-de-change is not. Preparing to explore Tripoli, I empty my rucksack, neatly arranging my belongings on the second bed in the room. Having travelled thus far in a pair of blue leather walking boots, it is time to don my Palestinian Ferraris, a pair of 'Ferrari' branded leather flip-flops that I found in the Jerusalem souq in the year of the Jubilee. Suitably attired, I walk through the Italian-built district with its colonial buildings and cropped white-painted trees into the Medina.

The Medina is a smaller, sleepier version of Tunis, mostly low ochre coloured buildings, with arcades and vines across the alleys providing shade. The fronts along the main street are entirely in Arabic, as it is forbidden to have any signs in Latin script. Indeed the only shop in Libya carrying English signage sells sports shoes and is owned by one of Qadhafi's sons, the footballer al-Saadi. Stylish and immaculate under Italian rule, the Medina now feels run down, with a distinctly African flavour in the lanes behind the main street. At the far end is the third-century Triumphal Arch of Oea, dedicated to Marcus Aurelius and Verus, and the only complete structure in Tripoli that survives from antiquity. The French traveller Henri

Méhier de Mathuisieulx related in 1903 that the arch's side-niches were filled in and the central space used as a tavern. Restored by the Italians, the marble today has an iridescent quality, as fresh as the Maison Carrée at Nîmes, with finely carved classical motifs, bas relief figures and vines.

Next to the arch is a friendly café whose clientele seem to be mainly black Africans. There is certainly no Bordeaux on the menu now. I sip my mint tea, the ubiquitous 'Berber whisky' of North Africa, and begin reading Qadhafi's *The Green Book*. This masterpiece is a cross between the Qur'an and the Communist Manifesto and is intended to provide the intellectual justification for the Great Socialist People's Libyan Arab Jamahiriya. Initial impressions are unpersuasive: it meanders along on a stream of grand-sounding words that amount to little more than that Libyans need Qadhafi to care for them.

I have to change my US dollar banknotes into Libyan dinars. Having been ripped off at the official bureau in the Qasr Hotel, I trawl the Medina for a more favourable exchange rate. A young English-speaking boy called Khalid has been following me around. So we make friends and he takes me to one of the Italian buildings off Green Square to eat stale flatbread and mouldy hummus. We walk to the gold souq in the Medina and Khalid introduces me to an engaging English-speaking trader called Salem Ali Baitro.

Libya is a pure cash economy: no bank accounts, no cheques, indeed no electronic money of any kind and not even any cash machines. Everyone is paid in physical cash which they hoard and use when required. Since there is a highly effective secret police force, and hence no crime in Libya, no one needs to worry about losing their savings. Since there is no financial system, and all investments are made by the state, which also keeps inflation low via the export surplus and strong fixed exchange rate, no one can earn a return on their savings, and no one imagines they need to. All loans are made with physical cash at zero interest rates, and money has a mental meaning equivalent to a physical commodity such as wheat or flour.

Since the financial crash of 1929, economists have flirted

with the idea of narrow banking, which eliminates fractional reserve expansion of the monetary base and has the advantage of preventing credit bubbles. But in the absence of a specie standard such as gold, the theory has always run up against the problem of how to back the currency. Even with a gold standard, as in nineteenth-century America, narrow banking kept money too tight, starving entrepreneurs of credit and funds for investment. Hence the Wizard of Oz.

In Libya's case, the monetary authority can hold dollars to match its dinar issuance, and those dollars are backed by oil exports. The tax raising power of the state to 'pay the bearer on demand' becomes irrelevant. All holders of dinars need to know is that the Great Leader will continue collecting petrodollars and will hand over enough of them to balance the internal accounts of the exchequer and the external accounts of the central bank. Simple Bedouin household economics. Perhaps reflecting the small population and the low velocity of transactions, Libyan dinars are extremely handsome notes in almost perfect condition. As I give Salem my dog-eared Yankee bills and take his pristine green dinars, inscribed in their elaborate geometric patterns, I feel I am holding something more beautiful and valuable in my hand.

Laughing at my description of the sandwich, Salem invites me to join him at a Turkish restaurant for a second, more appetising, lunch and tells me about his flourishing gold trading business. He buys worked gold in Italy and sells it in Tripoli to the locals who keep it as a parallel currency to dinars. He also sells to the Africans and buys unworked artisanal gold they have brought with them from producing countries such as Ghana to trade with the jewellers in Italy. Salem knows everyone in the souq and helps out other traders if they run into difficulties. He also explains that he does not pay any tax: he has a good relationship with the authorities and they leave him to his own devices. This is why he can give me a better exchange rate than the official bureau at the Qasr Hotel. I feel I have crossed a barrier and made friends with a local bigwig. Salem returns to his shop and tells me emphatically to call on him at any time if I need anything.

In the market behind the citadel I meet a compatriot, Jeremy Peacocke, who invites me for tea at the al-Kabir hotel with his brother Chris from the British Embassy. Chris gives an impressive direct translation from the local newspaper, and is insightful about the diplomatic processes aimed to restore relations with Libya and rehabilitate Qadhafi. But as we turn to the Iraq war, the predictable arrogance flows out: oh yes, we the experts (the vested administrative interests) know what we are doing, even it it involves killing thousands of innocent people, even if bombing presumed terrorists is only going to create legions more.

As the light fades, I wander in the lanes of the Medina and find a rooftop terrace to lie on my back and absorb the soundscape. The soft cacophony of the town decomposes into voices, birds and the wind, and at the appointed moment, the muezzins call the faithful to the Maghrib prayer on their loudspeakers. For several minutes the mellifluous chanting hypnotically rises and falls. It is unusual, I think, to lie on a rooftop at the centre of a capital city and not be deafened. What does one hear in London? Aircraft coming in to land, helicopters, police sirens, buses, trains and cars, barely the occasional church bell, and no birds—indeed hardly any natural sounds at all—and always in the background a pulsing hum, the low pitched menacing agglomeration of a million engines turning, a million rubber wheels on tar.

Delacroix, one of the early Orientalist painters, wrote in his diaries that industrial progress was proportional to the disintegration of artistic values. That is what is crushing in the metropolis: population density and industrialisation have destroyed our sound world. We are drowning in evil sounds. Like the inhabitants of the Bowery, we tune them out. As our inner ears close, our blood pressure rises, our horizons contract and our inspiration dies. But my reverie is interrupted by an uptick in sound that arrives with the darkness. I walk out of the Medina and discover that Green Square has become the focal point for the evening ritual of Tripolitans to drive around in circles honking their horns and exuberantly make a lot of noise, perhaps to shake off the stupor of the hot day. Perhaps people everywhere need noise to excite them?

TUESDAY 29 APRIL | TRIPOLI
Breakfast at the Qasr consists of a boiled egg and cheese with pitta, fava bean stew and chicory coffee from large urns on tables covered with white sheets. The Qasr is busy with African businessmen, mostly from Chad and Niger, dignified in their flowing white robes, and giving the impression of a harmonious commercial interchange between the North African coast and its distant hinterland. I walk past the lavish al-Kabir hotel and along Sharia al-Fatah by the seafront to Green Square, the central reference point of Tripoli. The National Museum of the Great Socialist People's Libyan Arab Jamahiriya is housed in the former citadel, the Assaria al-Hamra, looking over the square. The museum combines fine classical sculpture from the period of the Roman Principate with assorted Qadhafi memorabilia, including a photo exhibition of machine-gun-toting female warriors in jeeps. After admiring the statues of Hercules and Alexander, now protected by modern day Amazons, the Bedouin dictator's Praetorian Guard, I look for some local cuisine.

Salem takes me to Munir's restaurant on the first floor of a residential building behind the souqs. Munir's is a meeting place for the tiny Libyan underground movement—that is tolerated, even encouraged, by the regime—and cooks up excellent local dishes. Munir and his friend the painter Ali speak about life in Tripoli where everything is taken care of (except for health problems that require a trip to Tunis) but where no one except senior officials and a few independent traders like Salem has any money, and where nothing ever changes. With its quiet ambience and light open windows, Munir's is the perfect place to write.

Having thought I had exhaustively explored the Medina, I now find its most charming spot: an old courtyard khan with a low pool, black and white marble tiles and cacti in urns, whose languid shopkeepers ostensibly sell carpets and handicrafts, but mostly sit around drinking tea. The offset to a dictatorship that bribes its people with largesse is a certain ennui, a stifling sense that since it does not make much difference what one does, one might as well not do very much. It is ironic that investors and tourists look for the opposite qualities in an exotic foreign location. To an investor, Tripoli is a dead letter for its lack of velocity. But as with the anecdotal Mexican guitarist, who makes his fortune only to retire to his previous life playing music in the square, once the frontier market investor has made his money, he seeks out exactly the peace and harmony to enjoy his gains that he formerly eschewed in identifying money-making opportunities.

Absorbing the spirit of indolence, I return for a siesta at the Qasr before finding a serviceable grand piano on the mezzanine of the al-Kabir hotel. Against the background of phones constantly ringing, I take out my pages of Bach transcriptions and play away. I invent some chords, the beginnings of a composition, or at least an improvisation, and the waiter is so impressed he leaves a red rose for me on the piano. In the evening I smoke Amphora cigarettes on the boat-restaurant in the port as the sun sets over the harbour.

Wednesday 30 April | Tripoli

On a long journey, each new place of rest establishes a new routine. In Tripoli it begins with breakfast at the Qasr, then to Munir's to write. Today I have a problem: Khalid is waiting for me outside the Qasr Hotel and wants to be my guide. Trying not to offend him, I explain that I have no need for a guide and must hasten off. I return to Munir's and find a table in the corner to pass the morning taking notes from my books. Spacious and light, with the warm breeze coming through the open windows, it occurs to me that first-floor establishments are much more conducive to reading and writing than the ground floor. Is it the ideal of the *piano nobile* or perhaps simply the convenience of not being hassled by street noise and passers-by?

The first scene of *Tapwater*, a play in four parts about revisiting earlier versions of oneself, is going well, when Ali Agati arrives to interrupt my fledgling literary attempts. Ali is a wizened old translator who persuades me to accompany him to the former Spanish consulate which is now home to a colony of artists and writers. The nearest thing to dissidents, they grumble about Qadhafi and complain that, unlike the leaders of most other Arab countries, he does not patronise the arts. How can they make a decent showing at Arab artists' congresses when they are given no support at home? Fakhri's symbolic painting of Arab humiliation at the hands of Israel is touching. Salem had invited me to meet him after lunch to watch the Libyan football team play Argentina at the National Stadium on the outskirts of Tripoli. But I am so engaged with the dissidents that by the time I reach Salem's shop it is too late: he has already left for the stadium. So I miss the opportunity to watch Argentina beat Libya 3—1 despite the best efforts of al-Saadi Qadhafi, and return instead to the boat-restaurant in the port.

Tripoli harbour is breezy and expansive in the late afternoon light. The Amphora tobacco takes me into a ruminative state, but my pen is idle. When you sit down with the perfect conditions hoping for inspiration, nothing happens. The ideas seem to lose their immediacy: what ends up on the page seems to be only the pale memory or reconstruction of them. All I can think of is my doubt that for the 'metaphysical freedom from infinity' argument to work, it must be shown that realism holds in mathematics, for example that Cantor's Theorem is objectively true, and that this entails that nature-in-itself is continuous. How can this be achieved without using the Axiom of Infinity, the arbitrary assumption that our longed-for paradise must exist because we want it to? We cannot cross the threshold of hope by simply stipulating that we must. It is not enough to assume can opener. If nature is discrete as the quantum gravity theorists suppose, does that not undermine the argument for metaphysical freedom? I find an internet point with good connection speed on the top floor of an office block and enjoy the warm night air coming in through the windows.

THURSDAY 1 MAY | TRIPOLI

I return to the museum to photograph the well-preserved classical sculpture, and meet Salem for lunch at Munir's before sitting down to write. Again my literary inspiration is fleeting.

So I drink tea with Ali, who thinks I have potential, indeed could be the next Hemingway. Would I take his manuscripts to my publisher in London? After much expostulating, I convince him that I have never published anything, and cannot help him in his literary endeavours. The hoped for pages are returned to the satchel, and we discuss contemporary Arab writers, from Nizar Qabban and Rafik Schami in Syria to Taha Hussein and Naguib Mahfouz in Egypt, the Libyan Ibrahim Kuni and the Moroccan Tahar Ben Jelloun.

Restless, I walk along the coast road west from the Medina in the glaring sun, past the al-Imad towers, the Carinthia hotel, and a barracks with murals of Qadhafi's Amazons. Eventually I reach the British School. I knock on the door and am invited in for a gin and tonic by Charles and Maureen Weston, two kindly teachers from Yorkshire. Charles does not say a great deal but Maureen radiates enthusiasm, punctuating every observation about the Libyans with a glance at her husband, adding 'isn't that right, Charles?' They are enjoying Tripoli but lament the gulf in the mind world of their students, whose strict dedication to Islam makes it difficult for them to think freely and form an independent reasoned view of the world. As they drop me back in Green Square, they tell me that I am adventurous to be travelling like this.

Salem takes me for dinner at his friend Ramadan's place in a gloomy tower block on the edge of Tripoli. Ramadan is poor, henpecked and devout, and his Maltese wife Leila (formerly Maria) has a mighty tongue. They are raising five attractive children in their tiny apartment. The oldest, Sara, is beautiful and wants to study in England. Later Salem tells me that he helps Ramadan find jobs, and plans to help Sara too, although in case of any doubt, she is categorically off limits, even to his wandering eye. We talk about politics, and I explain that I have noticed the complete absence of any soldiers or police in official uniforms. 'That is because they are in plain clothes,' explains Salem. 'Have no doubt: we are being watched.'

Then I express my surprise at the large number of black Africans in Tripoli who have come mainly from Nigeria, Ghana and Chad to earn money and either cross to Europe or send clothes and other supplies back home. 'We don't much like the Africans,' they continue. 'Qadhafi turned to black Africa because his pan-Arab leadership ambitions were snubbed by the Gulfis. Mubarak was keen to take his money, but the Saudis didn't need it and they see themselves as the leaders of the Arab world. So Qadhafi proclaimed himself the Father of Africa, opened the southern border with Chad, and invested in the African Union. But we're Mediterranean people: we look to Italy and Europe for cultural influence, even if we are Muslims and Arabs, bound to our tribe, clan and family. Qadhafi has let a million black Africans come into the country from the south. But we're a small population of five million. There are too many of them and they have no skills or education. We make some money trading with the Africans, but it is not worth it.'

'Aren't they part of the 'umma too: are they not all God's children?' I ask. Salem explains that it is a mistake to dilute one's ethnic identity: it is best to marry from one's own tribe and let the Africans do the same. 'What is bred in the bone will out in the flesh,' I reply. 'Yes,' says Salem, 'white and black don't mix.' 'But if you're white, what am I?' I ask. 'Cheese, obviously,' says Salem: 'you're cheese!' 'What kind of cheese?' I reply. 'It doesn't matter,' they laugh: 'any cheese will do.' 'But it matters to me,' I say.

Salem drives me back to the Qasr and I reflect on what I have heard. The Libyans are articulating an instinct about identity that trumps their commitment to the 'umma (the community of the faithful). Their ample demonstration of Arab hospitality, deriving from the Abrahamic insight that a stranger could be an angel in disguise, coexists with a protective perimeter fence to their identity, defined by ethnicity, confession and tribe. The same problem arises whenever the indigenes of one society are confronted by an influx of aliens. As the introduction of grey squirrels into England almost eliminated the indigenous red squirrels, the untrammelled flow of capital sanctioned by the utility maximisation arguments of globalist libertarians must inevitably replace cultural diversity with a soulless internationalism. Any group has the right to preserve its identity. But the utopian ideal of a borderless world is a cipher for corruption. In extremis, globalist textbook models will eliminate the way of life and identity of anyone but the lowest cost producers.

FRIDAY 2 MAY | SABRATHA

Shared taxis to Zawiyah and the classical site of Sabratha leave from the Bab Jadeed at the southern end of the Medina. But it is Friday prayers and no one is going. After stopping some tourists, enquiring if anyone wants to visit Sabratha, I fall in with one Frank Cachia, a Maltese businessman, and his niece and nephew, Ann-Marie and Manuel. We visit the Orthodox Church in the Medina and stop to drink locally produced 'bitter' in green cans, which has the same flavour as Campari and is refreshing in the heat. Frank finds his driver Khalid and we set off for Sabratha, ninety minutes west of Tripoli along the coast.

Arriving at the site, we wander past the reconstructed theatre and public baths to enjoy the crystal purity of the blue sea below the ruins of the first-century Temple of Isis. Sabratha feels distinctly Mediterranean with fresh salty air and a soft breeze off the lapping waves, the scent of pines and ilex casting their needles and leaves like a carpet over the classical remains. The museum is closed but there is a row of statues arranged around the reconstructed colonnade outside. Emulating the ancient structures has become associated with the style of the fascistic period. But surely it makes sense to build with a simple, reliable aesthetic out of durable materials to a high standard?

On our way back to Tripoli we stop in one of the villages for lunch. There is no sign but the owner recognises Frank and treats us to an enormous meal. 'Qadhafi's Libya considers itself a modern Muslim country,' Frank explains. 'Alcohol is banned but women drive cars and walk arm-in-arm with their boyfriends. Mobile phones are heard ringing as often as calls to prayer. In the cities, everyone has electricity and water, while health care and schools are free.' I tell him that Qadhafi's Libya is as eccentric as its ruler, but charming once you penetrate the barrier of everything being in Arabic. Frank wants to talk about the consequences of Malta joining the EU. There are many opportunities in Libya, he tells me, and the Maltese are well placed to take advantage of them, with their proximity, linguistic facility and cultural similarity. Malta offers a route into the EU for the Libyan business community, although Frank is sketchy about how this relates to the corruption of the regime.

Passing through the towns and villages in Tunisia, one notices that all shopfronts, doors and window frames are uniformly painted bright sky blue, as if there is just one colour of paint available in the entire country. It was already dark when I arrived at the border, so it is not until now, driving through these villages, that I notice that in Libya, every shopfront, door and window frame is painted racing green. Frank drops me at the Qasr where I change and return to the piano at the al-Kabir. Today the waiter is less pleased and asks me to stop. After sending emails at the internet point, I meet Frank and his friend Victor for bitter on the roof of the Qasr. Following the intense heat of the day, the cool evening breeze on the roof terrace is revivifying.

SATURDAY 3 MAY | LEPTIS MAGNA

From the station near the Qasr I take the first bus to al-Khoms on the coast east of Tripoli. Fortified by strong coffee from an Italian espresso machine, I walk along the beach towards the ancient site of Leptis Magna, arriving on the seaward side of the city like a ship. Qadhafi has built a power station and an oil refinery near Leptis which emits a yellow gas cloud similar to the plant I observed on the coast north of Tunis. Environmental regulation might as well be non-existent in Arab dictatorships. As I walk by the crystal waters of the blue sea, I see the pillars and marble stones of the pristine Roman remains emerging from the reeds and dunes to reveal perhaps the most inspiring ancient site in the Mediterranean world.

The formal entrance and triumphal arches are on the landward side and I do not at first appreciate the layout of the city, which lies between the channel of the Wadi Lebda and the coast. I rest on the stones of the seaward baths imagining the scene of a ship embarking from a painting by Claude Lorraine. Leptis feels like the instantiation of a recurring dream, wandering timeless through the splendour of ancient ruins. I walk along the archaeologists' narrow-gauge railway to the Old Forum, and the vast enclosure of the Severan Forum. It is difficult to convey the grandeur of the forum, basilica and nymphaeum of Septimius Severus, built with stones imported from all over the empire when Rome was at the zenith of its power.

Imagine a wide open space paved with glowing marble, surrounded by sandstone walls, each block cut to perfection. To the north is the central doorway connecting the forum with the basilica, as massive as the emperor's entrance door at Hagia Sofia; on each side is a row of seven free standing smaller marble doorways surmounted by elaborate lintels. The floor of the forum is littered with the remnants of finely worked porphyry, marble and granite elements that have fallen down: columns, pedestals, capitals, lintels, cornices and the recurring circular Medusa medallions, which beam out from the spandrels in an arcade that has been rebuilt. The colours and intricacy of the stonework are astonishing. The forum is deserted and eerily quiet: the only sounds are the distant waves and the wind in the palms. I continue to the Via Trionfale and over to the theatre, then back along the Via Colonnata to Hadrian's Baths.

Drowsy from the early start I lie down in the shade of a broken tablet on the nymphaeum and imagine the Lepticians living carefree lives in this environment. After a time my reverie is broken by groups of school children, shouting and chattering as they pass by. The Leptis museum by the main entrance to the site is disappointing and contains little information. But beside the Arch of Hadrian I meet Ulrich, a German archaeologist from Mainz who lends me his guidebook over a sandwich at the roadside restaurant. According to the Italian archaeologists who excavated Leptis in the early twentieth century, what we see today dates primarily from the Augustan and Severan periods.

Leptis (or Lepcis, to use the Punic name) was founded by

Phoenicians who intermarried with the indigenous Numidians, developing a distinctive local identity and became the leading city of the Tripolitanian Emporia. After the Punic wars Leptis fell into the Roman orbit, forming an alliance with Rome at the beginning of the Jugurthine War in 111 BC. Backing Pompey, Leptis found itself on the wrong side of the first Roman civil war, leading Caesar to impose an enormous annual indemnity of 40,000 amphorae (one million litres) of olive oil. Once the Principate was established, Leptis was absolved from this burden and began to prosper again, exporting agricultural commodities throughout the Mediterranean. The leading families set about beautifying the city with public works, inspired by what they had seen in Rome herself. One man in particular, Hannibal Tapapius Rufus, poured his money into the white marble of the Old Forum and theatre, asserting the pride of the wealthy provincial city in the grandeur of its architecture.

A century and a half later the Lepticians Septimius Severus and his son Caracalla took control of Rome. They engaged in lavish building programmes across the empire and channelled its wealth into the beautification of Leptis. Following the competent government of the Antonines the Severan profligacy weakened the Roman state and contributed to the decline of the Western Empire. Which is causally prior? Is the extravagant construction the final flourish of economic vitality before the inevitable decadence that follows it? Or is decline the historical accident that follows the period of prosperity? Consider the building programme of the British at the start of the twentieth century, with grand constructions from the Victoria and Albert Museum to the Government Buildings in New Delhi that heralded imperial collapse.

Yet is there not more value in a beautifully carved piece of public architecture that lasts for centuries than in a cheap gadget with doubtful application that expires after a few years and clutters up the world with detritus? Our world has become de-aestheticised because in the coordinate frame of economic activity, there are not enough resources to go around. The purpose of production has shifted from the quality of the object produced to the provision of livelihoods to hands that would otherwise be idle. As the global population has expanded and as growth has become dependent on the ever more abstruse technologicisation of day-to-day life, increasing the complexity and computer intensity of economic activity, the quality of the resulting 'material culture' has deteriorated. Ulrich's guidebook is detailed. But nowhere can I find an explanation for the Medusa motif, repeated on medallions through the Severan Forum. Later I read that the Gorgon Heads, like Minerva's shield, symbolised victory: the might of Jupiter Capitolinus turning her enemies white with fear. But at Leptis they represent the hubris of Severan folly: 'Look on my works ye mighty and despair!' As dusk descends, I walk back to al-Khoms along the seashore and take a taxi to Tripoli.

Sunday 4 May | Tripoli

I wander through the Medina taking photographs of the charming buildings. Next to the old mosque by the Aurelian Arch, which is used by resident African Muslims and has colourful tiles on the wall, I discover the library of the former English consulate and browse the volumes. After lunch at Munir's and bidding farewell to Ali and Fakhry, I return. The library is dusty, but quiet and focussed, and I regret not staying longer in Tripoli: once one has made friends and found favourite spots, it is difficult to leave.

Salem takes me for dinner at the house of his Tunisian friend Nasreen. Their apartment is in a colonial era building, with a terrace and pot plants. Salem talks about his business, explaining that with gold trading, the objective is the same as for any business: to generate the highest return on capital. He explains that according to Islamic economic principles, capital should not be passive. Money under the mattress is wasted and to earn interest on any risk-free investment such as a bank deposit is usury: investors must share in the uncertainty of the enterprise. I think of Qadhafi's billions lying idle in bank vaults, and it occurs to me that while the Jamahiriya is supposed to be socialist, in reality it conforms to Pareto's principles of asset concentration: merchants, operating outside the official economy are thriving, while everyone else is poor.

We are joined by Nasreen's family for Tunisian food and friendly conversation. Suggesting that I might feel homesick so far away from my country, they look through their satellite television menu to find something British. So our supper is accompanied by *Braveheart*, a costume drama about Scottish resistance to English rule. Struck by the contrast of that northern bleakness with the brightness of Libya, it is no wonder I think, that the Roman legions declined to invade Caledonia; no wonder that the Scots were induced to flee their dour peninsular to administer far flung provinces of the British Empire; no wonder that the British have a visceral longing to escape the windswept darkness of their Atlantic Isle and find solace in the southern sun.

Cyrenaica

MONDAY 5 MAY | LEPTIS MAGNA

The early bus to al-Khoms leaves me as dopey as before. But I am pleased to return to Leptis and take more time to absorb the site, once again enjoying the walk by the sea. At the edge of the ruins I find a sealed bath house buried in the dunes and by accident drop one of my flip-flops into the open cavity. Fortunately some young boys are able to recover the shoe by finding a secret passageway into the bath house through the sand. I walk around the site, exploring the ancient harbour and the lighthouse at the end of the point, as well as the circus and the amphitheatre before returning to the temples of Jove, Serapis and the Flavii.

Salem arrives in the afternoon and we chat in the communal marble latrines of the bath house. One imagines Romans passing the tablet from one to another as they relieve themselves. At the Severan Forum I reflect that frontier regions are creations of the imagination and that as the physical environment is degraded by demography and over-development, tourism becomes less attractive. Part of the joy of Leptis is that the well-preserved site feels untouched by modernity. But to Salem these are just old stones, lacking meaning or excitement, and after a couple of hours he is impatient to leave.

On the way back to Tripoli, Salem tells me his confessions. He is happily married to a Libyan lady, lives in a large house, and is devoted to his four children. But he has a weakness for African girls, and has any number of African customers who bank their earnings in gold jewellery and are willing to jump into his bed. As we whizz down the highway, Salem tells me with great joy in his face how he once met two Ghanaian ladies in his shop who invited him to join them 'to make wonderful sex'.

But Libya is a conservative Muslim country where women wear headscarves and men cannot shake a woman's hand in public. Traditional beliefs have a firm grip on men's minds, and Salem is extremely diligent about his Muslim observances. He tells me with all sincerity that he is mentally torn between his duties as a father and his pleasures with the African girls, and is genuinely worried by what Allah thinks about his improprieties. 'Will Allah forgive my illicit indulgences?' he asks me, to get an outsider's view. I assure him that Allah is merciful and compassionate and that his peccadillos will count for nought—so long as he does not allow his guilt to become too strong. When we arrive back in Tripoli Salem takes me to his house, which is modern and comfortable, tidy and ordered. His young son serves us couscous before I return to the Qasr and settle up in preparation for my journey east in the morning.

Tuesday 6 May | Benghazi
Salem catches me at dawn walking to the bus station. Touched by his going the second mile, we warmly embrace and he waves me off for fourteen tedious hours along the coast road to Benghazi. I read Albert Hourani's *History of the Arab Peoples* and fall into the rhythm of the slowly passing desiccated landscapes; alas, the air conditioning and the smokers and the loud Arab pop music in the bus make it quite unpleasant. The fumes are awful and, despite my protestations, my otherwise talkative and friendly fellow travellers resist opening the skylight in the roof. The only consolation is that at ten dollars it must be the cheapest 1,000 kilometres to travel anywhere in the world. The road is uniform for the entire journey as we pass the outskirts of Misrata and traverse the Gulf of Sirte. Some distance past Misrata, the bus stops at a roadside food stand where a man called Ramadan tells me that from Rabat to Baghdad all Arab countries are the same: failed dictatorships that crush the human spirit. We stop at dusk for shawarma beside a brightly lit new mosque. Benghazi is uninspiring but the driver takes me to a *funduq* (inn) near the bus station.

Wednesday 7 May | Cyrene

The bus to al-Bayda passes along the depopulated and unspoiled coastline, past hillsides and olive groves. Cyrenaica is an island of green, the gift of the Jebel Akhdar. The town of al-Bayda consists of a single straight street that passes up and down a hill, and there is just one funduq in the town, with spotlessly clean rooms. After unpacking my things, I take another bus the short distance to the ancient site of Cyrene along a tree lined road with white painted trunks. Cyrene lacks the grandeur and wealth of Leptis. But it was built into a watered spur of the Jebel Akhdar and has expansive views across the plain. After walking in a stupor of delight at the charm of the place, I explore the Hellenic temples in the lower site and agora, before returning to the spring of Apollo, the raison d'être of the city's foundation. Some Libyan visitors say they cannot believe that their country, which is almost entirely desert, contains such a place as this.

As I wash my feet in the spring, watching the local children jumping in and out of the pool, my digital camera—placed out of sight beneath my books and shoes and socks—is artfully whisked away. I leap up but it is too late: the camera is lost and with so many of them I cannot tell which child is the thief. So I initiate the process of calling upon authority, starting with the attendants at the gate who stop an English-speaking passer-by called Suleyman Omar al-Fitouri, and ultimately Abdul Hamid, the local party chief, whose son had been among the group of children. Presently the camera is recovered but without the memory card. The children trawl through the site in search of the card which eventually they find. Abdul Hamid asks in solemn tones if I am satisfied that all wrongs have been redressed and, if so, can he go? I feel embarrassed that the representative of this region in the national council should be waiting on the word of a foolhardy tourist who allowed his camera to be pinched by a group of raucus children. But Suleyman tells me not to worry and takes me to his house in the nearby village of Shahhat for dinner.

Suleyman is an electrical engineer who lives off government contracts. The eldest of seven brothers and barely a few years older than me, he already has several children. The house is essentially a concrete Bedouin tent furnished with cushions and an outsized television on wheels which receives all the world's satellite channels. One son brings in a round metal tray with a mountain of food. Suleyman switches the channel to Norwegian lesbian pornography and as we scoop our kofta, falafel and tabouleh with eyes on stalks, we talk of Qadhafi, Bedouin life and women. Suleyman explains that his wife and daughters have bird brains and that female education is pointless. All is noble simplicity, but with the women hidden from view. Suleyman extends his hand of friendship and seems interested to know more about life in Britain.

Suleyman's taste in pornography reminds me of the Ottoman fetish for blue-eyed Circassians. I had always thought that love was narcissistic, that deep down we search for the simulacrum of ourselves in the opposite sex, that sampling the exotic other is merely part of the adventure of youth, sowing one's wild oats, but that one's Platonic other half must be hewn from the exact same block, that true happiness lies with the girl next door or, like Ptolemy and Cleopatra, perhaps even from the same litter. But what if your own kind is commodified and sold? Catullus idealised white-skinned women that have the wealth not to work in the fields. Now here we are in the global marketplace for televisual erotic stimulation, and the demand is for the lean, firm-breasted Scandinavian blonde. After tea Suleyman drives me back to al-Bayda and promises to take me to the secret spring at Ras Hillel on Friday.

THURSDAY 8 MAY | AL-BAYDA
The Funduq al-Bayda has a comfortable dining room with tables clad in smooth green tablecloths, sturdy chairs and curtains that let in the right amount of bright sunlight. I drink chicory coffee, smoke a Toscano cigar and return to Qadhafi's *The Green Book* in which the dictator elaborates his system of Islamic Socialism. When breakfast hour is finished, I enjoy the tranquillity of the empty room with the bright light of the African sun falling across the dining table and take notes from my books. But the coffee stirs up my restlessness and it is

difficult to make sense of *The Green Book*. After lunch on the main street under another large image of Qadhafi, I return to Cyrene to explore the ruins more thoroughly.

According to Herodotus, Cyrene was founded by colonists from the island of Thera around 630 BC, their leader, Battus, being selected for the task by the Oracle of Delphi. The Greeks defeated the local tribes, then integrated them into the economy and the colony flourished. The new city was named after a nymph who had apparently strangled a lion, thereby allowing the colonists to settle there. Cyrenaica became a Persian satrapy after the conquest of Egypt by Cambyses, then an extension of Ptolemaic Egypt and was eventually united with Crete as a Greek speaking Roman Province. Libanius relates that Cyrene was rebuilt by the Emperor Claudius Gothicus after an earthquake in 262, and then abandoned for Ptolemais on the coast after a more severe quake in 365. The region was conquered by the Arabs in 643 and repopulated by the Bedouin tribes of Banu Hilal and Banu Sulaym in the eleventh century.

For nearly a thousand years, Cyrenaica was the southern outpost of the Hellenic world, connected with Egypt, Sicily and the Aegean. The Cyrenaic philosophers corresponded with the Epicureans and the Stoics, and were devoted advocates of a simple sensuous hedonism, believing that bodily pleasures are preferable to the intellectual pleasures of the soul. The most celebrated artefact to have been uncovered in Cyrene is the life-sized marble statue of Aphrodite Anadyomene ('from the sea'), in the style of Praxiteles, whose missing arms are thought to have been fixing her wet hair. The statue was discovered by the Temple of Apollo that was built over the mythical grove of myrtles where the sun god seduced the nymph Cyrene.

Above all Cyrene was known in the ancient world for *silphium*, a versatile plant whose sap was used as a perfume, aphrodisiac and general-purpose medicine. Silphium was the emblem of Cyrene and appeared on the city's coins. During the Roman period, demand for silphium jumped exponentially and its value became so distorted that Caesar kept some in the state treasury. Whether due to competition for land or demand for livestock that overgrazed on the herb, or whether the plant's peculiar botany made it difficult to cultivate, by the middle of the first century, stocks of silphium had plummeted. Pliny relates that in the time of Nero it had become impossible to obtain. No one is quite sure of the plant's exact identity. But descriptions by Theophrastus and the images on the coins, suggest that it may have been a variety of fennel or celery. Equally it is not known if the original plant became extinct or survives in a form not identified as silphium.

Looking over the ravine at the canteen along the road to Cyrene's ancient port of Apollonia, I watch the sunset with grilled lamb's kidneys and a can of bitter. It is easy to understand how the Cyrenaicans responded to the beauty of this place by developing a philosophy of simple sensuality. Three local lads invite me to smoke their water pipe with them. They speak no English but enjoy a laugh and like to be photographed with the pipe. The waiter gives me a lift back to al-Bayda where I switch on CNN in my hotel room to watch the American President talking about establishing a Middle East free trade area.

The Green Book
Lincoln described democracy as 'government of the people, by the people, for the people' but, according to Qadhafi, parliaments result in dictatorship under the cover of election. Any system of political parties leads to the rule of the part over the whole as people of one culture or belief control executive authority and impose their will on the others. The aim of any opposition party is merely to take power: they must belittle the achievements of the existing government, even if its policies are beneficial to society as a whole. Opposition does not challenge the ruling party: it opportunistically seeks to replace it. Only the absence of a blood relationship distinguishes the party system from the sectarian struggle of tribalism. The party system has led to government by a junta in which the wealthy minority elite dominates the majority. In contrast, Qadhafi explains, in the Jamahiriya, no one tribe or party can crush the interests of the others.

Given that it is impossible to gather all the people in one place to decide upon national policy, the Jamahiriya implements 'direct democracy' based on their collective views. The people are divided into Basic Popular Conferences and Sectoral Professional Conferences that choose Secretariats who form Nonbasic Popular Conferences to elect People's Committees that supervise the national executive in a General People's Congress. What could be more 'democratic' than the Swiss cantonal system transplanted to Libya? But then Qadhafi explains that it is 'undemocratic' for any assembly to draft laws. Natural law is grounded in custom and religion while constitutions only derive justification from their natural sources. So to protect freedom, the Jamahiriya must be subservient to sacred and immutable natural law. Any law not premised on tradition and Islam is the instrument of oppression. Information is critical to decision making. So individuals and corporate bodies have the right to free expression except concerning any subject that affects the good of the whole. In the Jamahiriya only the General People's Congress can disseminate public information: there can be no privately owned free press, as this could only serve the interest of a junta.

FRIDAY 9 MAY | RAS HILLEL
Suleyman arrives on time at the funduq. We buy food and drive through the hills, stopping in a village called Gayab where Suleyman collects some money he is owed and prays at a mosque which is crowded for the Friday sermon. We traverse the long flat ridge of the Jebel Akhdar, which rises to about 900 metres, past various ruins and down into the valley of Ras Hillel. There we make a fire by the spring to grill chicken and heat Bedouin tea. Sitting around the picnic blanket in the perfect stillness of this isolated valley, we are joined by Mahmoud and Saleh, who have come from Derna. Mahmoud Shennib is a gynaecologist in his mid-fifties who studied medicine at Manchester in the 1970s and now administers the hospital and the one bank in Derna. Mahmoud tells us the story of the fossil water of the Jebel Akhdar and how it was a key factor

determining the outcome of the North African campaign. Rommel knew there was water in the hills, which he needed to supply his troops as they retreated from al-Alamein. But the local population, led by the Senoussi Order, refused to cooperate with Axis forces, seeing them as a continuation of Italian repression.

Following the first Italian occupation of 1911, and the subsequent re-invasion of Libya by Mussolini in 1922, the Jebel Akhdar was used as a base by the Senoussi resistance leader Omar Mukhtar. Seeking to settle Italian colonists in the fertile region, General Graziani fought against Mukhtar's guerrillas. In the summer of 1930, the Italians launched a major offensive that failed to achieve its purpose due to civilian support for the resistance. The Italians responded by deporting the population of the Jebel Akhdar into concentration camps, killing by some estimates up to a third of them. Eventually Mukhtar was captured and executed in September 1931. During the Second World War, British and Axis forces fought fierce battles in the Jebel Akhdar, with the Senoussi-led Libyans supporting the British and guiding them to the springs at Ras Hillel. As the sun begins to set, the conversation turns to the contemporary situation, and whether a socialist economy can exist without political repression. Mahmoud invites me to visit him the following day in Derna. Suleyman drives me back to al-Bayda where I eat kebab and watch more CNN.

The Green Book continued
Qadhafi explains that wage-earners are slaves to the masters who hire them. So in a just society the wage system must be replaced by 'natural socialism' based on equality among the components of production while maintaining public consumption equal to natural production. Natural law is the basic rule for freedom. Corruption begins with the exploitation of man by man and the possession by some individuals of more of the general wealth than their needs require. No one has the right to acquire property surplus to the dwelling needs of their family and dependents because this additional property is the need of someone else.

Just economic activity aims at the satisfaction of needs and does not seek profit beyond this. Additional accumulations deprive the rights of others or involve the exploitation of others' labour. Recognition of profit is an acknowledgment of exploitation, for profit has no limit. Socialism achieves freedom through the liberation of man's material needs from the control of others, turning wage earners into partners. The optimal system is one of self-employed workers who cannot exceed satisfaction of their needs. But who fixes the level of income at which a person's needs are satisfied? How does one determine 'natural law', when even primitive societies are themselves the product of reason? If coercion and exploitation exist 'naturally' in a society then those features must also be natural according to Qadhafi's principles.

Qadhafi continues that every nation must have a single religion to maintain harmony and ensure the growth of a stable community. The family is the plant, society the garden: the individual without a family has no value. Tribes are enlarged families that provide solidarity, cohesiveness, unity and love, while nations are enlarged tribes. Social bonds at different levels must be kept in balance: tribal allegiance can weaken national loyalty, but excessive patriotism can threaten humanity. National fanaticism expressed as the use of force against weak nations is evil. But progressive, productive and civilised nations are useful to the world, just as strong, self-respecting, responsible individuals are useful to the tribe.

SATURDAY 10 MAY | DERNA

Suleyman puts me in a taxi with his friend Saad and after passing various sites of Greek Cyrenaica we meet Mahmoud at the Wahda Hospital in Derna. We drink tea with a group of hospital administrators, and Mahmoud explains that all across Libya, but especially here in Cyrenaica, there is a severe shortage of trained staff and equipment. The Derna hospital is an institution for diagnosis only: sick patients are told what ails them and are sent home to die. The regime used to blame sanctions for the poor state of medical services in Libyan hospitals. But four years after the embargo was lifted, drugs and medical equipment are still in short supply, despite the fact that this country of five million people exports two million barrels of oil per day. The funds that would pay for this basic welfare expenditure are collected by 'the monkey' at the port, sometimes as crates of 'Benjamins' (100 dollar bills), and sent to private accounts in Switzerland.

Mahmoud takes me to the gentlemen's club of Derna where the town's elders drink tea and cherish the relics of Omar Mukhtar. As well as items linked to the person of Omar, the club's museum contains memorabilia from the Second World War, prehistoric remains from caves in the Jebel Akhdar, and stuffed animals from the desert such as mongoose, a cobra and Siamese calves. The general Libyan view of the North African campaign is that the British helped them by throwing out the Italians, and that the post-war years of British rule were benign in comparison with the preceding Italian brutality. Libya achieved full independence in 1951 and became a united monarchy under King Idris, leader of the Senoussi Order since 1913. Idris had previously been Emir of Cyrenaica between 1920 and the Italian Riconquista of 1922.

We are joined for lunch nearby by Mahmoud's friend Saleh and talk about contemporary politics. Having overthrown King Idris in 1969, Qadhafi was linked to state-sponsored terror in the 1970s and 1980s, supporting such organisations as the IRA and PLO in the name of anti-imperialism. This policy culminated in Reagan's 1986 air strikes on Tripoli, including on Qadhafi's compound, and the retaliatory bombing of Pan Am Flight 103 over Lockerbie in 1988. The thaw in relations in the late 1990s led to Qadhafi being depicted as an eccentric clown. But despite attempts to reach a new accommodation with the Libyan dictator, Mahmoud explains that, in reality, Qadhafi is just as much a brutal gangster as Saddam Hussein. Instead of being as wealthy as Norway or Qatar, whose wealth its per-capita production of hydrocarbons ought to sustain, Libya is a shambolic mess. The wasted opportunities are staggering.

Mahmoud's great-uncle had been minister of defence after independence and his uncle had served as secretary to King Idris. Since the king had drawn his support from here, Qadhafi always knew that Cyrenaica was his weakest point. During the last years of King Idris, corruption had become rampant as oil revenues flowed. But the east had been the primary beneficiary and therefore the most resentful against the substitution of economic rent extraction by the new regime. Qadhafi knows who his enemies are and keeps them closer than his friends. Although Mahmoud spent four years in prison, ostensibly because his cousin once spoke against the regime, he is required to maintain a 'friendship' with the dictator. Twice a year Mahmoud is collected at his house, blindfolded and driven with Saleh to an unknown location. There they must have a long lunch with Qadhafi in his tent, sitting by his side as if they are the closest of friends, making conversation to entertain and praise the Great Leader, while recounting everything that is happening in Derna. But the relationship is more subtle, as one senses that Qadhafi respects the Senoussi Order, with its Sufi interpretation of Islamic law and society, taking from it many of the ideas in *The Green Book*.

Mahmoud takes me to his bachelor's house at Omar Shennib Street for tea. The substantial property feels like a normal middle class home in any European country, comfortable, clean and well furnished. We chat for a while on the sofa and then he takes me up to the first floor terrace and shows me the land his family once owned stretching into the distance to the west of Derna, and which, if he can get his construction business going, he hopes to recover—minus the road that has been built through it. His wife and children live in Benghazi. In contrast to Suleyman's seemingly contemptuous attitude to his wife, Mahmoud explains that now the children are a bit older, he has helped his wife to establish a business in Benghazi, and that she enjoys her freedom and independence. I wonder if the difference is not due to Mahmoud's exposure to Western culture during his medical training in Manchester, or whether this was a fundamental difference between the Bedouin and the educated class who belonged to the Senoussi Order.

Mahmoud tells me about a certain plant that camels chew in the desert and which he believes has an anti-viral effect. Its name in Arabic means 'control plant' because it controls the behaviour of camels. Whenever the Bedouin lose their camels in the wilderness, they look for where this plant is growing and always find them eating it. But the camels rarely get sick. Something in their diet or the environment prevents them from catching viral infections, and Mahmoud speculates that the key ingredient is the control plant. He hopes that the active agent can be isolated, tested in clinical trials for its anti-viral effect, especially against Hepatitis C, and then patented and marketed. Is it related to silphium, I wonder?

Saleh arrives and drives me to a farm on the hill above the town. There we look at the beehives and the groves of plums and tomatoes in the red, fertile soil that the farmer irrigates with fossil water from deep under the jebel. The farmer prepares us the most delicious tea from a concoction of Bedouin herbs and hibiscus, and as we sip the tea he gives me a sprig of the curious control plant. The afternoon light on the hill is other-worldly. There is something confusing in the air: we could be in Provence, but we are on the edge of the North African desert. Saleh and I explore the wadi where men eke out a living growing trees, and return to the gentlemen's club to look more closely at the collection of artefacts. We eat dinner at Malim's restaurant on the corniche to the sound of the waves, and afterwards join Mahmoud at the garage of the shopkeeper Ahmad, where we drink more tea with nargileh on cushions, talking and talking.

Sunday 11 May | Sollum
Over breakfast Mahmoud invites me to stay another day and to talk more about weighty matters. For Mahmoud, Islam and the Qur'an provide an external ethical anchor to a corrupt and violent political economy. He tells me that the purpose of each man's life is to sacrifice himself for his family. That is what Islam calls us to do and that is why Muhammad despised monasticism. In Islam, producing new members of the 'umma is an essential part of one's service to the community. The Byzantine east, riven by doctrinal squabbles and fighting with the Persians, was the mirror against which Islam defined itself.

Islam subordinates the will and interest of individuals to that of the 'umma. But Muhammad was a merchant. Thus Islam is a way of life devised for a merchant's way of thinking: it is fundamentally about working to make money to support one's family and in this sense is about living in harmony with nature. If, I counter, nature is rough in tooth and claw, should we not strive to overcome it? By narrowly restricting life to this 'natural' form, is Islam not repressive of the human spirit and the individual imagination?

But I am impressed by everything he has told me, and am struck by the picture of the White House on his mouse mat and the statue of Saddam being toppled on the screen saver of his desktop computer. Mahmoud is intelligent and sagacious and has a cynical view of politics. He longs for his country to be rid of its dictatorship, and prays every day that the Americans will come and remove 'the monkey'. But he knows that a Damocles sword hangs above his every move and is afraid to give me an email address in case he catches a 'political virus'. Derna is comfortable, and Mahmoud has made me feel so much at home that I almost feel as if I am visiting a close uncle who happens to live far away. But something prompts me to make my excuses, and when I say that I must continue my journey, Mahmoud expresses his disappointment that I cannot stay longer and talk further. I feel embarrassed, and he can see that I feel sad not to continue this new friendship that has been so warmly and sincerely offered. He takes me to the taxi station where I thank him profusely for all his kindness and tell him that I very much hope to return to Derna.

I reflect that Mahmoud's admiration for President Bush is as desperate as his hatred of Qadhafi. For freedom is an elusive phantom that each person in each generation must fight for, whether it is against the obvious tyrants or those who advertise themselves as defending liberty. Individual freedom is contingent, against the natural order of things and always precarious. The sapling of liberty is vulnerable. For we are not born free, rather only with the potential to make ourselves free. But as I continue my journey, I regret not staying longer with Mahmoud, suddenly feeling foolish to have left such a place of warmth, shelter and engaging conversation, wondering how I can stay in contact with him, if indeed I will ever meet him again, and apprehensive now that I am alone and must fend for myself once more. It would subsequently be Mahmoud and others in the east of Libya who would lead the 2011 insurrection against the 'monkey'.

The shared taxi takes me to Tobruq, and after a change, to the Egyptian border at Sollum. It is fearfully hot at the frontier: all the border cubicles are closed with the officials inside, and there is no shade at the crossing point. Hundreds of people are sitting on the ground waiting, most of them wearing white cotton robes called holis, pulled over their heads. I try to jump the queue to find shade in the customs area ahead. But I am sent back into the sun, and in the end give my passport to a man who seems to be an official and assures me he can help. To sit on the ground in the direct sun in the middle of the day in the early North African summer, and allow time to pass for what seems like an eternity without becoming anxious, takes considerable strength of mind. When at last the cubicles reopen after more than two hours, everyone stands up and rushes towards the nearest open counter with their sacks of goods and old suitcases.

In the melee I am abruptly accosted by a smartly dressed man, presumably a secret policeman, who presses his revolver into my side through the pocket of his suit and asks me in Queen's English why I gave my passport away so freely to a complete stranger. He takes my arm, walks me away from the crowd, admonishes me for attempting to jump the queue in order to avoid the sun, and produces my passport. Why, he demands to know, am I not escorted by a tourist guide and where is my currency declaration? Suddenly aware of the extreme vulnerability of my situation, I try to be as respectfully compliant and as likeable as possible. I explain the circumstances of my entry into the Great Socialist People's Libyan Arab Jamahiriya whereupon he interrogates me thoroughly about exactly where I have stayed and every person I have spoken to in Libya. Despite the intense questioning, I manage to be suitably vague, mentioning only the funduqs, the helpful traders in the souqs, the various bus journeys and shared taxis, and as abruptly as I was arrested, I am released and escorted firmly through the Libyan side of the border into no man's land.

The Egyptians are pleasant but shambolic: leaving my bags in their care I must walk a mile in the heat to buy stamps for the visa as they do not keep them at the frontier post. After nearly four hours at the border I finally enter Egypt, only to wait in a shared taxi for what feels like another eternity. Despite the discomfort it is paradisiacal after my ordeal on the Libyan side. Eventually the car fills up and departs. It is two hours along the coast to Matrough, and I am delighted to be in motion again, sitting in the front with the evening breeze streaming through the open windows. At Matrough I take a tiny, mosquito infested room in the town centre for ten Egyptian pounds (one British pound). It could not be further from the comfort of Mahmoud's guest room. Before attempting to sleep, I close the windows and spat every mosquito I can see with the heel of my shoe. No sooner do I close my eyes than I am assaulted by the intermittent tyrannical whine of one I have missed. I cover my head with the sheet and the mosquito bites my hand through the cotton. I turn on the light and brandish my shoe; but the creature is canny and hides. So this is what it is to wander the earth in search of one's long lost other half: brutal officials at frontier posts, sleepless nights and mosquitoes.

Siwa

MONDAY 12 MAY | MERSA MATROUGH
Matrough, or Greek Paraitónion, was known to the ancient world as the port of the oasis of Jupiter-Amun. Today it is a small town with little of interest, apart from the Rommel Museum. After tending to my mosquito bites I take a taxi to the museum on the peninsular across the bay. In contrast to the Libyans, the Egyptians honour the losing general of the North Africa campaigns because he was their best chance of seeing their British colonisers chased out of Egypt. The museum displays Erwin Rommel's bunker exactly as it was on 31 August 1942, the day it was abandoned, with photographs of the German commander in various lengths of black leather coat. What does this say about Egypt, that it offers such homage to the might-have-been, knowing full well that it would not have been that great? For as the Grand Mufti of Jerusalem Hajj Amin al-Husseini discovered to his cost, in the Nazi ideology, Arabs were worth little more than Jews. Returning to the station, I wait for the bus to Siwa and resign myself to a glass of stale shay.

Before the road was tarred in the 1980s it took ten hours to reach Siwa from Matrough; before there was a road at all, which was completed in anticipation of the Khedive Abbas Hilmi II's visit to Siwa in 1905, it took six days on a trotting camel. Now it takes six hours in the bus to cross the 300 kilometres of featureless stony gravel. Despite the relative consolation of modernity, the journey feels hot and slow. The only distraction comes from the Egyptian feature film on the small screen above the driver's head and the occasional chuckles of the Siwis on the bus. The film is about a pair of wealthy businessmen in pursuit of hysterical young girls who are simultaneously attracted and repelled by their advances. The style could be from the 1960s, with technicolour and distorted sound, advocating the carefree absurdity of mid-twentieth century life to an inherently conservative audience. Only it turns out that the film has been made recently. Halfway across the blank expanse the bus stops at an austere breeze block building with plastic tables and more tasteless tea. I begin reading Bruce Chatwin's *The Songlines* as the driver takes his statutory rest.

Approaching the oasis, the bus descends through a rocky passage from the barren plateau into the depression which lies twenty metres below sea level. I am shaken out of my stupor by the intense green of the palms on one side and the deep blue of the salt lake on the other, shimmering brightly into the distance in the late afternoon sun. On arriving at the terminus in Siwa Town I shake off a pack of children who mob visitors in search of money and biros, and instal myself off the main square in Room 16 at the Palm Trees Hotel. On the second floor of a concrete block hopelessly unsuited to its environment, the room is hot and stamped with mosquito marks on the walls. The bathroom has multiple cubicles, none of which contain a functioning shower, only leaking pipes. But there are French windows on to a balcony looking over the wicker furniture and tall palms in the courtyard. Enchanted, I put my notebooks on the table by the window and reflect that I will be here for nine days in this remote place deep in the desert.

TUESDAY 13 MAY | OASIS OF JUPITER-AMUN

The word oasis derives from the Demotic (hence Coptic) word *ouahe*, meaning to dwell, as Siwa was believed by the ancient Egyptians to be the dwelling place of the sun god Amun-Ra. Thus Siwa is the original oasis, and geographically it is the last in a chain that runs along a subterranean branch of the Nile from Kharga to Farafra, Bahariya and Siwa. The oases were colonised and integrated into Egypt by the New Kingdom Pharaoh Ramesses III around 1175 BC, although Diodorus tells us that the earliest Temple of Amun-Ra predates this. The Amunians were governed by a priest-king, and the oasis of Jupiter-Amun was known throughout the ancient world for the perspicacity of its oracle.

The Greeks venerated the oasis and sent many ambassadors to consult it, believing that the art of prophecy had reached the earliest oracle in Greece at Dodona from the Oracle of Jupiter-Amun. Following his conquest of Egypt in 525 BC Cambyses the Persian dispatched an army to rob and burn the wealthy oracular temple. But the expedition lost its way in a sandstorm somewhere between Kharga and Siwa, and the entire army perished in the barren expanse of the western desert. The ruined temple at Aghurmi, which stands on a rock visible from all around the oasis, dates from around this time. In 499 BC the Athenian General Cimon consulted the oracle which correctly foretold his death in battle, greatly increasing its reputation. In 331 BC Alexander travelled to the oasis to enquire about the origins of his birth. The expedition nearly suffered the same fate as Cambyses's army. But as Arrian relates, the parched Macedonians were saved by a sudden rainstorm, and guided to the oasis by two ravens. The Amunians received Alexander with divine honours as the son of Zeus (i.e. Amun-Ra), legitimising his rule over Egypt.

By late antiquity the oracle had declined and the historical record falls silent. Siwa may have become a place of banishment, or possibly a thriving settlement, admired for its fertile gardens, good climate and the clarity of its air—certainly there are large numbers of ancient tombs scattered all over the oasis. It is also possible that Siwa was abandoned due to salination of the springs. The present inhabitants derive from Berber tribes who repopulated the oasis in the Middle Ages, settling the new town of Siwa around the watered fortress of Shali. Subsequently the Siwis were converted to Islam by the Banu Hilal or possibly by holy men from the Hijaz: the mosque of al-Atik in the citadel dates from the 1300s. A succession of Egyptian rulers sought to conquer the oasis, now called Shantarieh. But they either could not find it or were repulsed by the Berbers, who retreated behind the high walls of the Shali. Eventually Muhammad Ali Pasha brought anarchic and quarrelsome Siwa under notional central government control in 1820.

Before the twentieth century, Siwa was governed by a

Council of Seven Sheikhs, representatives of the Berber families who are recorded in a local manuscript to have settled the oasis by the year 1203. Siwi society was divided into two factions under five western sheikhs at Shali and two eastern sheikhs at Aghurmi. The two groups would come into periodic conflict, settling disputes through ritualised battles that would sometimes spill over into actual violence. The Siwis lived behind the high walls of the Shali in houses constructed from *kersheef*. This traditional building material consists of dried salt-mud supported by mature palm trunks that remains cool in the day and insulates at night but has one significant drawback: it dissolves in the rain. Since it only rains heavily once every few decades in Siwa, there is a logic to the technique. In 1926 a rainstorm destroyed the walls of the Shali, and the oasis is dotted with the remains of abandoned kersheef houses.

Men below the age of forty, known as Zaghala, or club bearers, worked in the gardens and defended the town, but were not permitted to marry or sleep inside the walls of Shali. Women were completely veiled, not even leaving eye slits in their burqas. Siwa therefore developed a culture of homosexuality practised by the young men in the palm groves until they reached forty. Since this custom was banned by King Fouad in 1928 Siwi men have been allowed to marry at twenty, but the Zaghala clubs still survive. During the First World War, at the instigation of the deposed Khedive Abbas Hilmi II, with materiel provided by Enver Pasha, the western desert and Siwa were invaded by the Senoussi Order under Sayed Ahmed. The British drove the Senoussi back to Cyrenaica in 1917, and Ahmed was replaced by his cousin Sidi Muhammad Idris, the same Idris who later became king of Libya. In the 1920s the Senoussi Order was suppressed by the government of King Fouad. The Siwis then reverted from the Sufi influence of the Senoussi to their own interpretation of Islam directed by the Council of Seven Sheikhs.

The courtyard of the Palm Trees Hotel is the hub for visitors and researchers studying Siwi culture. The hotel has several volumes about the oasis, from the conventional history written in the 1920s by an official of the Frontier Districts Administration, C. Dalrymple Belgrave, to ethnographic accounts by the Siwi-Egyptian Fathi Malim and the Swiss anthropologist Bettina Leopoldi. Immobilised by the heat, I browse through them in the courtyard with tea, honeyed pancakes and crushed cane juice, before walking through the groves to the oracular Fountain of the Sun at Aghurmi, now called Cleopatra's Bath. It is over forty degrees and I am glad to swim in the ancient spring and recline under the palms.

As the air begins to cool I walk back to the main square, past the ruined citadel and al-Atik mosque, through the streets of ruined kersheef houses beyond the Shali, up the steps to the modern mosque and climb to the summit of the rocky outcrop above. From this vantage point, you can see at least twenty kilometres in all directions, from the White Mountain at the far end of the salt lake to the west, to the Hill of the Dead by the Matrough road to the north, to the oracular Temple of Jupiter-Amun on its rock at Aghurmi and the Gebel Dakrour to the east, and the white sand sea receding into the distance to the south.

The sun passes over the horizon on the edge of the depression and the evening wind picks up with the drop in temperature, like a diurnal sea breeze. Doves fly to their nests in the palms, while the muezzins chant the summons to Maghrib prayers and the donkeys respond in a cacophony of braying. For ten to fifteen minutes, as the desaturated colours of the salt lakes and the palms and the sands fade into darkness, the entire oasis is electrified in a sonic celebration of the night. Looking out over the Sahara, whose star-guided crossing by nocturnal caravans is now the fiefdom of terror groups and insurgencies, the prehistoric civilisations of the Hoggar and Tibesti ranges feel incomprehensibly distant, as if our world has contracted and the wonder of discovery has become ever more remote. Darkness falls completely and I retrace my steps to eat chicken and tahina at the brightly lit East West Restaurant, culinary symbol of peace in Siwa.

Wednesday 14 May | Eastern Oasis

At breakfast I meet Petra, an energetic Slovenian researching Siwa as a tourist destination. We visit the museum with its displays of silver jewellery and costumes, and Petra invites me to join her tour of the eastern oasis with Magdi, the head of the tourist office. Explaining that I am suffering from the heat, Magdi sells me a pair of cool white cotton sirwal undertrousers that become my second skin. We drive in a pick-up truck past the east salt lake and the ruined village of Zeitoun, and swim in the stone lined rectangular spring at Abu Shreif. For twelve lengths, I enjoy the warm sun on the clear blue water surrounded by palms, admiring Petra's svelte form as it glides through the pool. We stop at a village for tea and discuss the travails of Bedouin life, enjoying the respite from the heat in their breeze block house. They show us their olive groves, and we visit some tombs and an island across a causeway in the salt lake. I disembark to explore Aghurmi and return to Siwa Town on the back of a donkey cart.

Over evening coffee at the Palm Trees Hotel, the proprietor suggests that he knows some young boys from a Zaghala club who might be interested to pass the evening with me. I explain that I am rather more interested in Petra, who at that moment walks into the courtyard. We climb the concrete staircase to the roof and look up at the night sky. Despite the electric lights, the stars shine out brightly against the Saharan night. Mars and Jupiter are plainly visible as discs rather than points, with an angle of arc across their surface, and I wonder if the visibility of Jupiter might be related to the latitude as well as the clear air. If the ancients saw the natural world more clearly than we do and dedicated the oasis to Jupiter-Amun, perhaps they noticed something in the celestial spheres that has been forgotten or that escapes our attention?

Thursday 15 May | Dakrour

Waking at dawn, I steal down to Petra's room on the courtyard to chat with her before she leaves Siwa. We run for the honking bus in the fresh morning air and Petra climbs in as it moves off. Dismayed by her sudden appearance and disappearance, I walk through the groves towards Dakrour. As the donkey carts rumble past in the morning rush hour, I stop at a food stand that serves hot *fuul* (fava bean stew with olive oil) from a large urn. Dakrour consists of a few houses near the east salt lake with the twin-peaked gebel rising above them. In classical times there were references to emerald mines in the oasis. According to Siwi tradition the gebel still contains precious stones, but the entrance to the cave is guarded by a jinn who will only open it to a person who has drunk from a secret spring at an unknown location in the desert. The open area below the rock is used for a lavish harvest festival in October, when Siwis come together to bury the hatchet from their quarrels in the preceding year. I find a shaded ledge under the gebel looking out over the desert and sleep for two hours in perfect silence.

At Cleo's in Siwa Town, I fall into conversation with the Breton-Corse ethnologist Vincent Battesti. Vincent has been studying the Siwis for several years. 'In Europe the palm tree is the symbol of the exotic,' he explains, 'but in Siwa the trees and the donkeys are functional objects, practical tools for survival.' 'What do we have to learn from the Siwis?' I ask him. Vincent believes it is ignoble to work for money and that every citizen has the right to a basic income dispensed by the state. The problem with Western societies is the 'I'm all right Jack' mentality of methodological individualism that leads to alienation, inequality and *l'horreur économique*. In Siwa, the governing council makes sure that everyone in the oasis is provided for. The West needs a revolution in metaphysics. 'Is Siwa really an ideal society of enlightened communitarianism or do factional conflict and disaffection lie below the surface?' I reply. So we embark upon a fierce discussion, relieved only by an evening swim in Cleopatra's Bath, surrounded by the delightfully 'exotic' palms. Unable to sleep, I return to the rock above Shali and look at the stars.

The eternal contingencies
What to do about Pyrrha who demands a 'provider husband' to endure economic coggery: Karim's gilded cage of marriage? Are there not symmetries in all human relations? A house

cannot be a place of security if it can be taken away at any time. A man cannot be a slave to biology; better to be poor and free than rich and bound. Does poverty mean having insufficient money or enduring the tedium of earning it? The restless freedom of the spirit seems to be incompatible with a traditional marriage—that trade between financial and emotional security. In a Siwi household the man is absolute ruler: his wife may not even leave the house without his permission. The quid pro quo is that the man bears full responsibility for earning money to support his family. In a local traditional society, the man knows that so long as he is honest and honourable, he can depend on the community. But in a global society, there is no such support: he must face external competition and prove himself in the market. If he fails the test he is expendable or condemned to drudgery.

In Siwa, a man may lament that the cost of keeping his family is sweat and toil. But he knows the conditions of his work in advance and he knows that they are manageable. The modern man, in contrast, must face a sea of uncertainty. In the traditional system, sex provided the incentive to enter the gilded cage—to become settled and accept duties and obligations. The system ensured that children were raised in a stable environment. Very Frommian: father the source of security and authority; mother the source of love and affection. In pre-modern Siwa, existential joie de vivre was expressed in socially harmless Bacchanalia in the palm groves. The result was good parenting and population control: all desires well channelled and the community protected. Has Siwa lost its freedom now: is there no longer any joy before accepting responsibility? Pyrrha seeks the traditional way, whereas I am the wild man, the toil-hating rationalist misfit. All her sweetness and affection cannot seduce me into the gilded cage. I refuse to submit to its demands, preferring the path of enlightenment, the Epicurean life of reflection and friendship.

Friday 16 May | Siwa Town
I take notes from *The Songlines* at the Palm Trees Hotel, stepping out to replenish my glass of crushed sugar cane at

Khaled's juice bar on the square. Khaled passes the canes into the industrial sized machine and collects the thick green juice at the bottom. Between the hotel and the square is Ahmed's internet point. Illiana writes to explain that she believes in love but does not want to own or be owned. I reply that I want that openness which is free from the anxieties and expectations that seem to ruin so many bonds of passion and friendship. As my emails send, Ahmed discusses the Siwis' mixed feelings about tourism, happy to take the money but wary of alien influence. He tells me about the campaign to 'Keep Siwa Beautiful' and preserve the character of the oasis. Already there are buses of Alexandrian tourists who disturb the peace but regular flights from Cairo would destroy Siwi culture completely.

In the evening I return to the rock above the Shali to watch the sunset, and slip into the new mosque to listen to the imam leading a group of old men chanting sacred verses. As I sit on the green mat, leaning against the wall under the slow fans with the cool air blowing through the open space, I am entranced. 'Why do you come here when it is only allowed for Muslims?' the imam asks me after the chanting has finished. 'Because I respect your mosques, with their tranquil feeling of time suspended, and especially the singing. All religions have an aspect of the truth and we should learn more about one another,' I tell him. 'To follow Al-lah is to be straight and strong,' he says, forming a fist with his right hand and hitting his left palm against his upper arm. 'But many people are not good: they twist and turn like snakes.'

At the Palm Trees Hotel I run into Vincent who takes me to a new restaurant called Kanooz on the road to Aghurmi. There we meet Ali, the wiry, talkative major-domo, who, when not evangelising Islam to European tourists, works for Dr Mounir Neamatalla, sustainable tourism entrepreneur and expert on Siwi architecture. Ali tells us about their plans to build a new hotel in the kersheef style, but with baked bricks under the salt-mud walls to make them rain resistant. After we finish our Om Ali bread pudding, Ali shows us around the soon to be completed Shali Lodge over the road, which certainly promises to be more comfortable than the dilapidated Palm Trees Hotel.

Saturday 17 May | Aghurmi

A new routine: fava beans for breakfast and writing confinement at the Palm Trees fortified with cane juice. As the heat wanes, I walk out to Aghurmi to explore the Oracle of Jupiter-Amun, the Fountain of Divine Wisdom. Stone steps lead from the village up to the acropolis, which consists of a raised open space with views across the oasis, the mediaeval kersheef mosque on one side and the oracular temple on the other. The well-preserved stones of the oracle form part of the fortification of the acropolis. The temple is effectively a consulting room with three consecutive doorways leading to the innermost chamber whose channel of communication to the gods became the obsession of ancient potentates. Unlike at Delphi, there are no inscriptions, no comforting words of wisdom. Of Omm Beyda, the smaller temple that was connected with the acropolis by an underground passage, nothing remains except for a section of wall decorated with hieroglyphs on the lintel and pharaonic figures making offerings to Amun.

From Aghurmi I continue to Cleopatra's Bath. Sipping tea in the shade by the spring is an elderly watery-eyed Englishman called Martin Leslie Savage. 'What are you doing in Siwa?' he asks. I describe my journey and my flight from Pyrrha and the domestic project and my quest to find inspiration and enchantment in these ancient lands of the Levant. Martin tells me that after several foreign office postings across the Arab world, he decided to retire to Siwa. He has bought some gardens, as the small plots of date palms around the oasis are known, and has converted the former police station into a comfortable residence. We discover a shared experience of Anglo-Catholicism and Martin invites me for dinner at Kanooz.

After watching the sunset from the parapet of the oracle, I walk through the groves to the restaurant. Martin produces a bottle of Cleopatra wine and we sit on the low cushions of the roof terrace surrounded by candles and palm fronds. Under the moon and stars we talk about Siwa and my earlier conversation with Vincent. 'The Corsican is definitely coarse,' Martin remarks. 'Behind the allure of its natural beauty, the utopian domain of the noble savage, Siwi society is in reality brutal and primitive, more Hobbesian than Gauguinesque. Everything here,' he tells me, 'is governed by superstition, the fear of jinns or evil spirits and belief in magic. Although they are known to be fanatical Muslims, the Siwi form of Islam is really a syncretism with their pre-Islamic Berber way of life. Take their enthusiasm for lubki, the palm wine that often fuels their disputes. The Qur'an forbids intoxication. But the Siwi sheikhs justify the consumption of lubki on the grounds that the Prophet also commended all the products of the palm tree.'

Martin takes pleasure from restoring his house and cultivating the olives and dates in his gardens. But above all else, he is proudest of his donkey, the most beautiful and expensive donkey in the whole oasis. Siwi donkeys are a robust indigenous variety with stripes on their backs, somewhere crossed with an ancient equine beast, possibly a proto-zebra. After spring water and the trees, they are the most valuable things in Siwa, relied upon entirely for transportation. Martin tells me about how in this den of Siwi Islam, he re-enacts on Palm Sundays our Lord's entry into Jerusalem, with the workers he employs in his gardens throwing down palm fronds in front of him as he passes through the groves on his beloved Pascal donkey. After dinner we take a late night tea on the main square with Martin's Swedish friend Mats, who tells us about a Zaghala party he has just come from, with reed pipes, chunks of grilled camel and lubki wine.

SUNDAY 18 MAY | MARTIN'S SHRINE

Martin meets me on the square with his estate manager, Abdu Rahman. After fuul and falafel we drive in his pick-up truck to visit his gardens in the western oasis. As we walk through the groves Abdu Rahman explains that the cultivation of the palms and olives is an elaborate craft. In the early spring, the palms must be pollinated artificially or the resulting fruit can be very small; in the summer they require careful watering and manuring; in the winter they must be trimmed and pruned. Siwis take great pride in their tree husbandry and show off the quality of the product in the markets but the workers require considerable coaxing, particularly at harvest time, when there is a shortage of labour and the fruit can quickly perish.

Martin drives me to his house, the former police station halfway along the road to Aghurmi. Apart from the oracular temple, it is the only stone building in Siwa and may have been constructed with blocks plundered from the small temple. All the other structures in the oasis are built from kersheef and breeze blocks. In the yard is his donkey, for which he has just bought in Alexandria a carriage with a black leather bench and brass lamps. The house is bright and airy with comfortable furniture. 'Before the police station was moved to the new government offices,' Martin explains, 'this building was feared by the Siwis as a place of brutality.' Even today they do not like to accept his invitations and he was only able to buy the house because none of the locals wanted to live in it. Martin tells me that the cellar was the gaol of Siwa, and that he has exorcised it, converting it into a shrine to Alexander that he uses as a meditation chamber.

From the room at the back of the house, a stone spiral staircase leads down to the cellar. Martin takes a splint and walks down the steps ahead of me, lighting candles that rest on the inside of the steps. The floor at the bottom is wet and in the gloom I can see there is a sunken bath that Martin illuminates with the splint. We sit in silence on the lowest step and after a while Martin tells me his theories about Alexander. After his death, Alexander's body was taken from Babylon to Alexandria, embalmed, put under a transparent crystal cover and displayed there, like Lenin lying in state on Red Square. The tomb-temple was visited by Caesar and Hadrian, and the physical presence of Alexander, as well as the many biographies of antiquity, contributed to the influence his cult had on senators, kings and emperors. Septimius Severus closed the tomb and it was presumed to have been later destroyed, either by Christians or in an earthquake, and its remains lie buried somewhere under Alexandria.

That at least is the official version. But there was always a legend that the embalmed body on display in Alexandria was not the real one and that Alexander had in fact been buried at a secret location in the oasis. Many ancient writers from Arrian to Plutarch emphasised the personal impact that his visit to the oracle had had on Alexander and that he believed himself to be the son of Zeus. Since the oasis was the dwelling place of Jupiter-Amun, the supreme god, it is plausible that Alexander wished to be buried in the oasis. In the 1980s a team of archaeologists from the Egyptian Ministry of Antiquities discovered a 525-square-metre Hellenistic tomb guarded by a series of lion statues at a place called al-Maraki near Siwa. The ministry's assessment was that it is an important Macedonian tomb possibly intended for Hephaestion or Ptolemy. But the inner chamber has not been penetrated and the site has since been closed by the authorities.

We ascend the stairs and Martin prepares lunch. 'Without Alexander there could have been no Christ,' he tells me. Heros merged with deities in the Greek mind: if Heracles was semi-divine then it was natural that Alexander also had divine lineage. The spread of Hellenism around the Levant, Epicureanism as a staging post and the syncretism of the personalities of the Greek Pantheon with the oriental mystery religions were all necessary foundations to the arrival of the Christ. 'If you reach the Euphrates on your journey,' Martin tells me, 'then you must read Freya Stark.' He relates the thesis of that indefatigable traveller that Rome's victory at Magnesia broke Alexander's bridge between the Mediterranean and Central Asia, marking the Euphrates as the permanent frontier of the Western world. If the Hellenic bridge had remained, Christianity would have spread throughout Persia and the Indian subcontinent. But the Byzantines and Sassanians threw their forces to exhaustion against this frontier and Islam crushed both the Christians and the Zoroastrians.

'And before Alexander?' I ask. 'Was he not re-enacting the hero journey of Odysseus? After the Battle of the Hydaspe (Jhelum), Alexander wanted to continue, to conquer all of Asia and see the edge of the world. But his companions had had enough: after ten years of wandering, fame and fortune were theirs and now they wanted to return home. The Indian monsoon broke their spirit; their mutiny broke Alexander's. What else could he really have been seeking, if not eternal life? Does it not all go back to Gilgamesh?'

I tell Martin the story of the oldest epic, the first written hero journey. Gilgamesh, the restless king of Uruk, is challenged to a duel by Enkidu, the wild man sent by the gods. Recognising his equal companion, Gilgamesh befriends Enkidu, and they travel together for adventure to cleanse the land of monsters. When Enkidu is killed, Gilgamesh is grief stricken to lose his friend and wanders the earth in search of eternal life. After passing through the Forest of Cedars, the Mountains of Mashim and the Garden of Jewels, Gilgamesh meets Utanapishtim, the Babylonian Noah. Utanapishtim tells him to shave his beard and pull himself together. The sage explains that he cannot find eternal life but must return to Uruk and serve his subjects, respectful of his duties of kingship. For we can only live forever in others' memories of the good we have done and it occurs to me that if I am Gilgamesh, Martin is the reincarnation of the sage Utanapishtim.

We talk more about his life in Siwa, far from family and friends, and Martin tells me that the rewards of solitude only ever increase. 'God speaks through chance occurrences: being open and forgetting the self always eliminates loneliness. If the epics reach back to the soul of early man, then so too does the silence of the desert.' But then Martin confesses that he is going blind, and I sense that he does not have many years left to tend his gardens. Martin asks me about my personal life. He tells me to keep Pyrrha as a friend and not to worry about the livelihood question. 'Being responsible for the welfare of a family is no more onerous than discharging the duty of realising one's own potential.' I look at this brilliant elderly man who has created for his autumn years a charming haven from the world, in whose shrine-cellar not far from the intended resting place of the demigod one can feel the spirit of Alexander, and I think to myself, we are alike you and I, we both love life too much to let it go—that's the tragedy of it isn't it? Martin tells me about a hot spring past Dakrour and drives me there to sit in the warm water under the stars.

Alexandria

MONDAY 19 MAY | SIWA TOWN
After an early swim at the spring and fuul on the road to Dakrour, I write at my desk looking over the courtyard of the Palm Trees Hotel. Wearying somewhat at the dankness and the mosquitoes, but still delighted by the simplicity and the softness of Siwa in the fullness of its colours, I sit on the rock above the ruins of Shali, watching the intense light fade, listening to the donkeys braying and the night wind picking up across the desert. One could sit on this spot again and again and its splendour would never lose its force.

Martin and Mats meet me for a late-night tea on the square. 'The erotic should not be taken lightly,' Martin says, and I am not sure if this is directed at Mats or myself. 'A little fun is alright. But the erotic experience of another being changes one irrevocably each time. The traces never vanish or dissipate. What comes to be erotically and emotionally meaningful through particular experiences is fixed immutable. What is unhygienic for the soul is in the end the cause of more pain than joy.' Martin often reverts in his conversation to the themes of sin, sex and death. 'What does sex have to do with death?' I reply. There is the obvious connection that if we did not have to die, we would not need to reproduce. But nowadays sex has no more to do with reproduction than the activities of the mind have to do with hunter-gathering. The erotic force stands to reproduction as chess playing or musical composition or theorem-proving stand to replication of our genes. Humans play chess, make music and prove theorems, all of which apply the mind to uses for which it was not originally intended. 'Isn't the erotic the same?' I argue.

Boredom is the absence of stimulation and the impetus for excitement. Even without a drive that needs to be alleviated, channelled or sublimated, the wish for sexual experience still remains, in the full knowledge of the pleasures and joys that could be had. This is the real Pandora's box: once opened how can those wishes be expunged? They cannot and they should not. Perhaps it is best to stop all the mortification and just get on with being sensual not worrying all the while. Freud thought that the sexual drive is an itch to be removed by satisfaction. But in fact desire gives us the opportunity to experience pleasure.

The wisdom of Martin Savage
Ancient minds are not the same as modern ones. The ancients *saw* the gods and experienced the supernatural in their daily lives. It was not until the late renaissance that Europeans read silently to themselves without speaking the words aloud. Alexander, the son of Zeus, was the precursor of the Christ. The biographical character of the Gospels is inspired by the Hellenic style. Nature threw up many prior versions in the evolution of religious, moral and aesthetic experience. But Alexander gave in to the temptation to rule the world. There is a devil, an active force of evil. You see it every day in Siwa, where life is precarious and people die randomly with great frequency. A cyclist might cut his leg, get septicaemia and die. Or people get drunk and fight: they have not yet evolved any discipline or emotional control.

The parable of the farm workers may seem to dispense economic irrationality because people are paid the same for working different hours. But the workers hired at the end of the day had still sat in the sun and waited for nearly the whole day not knowing if they would find work by the end of it. They could have given up and gone home. The point is never to give up the quest. Islam may seem simpler than Christianity, making fewer demands on the credulity of the faithful, but it ignores the Christian revolution. It fails to consider grace in the transformation of the sacraments in communion with others. By contrast Islam seeks to micromanage one's life by divine decree. We should not speak of 'conservative' versus 'liberal' societies but of the degree to which people have the resources to think for themselves. If a rule is sensible, it should be followed; if it is an arbitrary dictat or an irrelevant relic it should be defiantly ignored.

Tuesday 20 May | Siwa Town
On this final day in the oasis, I walk through the groves to Dakrour, taking photographs of Cleopatra's spring, of Aghurmi and of Martin in his house. Abruptly I am stunned by the beauty of a young Siwi who walks past with a smiling open face. It is too hot to write so I send emails and finish *The Songlines*. One last time I climb to the rock above the Shali, sad to leave the sanctuary of Siwa. After prayers, I sit in silence on the green carpet in the mosque, resting my back against the wall. Without the chanting, I notice the absence of any music in Siwa. Martin and Vincent join me for a farewell dinner at Kanooz. Retiring early to prepare for my departure, I embrace Martin warmly and put *The Songlines* in his hand: he has had the same idea and gives me Freya Stark's *Rome on the Euphrates* in return.

Chatwinism
Restlessness, wanderlust and nomadism; distant horizons, travelling light and the tyranny of hours unbound. In *The Songlines*, his study of Australian Aboriginals that develops themes he explored in an earlier unpublished work *The Nomadic Alternative*, Bruce Chatwin reproduced notebooks of his travels around the pre-modern regions of the world. Reflecting on the depression that prolonged stasis caused him, Chatwin observed that while woman is the guardian of the hearth, man was born migratory. We evolved in the adversity of the arid steppe with ingenuity and inventiveness our protection from thirst and predation. To be fixed in one place is to wither and contract. Habit, routine and stasis are repressive to idea, intuition and imagination. There is security in fixed routine; but discovery and inspiration require motion.

Civilisation means the formation of cities: the city is a sheepfold superimposed on a garden; the state is the fusion of the herdsman and the planter; the nomad chief presides over the allocation of pasture. Common defence began as collective aggression against the primaeval Beast. But rival nomadic tribes would fight each other and raid the city. War is ritualised squabble, channelling the defensive aggressive instinct into the division of territory and space. Settlers turned to nomads to defend them; but once recruited these mercenaries always became the rulers. As kings these pastoral 'shepherds of the people' applied the same methods of coercion from their herds to the peasant mass, who were corralled, milked and slaughtered. Law comes from *nomos* meaning pasture; justice comes from *nemesis* meaning to graze; the words capital, chattel and pecuniary derive from head of livestock, and currency from running animals.

The corruption of the city is the internal defence against its constraint: distraction, hoarding, gadgetitis and the mania for the novel are substitutes for the despair of motionlessness. In *Muqaddimah*, the fourteenth-century Tunisian Sufi sage Ibn Khaldun observed that the people of the desert kept themselves abstemious, free and healthy; hence the prophets always came from the desert. Ibn Khaldun developed a cyclical theory of history, taking into account geography, economics and culture. For human existence to continue in the face of nature's challenge, societies need strong bonds of *asabiya*, or group solidarity, that is the source of laws, customs and skills. The strongest asabiya develops among desert nomads. As settled societies become more prosperous and their culture grows more sophisticated, corruption sets in and the bonds of communal solidarity grow thinner. The combination of prosperity and weakness invites conquest by nomads who bring a stricter moral sensibility to restore asabiya and the process repeats.

Spatial compression of rival tribes, preventing their separation, led to gift exchange replacing aggression, to trade replacing war, with violence only following from unjust exchange. Modernity broke the aristocratic power of the feudal nomad, replacing it with rule by knowledge. But the power of settlers is based on innovation; innovation requires idea and idea requires motion. Pilgrimage is the reversion to our primaeval migratory instinct, the hard journey to escape the dominance hierarchies of the city and face ourselves. Strehlow observed that the Sahelian Aranda nomads are always laughing: apparently they cannot help it.

WEDNESDAY 21 MAY | PHAROS
Accepting the nomadic imperative, I catch the dawn bus. The hours pass slowly and the 600 kilometres of interminable nothingness are relieved only by tea breaks at the halfway point and then at Matrough. The bus passes the war memorials at al-Alamein, first the Italian octagonal tower, then the German fortress and finally rows of British Commonwealth war graves spread along the dusty hills above the highway.

Approaching Alexandria, the density of new buildings along the coast increases. As we pass the city limits the transition from desert purity to dystopian industrial sprawl begins to bite. Along the isthmus between Lake Mareotis and the marshy inlets around the port there are steel plants and oil tanks, slag heaps and gas flares: charmless industrial detritus blotting out the sky. After the light of Siwa, Alexandria feels heavy and dismal. From the Sidi Gabr bus terminus a decrepit black and yellow Lada taxi takes me to Amin Fikhry Street by the Ramleh tram station. My former haunt, the Hotel Ailema on the seventh floor of a belle époque building, no longer exists. But I settle for the Hyde Park on the sixth floor, and rest on the art nouveau bed listening to the traffic and the clanking of the trams below.

Wander aimlessly, advises E.M. Forster in his guide to Alexandria, to hear the noise of the sea and the echoes of an extraordinary history. An evening walk in a new city gives one a sense of detachment, to observe people going about their business while free from any compulsion to participate. As at Mergellina, I follow the corniche around the harbour from Midan Zaghloul to the Qaitbay Fortress on the Pharos. Pharos was an island, mentioned in Homer, that guided ships to safety along the reefs and shoals of the coast; Pharos was the lighthouse that shone over the port city of classical civilisation; Pharos was a metaphor for Hellenism, transmitting Greek thought across the Mediterranean world, from science and mathematics to the syncretism that became Christianity; Pharos was the fortress that fell to the city's conquerors: Caesar in 48 BC, Octavian in 30 BC, Amr in 641, Selim in 1517 and Britain in 1882.

The actual lighthouse was designed by Sostratus and constructed in white marble from 297–283 BC. Possibly 130 metres high, the tower had a permanent flame at its summit, with a system of mirrors to beam it out to sea and an observatory with state-of-the-art scientific instruments. Following the Arab invasion, the structure ceased to be maintained and eventually collapsed from neglect, earthquake and pillage. All that remains of the original monument are a few carved stone blocks dimly lit in the basement of the mediaeval fortress of Qaitbay. But the Pharos is closed for restoration, and no amount of inducement can persuade the guards to open it. When I enquire about the marble blocks I saw on my earlier visit, I am told that they have been removed for safe keeping and will be housed in the Graeco-Roman museum.

Looking over the eastern harbour, I imagine what the classical city would have looked like. Founded by Alexander in 331 BC and brought to its zenith by the first three Ptolemies, Alexandria burst into the world *ex nihilo* in bright white marble. Facing the Mediterranean with its sea harbours as well as the Nile valley via a canal to the city's freshwater port on Lake Mareotis, Alexandria harnessed the agricultural wealth of the Nile and turned Egypt into the granary of the Mediterranean. Ruling over a small maritime empire that encompassed most of the Levant and its littoral, the Ptolemies converted this wealth into the grandest city the world had ever seen and incubated the late flowering of Greek science and mathematics.

Walls surrounded Alexandria on the three landward sides, enclosing the lake port and the canals. A causeway called the Heptastadion connected the city to Pharos Island, with arches that allowed ships to pass between the two primary harbours. The Ptolemaic palace was at the eastern end of the city with its own royal harbour. At the central crossroads of the east-west canopic way and the street running north-south between the lake and the sea stood Alexander's tomb, and attached to it, the public institutions of the Mouseion and the Library. Unlike their Seleucid rivals in Antioch, the Ptolemies granted autonomy to all communities in the city, encouraging migration from across their orbit. The Delta district outside the eastern wall accommodated the leading Jewish community on the Mediterranean. By the time of Cleopatra, the last Hellenic ruler of Egypt, there were almost as many Jews as Greeks in Alexandria.

I sit on the stone parapet above Anfushi bay as the sun sets over Muhammad Ali Pasha's lavish palace at Ras el-Tin—the Cape of Figs. After the Arab conquest and the founding of Cairo, Alexandria decayed. The coup de grace was the silting up of the Canopic mouth of the Nile in the twelfth century that disconnected the flow from the Nile into Lake Mareotis. Modern Alexandria is above all the creation of Muhammad Ali who in 1819 dug the Mahmoudiya canal that brought back the water, the foreign communities and trade.

Walking through Anfushi I am drawn to the mosque of Sidi al-Abbas al-Morsi, whose domes and minaret seem completely at one with the palms as its green strip lights flash on at dusk. Sitting on the thick carpets under the carved stone in the warm evening breeze I sense again the cosiness of the mosque after prayers. To a busy Westerner time-crushed by the work-hard play-hard way of life, it might seem a preposterous intrusion to pray five times a day. Yet the prayers themselves serve as a zero point—a grounding of equilibrium—evensong without the Aquinas hymns. From the mosque I walk past the fishing boats to the Windsor Palace Hotel whose Spencer Terrace shows the taste of Anglo-Egypt, with its aristocratic aspiration transplanted to the Protectorate as if the British Empire were destined to prosper forever.

Near Ramleh I find Elite, a French restaurant whose ancient patroness Christina is one of the last surviving Greeks born in Egypt. The Alexandria of Forster, Cavafy and Durrell was a polyglot city of 500,000 souls, with Jews, Greeks, Armenians, Europeans and Egyptians. That world vanished after the 1952 revolution with Nasr's Arab nationalism, the

Suez Crisis of 1956 and the tenfold demographic expansion of the later twentieth century. The restaurant has comfortable blue-backed leather settles and serves local Cleopatra and Omar Khayyam wines. But something about the offhand manner of the staff suggests that once the old lady pays her obol, even this residual influence will vanish.

As I sip the wine and Christina's onion soup, I read Naguib Mahfouz's novella *Miramar*. Published in 1967, shortly before the Six-Day War, *Miramar* conveys the flavour of post-colonial Egypt through the eyes of the inhabitants of an Alexandrian pension whose Greek owner could be Christina. Four characters narrate the story of Sarhan al-Beheiry's apparent suicide for love of the beautiful *fellaha*, Zohra. Through the Arab tradition of storytelling, Mahfouz expresses the pessimism of the era. None of his characters achieves fulfilment: regardless of background, service to the revolution or legitimacy of expectation, all their hopes are crushed by the regime. But then I reflect that perhaps all our hopes are dependent on chance events.

THURSDAY 22 MAY | ALEXANDRIA

A genial Nubian, tall and dark-skinned, serves me tea, rolls and a boiled egg. The breakfast room of the pension has a Regency style glass covered terrace. The sun reflects on the mirror above the dresser, and I feel better about the city. It is a shock to move from serene natural beauty to the dirty metropolis. But Alexandria improves when the sun comes out. I walk past the closed Eliahu Hanavi Synagogue to the Coptic Patriarchate and seek permission to stay overnight at the Wadi Natrun. But I have no luck. So I find the Anglican church of St Mark, built in the Moorish style in the 1840s, and play on an upright piano in the side aisle. A Dutch missionary called Pieter interrupts me and insists that I accompany him for a coffee.

Pieter walks me at speed from the corniche to his favourite noisy coffee shop where we cannot be overheard by his enemies. He talks about corruption in the Coptic Church, how wealth is the source of unhappiness in the rich countries of northern Europe and how Egypt is a nation of thieves and liars. Pieter is interested in my travels but he thinks they will be fruitless unless I devote myself to a social cause and suggests that I minister to Sudanese refugees. We are joined by his friend William Hepper who continues that Egypt's problems come down to a lack of transparency and a culture of obfuscation in public institutions. William believes that democratisation will improve the quality of decision-making, leading to economic growth and wealth creation. But I wonder if the hopelessness Mahfouz describes is not endemic.

Pieter observes that Northern Europe has a suicide problem, even—or rather especially—among the rich. 'Our Lord is the only sustenance that will sustain,' he says. But as Metropolitan Anthony of Sourozh once said, 'There is scant spiritual succour in poverty.' To be sure, navel-gazing presupposes the luxury of a full belly but full bellies are not the *cause* of suicide: matters of the belly and the soul are quite distinct. The plight of Sudanese refugees will not be improved without a political economic solution; but nor will Swiss suicides be saved from their meaninglessness without a psychological solution. The will to live and the desire for freedom—for individual self-actualisation harmoniously achieved with others—are the same. As Epicurus understood, a basic level of material prosperity is a prerequisite for the realisation of freedom. But freedom from absurd laws, arbitrary tyranny and the senseless harm of others all matter too.

I extricate myself and find the Café Viennous on the corner of Nebi Daniel and Sharia al-Hurriya, somewhere near the site of the Mouseion. Local Arab legend merged the Prophet Daniel with the figure of Alexander. But archaeological consensus is that Alexander's tomb-temple may have been located under the mosque of Nebi Daniel. Once the haunt of Cavafy and Forster at the very centre of Alexandria, the Viennous is empty now apart from the odd stray cat. The marble tables, wooden chairs and even the prices are unchanged since my previous visit five years earlier. The patron is friendly and makes me a strong Turkish coffee. Whether from jealousy or competitive disadvantage or manipulation by the regime, the

Muslim Arab majority came to resent any Jews and Greeks in Alexandria who were better off than themselves. But with its art-nouveau mirrors, chandeliers and cabinets, the Café Viennous still carries vestiges of their splendour.

Alexandria is the capital of memories because it encapsulates universal decline. Yet for all the stifling drabness of the contemporary city, the beauty of the nineteenth-century conception is still visible, with its elements of a pan-Mediterranean style. Beyond the junction, Nebi Daniel Street is closed to traffic and there is a row of book stands and market stalls shaded by trees. Along the streets are elegant stone houses with decorative cornices, painted wooden shutters and wrought iron balconies. Trade and capitalist competition generated the financial wealth that allowed the Levantine merchants to construct these townhouses. But the taste, style and judgement, the craftsmanship, proportion and materials of their world represented a very different cultural landscape from twenty-first century hi-tech globalised capitalism.

After a bowl of onion soup I set off for the Biblioteca Alexandrina. I imagine a spacious, well-proportioned classical building such as the library in Palermo, situated by the water, with the illumination of divine wisdom streaming through the windows into the readers' minds. From the outside, the modern Biblioteca looks ungainly but it derives beauty on the inside from its staircases and bookshelves under a single central skylight. A World Press Photo exhibition displays pictures of Palestinian gunmen holed up inside the Church of the Nativity in Bethlehem. Likewise there are photographs of Alexandria from July 1882 showing the extent of the destruction following riots and British shelling. At the Planetarium next door, there is an exhibition of the scientific contribution made by ancient and mediaeval Alexandrians.

Founded by Ptolemy I (Soter) and funded by the palace treasury, the Mouseion of Alexandria allowed scholars to pursue their research interests without financial constraints or teaching responsibilities. Initially rivalled by Athens, Rhodes and Pergamum, the Mouseion's library collected more papyri and parchments than ever before, possibly 500,000 items, and became the repository of all knowledge. The first librarian, Demetrius Phalerus, was a student of Aristotle and modelled the new institution on the Mouseion of Athens. Under Ptolemy II (Philadelphus), Euclid wrote his thirteen-volume *Elements*. This text is the most complete surviving work of Greek mathematics and defined the method of axiomatic proof: apart from its presentation of geometry, it summarised earlier mathematics going back to Pythagoras, including studies of optics and the earliest surviving proof that there is no greatest prime number.

Euclid's colleague Aristarchus proposed a heliocentric model of the heavens and devised geometric methods to calculate the relative distance from the Earth of the Moon and the Sun. Meanwhile, Erasistratus and Herophilus correctly identified the functions of the various organs of the body including the lungs and the brain. In the following generation Euclid's pupil Apollonius defined the ellipse, parabola and hyperbola as species of conic section and may have worked with Archimedes. Eratosthenes of Cyrene, librarian under the third Ptolemy (Euergertes), devised his sieve algorithm to test numbers for primality, calculated the circumference of the Earth to within a few seconds of arc of its modern known value and was the first to compile systematic geographic maps of the world.

Cleopatra's defeat at Actium marked the extinction of any independent Greek polity. Augustus absorbed Egypt into Rome as the personal bounty of the Imperator and the vigour of Alexandria turned inwards. But the city remained intellectually active: Claudius Ptolemy's first-century mathematical model of planetary motion was not surpassed in predictive accuracy until the 1600s; in the second century Diophantus pioneered algebra, giving representation to the unknown variable and solving polynomial equations.

As Christianity spread around the Roman world in the first three centuries, it was primarily at Alexandria that the cut and thrust of intellectual disputation led to the definition and elaboration of theological positions, as if the new faith supplied new thought-exercises to the old Hellenic mind. The Gnostics explored stories of the Christ in terms of secret messages from the (implicitly pagan) gods; Clement and Origen grounded Christian thought in Greek philosophy; in the third century, Plotinus and Porphyry elaborated Christian Platonism; and in the early fourth century Arius and Athanasius used Aristotelian metaphysics to debate the trinity and divinity of Christ. It was only when imperial arms imposed Orthodoxy by force that free enquiry and creative intellectual activity gave up the ghost at Alexandria.

Heading towards Mareotis at the southern limit of the Ptolemaic city, I reach the archaeological site known as Pompey's Pillar. This garden around a small hill lay at the centre of Rhakotis, the New Kingdom pharaonic town that Alexander would have seen. Later it became the location of the Temple of Serapis, the Ptolemaic syncretic deity that integrated Osiris and Apis with Zeus and Dionysius into an overarching one-God conveniently cementing Hellenistic rule into the prior mind world of their Egyptian subjects. After the original 'mother' library of Alexandria was accidentally burned during the war with Caesar, Cleopatra refounded the second more extensive 'daughter' library and attached it to the Serapeum.

Four centuries later, in the year 380, the Edict of Thessalonica declared any persons deviating from Nicene Orthodoxy to be 'foolish madmen' and heretics. Greek science and mathematics became suspect and the authorities began to systematically destroy ancient texts seen as inconsistent with Christian doctrine. In 391, the Patriarch Theophilus orchestrated a gang of desert monks to demolish the Serapeum, and Cleopatra's library was destroyed along with it. Possibly 500,000 papyrus scrolls and parchments were lost, marking the full rupture with the Hellenistic world. Later in 415, during the Patriarchate of Cyril, another fanatical mob killed the pagan mathematician and philosopher Hypatia in the streets of Alexandria. Today there is a lonely sphinx on the site of the temple and beneath it stands an outsized granite Corinthian column: the inscription states that it was erected to the worship of Diocletian in the year 297, the period of the Great Persecution.

The Coptic Church broke with Orthodoxy at the Council of

Chalcedon in the year 451, along with the Armenian, Syriac and Ethiopian Churches. It is ironic that the edict issued to provide imperial support for Orthodoxy over its doctrinal alternatives led to the destruction of the Serapeum by Egyptian Christians who then, within a few more decades, broke away from Orthodoxy themselves. Imagine how different history would have been if the Patriarch's fanatical monks had knocked down the pillar and spared the library.

FRIDAY 23 MAY | ALEXANDRIA

I take the tram from Ramleh to Stanley Beach for Sunday mass on a Friday at the Anglican All Saints church. After the service, William and Morrat Hepper invite me to their house for lunch with two American missionaries called John and Sandy. There is something reassuring about attending an institutional Anglican service in a foreign country and receiving the welcoming hospitality after. But listening to the Americans, I wonder what a crusading Hospitaller knight would think of American evangelical Christianity. Has Christendom come to soft rock, drums and guitars? The discussions continue into the evening. We talk about everything from Iraq to creationism, Christian Zionism (derived from John Nelson Derby's dispensationalism) and the American Bible Society. I argue that to believe literally in New Testament doctrine in the post-enlightenment age is tantamount to psychosis. John blames individualism for the American malaise. I blame corporate power and the inability of the polity to apply principles consistently.

William walks me to the tram stop and recommends Tsirkas's *Drifting Cities* about the multicultural life of Alexandria before Nasr expelled the Greeks and Europeans, and forced the Jews to leave for Israel. The return journey on the tram is delightful in the evening light, and the city seems almost tropical with the bougainvillea of the sports clubs and gardens. I sit in Anfushi reading *Miramar* and find my way to the Santa Lucia restaurant opposite Elite. The restaurant is empty so I play through some Bach preludes and fugues with my inarticulate fingers until George the jazz pianist arrives. George is kindly impressed with my efforts and plays *Dark Eyes* and other jazz numbers that the diners appreciate more than the Bach.

Saturday 24 May | Alexandria

In the morning I explore the Cavafy Museum. Constantine Cavafy's apartment is on the second floor of a corner building, light on both sides. There is no through traffic: from the balcony all you hear is the chattering of nargileh smokers opposite and birds rustling in the enormous ficus tree above. This mellifluous background noise provides *sotto voce* companionship to poetic invention. The bookshelves and Cavafy memorabilia transport the visitor to a simpler, more charming era when the poet sat in these rooms, to compose, fret and receive visitors. I look attentively through the photographs, read the poems, newspaper articles and vignettes from Cavafy's life, and examine the line drawings of Cavafy's naked male friends by Andreas Karayan, discretely placed behind a curtain at the back of the museum.

As I sit in the throne-like chair in the drawing room, imagining Cavafy's world, my reverie is disturbed by two new arrivals: Anne and François are French diplomats posted to Cairo. We decide to pass the day together and head through the streets of the former Greek district to the Graeco-Roman museum. After enjoying the bas-reliefs and statue of Venus, we take coffee in the garden, and I tell them about my travels. We walk across to Christina's place for some fish where Anne takes Cavafy from her bag and reads the poignant lines of his poem *Ithaka* at the table. I return to the Café Viennous for a late night hot chocolate with *Miramar* and ponder the endlessly complex aspects of life and love.

Logos

'In the beginning was the Word, and the Word was with God and the Word was God.' *The Gospel of John* chapter one, verse one. All over the world this sentence is read aloud at Christmas time, and in this simple statement of Christian cosmology, something magisterially poetic captures the ear of the listener. But what does it mean? The English sentence in the King

James Bible closely matches the vulgate, St Jerome's Latin translation commissioned in 382. '*In principio erat Verbum et Verbum erat apud Deum et Deus erat Verbum.*' The text of the original Koine, the 'common' Greek of the Hellenised Levant, reads as follows: Ἐν ἀρχῇ ἦν ὁ Λόγος, καὶ ὁ Λόγος ἦν πρὸς τὸν Θεόν, καὶ Θεὸς ἦν ὁ Λόγος.

In *Readings in St. John's Gospel*, William Temple explains that the word *logos* combines two meanings: the command of the creator by which the cosmos came into existence and an unfolding principle of divine reason which lies at the root of the cosmos. The first meaning descends from the creation story of the Hebrew book of Genesis: 'Let there be light'. The second meaning derives from Greek philosophy. Philo of Alexandria, the head of the Jewish community in the city in the early first century, joined the two and identified divine logos with the concept of love. As St John elaborated the concept, logos is the source of life, the light that shines in the darkness —the cosmic force that imposes order on chaos.

From the time of Philo to Athanasius and the formulation of the Nicene Creed in 325, Alexandria was the incubator of Christian theology. Without the Hellenisation of the Alexandrian Jewish community, the Nazarenes would have remained a marginal sect, destined to vanish. But when the Christian seed was planted in Alexandria, according to tradition by St Mark, it fell on fertile ground. That seed bore fruit in Egypt because the Jews had created the conditions to frame the gospel message in the terms of the Greek worldview. Without Philo's syncretism and its Hellenistic intellectual scaffolding, the new religion could not have unshackled itself from the Jewish cultural tradition and found a broader appeal among the gentiles.

Concerning the origin of the idea of logos, Temple quotes Heraclitus, who wrote around 500 BC that the principle of divine reason existed from the beginning of time and is the source of human and natural law. We do not know for sure what Heraclitus or any of the early Greek philosophers really thought because there are no original sources: the earliest surviving documents are mediaeval fragments of texts and references, recopied on papyrus or parchment over the centuries. In his *History of Western Philosophy* Bertrand Russell speculates that the idea came from Pythagoras in the generation prior to Heraclitus.

Pythagoras's Theorem about right-angled triangles led to the discovery of incommensurables and irrational numbers. Two line segments are incommensurable if there exists no common line segment that each are integer multiples of, or equivalently, if the ratio of their lengths does not equal a ratio of natural numbers. The proof (by contradiction) of their existence was probably discovered by the Pythagoreans and can be found in book ten of Euclid. The proof shows that if the hypotenuse of a right-angled triangle with sides of unit length is the ratio of two whole numbers, one of them must be odd if it is even. Therefore no ratio of whole numbers measures the hypotenuse and the square root of two is irrational. The word used by Euclid to mean irrational in this mathematical sense is ἀρλόγος. As in Modern Greek, the word λόγος can mean both speech and reason: likewise the logos of Philo and St John means both verbum and ratio in Latin.

Russell explains that the Pythagoreans were the first Greek thinkers to link mathematics and theology; or to put it another way, they intertwined the hypothetico-deductive with the transcendent. What is often called Platonism is at its root Pythagoreanism. Geometry deals with exact circles while no natural object is exactly circular. So mathematical reasoning applies only to abstract objects, ideal Platonic forms, and not to any physical reality. Yet from the time of Pythagoras up to the speculations of modern physics, mathematics has been the instrument to describe, understand and predict the natural world. Before Pythagoras, Greek theology was akin to creation myths and the propitiation of arbitrary external forces. Pythagoras introduced the concept of an eternal world revealed to the intellect and hence the idea of reasoning about the divine.

In pre-Socratic thought, λόγος (reason) was distinct from αἰτία (cause). Aitia relates to natural explanation, developed by Aristotle into four kinds of cause. If every event has a cause, then the network of events in nature must go back in time to a first event. But this first aitia does not give reason, structure or law to the cosmos: it is merely a spark or trigger, inanimate mover of the first domino. The historical tension in Greek philosophy is often cast between the abstract idealism of Plato and the material naturalism of Aristotle, hence the direction of the two mens' arms in Raphael's *The School of Athens*. This division continued into the enlightenment bifurcation between rationalism and empiricism, between *a priori* and *a posteriori* knowledge. Logos combines the two and makes the 'first mover' not so much a spark as an eternal flame.

Logos is the channel by which the transcendent impresses itself upon the human mind. Even if the concept of Philo and St John could be interpreted metaphorically, it cannot be dismissed as nonsense. To reject the transcendent altogether is cavalier: too much is unknown. There remains a fundamental gap between inanimate matter and that which lies beyond, between the physical world and our sentient conscious selves whose mathematical creations inexplicably fit that world. Logos is the eternal source of light divine and the unfolding revelation of the cosmos. Logos connects our sentient being to the transcendent and our rational faculties to nature so that we can gain insight and understanding. Logos leads us along a personal path to peace and freedom, the source of everything we seek, regardless of the –isms and –ologies of the millennia.

SUNDAY 25 MAY | WADI NATRUN

Alexandria! Alexandria! White-marbled capital of nostalgia! After Muhammad Ali Pasha's inspired refounding, have you not faded once again? I continue my journey towards Cairo and stop along the way to visit the Coptic monasteries of the Wadi Natrun in the western desert of Scetis. In antiquity the way to Scetis began at the low gebel of Nitria on the edge of the delta; or the valley could be reached from Tarraneh on the Canopic branch of the Nile further to the east. Today I take the microbus along the Cairo-Alexandria desert highway. After being dropped at the Rest House junction I hitch a lift into the valley with a Coptic family. The narrow straight road descends past fields and salt lakes into a watered depression running parallel to the highway. The road divides near the monastery of Deir Bishoi and the family leave me at a stall selling sesame seed bars and mother of pearl inlaid Coptic crosses.

The present structures of the monasteries date mostly from the sixth and seventh centuries, rebuilt and restored several times following devastations by Berber nomads. They resemble military forts with ten-metre-high walls built in sand-mortar, stone and timber from the delta. The entrance porch typically has a single small doorway and above it a high square tower, or *qasr*, blind to the exterior. Three-dimensional crosses surmounting the cupolas and domes are visible from below amid the tops of the palms in the gardens. Their fortunes have waxed and waned, but today there are several hundred monks living in the four monasteries of the Wadi Natrun: Baramus, Suriani, Bishoi and Macarius.

Leaving my belongings in the porch of Bishoi, I walk the short distance to Deir al-Suriani and join a tour group. Coptic monks wear black habits and a head-dress decorated with crosses: our guide has a grey beard and bright eyes, and alternates between Arabic and flawless English and German. As we walk through the gardens to the church he relates the history of the monastery. Deir al-Suriani was founded as a result of a theological dispute about the incorruptibility of the body of Christ, and came to be inhabited by Syrians. In 927 the Abbot Moses travelled to Baghdad to negotiate a tax exemption from the Abbasid caliph and collected 250 Syriac manuscripts. Deir al-Suriani still has the richest library in the Wadi Natrun. Above all the monastery is famous for its tenth-century Door of Prophecies which is divided into seven rows inlaid with ivory emblems representing the epochs of the church: Apostolic (figures of Christ, Mary and St Mark); Patristic (circles), Constantinian (crosses representing the Patriarchates); Islamic (crescents); Frankish (swastikas); disunity (divided crosses) and a radiating final epoch. A Syriac inscription states that the doors were made in the reigns of Gabriel I, fifty-seventh Patriarch of Alexandria, and John IV, twenty-fifth Patriarch of Antioch.

I return to Deir Bishoi, retreat of the Coptic Pope Shenouda

III, and am invited for lunch by Father Joachim. The refectory is in the qasr on the first floor, and I sit by the window looking out over the tamarinds and palms in the garden, absorbing the bright and airy, reedy-breezy atmosphere. The lunch is simple and delicious: fuul, olive oil, salted flat bread and tiny lemons which are juicy and sweet. Many Copts visit the Wadi Natrun on Sundays and Father Joachim finds me another family with space in their car. They drive me to Cairo and drop me by Ramses Station. From there I walk in the heat to Pension Roma on Sharia Muhammad Farid where Madame Cressaty remembers me and gives me Room 16 in the corner.

The desert a city
It began with the religious persecution and crippling taxation of the late third century: Christian men and women, saints and vagabonds, abandoned the world of the cities for the fringes of the desert. Around the year 250, Pax Romana collapsed as the new Sasanian dynasty assaulted the empire across its eastern frontiers and the Roman state targeted the Christian communities. Roman military reorganisation led to the emergence of a technocratic warrior class and reinvigorated emperor worship. The repression of Christianity reached its peak under the Tetrarchy and the Great Persecution of Diocletian. In the ensuing civil war, Constantine saw a vision of the cross before defeating Maxentius at the Milvian Bridge in 312. With the Edict of Milan in 313, the age of martyrdom transitioned into the Christian Empire; yet the migration into the desert only gained momentum, as if once tasted, life in the wilderness was too sweet to give up. According to contemporary writers, by the end of the fourth century the desert had become a city.

The founders of the movement were Anthony and Pachomius. St Anthony was the father to the anchorites (the displaced), who lived alone in caves and cells. Athanasius, leading advocate of Trinitarian doctrine at the Council of Nicaea in 325 and later Patriarch of Alexandria, wrote the *Vita San Antonii* shortly after Anthony's death in 356. Widely disseminated across the Roman world, the *Vita* became the manifesto of monasticism. Meanwhile the former soldier

Pachomius, whose biography survives in the *Vita Prima Pachomii*, organised the first coenobitic, or communal, house and constructed the prototype monastery at Tabenna. His daily regime of prayer and work—building, tending kitchen gardens and weaving mats and baskets to sell—was taken up by St Basil of Cappadocia, whose *Asketikon* served as the basis for the Rule of St Benedict in the Latin West. Anthony himself lived at the foot of a mountain in the eastern desert where the monastery dedicated to him stands today. The Pachomian communities initially flourished at the Gebel Nitria on the edge of the delta, accessible by boat from Alexandria. As Nitria became more populous, monks and hermits migrated to Scetis in search of the silence of the desert.

Some have interpreted this retreat to the desert as a response to the Constantinian triumph of Christianity, whose very adoption as the official religion of the wealthy classes undermined its other-worldly spirit. Later, after the Oriental Churches split from Orthodoxy at the Council of Chalcedon in 451, Coptic monasticism became linked to an assertion of national identity against a revived Greek Empire whose doctrines were imposed at Alexandria. From its earliest days monasticism embraced varying degrees of asceticism: Anthony himself lived alone for decades in the eastern desert, passing away at the age of 105. His friend Paul lived to be 113, which suggests their regimen of mental discipline and a perpetual Lenten diet was at least conducive to longevity. The majority formed themselves into Pachomian communities— *monachos* meant a station or lodge—and a network of monasteries grew up across Egypt and the Levant.

The monks of Nitria and Scetis were often devoted Origenists, interpreting Christian doctrine as the innocent joy of the Hebrew *Song of Songs*. Origen, who died in Alexandria shortly after Anthony's birth, argued that since the external world is brittle and fragile, any attempt to find a path to light through material security must fail. Salvation lies in the creation of an internal tranquillity made alive by the power of the imagination and by the love of God. The *Life of St Anthony* tells of the anchorite's quest to regain paradise lost through the vanquishing of demons. The first stage on the path is to overcome the inner conflict of temptations and malign thoughts from within; then the soul must confront disturbances from without, before returning to the world to reconcile mankind with God, society with the transcendent.

In *The Wisdom of the Desert* Thomas Merton situates the Desert Fathers as 'axial men' who fled from the world of cities because they neither wanted to dominate nor be dominated by others. Instead they wanted to liberate themselves from the exploitation of a worldly society and live in true equality under the sole authority of divine love. Merton describes the Fathers as seeking their true selves with pure hearts, swimming for their lives into an apparently irrational void. 'What can we gain by sailing to the moon if we are not able to cross the abyss that separates us from ourselves?' The purpose of the internal journey is the transformation of our subjective experience to a state of *hesychia* or sweet repose. To keep the mind still the body must be active, and the Fathers practised physical work alongside their prayers. The challenge for us who live in the world of cities is to find this zero point of quies or silent absorption, avoiding unnecessary distraction, and instead engaging in reflective activity much like the flow state of Mihály Csíkszentmihályi.

The monasteries of Scetis could be Epicurean gardens that have adopted the distinctively Christian elements of love and forgiveness. The sayings of the Desert Fathers, the *Verba Seniorum* or *Apothegmata*, survive in many collections, copied and re-edited over the centuries. Sometimes they are laconic. Patriarch Theophilus, the very same destroyer of the Serapeum, went to Scetis and called upon Abbot Pambo to speak with him to edify his soul. Pambo replied that: 'If the Patriarch is not edified by his silence then his words must be hopeless too.' Likewise another saying: 'The worldly ruined Rome and now the monks ruin Scetis.' Above all their spirit is one of detached humanism run through with love.

There was an abbot at Scetis called Anastasius who possessed a beautiful bible: it was finely inscribed in the highest quality parchment and was worth eighteen pounds.

One day a novice came to visit him and stole the book. The abbot went to read his bible and realised that the novice had taken it. But he did not pursue the brother because he feared that the novice would harm himself with perjury, in addition to the theft.

Now the novice went down to Alexandria to try and sell the book: the price he asked was sixteen pounds. A bookdealer said to the novice, 'Lend me the book so that I can find out how much it is worth.' The dealer took the book to the abbot at Scetis and said, 'Holy father, tell me if you think this book is worth sixteen pounds.' The abbot said to the book dealer, 'Yes, it is a fine book and worth at least that much.'

So the bookdealer went back to the novice and said, 'Here is your money. I showed the book to Abbot Anastasius who said it is a fine book and worth at least sixteen pounds.' The novice asked, 'Was that all he said? Did he make any other remarks?' 'No,' said the book dealer, 'he did not say another word.' 'Then I have changed my mind,' said the novice, 'and do not wish to sell the book after all.' The novice hastened back to Abbot Anastasius and begged him on his knees to take back the bible. But the abbot would not accept it and said, 'Go in peace my son. You may keep the book: I make you a present of it.' The novice replied that if the abbot did not take back the book he would never have any peace, and he lived with Abbot Anastasius at Scetis to the end of his life.

Cairo

MONDAY 26 MAY | EGYPTIAN MUSEUM

Madame Cressaty's pension is on the fourth floor of a grand building in the Ismailia district that dates from the 1940s with shuttered windows, pot plants and an upright piano in the hallway. I discovered it on an earlier visit to Cairo, when initially I stayed in the Hussein Hotel opposite al-Azhar for the immersive Cairene experience, but whose bathrooms carried the residue of their former occupants, and fled to the comfort of the Roma. Cairo is a desert encampment that has morphed into a dystopian megalopolis. But the Pension Roma is a haven above the hubbub, and there is always someone interesting to chat to over breakfast of tea and rolls. After speaking with a French woman who apparently resides permanently at the pension in emulation of Coco Chanel, I drop into the Anglo-Egyptian bookshop next door. This Cairo institution, founded in 1928, has a superb stock of Arabic literature and books about Egypt.

From the bookshop I walk down Qasr al-Nil to the Egyptian Museum. The antiquities are astonishing but it is odd to breeze through three millennia of history from Menes to Cleopatra in three hours. There is something static about the ancient Egyptians, as if they found that life as it was was too good to change. From the depth of their fastness on the Nile, they periodically expanded across the Levant as far as Anatolia and then retreated into domestic isolation. Perhaps the security of their land, punctuated by incursions from the Hyksos and Sea Peoples, allowed them to preserve the old ways of the rhythms of the sun over the Nile and its floods. There is so much that remains obscure: how did the genius of the Old Kingdom spring out of this land with its pyramids and statues, temples and hieroglyphs? Was the reaction against

Akhenaten really about monotheism or was it the politics of a priest-class seeking to protect its interests?

I pay the surcharge to the reserved gallery and examine the collection of Royal Mummies. The ancient Egyptians saw the afterworld as a more perfect version of this one. But to guarantee safe passage of the departed it was necessary to preserve the body as the conduit of the soul. Techniques of mummification developed in the Old Kingdom by desiccating the bodies in natron salts. In the New Kingdom, funerary texts of spells to answer the questions of the gods were written on papyrus and placed in the coffin. The Royal Mummies were discovered in the tomb of Pinedjem II in the Dayr al-Bahri, to which they had been transferred from their original sites in antiquity to protect them from robbers. The site was excavated by the Antiquities Department in 1881 and a second cache was discovered in the tomb of Amenhotep II in 1898. Scientific analysis of the bodies, including DNA testing, has established their familial relationships, and the New Kingdom mummies show a clear facial resemblance to one another.

One mummy stands out as physiognomically distinct from the others with his broad serene face: 'Yuya', Chief Minister of Egypt, the father of Tiye—wife of the eighteenth dynasty Pharaoh Amenhotep III and grandfather of Akhenaten—is thought to have been of Syrian ancestry. Could Yuya be Joseph? Could his Semitic influence have precipitated the revolution of Akhenaten, who refocussed Egyptian religion around the omnipotent creator Ra-Horus, the solar disc Aten? Akhenaten's body has not been found, possibly because it was destroyed along with his city of Akhetaten (Amarna); but the statue of him that survives in the museum shows his face to carry distinct features. It has been speculated that the face is deliberately elongated in a symbolic representation of his Ra-worship. But perhaps it is simply a likeness?

And there is Ramesses II, imperious as Ozymandias, complete with nasal hair, broken teeth and fingernails. Post-enlightenment materialism argues that religion is a pre-modern relic, an instrument of social control through the exercise of superstition. But records of the earliest societies suggest that the religious impulse has always been about the awareness of mortality. Did the Egyptians really believe in the afterlife with the same confidence as their belief in stones and trees and crops? Was their afterworld a collective delusion that satisfied minds more accustomed to natural cycles than to dialectic and logical analysis? The Pharaohs certainly invested considerable resources in their tombs.

Yet in the Sumerian *Epic of Gilgamesh* that dates back to the era of the first pyramid builders Zoser and Imhotep, we find a longing for immortality that cannot be satisfied by any funeral rite. In the natural cycle, passing on our culture to our children is supposed to mollify the horror. But it does not work. Ramesses has survived in our apprehension of his slender frame; but the continuation of his present experience was terminated as abruptly as that of the Unknown Soldier. Nothing has changed in human experience since the beginning: the Epicurean arguments to rationalise away our fear of death are as futile as the attempts of Gilgamesh and Ramesses to escape it or the Christian denial of its finality.

I amble across the square to the Nile Hilton for tea and a water pipe with Max Rodenbeck. The Hilton terrace is a comfortable enclave where business people and foreign visitors can enjoy first-world comfort in the cool Nile breeze—the sort of place where foreign correspondents tap out their copy while the streets are in flames. Max is a journalist whose book *Cairo: The City Victorious* remains the most empathetic biography of Cairo. Max's father taught at the American University in Cairo and Max grew up in the city. Urbane and engaging, he tells stories of Egypt's writers and conspiracy theories of the Arab street.

Al-Qahira 'the Victorious', was founded by the Fatimids in 969 and became the dominant city of the Dar al-Islam. Writing in the 1340s the Maghrebi traveller Ibn Battuta described Cairo as the mother of cities, the navel of the world, peerless in the beauty and splendour of its mosques, souqs and palaces. Mediaeval Cairo was the centre of a trade bloc extending from the Atlantic to the Hindu Kush, with free movement of goods, labour, capital and business. But the Portuguese voyages of discovery and the rise of European empires undermined Cairo's position and Egypt has been in decline ever since. Muhammad Ali reversed the trend during his long reign. But his grandson Khedive Ismail overspent, leading to debt diplomacy and the British Occupation. Today Cairo is among the most densely crowded cities on the planet, most of whose people lived precarious lives in shabby tenements, even as the architectural heritage survives as the reminder of a glorious past. Since the military coup of 1952, the population shock has overwhelmed the infrastructure while successive venal governments have failed to address Egypt's economic challenges.

The Arabic name for the country and its capital is Misr, whose Semitic root means grain. But the ancient local name was *hut-ka-ptah*, the house or essence of *ptah*, which became 'Egypt' via the Greeks. Ptah was the source of life, the radiation of the energy of Ra, the sun itself represented in human form by Amun. Solar radiation and the Nile's flood created the breadbasket and the flowering of the Old Kingdom. As the country continues to carry the weight of Nile silt in its habits of inertia, so the sense of divine inevitability is never far away in Egypt: 'in sha'allah' and 'al'ham dal'allah' are the motifs of contemporary Misry speech. Max laments Cairo's inexorable slide into an impatient, less charming city of ugly modern buildings but writes that Misr is as comfortable as an old shoe —reflecting the enduring warmth of its people.

Returning to the pension I play the piano in the corridor and prepare for dinner with some business people introduced through a family connection. From somewhere among my belongings I fish out a grey sweater, a pair of black leather shoes and a white shirt that Madame Cressaty's assistant kindly irons. Looking presentable, I wait in the street outside the heavily protected synagogue on the corner. Abbas Hilmi arrives with his son Daoud in a black four-by-four jeep and we drive to a 'pre-sunk' restaurant boat on the Nile.

Abbas seats me beside Muhammad Younes, founder of the Concord Group, a private equity firm investing in Egypt. Younes explains that after decades of stagnation since the 1952 revolution, Egypt is in the midst of a new revolution that will invigorate the economy. Having taken the prescription of the Washington Consensus, the government began privatising state-owned enterprises in the 1990s and is now opening the capital account to attract foreign investment. The new system will bridge the gulf between foreign educated business people who have learned best practice in international firms and the domestic community that often perpetuates the mentality of protectionism and shoddy goods of the old statist era.

Since capital flows out as well as in, I wonder if the medicine is really a prescription for value creation. Younes believes that liberalisation will allow the business community and foreign investors to earn good returns on capital while growing the economy and raising living standards for ordinary Egyptians. Yet many members of the business elite are closely linked to the government, which raises questions about conflicts of interest between private corporations and public administration, as well as the basic nature of governance in Egypt. Abbas drives me back to the Pension Roma and invites me to take tea with him later in the week. Around the corner from the pension on Talaat Haab, up a flight of stairs, I find the Internet Point Hany suffused in diesel exhaust through the open windows from the heavy evening traffic below.

Dialogues
Dear Illiana, Cairo is uncomfortably hot. So I am wearing my Siwi sirwal trousers which attracts laughs from the locals as people think they are undergarments. It may sound amusing but below the surface I sense anti-Western feeling in Egypt. I had to smarten up for dinner this evening and bought a pair of tan-coloured Egyptian cotton chinos. Quite a contrast to backpacking, I was the guest of the direct descendant of Muhammad Ali Pasha: Prince Abbas and his family were forced to leave Egypt after the 1952 revolution but returned to the country nine years ago. If I meet him again I will ask him what he thinks about politics, religion and economic development in Egypt. Yesterday in the Wadi Natrun I met a woman who works with refugees and human-rights groups. Beatings and torture are routine methods of police investigation in Egypt,

presumably occurring with the sanction of President Mubarak and his ministers. Rupert.

TUESDAY 27 MAY | ISLAMIC CAIRO

Khamseen, meaning fifty, is a seasonal wind that blows off the desert and the city is covered in dust. On first inspection, the streets of the nineteenth-century Ismailia quarter resemble the business district of any modern capital: there are traffic jams and people dressed in Western clothes heading to work in offices. But one block east of the Midan al-Opera, the European city transitions into the districts of mediaeval Cairo. The Azbakiyya Park was once a lake along the western edge of the Fatimid city wall, then became pleasure gardens as Cairo expanded to the Nile and was laid out as a small park. There are camels and rural *fellahin* wearing *galabiyya* and a sense of urban hubbub at this juncture that used to have rows of book stalls. During the digging of the third metro line that went on forever, the once charming gardens were ripped up, including a giant banyan tree. After an outcry the book stalls were relocated to the far side of the garden.

In search of the romance of the *Thousand and One Nights*, I begin walking along Sharia al-Muski towards the Khan-al-Khalili, the sprawling mediaeval markets at the heart of Fatimid al-Qahira. It is safe to walk everywhere in Cairo: you may be pestered by pedlars but you will never be robbed or assaulted. After a short distance I realise that the heat is overpowering. So I hail a black and white decrepit old Lada taxi that drives me along the winding flyover past the ochre buildings of al-Musky district down to Sharia al-Azhar. A passageway leads to the art deco al-Hussein Hotel that looks over the Midan al-Hussein. I climb the stairs to the fifth floor roof restaurant and ensconce myself with a water pipe and hibiscus tea.

Cairo's greatest glories are its mosques, madrasas and mausolea constructed over twelve centuries, and nowhere is the grandeur and style of mediaeval Islam better preserved. To visit them involves wandering through the narrow streets, stopping for gunpowder tea with the guardians, and shedding shoes to study the interiors and climb minarets. In 1992 an earthquake damaged many of Cairo's monuments. This event catalysed the formation of the Historic Cairo Restoration Project and led to a substantial renovation programme. The narrow primary route of mediaeval Cairo, al-Qasaba, runs from the Bab al-Futuh in the north to the mosque of Ibn Tulun in the south. A series of markets along the route and off its side streets sells everything from skinned lamb's heads and vegetables to brassware and textiles.

The al-Hussein roof restaurant gives a panoramic view from the mosque of Hussein on the square below up to the Muhammad Ali Mosque on the citadel. This fortress, built by Salah ad-Din and his successors, rests on a spur of the Muqattam Hills whose limestone blocks have been the primary source of stone since the Old Kingdom. The minarets of Misr are distinctive and local, their basic form with balconies and cupola derived from the tiered structure of the Pharos at Alexandria. An open terrace extends behind the restaurant with a large carved wooden mirror that affords a roofscape view of broken detritus and satellite dishes.

By the pedestrian bridge over the congested Sharia al-Azhar, I find a juice bar and observe the crowded street with several glasses of pulped sugar cane mixed with sweet fresh orange. As at Siwa, the juice is a life saver in the heat and there are stand-up juice bars all over the city. I continue over the bridge and walk along to the al-Ghuri complex. The covered space between the mosque and mausoleum is a thriving street market selling spices and perfumes. Constructed by the penultimate Mamluk sultan who died fighting the Ottomans in 1516, al-Ghuri's fully enclosed mosque has fine polychrome inlaid marble panels. From the minaret one can see across the roofs from the al-Azhar Mosque-University to the double minarets of the al-Mu'ayyad Mosque that stand over the Bab Zuwayla, the southern gate of Fatimid al-Qahira.

Endowed as a madrasa with a library in the 1410s, the mosque of al-Mu'ayyad is perhaps the most serene of all Cairene Islamic monuments, and the last open-courtyard congregational mosque to be built. Steps lead to the characteristic Mamluk portal with stalactitic decoration and striped dressed stone into the hypostyle prayer hall with tie beams, hanging lamps and marble mihrab. The sultan's mausoleum is on one side and the arcaded courtyard with ablution fountain on the other. These enclosed gardens of tranquillity are a cultural parallel to Oxford colleges, foundations for the incubation of poor scholars. Cairo has several hundred mosques and madrasas built with common elements but developed into a wide range of styles.

Continuing south, the Qasaba passes through the wood-covered souq of the tentmakers past a succession of workshops and stalls. This souq is the centre of a tradition of textiles with elaborate designs hand stitched to order that has continued unbroken since the Fatimid period. The souq is known for making pavilions, or *suradeq*, out of appliqued cloth patterns. These tents are lined inside with geometric patterns in bright colours painstakingly sewn by hand, and are used for social gatherings, but especially during Ramadan for singers and dancers and the dispensing of food. Suradeq commissions come from all across the Arab world while the designs derive from coloured marble inlay patterns found in the walls and floors of the mosques.

Along the Sharia Darb al-Ahmar at the edge of the al-Ghuriyya district, I pass a workshop where a leather-jacketed German tells me that his project is one of many in Cairo funded by European development agencies to foster tradit-ional craft and building techniques. Further along is the garden mosque of al-Maridani, dating from 1340, whose lovely courtyard has trees with chirping sparrows. I ask the guardian about Cairo's bath houses. Following a tradition going back to the Roman Empire, hammams were a central part of the daily life of mediaeval Islam. In many Arab countries they survive, maintained as historical buildings and as a practical solution to staying clean. As recently as the 1990s, the thirteenth-century Hammam al-Sultan on the Sharia al-Muizz in Cairo was still in operation. But it has since closed down, along with half-a-dozen others, while the former Hammam Bashtak in the al-Darb al-Ahmar district is in ruins. The guardian explains that cultural change in modern Egypt has rendered the hammams obsolete.

Leaving the mosque I am assailed by a man who asks me to change US dollars and cheats me out of ten Egyptian pounds. So I challenge him, whereupon he produces the note, explaining that he lost his job as a civil servant and cannot afford shoes for his three daughters. Judging by his appearance I find it hard to believe that he once worked for the state. But I ask him why he has three children when his situation is so precarious. 'Three is very few,' he replies, saying that it is normal in Egypt to have seven or more children. 'Whether Christian or Muslim, Egyptians believe that children are given and that Allah will look after them.' 'If Allah gave us reason,' I reply, 'is it not to work out how best to live? We can only depend on ourselves.' I give him back the note, wondering if the second part is the elaborate plan B to the con. But his story seems too well embellished. There is great wealth in Egypt; yet ten million Cairenes live off dirty water and subsidised bread, and any kind of social movement meets with repression. How does one reconcile this with the splendour and cultural richness of mediaeval Cairo?

From the terrace of the Muhammad Ali Mosque on the citadel, built in the Ottoman style with massive central dome, the dusty metropolis stretches to the horizon. At the Sultan Hassan Mosque I ponder the swaying glass mosque lamps set against the stucco calligraphy on the ochre rendered walls. In the Rifai mosque opposite, I admire the tombs of Kings Faoud and Farouq and the Shah of Iran: all Victorian neo-Mamluk splendour to rival the mausolea in the mediaeval cemeteries. But for scale and wonder, nothing surpasses the vast congregational mosque of Ibn Tulun, built in the 870s and comparable in its austere simplicity to Kairouan. The architect is thought to have come from Abbasid Samarra and the square-spiral minaret is more the descendent of Ziggurat than Pharos. The mosque is enclosed by double walls and the courtyard has double arcades on all sides. The rendered walls and limestone paving contrast with the carved stucco and the vine leaf capitals on the piers of the arcades. The sanctuary has

Kufic calligraphy around its sycamore ceiling, including the Shi'a statement that 'Ali is the friend of Allah'.

Over chicken shawarma at Gad near the pension, I reflect on how this grandeur became smothered by the cheap concrete of modernity, the stupor of political stagnation and the squalor of over-population.

Demography and development
In polluted, crowded Cairo, one cannot feel more strongly the impact of demography on development. Egypt was once the wealthiest province of the Roman Empire, the source of the largesse that funded bread and circuses. During its second golden age in the later Middle Ages, Egypt was again a prosperous and well administered state before declining under the Ottomans and reviving briefly under Muhammad Ali. Alas state bankruptcy in the 1870s, the British occupation from 1882 to 1922 and ensuing partial independence led to the 1952 revolution, nationalisation programme and exodus of human capital. This historical path permanently damaged Egypt and interrupted the natural flow of development of the country. Since the early 1990s, structural reform and liberalisation have resulted in higher nominal economic growth rates.

But the overwhelming factor militating against a general rise in Egyptian living standards has been demographic. When in the 1960s the Club of Rome forecast a global population of six billion by the end of the century, their estimates seemed outlandish. But demographic models have few, easily measured parameters and their forecasts turned out to be accurate. In Egypt's case, her population grew from 10 million in 1900 to 70 million in 2000 and 100 million in 2020. But during this expansion the carrying capacity of the country has remained the same: Egypt is a river valley plus delta surrounded by desert.

Investors are interested in the aggregate nominal economic growth that determines market size. But *ceteris paribus*, more people means less environment per person. So the key welfare measure is per-capita income growth, which is a function of accumulated investment and higher productivity. The yardstick of economic development is capital accumulation per-capita: physical (housing, industrial plant and infrastructure) and human (education, skills and institutions). No country can develop if it produces babies faster than teachers. Malthus argued in 1798 that since population growth is geometric while food production grows arithmetically, the recurring constraints on progress of famine, war and plague are inevitable.

It has been argued that Malthus failed to consider the effects of technological innovation. Over the course of the twentieth century, agricultural mechanisation and irrigation expanded the supply of cultivable land, while the Green Revolution—including hybridised cereal grains, fertiliser and pesticide—tripled global crop yields. International agencies such as the UN Food and Agriculture Organisation project that population growth in low-income countries has slowed sufficiently to absorb the expanded food supply without reaching Malthusian limits. Demographers forecast that due to the adoption of family planning, increased urbanisation and higher incomes, birth rates are falling and the global population will peak in the mid-twenty-first century. But does this scenario still not leave many poor countries with large populations facing a future of permanent lower living standards? If the Newly Industrialised Countries of Asia such as South Korea and Taiwan have converged with the higher income countries, why should Egyptians not also aspire to the affordances and amenities of America, Britain or France?

For there are two distinct Malthusian arguments. The first is the incomplete theory of Malthus himself: since the 1960s, food prices have indeed been kept down by agricultural innovation, and populations have not exceeded the carrying capacity of the resource base. But the second argument is more subtle. Rather than a unitary constraint of food versus population, living standards as a whole reflect the intersection of multiple factors of well-being against multiple limits. As economies develop, food production becomes a smaller share of the total economy. So Malthusian constraint becomes reflected in all forms of capital accumulation, from the environmental damage caused by the industrial economy to the absolute compression of space and an intensification of the competitive struggle to divide the spoils of the inherited capital stock. The Green Revolution was only a temporary reprieve: in terms of capital accumulation and income per-capita, the poor countries are where they were at the beginning, only now with a greater population, having already absorbed the one-off step-change in agricultural productivity.

Furthermore, nineteenth-century European demographic transition was alleviated by emigration. Britain grew from 10 million in 1800 to 38 million in 1900 and 58 million in 2000. But during this period at least 40 million emigrants left the British Isles for the settler colonies of North America and Australasia. Today the low-income countries have no vent for surplus population but they still have the benefit of medical and public-health knowledge that has extended life expectancy. The burden of the demographic challenge is carried primarily by the overcrowded low-income countries themselves. But even with relatively closed borders, it is also paid by the developed world through the free movement of goods and capital. Demographic expansion has led to the global excess supply of labour that has created the structural condition of excess demand for employment, bargaining down wages while constraining the global accumulation of capital per-capita; all this despite the increase in productivity arising from innovation.

What about the belief that desired family size is an inalienable right that no one can infringe? The conventional view is that fecundity is high in poor countries because the absence of public welfare systems force young people to support the old: so the best way to maintain a favourable dependency ratio is to have more children. The theory goes that as incomes rise, the working generation invests more per child. But consider Bangladesh, a densely populated low-income country with limited resource endowments and a traditional society. Fecundity has fallen from 5.0 per woman in the 1960s to the replacement rate of 2.1, even as annual per capita income remained below $5,000 (considered by purchasing power parity). It is as if the society collectively understood that the country cannot absorb more people, and attitudes to family size adjusted down. Women were encouraged to marry later and patriarchal aggrandisement has been abandoned. If that cultural shift has occurred in Bangladesh then it must be possible anywhere.

Another argument deployed against Malthusianism is that large populations are good in and of themselves. Endogenous growth theorists believe that once investment in physical capital has plateaued, growth derives from ingenuity: twice as many brains equals twice as many sources of ideas. At the technological frontier, innovation improves the efficiency of capital equipment and industrial processes and has reduced the energy intensity and polluting effect per unit of output. Since the 1930s America has attracted the world's best brains, from Europeans fleeing Nazis and Soviets to the émigrés of poorer countries such as Egypt fleeing stagnation and repression. These talented people have been richly compensated to develop techniques in basic research as well as new products such as personal computers and portable telephones. *But what about the rump?* Clean energy may be in the vanguard to reduce emissions at the frontier. Yet global carbon generation has continued to mushroom as large middle-income economies operate the dirty factories of the world that sustain high consumption levels in the developed countries. Away from the elite research institutes and their hi-tech spin-offs, the vast share of global economic activity is more humdrum.

American growth theorists see the world as like America, with its freeways and malls and suburban houses, its city-centre grids of skyscrapers with elevators and air-conditioned offices. For their world is a country of limitless land, of industrial mass production and of the technology prevailing in the period of their keenest expansion. But which of these ideas are truly growth-enhancing to a poor Egyptian? The revolution in information and communication technology has enabled Cairenes to communicate with their families in the villages and given them access to the information superhighway of the World Wide Web. But the daily reality for most Egyptians is long working hours for basic living in poorly built apartment blocks, worrying about food prices, traffic jams and untreated health problems. The knowledge theory may be true at the frontier. But for the rump, the environmental constraint of basic physical infrastructure is far more pressing. On its own, more people do not equal more brains to solve problems: brains require education to generate ideas. Education requires investment in human capital. To stand on the shoulders of giants, one must first reach up to their shoulders.

WEDNESDAY 28 MAY | COPTIC CAIRO

From the taxi stop at al-Azhar it is a short walk to al-Fishawy in the Khan al-Khalili where I meet Anne from the Cavafy Museum. Fishawy's opened in 1797 and used to be the haunt of the Cairene literati: it is said that Naguib Mahfouz wrote much of his *Cairo Trilogy* here. The writers have vanished, but the café still has carved wooden benches under rows of mirrors and is busy with locals. We take the metro to Misr al-Fustat (Old Cairo), the settlement founded in 641 following the Arab conquest. After looking into the congregational mosque of 'Amr ibn al-'As, whose spirit of early Islam is so well captured by the academic French painter Jean-Léon Gérôme, we pass the closed Ben Ezra synagogue and explore the Coptic Museum.

Coptic art is primarily of interest for its antiquity and there are charming portraits from the early centuries that show the faces of these distant people as well as wood carvings of idyllic Nile scenes. The tenth-century 'Hanging' Church of Mariam al-Azraa has a lovely atmosphere: wide marble steps lead up to the sanctuary which has arcades with ancient columns. Official portraits of the Coptic Patriarchs going back to St Mark hang in the corridor, with the incumbent Pope Shenouda III displayed in a joint portrait with Mubarak. The Copts are the true inheritors of ancient Egypt and their very name derives from hut-ka-ptah. The Ankh was the pharaonic emblem of eternal life, adapted by the Copts as the symbol of divine love; their language (Sahidic and Bohairic in the contemporary dialects) is the continuation of Ptolemaic demotic and is now used only in the liturgy. Post-Akhenaten, pharaonic religion became focussed on divine unity: ptah, the essence of Amun-Ra became the divine shepherd who spoke in oracles. So the essence of ptah is not far from the divine light that shines in the darkness—perhaps this was the source of Philo's concept?

In pharaonic myth, Osiris, deity of the Nile valley, was killed by his brother Seth, master of the desert. Isis impregnated herself with the seed of her brother Osiris and their son Horus avenged the murder of his father. Osiris was mummified and resurrected in mythic representation of the annual flooding of the Nile that fertilised the land. The Copts adapted the cult of Isis and one can see how Osiris, Isis and Horus form a proto-Holy Family. The worship of Isis herself continued in Egypt until the Temple at Philae was closed by Justinian in 537. Likewise belief in the physical reality of the afterlife persisted as the Copts continued the practices of mummification and painted funerary portraits. Even today Copts believe in the active presence of the divine in their worship, a remarkable consistency with the Pentecostalists. After all, the post-reformation nonconformists looked back nostalgically to the purity of the Church before Constantine.

In the pre-Constantinian period the Catechetical school of Alexandria lay at the centre of Orthodoxy, with Clement and others defining Christian theology through the application of Greek philosophy. But at the Council of Chalcedon in 451, where the Copts split with Orthodoxy, Dioscorus of Alexandria argued that the humanity of Christ was fully absorbed by the divinity, so that the Christ had one nature, or *physis*. Porphyry had earlier described how the omnipresent creator dominated all other elements. Perhaps it was the implicit perpetuation of the pharaonic concepts that led to the schism at Chalcedon.

After the Islamic conquest, Copts were in theory free to practise their faith, following the verse in the second surah of the Qur'an that there be 'no compulsion in religion'. Islam had been interpreted by Sophronius the Patriarch of Jerusalem as a form of Arianism, according to which Christ was wholly created and the father was uniquely divine. But it soon became apparent that Islam was not a Christian sect: rather it was an alien and conquering force from a different cultural tradition. Christians were forced to pay special *jizya* (poll) and *kharaj* (land) taxes to the authorities; the child of any mixed union was deemed Muslim under the law, while apostasy was considered treasonous to the 'umma and a capital offence. As Egypt became more Arab and more Muslim dominated towards the end of the Fatimid period, the Christian share of the population fell to less than a quarter and the Coptic language fell out of common use.

Under Salah ad-Din and the early Mamluks, the Copts experienced a cultural renaissance. But from the 1320s onwards they became an intermittently persecuted minority. Muhammad Ali Pasha revived their fortunes and they achieved equal citizenship with Muslims during the Khedivate of Tewfiq. Later during the independence struggle from British rule, leading Copts were active members of Saad Zaaghloul's nationalist Wafd party. Successive governments of Nasr, Sadat and Mubarak have stated that their duty is to serve all Egyptians equally regardless of confession. But Isat who works in the Pension Roma suggests that today the Copts have become once again a persecuted minority who accept their status, knowing that to resist would only worsen their situation. At least the relics of St Mark, stolen by the Venetians in the ninth century, were returned to Egypt in 1968 and are now in the Abbasiya Coptic Cathedral.

I return on the metro to meet Prince Abbas Hilmi at the Semiramis Hotel. Abbas is the grandson of Khedive Abbas Hilmi II who built the Egyptian Museum and visited Siwa in 1905. Following Britain's declaration of war against the Ottoman Empire on 5 November 1914, the Khedive found himself notionally subject to the Sublime Porte while *de facto* subject to the enemy occupying power. In light of his clandestine activities, the British deposed him in place of his more pliable uncle. After the 1952 revolution the family was forced into exile. Abbas was allowed to return in the 1990s on condition that he remain aloof from politics. Over tea and baklava Abbas tells me about his ancestors going back to Muhammad Ali Pasha and talks about the 1827 Battle of Navarino at which the Royal Navy eviscerated the Turkish-Egyptian fleet, effectively eliminating Ottoman naval power.

Abbas's mother descends from the Osmanoğlu line, and I sense his nostalgia for the *ancien régime* that maintained stability in the Levant for four centuries.

We discuss the contemporary international situation as well as Ibn Khaldun, whose social theories prefigure the cycles of modern democratic politics—of the balance between growth economics and welfarism. Abbas is reluctant to comment on Egyptian politics, except to note that having floated the exchange rate, the government is continuing to liberalise the economy, privatise inefficient state-owned enterprises and incentivise foreign investment. As a private equity investor Abbas is optimistic about the outlook for Egypt and believes that the country is well placed to prosper and grow. Abbas suggests that human rights abuses are not as bad in the country as some claim, and that for political reform to proceed without leading to a rupture, economic development is the prior consideration. As for the legacy of the British Occupation, he recommends that I should read his grandfather's 1930 *Anglo-Egyptian Settlement*.

I ask him about the Muslim Brotherhood. Abbas explains that at the time his illustrious ancestors took control of Egypt, the form of Islam practised in the country was enlightened and that Islam does respect women and give them freedom. In the nineteenth century, Egyptian women had authority to administer the household, own property and run businesses—like Mahmoud's wife in Benghazi. As for the Copts, they were always protected under Islamic law, and this is still the case in modern secular Egypt. Coptic families such as Ghabbour and Sawiris are prominent in the business community. I tell Abbas my story about the man at the Maridani Mosque and he explains that any policy of population control would never be accepted by the inherently religious Egyptians. We talk about architecture and Abbas promises to introduce me to his friend Dr Nawal Hassan, student of the architect Hassan Fathy.

THURSDAY 29 MAY | AL-AZHAR
Once again a new routine: I pass the morning at the top-floor restaurant of the al-Hussein Hotel taking hibiscus tea and

writing notes from my books. Once again the air is so thick with dust outside that the hotel's long room seems cut off from the rest of the world. Everything is relieved when a short downpour clears the air. After honey pancakes I walk across the street, past a meat market with cows standing nonchalantly waiting to be slaughtered, and enter the precincts of al-Azhar. Founded by the Fatimids, al-Azhar University remains the leading authoritative institution of Sunni Islam. The mosque itself is a popular location for students and young pilgrims to congregate. While madrasa students memorise passages from the Qu'ran, I pace under the fans over the lush carpets and ponder the inspiration of Islamic architecture. The pale marble stones of the courtyard contrast with the stucco of the arches to create a glittering effect.

During its golden age the Islamic world lay at the frontier of scientific progress. The Abbasid Caliphate united Mesopotamia and the Mediterranean for the first time since Alexander. It is unlikely that anything from ancient Babylon was transmitted directly to the Abbasids, as the Arabs never deciphered cuneiform. But in Baghdad, Indian arithmetic intersected with Greek geometry and the Syriac and Coptic cultures of the former Byzantine provinces. The Arabs combined the methods of Euclid, Archimedes and Diophantus, with the use of zero and the Indian numerical place-value system. In *Pathfinders*, his book about Arabic science, Jim al-Khalili relates that the Caliph al-Ma'mun founded Bayt al-Hikma at Baghdad as a prototype national academy. The translation of the surviving Greek texts into Arabic was initiated by Hunayn ibn Ishaq (809–877), a Nestorian Christian from Edessa, and the early flowering of Arabic science was led by scholars such as the mathematician al-Khwarizmi (780–850) and the philosopher al-Kindi (800–873).

Ibn Ishaq al-Kindi created a synthesis between Aristotelian philosophy and Islamic theology by which revelation can be interpreted through *kalam*, or rational argument, leading to the discovery of truths about nature and mankind's place in god's created universe. Like St Augustine before him, al-Kindi argued that there are no infinite quantities in nature so the universe cannot have existed forever and time must have been created along with the cosmos. Al-Kindi was also the leading Arab music theorist but sadly most of his work was lost in the Mongol sack of Baghdad. In his treatise on algebra, al-Khwarizmi established a system of procedures or 'algorithms' to manipulate algebraic expressions and solve equations for unknown quantities, with thousands of worked examples of practical problems in applied mathematics.

With the rise of the Fatimid dynasty, Cairo became a second pole after Baghdad, attracting scholars from across the Dar al-Islam. In emulation of al-Ma'mun, the Fatimids established a House of Wisdom at Cairo in the early 1000s, reviving the tradition of the Mouseion and Serapeum. Its greatest son was the Iraqi scholar al-Hassan ibn al-Haytham (Alhazen) who lived near al-Azhar from 1021 to 1039. Al-Haytham's *Treatise on Optics* gave the first understanding of vision by which light rays radiate in straight lines and enter the eye to form images, as well as speculating that light travelled at different speeds in different media and advancing the sine law of refraction. Al-Haytham wrote texts on perspective in painting and anticipated Kepler's laws. The general method of framing a problem through representation in a mathematical model and testing it by fit to nature through measurement and experimentation is credited to al-Haytham. Later Ibn al-Nafis, who died in Cairo, in 1288 pioneered the dissection of cadavers and theorised about the circulation of the blood.

By the time of the Ottoman conquest in 1517 the scientific flame had already dimmed in Cairo, but the following three centuries of stasis extinguished it altogether. In the 1830s, Muhammad Ali Pasha reportedly asked the Rector of al-Azhar to solve an engineering problem and discovered that the university's scholars were still using al-Haytham's mathematical tables. In contrast to the European states that developed National Academies from the 1600s, the Ottoman sultans saw no purpose for scientific enquiry and closed the only remaining astronomical observatory in the Islamic world at Galata in 1580. Lack of patronage led to the narrower dissemination of ideas and the printing press itself did not reach Constantinople until 1830.

What caused the decline? In *Pathfinders* al-Khalili cites the sack of Baghdad by Hulagu's Mongol horde in 1258; the change in attitude of the Muslim clergy towards reasoning about nature; and the influence of the eleventh-century Persian theologian Abu Hamid al-Ghazali who argued against rationalist Mu'tazilism and wrote that divine will and justice are to be found only in the Qur'an and hadiths. Revealed Islam considers itself the final completion of all preceding revelations. But if logos is the continuous illumination of the cosmos to the mind, there can be no final revelation. Within the Islamic community the two tendencies of *taqlid* (religious authority) and *ijtihad* (independent reasoning) seem always to have jostled for dominance.

Hassan al-Attar, Rector of al-Azhar from 1831 to 1835, tried to modernise the curriculum, including logic, mathematics, astronomy and anatomy. But his programme was sabotaged by conservative sheikhs. Attar's student Rifaa al-Tahtawi sought to show that Islam is compatible with progressive modernism —that Islamic ideals of governance, justice and charity are close to representative democracy, equality before the law and social welfare. Sheikh Abduh, Grand Mufti of Egypt in the 1890s revived Mu'tazilism, absorbing nineteenth-century science, while the Khedive Abbas Hilmi II supported reforms to al-Azhar, funding new disciplines that allowed its students to become employable in business and the civil service.

Leaving al-Azhar, I pick up some pamphlets from the bookshop by a professor at the King Abdul al-Aziz University in Jeddah, including one entitled *Islam and Sex* and walk up to the Bab al-Futuh. The courtyard of the mosque of al-Hakim, over-restored by the Aga Khan Foundation, is impressive but lacks the spirit of Amr's earlier version. It was al-Hakim the 'mad caliph' whose destruction of the fourth-century Church of the Holy Sepulchre in Jerusalem was cited by Pope Urban II in 1095 in his call for the First Crusade.

At the mosque of al-Ustadar in the al-Gamaliyya district, named after the Mamluk vizier who constructed it in 1407, I fall into conversation with a talkative young man who assists the custodian. Ahmed talks about *jihad* as the struggle to master oneself, and the concept of *taqwa* as the seeking of divine guidance. Ahmed takes me to the *wikala* of al-Ghuri to experience the 'peace of the garden of Islam', part of the International Sama'a Festival. Sama is the Sufi musical ceremony that is performed in dedicated *zawiyas* (tombs) or *tekkes* (spiritual retreats or lodges). The performance by the Morlawiyya is contrived for visitors and is not formally a religious activity but the display of Sufi dance is immediately compelling. As the dervishes spin and shed their coloured cloaks to the *maqam* (modes) and *wazn* (rhythms) of the Sama performed with ney, oud, tanbur, kanun and cymbals, I wonder why the ceremony is so beguiling: with the conquest of the self and the experience of joy in the trance state, who needs all the complexity of the modern world?

Anscombe versus Azhar

As many as a quarter of Egyptian men under forty are unmarried because they lack financial resources. *Islam and sex* is a practical manual advising these turbo charged young men who cannot afford to marry. In some ways it reads like a guide for teenagers by evangelical Christians with distinctions between light and heavy petting. Like many aspects of the two religions, their roots are the same, deriving from the Pauline attitude that sex is inherently bad. The manual encourages young men to avoid spicy food and drinks with stimulants (which is a tall order in Egypt), take regular exercise and sleep facing Mecca. If necessary, a prostitute may be used to release excess energy than cannot be controlled in any other way.

In strict Islamic traditional society, married women are veiled and forbidden to meet male visitors not closely related to the family. In part this may be because men do not trust other men and fear that if allowed to do as they pleased, their wives might seek another man. The social attitudes of Copts and Muslims in Egypt tend to be similar. At al-Suriani in the Wadi Natrun, another visitor, on discovering that I was not married, explained at length the virtues of Coptic women—prime among them their loyalty and devotion to their husbands. 'Unlike Western women,' he said, 'you can have complete confidence that your wife will never go off with another man. Look at the divorce rate in Western society, he argued, where women get the seven-year itch. Isn't the traditional society a superior system?'

In the West, female circumcision is regarded as a savage atavistic practice yet in Egypt there are adult women who voluntarily go through a surgical procedure with a local anaesthetic. They do not do this because they are acting under the duress of a jealous husband; they do it to remove temptation and enable them to focus on their domestic life. In a sense these women rationally choose public duty—to devote their lives to maintaining a home and raising children—over individual, personal pleasure. Influenced perhaps by the prudish atmosphere of pre-war ladies colleges and her Roman Catholic faith, the philosopher Elizabeth Anscombe argued that sex ought to be engaged in purely for reproductive purposes and not for 'recreational pleasure'. She went on to have seven children.

The conclusion must be that the constraints and dilemmas that confront people are similar regardless of the cultural wallpaper that surrounds them. Sex is a natural pleasure, no different from any other form of sensory stimulation; it has no more to do with reproduction than fine cuisine has to do with maintaining critical nutrients within the required limits of homeostatic space, or playing the piano has to do with attracting a mate. Family size on the other hand is a key determinant of the long-term living standards and economic well-being of a society. Anscombe recommends that we triple our population every generation (which is what having seven children amounts to), while abstaining from practices that give pleasure and do not, if engaged in responsibly, cause harm or carry any economic cost. In developed liberal societies, a relaxed social attitude to sexuality is compatible with a stable population. Sadly for frustrated young Egyptians, something similar to Anscombe's worldview seems to be the norm.

FRIDAY 30 MAY | SAYYIDA ZEINAB
Rebecca, a friend from London, meets me at the pension and we walk to Talaat Harb Street for lunch at Café Riche. Another

Cairene literary institution since it opened in 1908, the restaurant has black-and-white photographs of Egyptian writers around the walls. The waiters wear smart blue outfits, and we order a small bottle of Omar Khayyam red wine to drink with our chicken. Rebecca has been working with refugees for a charity and is due to begin a Master's degree in Development Studies. We are both outsiders in Cairo but look at the problems of the city with different reference frames. We exchange ideas—hers driven by empathy for the poor, mine wanting to analyse the problems of political economy and find solutions. Despite being in Egypt for several months, Rebecca has not explored the city's ancient districts.

From the terrace of al-Hussein Hotel we look over the tangled mass of Islamic Cairo as the imams blast out their Friday sermons. Rebecca is focused on bringing relief to people in need while I talk about the structural causes of poverty and how they can be addressed. Why have the hammams been abandoned when they thrive in other Arab countries as an efficient way for the poor to stay clean and are such a focal point for those communities? Why has Egypt been unable to confront its demographic challenges or create well-paid employment for its youth? Why does this hotel in the best location of mediaeval Cairo remain so poorly maintained? Why is its tremendous potential unrealised? The manager joins our conversation and I suggest that with some upgrading, they could raise the room rates tenfold and the hotel would still be full. But the manager explains that it is owned by over 100 business partners who cannot agree on how to develop it and so it continues in its present state.

We walk down al-Ganbakiyya and discover a musical performance at Beit Taz. We are invited into the courtyard and absorb the atmosphere of families enjoying Arabic music with oud and voice. At the restaurant opposite, we eat grilled lamb with shatta, a Sudanese chilli pepper that brings out the flavour: the lamb is weighed and charged for by the gram, a reminder of the luxury of meat in Cairo. We continue to the Shattanj (chess) Café on Bur Said near the Sayyida Zeinab Mosque and find my old friend Wagdi Kamal. When not playing speed chess, Wagdi is an engineer who makes integrated circuit boards and applications for educational electronics at the Cairo and Ainshams Engineering faculty. The café is an extension of his home and he offers us sahlab and tea while proceeding to humiliate us on the chess board.

Wagdi tells us that in Egypt the president beats the minister who beats the bureaucrat who beats the taxi driver who beats his wife who beats her son who beats his sister who beats the dog who beats the cat who beats the rats who beat the cockroaches who bite the president in his bed: and so it goes. Wagdi adores Rebecca and suggests we visit his office in a run-down nineteenth-century building near the Azbekiyya Park. Wagdi is a brilliant man and if he had been given the opportunity along a different life path, he could have been running a semiconductor company in Silicon Valley. But in Cairo the obsolete technology he deals with feels like a time warp—as if whole sections of the economy, having fallen behind the frontier, continue in a suspended state that has no external value but only a peculiar internal logic within its own system.

We return to al-Hussein Hotel and talk about Orientalism. Edward Said argued that this nineteenth-century art movement was an instrument of colonial exploitation. When painters like Delacroix travelled in the Arab world, they followed the habits of their own culture of painting, while delighting in the colours, light and exoticism of what they saw in contrast to the cold bleak North. Now the paintings are in high demand, especially from Egyptian business people, and I suggest that they should be seen on their own artistic terms.

Oriental Weavers versus Axminster

From an Olympian perspective, the human spirit ought to strive in the direction of the beautification of the world. So what could be more alluring than the commercial fabrication of carpets in Cairo, of Axminster going Levantine? Egypt was not known for its weaving but nor was Devon until someone made it so. Oriental Weavers is a profitable company, listed on the Cairo and Alexandria stock exchange, whose flagship retail outlet is on Sharia al-Azhar. The toast of adventure capitalists, Oriental Weavers is well managed, provides its target market with a variety of carpets at attractive prices and grows its earnings at a healthy rate. But look at the product! Oriental Weavers is no Axminster: the colours are drab, the materials synthetic, the weave crude and the patterns lacking in imagination. The company's controlling shareholder also privately owns Oriental's supplier and it remains opaque how much value is transferred from minority shareholders to the petrochemical company whose product it takes as input.

What is the difference between the economics of Axminster and Oriental Weavers? Comparison of their financial statements at equivalent points in their lifecycles would reveal nothing. For the mechanism of business efficiency and capital allocation is entirely neutral with respect to the aesthetic and cultural value of its output. The difference lies in the taste and mentality of the target market. The poor quality of the product reflects the poverty of discrimination of the customers and the unwillingness of the entrepreneur to educate them. A well-furnished house should follow the principle of Occam's Razor: ontological parsimony. It would contain just as many well-arranged objects as are required, purged of any excess clutter. A well-furnished world ought to be the same: we need fewer objects overall, of higher quality and less waste. But we have lived through a century of global demographic expansion accompanied by the continuous downgrading of taste. We are moving in the opposite direction from the Olympian ideal.

John Masefield's poem *Quinquireme of Nineveh* expresses the idea that the wealth created by British industrialisation was somehow spurious because of the ugliness of its product. But in the nineteenth century, canals and bridges and factories were built with aesthetic awareness and a sense of craftsmanship to benefit the material inheritance of the country. In a civilised society, one of the aims of accumulation should be to produce artefacts of cultural value. But contemporary capitalism tends to value money for its own sake, disconnected from its fruits. Consider the quality of the artefacts collected by

Gulbenkian at Lisbon: is not each one of them worth more than all the stock of Oriental Weavers?

SATURDAY 31 MAY | AL-QARAFA

I take a dawn taxi to Sayyida Zeinab and walk to the street market of al-Khalifa with its birds in cages and continue across the Salah Salem highway into the Southern Cemetery. This district, known as al-Qarafa, was the original pre-Fatimid necropolis of Misr al-Fustat. Ibn Battuta described al-Qarafa in 1325 as a 'place of blessed power, for Allah has promised that it shall be one of the gardens of paradise'. Walking down the deserted Sharia al-Imam al-Shafi'i in the early morning sunshine, past jacaranda trees and stone carved tombs, I sense what he meant. Like its northern counterpart which contains the mausolea of Mamluk sultans, the Southern Cemetery is inhabited by people with nowhere else to sleep. Unlike the Northern Cemetery, which is wedged between two highways, al-Qarafa is otherworldly and silent.

The Ayyubid shrine mausoleum of the imam al-Shafi'i is the principal monument of the district. The imam was descended from the Prophet's uncle Abu Talib and died in 820. But the elaborately decorated mausoleum with its large dome and unusual grain-boat weathervane was completed in 1211. Imam al-Shafi'i was the founder of a leading school of Sunni *fiqh* (jurisprudence) and it was at his tomb that Salah ad-Din founded a Sunni madrasa after the end of Shi'ite Fatimid rule. Normally the shrine is busy with pilgrims who recite prayers but today I have the tomb to myself and can study its polychrome inlay, wooden beams and stalactitic squinches. The light shaft falling through the dome windows against the marble panels of the lower walls carries the sense of *baraka* (healing peace) that attracts pilgrims. Behind the imam's shrine is the Hosh al-Basha that contains the tombs of the children of Muhammad Ali Pasha.

Returning to the Sultan Hassan Mosque, I sit against the wall and observe the swaying mosque lamps: these distinctive glass forms have a waist with chains attached to a metal ring that reach up to the roof. In the central *iwan* is the elaborately decorated prayer niche. Mihrabs in mosque architecture derive from the Arabisation of Roman niches surrounded by pillars that make them seem like a doorway: doors of perception to a reality beyond the material. What joy did these craftsmen derive from their work, I wonder, like the European masons carving sacred geometry into the physical representation of the transcendent?

I take a taxi to the island of Zamalek and browse the Diwan Bookshop before meeting Anne at an American-style coffee shop popular with the teenage elite of Cairo. François and Anne's expansive apartment looks over the Nile adjacent to the Vatican embassy. As diplomats residing in Egypt, their way of life feels far from the mass of Cairo beyond the river. They have organised a dinner party with some expatriates and an Iraqi American photographer who teaches at the American University. Their Jewish friends the Maaris have been doing business in Egypt for three generations but are talking about leaving the country for good.

The insufficiency of materialism
Materialists regard the word 'mystical' pejoratively, as if it conveys a primitive world view. Yet they concede that there is no explanation for mathematical fit in physics: no one knows why models using vector calculus and infinite dimensional spaces defined over the complex numbers predict cosmic and subatomic patterns. Some physicists suggest that the explanation of fit lies beyond the limits of understanding; others believe that once the mathematics has been discovered that unifies all physics, the universe will have been mastered. The question of how something came from nothing will be answered as the actualisation of *possibilia* by chance. Materialists put their faith in mathematical models as absolutely as theists. Yet the understanding of each is the same unfolding illumination.

Within its original domain of application, natural selection was a great leap forward. The zenith of the nineteenth-century mechanical world, Darwin's theory explained speciation and biodiversity, and situated humanity in the common tree of life going back to the first living organisms. Twentieth-century molecular biology put flesh on the bones of the mechanism of heredity, identifying genetic mutation as the source of variation. As the genotype varies so does the fitness of the phenotype: specimens are selected by the survival of their progeny in the competitive struggle to optimise their adaptation to a changing environment. This mechanism extends to mind: reason and logic emerged as mental faculties through the process of natural selection. Ethologists theorise that motivation is subordinate to selection: the outcomes we value are those that our genetic history has encoded as the goals whose pursuit maximises our adaptive fitness.

Physicists have groped towards evolutionary theory to complete the circle of the problem to fit. If the cosmos is a mathematical structure, as the Pythagoreans may have believed, then logic as the foundation of mathematics is in the cosmos. If logic is in the cosmos, then it is also within our environment and our minds will have become imbued with it by natural selection. It is logic that lies at the foundation of the mathematics that models the physical world, so our brains reflect the structure of the physical world, which is why they can generate the mathematical creations that explain it: mind, matter and number are mutually entwined. But this circle remains as arbitrary as the Axiom of Infinity: an axiom cannot be proved by reasoning or verified by experiment, and if it is not 'self-evident' then there are only weak grounds for believing it.

Nor does the ethological explanation of conscious motivation hold water, for natural selection explains very little about what makes us us. After all, we share ninety-nine per cent of our DNA with chimpanzees; but our personhood, our soul, our sentient presence is qualitatively different from anything that can be captured by the tiniest difference in DNA. Advances in epigenetics diminish the significance of reading DNA as the sole determinant of cell activity and hence of the expression of the phenotype of the organism. However close the DNA sequence with chimpanzees, the gap in the phenotype represents a qualitative difference in those faculties that are uniquely human, for the human mind has broken out of the mechanical constraint that led to its genesis through natural selection. To prove theorems or speculate about the cosmos, to compose music and poetry or construct fine buildings, cannot be functions of adaptive fitness: they are merely its by-products.

Natural selection was an inspired description of the mechanism of biodiversity and speciation, a process so simple that a child can understand it with the minimum of instruction. Yet Darwinism leaves unanswered why random events have their particular patterns. Is chance a basic element of the cosmos? Darwinists regard the evolution of the cosmos as a blind mechanistic process whose wellspring is chance, the randomness inherent in nature. But how does one explain chance, and the particular patterns that ensue, for example in the distribution of prime numbers? Chance as an explanatory primitive is as much an axiom as the circle of logic from matter to mind. As Unamuno observed, modern science tends to suffer from mechanistic triumphalism while the ancients were more humble about admitting what they could not explain.

If astronomical observations and experiments in cloud chambers and particle accelerators are sources of data about the material world, then the interior stream of conscious experience is equally valid as a datum. Examination of this interior datum shows the fabric of our mental texture to be hardly logical at all. Nor is there any mathematical 'fit' to subjective conscious experience. A conscious life extended through time cannot be merely a series of actions. What happens between them? *Being* between actions is like the void between pieces of matter or the time between events—shadowy and difficult to report on, but there all the same. Birdsong, the swaying of the mosque lamps, people passing by —all the passive fabric of *being* for a short time doing nothing. Examination of interior experience shows that mechanical theories of the mind cannot capture the nature of subjective conscious experience. Any attempt to give a mechanistic model of 'consciousness', whether inspired by Turing or Darwin, is seeking to answer the wrong question.

The theory that consciousness is how pain and pleasure

guide intentional behaviour describes how we assign values to outcomes through direct contact with them; it does not explain how the internal experience of sensory contact has its *qualia* or particular character. So it is a mistake to map consciousness (or subjectivity or sentience) onto any behavioural or cognitive function. Consciousness is the by-product of the emergent complexity of the brain-mind and has no function: it is merely internal experience. Humans share behavioural elements with lower animals as well as the reasoning capabilities of higher animals. Language distinguishes humans. But the linguistic consciousness of birds and bats and dolphins and whales is distinctive to each of them and they live in their own worlds.

If our minds were like computers, the event stream would stop once all tasks in the stack had been executed and there would be nothing but waiting until another action was requested or the power switched off. Then what? Knowing how to *be* between tasks can be disorientating, as if there is no floor to stand on, just empty space. Actions provide the comfort of a solid surface. Yet there is a difference between waiting indefinitely to perform the next action and switching off the power. One is the essence of life while the other is death. When the gaze is turned inwards, it is tempting to think as Hume did that the self is an empty sarcophagus. But reflecting —*being* between actions—is the ground of confidence in our subjective experience. As clearly as experimental physics has verified the mechanical mathematics of the cosmos, the interior event stream of our private conscious experience shows that we are not machines. Yet in the automation of our present era, our lives become ever more programmed like clock ticks in a sequence of mechanical actions. Hence the imperative to find flow activities and experience for their own sake.

Sunday 1 June | Hassan Fathy

Returning to al-Ghuri I pass down an alley through the wool souqs to find the 'Centre for Egyptian Civilisation Studies' and take tea with its founder Dr Nawal Hassan. Nawal's offices are up a stone staircase on the second floor of an Ottoman era building. Greeting me at the door, Nawal takes me along the corridor past bookshelves and tables stacked with papers. Everything about her reception rooms speaks of elegant simplicity, from the rugs and chequer-tiled floors to the green doors and window frames to the inlaid tables and benches under architectural prints along the white walls. This is a space for conversation.

Nawal was the student of the architect Hassan Fathy, known especially for building in traditional styles out of local materials. Fathy's 1973 magnum opus *Architecture for the Poor* remains a manifesto for an alternative modernism that would now be called Sustainable Development. Nawal explains that Fathy used methods of construction that fit the Egyptian environment, and that his buildings breathe naturally instead of requiring air-conditioning to ameliorate heat-trapping concrete. Fathy stood for the authenticity of the particular against the blandness of an alien standardised internationalism. As the kersheef and date-palm trunks of Siwa or the sand-mud timber walls of Scetis were adapted to their environments, so the dressed stone of Cairo worked for centuries. Yet in his lifetime Fathy was vilified as anachronistic: the public authorities in Egypt refused to work with him and criticised the maintenance demands of his architecture. The result is the concrete tenement housing that surrounds Cairo.

Hassan Fathy believed in social responsibility and channelled the money he earned designing luxury villas into buildings for the fellahin. Fathy argued that poverty is mistakenly associated with ugliness when in fact the less expensive the project the more concern and attention should be paid to aesthetic matters. The fabric of mediaeval Cairo developed organically in response to indigenous culture, the environment and the patronage of rulers—hence alleys for donkeys and pedestrians, *khans* with internal courtyards and merchant houses screened from the public space by walls. Modernity brought districts with wide streets for automobiles, tower blocks and the materials of industrial capitalism.

'The fabric of Islamic Cairo is changing,' Nawal explains, 'with concrete structures taking the place of the old houses as the souqs thin out and the quality of the stock deteriorates.

Local artisanal production of everything, from apparel to pottery, is being replaced by cheaper, inferior goods sourced from global markets.' Nawal points at the pale green camel-hair shawl I have bought in the market outside al-Ghuri Mosque, embroidered with lotus and papyrus motifs. 'These shawls and galabiyya have been worn by the fellahin for centuries. Now al-Ghuri market suffers from the influx of low-quality Asian products driving down the cultural level of the Egyptian consumer as well as the income level of the Egyptian producer.'

Nasser and successive military regimes cut funding for the restoration of the old districts and the gap was filled by charities and development agencies. The Aga Khan Foundation also restored many of the mosques and laid out the Azhar Park over the former rubbish dump between Fatimid al-Qahira and the Northern Cemetery. Ironically, the restoration movement came from the savants of the Napoleonic invasion, even if the European city was culturally alien from the world of mediaeval Islam. The techniques of craftsmanship that created 'The City of a Thousand Minarets' represent a way of life disconnected from the modern international economy. Tourism brings in hard currency and some cultural appreciation, but this is an enclave, not an embedding of the building-craft economy in the politico-economic fabric of the city.

Nawal established the CECS in 1977 to preserve the heritage of Islamic Cairo, organising lectures and exhibitions and linking voluntary organisations with donors. Following the earthquake of 1992, the centre has worked in parallel with the Historic Cairo Restoration Project to support craftsmen and artisans. In *The Building Crafts of Cairo*, Nawal's associate Agnieszka Dobrowolska summarises the traditional techniques. The primary historical sources are Jomard's *Arts et Metiers* volume of the Napoleonic *Description de l'Egypte*, which systematically described the work of Egyptian craftsmen around the year 1800 with illustrations of their workshops and tools, as well as Arabic documents of their legal organisation. 'For centuries the craftsmen of Cairo produced work of beauty, ingenuity and high skill. They remained humble and anonymous ... yet it was their work that created the city, not the deeds of the mighty and famous.'

Nawal suggests that I should visit Bayt al-Suhaymi and I wander through the streets to this fine Ottoman merchant house built in 1648 around two courtyards with plants and trees. Sitting by the fountain, looking up at the carved wooden ceilings and *mashrabiyya*, I wonder why it is no longer possible to construct a beautiful built environment as Europe did in the eighteenth and nineteenth centuries. 'It's too expensive!' we are often told. But is this not a false economy, reflecting a false theory of political value? For *civilisation is craftsmanship* and the cultural affordances that shape the built environment are entirely contingent and chosen. The quality of the housing stock is a greater determinant of living standards for the population than access to continuously upgraded gadgets or the endless proliferation of inconsequential media content. There is no logical impediment to the construction of low-cost well-built houses in traditional materials at an economic rate of return: the practical embodiment of flow.

From Bab Zuwayla, I proceed to the Townhouse picture gallery on Qasr el-Nil to join Anne and François for a photographic exhibition of Damascus. We return to the chess café on Bur Said and I introduce them to Wagdi. From his perspective in the French mission François discusses the corruption of public procurement in Egypt. But Wagdi is too small to stand a chance against the monolithic weight of the authorities. François will shortly leave for another posting but the inertia of Misr will continue for eternity.

Sinai

MONDAY 2 JUNE | SUEZ

From to the Turgoman bus station it is an eight-hour journey to St Catherine's. At Suez the bus crosses under the canal from Africa to Asia and we can see only the tops of the masts of ships passing through it. We continue south along the Gulf of Suez, gaining occasional views of the stunning blue water against the desert bluffs. As the bus rattles along the highway, ticking off distance posts at ten kilometre intervals, I remember my previous visits to the Holy Land: sleeping under the stars in the craters of the Negev desert; walking to the monastery of St George Choziba in the Wadi Qelt and from Bethlehem to Mar Sabas above the Kidron; travelling to Sinai with Pyrrha, meeting Father Justin, and accompanying him to the summit of Gebel Catarina, the highest point in Sinai at 2,637 metres.

Some distance before the ancient port of Tur, the bus turns inland and we ascend the wadis of the interior in the evening light. The route passes the oasis of Wadi Feiran, the principal urban centre of Sinai in antiquity, whose settlements were destroyed in the seventh century. The landscape is entirely barren except for the occasional tree and isolated walled orchard that stand out from the red granite background. St Catherine's is the seat of the Archbishop of the Autonomous Orthodox diocese of Sinai that used to claim title over most of this wilderness. After the Israeli withdrawal in 1982, the Egyptian government nationalised any land on the peninsula that was not enclosed within a wall. We reach St Catherine's in the dark, and I take a place at the Desert Fox Camp on the plain of al-Raha, the traditional site of the Israelites' encampment. It is perfectly silent and I am glad to breathe the clear air after all that Cairene dust.

I read through my notes written over cardamom coffee at the Yerevan coffee house in Jerusalem. The divine is the unknowable void that lies beyond the limits of our possible comprehension. Christianity speaks of a personal god. But this is the legacy of the prior polytheism and cults of appeasement of supernatural powers. Faith is not belief in articles of doctrine and nor could those beliefs be the rational deductions from some datum. Faith is not an attitude of optimistic confidence in the goodness of things nor the naïve expression of longing for the cosmos to be a certain way. Faith is the desire to experience ultimate reality. But there cannot be a direct flow of information between the human mind and the transcendent, so the best we can hope for is hesychia, or sweet repose, and eliminate all disturbance from the soul. It is bad enough that have to die: can we not be good to one another, starting with ourselves?

Tuesday 3 June | St Catherine's

Mount Sinai, or Horeb, has been a sacred place for millennia: the name Horeb is linked to the god Horus in the Egyptian cosmology. According to *Exodus* it was at Horeb, across the wilderness from Midian, that Moses met Yahweh in the Burning Bush as he was tending Jethro's flocks. Moses led the Israelites out of Egypt to Sinai where Yahweh entered into the Old Covenant with his chosen people. Moses came down from Horeb with the Ten Commandments and led the Israelites to the Promised Land. In *Kings* we read that Elijah travelled from Beersheba to Horeb where, after wind, earthquake and fire, he heard Yahweh in the voice of a gentle breeze. The Hebrew bible is scattered with geographical references that place Horeb and the nearby wilderness of Paran between Egypt and Midian. Some have claimed that Gebel Serbal above the Wadi Feiran is the real mountain of God but from at least the time of the Decian Persecution in the year 250, anchorites identified Horeb with this Mount Sinai and venerated its summit as Gebel Musa.

According to Eusebius, St Helena the mother of Constantine went on pilgrimage to the Holy Land in the year 326 and encouraged her son to construct basilicas at the most important sites. From this period date the Sepulchre complex in Jerusalem, the Church of the Nativity in Bethlehem and the Golden Church in Antioch. At Sinai a small church was built around the site of the Burning Bush at the foot of the mountain, with a tower attached for the protection of the hermits. A few decades later, the Syrian monk Julian Saba built a shrine on the summit itself. Accounts by Theodoret in the early fourth century and the Spanish pilgrim Egeria, who climbed Gebel Musa in the 380s, describe the community of hermits scattered around the mountain as well as speaking of the flourishing Bush as 'giving forth shoots'. Meanwhile a legend developed that the remains of the Alexandrian martyr Catherine had been carried by angels to the peak that bears her name.

Through the doctrinal disputes over the Trinity and Christology, the monks at Sinai remained aloof from theological debate while adhering firmly to Orthodoxy. In the sixth century the community appealed for protection to the Emperor Justinian who ordered the construction of the fortress walls and *katholikon* (basilica). The works were completed by the year 565 and the monastery was dedicated to St Catherine and the Transfiguration: the church's apse mosaic depicts Jesus transfigured with Moses and Elijah, while either side of the window above the apse are figures of Moses before the Burning Bush and receiving the tablets of the law. The library grew to become the largest collection of early Christian manuscripts outside the Vatican. Today the monastery holds over 4,500 scrolls and manuscripts in eleven languages. Its most valuable treasure was the *Codex Sinaiticus*, the earliest extant complete copy of the Septuagint and New Testament, only a small part of which remains at Sinai.

With the coming of Islam, and despite his general antipathy to the monastic movement, tradition relates that Muhammad gave his personal protection over St Catherine's. This act is recorded in the *Ahtiname*, or Covenant of Peace, purportedly written by 'Ali circa 625 and sealed with an imprint of the Prophet's hand. The library retains a copy of this document while the original was supposed to have been taken to Constantinople by Selim the Grim. Under the Fatimid Caliph Hakim, the monks felt it necessary to convert the original refectory into a mosque that still stands with its minaret opposite the narthex of the church. There are no references to the *Ahtiname* prior to the 1500s: so its purpose may have been to protect the monks from their new Turkish rulers and its authenticity remains unclear. Justinian maintained a garrison of 200 soldiers at St Catherine's who converted to Islam after the Arab conquest. The Gebeliya Bedouin trace their descent from these troops and serve the monastery to this day.

At first light the special beauty of the desolate landscape becomes clear: there is a clarity to the silence that seems to slow down time. At breakfast in the camp I fall in with a group of French pilgrims and walk with them up to the monastery. Our tour stops at the Holy Bramble in the courtyard, whose continuously regrowing root system is the source of its longevity, and continues to the narthex of the katholikon. During the period of iconoclasm from 726 to 842, icons were rejected as the worship of graven images. Following the Seventh Ecumenical Council, their veneration as symbols of divine presence was restored to Orthodox practice. As Sinai was under Islamic control, its icons were spared and the monastery possesses the only surviving sixth-century Byzantine icons. The paintings of St Peter and Christ Pantocrator in the narthex used the encaustic melted wax method that gives them a special luminance: this image of the Pantocrator became the model for mosaics across the Byzantine world and as far away as Monreale.

Standing by the iconostasis is Father Justin, tall and exuberant, who invites me to stay within the walls of the monastery itself. For the next six days, a new routine establishes itself around the staging posts of monastic life: reading in the guest house canteen or on the library roof, lunch in the refectory, more reading, vespers, wandering into the desert or ascending the steps to Gebel Musa and returning in the twilight for supper with the other visitors. Father Justin walks with me to the camp to recover my belongings, talking of false monks and unholy frauds. We return to the monastery and Father Nilus shows me to my room in the guest quarters. I meet one of the resident archaeologists, George Manginis, who is writing a history of Mount Sinai and Brother Porphyrius who delights in feeding the pot plants around the cells. After vespers, I join the visitors for coffee and baklava with Archbishop Damianos in the *salone* above the entrance gate.

In the evening Father Justin invites me to sit with him on the porch, a corner section of the roof that faces down the valley towards al-Raha. Father Justin departs in the morning for Thessalonica but he has enjoyed the books I sent him, especially *The Captive Mind*. In return he gives me Andrew Louth's *Origins of the Christian Mystical Tradition* and *Orthodox Theology* by Vladimir Lossky. We talk about the history of the monastery, Tischendorf's theft of the *Codex Sinaiticus* in 1859 and the planned facsimile of the complete codex. The library building is due to be reconstructed and a digital archive created. Father Justin tells me about *The Ladder of Divine Ascent*, written by the seventh-century abbot of Sinai, John Klimakos. The ladder describes thirty stages of a mystical journey that involves taming the passions and finding hesychia. The spiritual exercises aim to ascend to the summit of transfiguration in anticipation of the *apocatastasis*, the divine restitution of all things. But like the angels of Jacob's Ladder, one never reaches the summit, for there is only one limit in perfection—that it has no limit.

Father Justin suggests that as the mind is the frontier between biological specimen and sentient being, and as the desert is a boundary between the inhabitable and the uninhabitable, so spirituality is another frontier between the material world and a transcendent one. I explain that despite the kindness of the monks, I suffer from the doubt of an instinctive rationality. Father Justin encourages me to read the books he has given me. I promise to read diligently but confess that I am unlikely to rise for the dawn office. Father Justin laughs and suggests I speak with Brother John in the bakery. Brother John has similar difficulties and has never become a monk. But he loves making bread each day for the community in the ancient stone oven of the monastery and enjoys smoking cigarettes in the courtyard.

WEDNESDAY 4 JUNE | ST CATHERINE'S
Heterodoxy

Reading in the guest house garden, I begin with Kallistos Ware's *The Orthodox Church*. Ware explains the disputes over doctrine that gave rise to the Seven Ecumenical Councils, whose definitions of Orthodoxy have continued to this day. The central axiom is that to save mankind, the Incarnate Christ must be fully human and fully divine. At Nicaea in 325, the Council of Bishops proclaimed the Athanasian formula that God became human so that mankind could become divine. The 'Word became flesh' yet Christ is as divine as the Father and not a man among created things, as Arius argued. Father, Son and Holy Spirit are three entities (*hypostases*) in one essence (*homoousios*). All forms of heterodoxy deviate from these statements.

But the Nicaean consensus left unanswered questions about the dual nature of Christ. A century after Nicaea, Nestorius argued that Mary could not be the mother of God but only the mother of Christ's humanity and hence that the two natures of Christ must be joined in a *prosopic* union, as if Christ had divine and human faces. Meanwhile another faction argued that since Christ was God come down to earth, the divine must have absorbed the human and hence Christ must have only a single nature. At the Council of Ephesus in 431, led by Cyril of Alexandria, it was proclaimed contra-Nestorius that Mary was *theotokos* and that Christ was a single person. This resulted in the first schism when the Christians of the Persian Sasanian Empire, the so-called Nestorian Church of the East, broke from communion with Orthodoxy.

Twenty years later at Chalcedon in 451, the Council declared Orthodox Christology to be *dyophysite*, expressed as the hypostatic union of the divine and human natures (*physes*). Chalcedon led to the fracturing of Christianity within the Byzantine Empire, as the Churches of the non-Greek speaking provinces broke away from Orthodoxy. It is thought that the non-Chalcedonian *miaphysite* position held that Christ is divine and human in one composite nature. The Syriac scholar Sebastian Brock has suggested that the emotional root of the dispute lay in the question of *when* the divine and human natures were combined in the Christ-Messiah, the Kyrie-Adonai. If the essence of the Christian proposition is salvation through belief in the Resurrection, then it is not enough to hold that we are 'saved by grace through faith in Christ'. Rather it matters that one's beliefs about the Christ are correct: did the union of the two natures occur at conception (miaphysite) or at the Ascension (dyophysite)?

The apostles told that Jesus was the son of God who died to save all mankind. They called the resurrected Jesus Kyrios, the Greek word in the Septuagint for the Hebrew Adonai, used in Jewish prayer for Yahweh. So the divinity of Christ was asserted from the beginning. Yet doctrinal problems emerged as soon as the Apostolic Age passed away. In the second century, Justin Martyr asked what it meant to be the son of God and elaborated logos to explain how Jesus was both transcendent creator and incarnate son. Neither apostolic authority nor reference to mysteries that surpass understanding give definitive answers to logical questions: theology has never been an exact science. So heterodoxy was inevitable. But the Church Fathers saw Gnostic and neo-Platonist interpretations of the Christian message as threats to their beliefs. Irenaeus wrote *Against Heresies* around 180 to defend Orthodoxy as passed down from the apostles. By 144, Marcion was excommunicated at Rome despite being the first to collect together the Epistles of Paul.

In reading the history of the early church one must be struck by its sadness: the New Testament has been as fought over as the Holy Land. From the followers of Arius and Nestorius to the devotees of Origen and Pelagius and even John Chrysostom, whose liturgy remains the standard for the Orthodox Church, countless thinkers were exiled or suppressed at the hands of their co-religionists. The factional politics of the Church gathered pace after the military victory of Constantine, when doctrine came to depend as much on the confidence of the emperor as on reasoning and reflection. The central axiom of the faith was clear from the beginning. But the final statements of Orthodoxy seem more the result of politics than divine inspiration.

After the schism that followed Chalcedon, the Byzantine emperors periodically tried to reconcile the Greek Patriarchates with Rome on one side and the non-Chalcedonian Oriental Churches on the other. But any formula that deviated from Orthodoxy, such as the Henotikon of Zeno in 482 or the *monolethitism* of Heraclius in 638, appeased the Oriental Churches to a degree but was rejected by Rome. Justinian sought to build a unified empire of doctrinal Orthodox purity and repressed the mostly non-Greek speaking Oriental Churches who believed in the pure divinity of Christ from conception. To what extent did the doctrinal conflicts between Byzantium and the Syriacs and Assyrians, Copts and Armenians pave the way for the seventh-century Arab conquests? The schisms of 451 and 1054 over seemingly arcane doctrines were in reality the result of misunderstanding and disputes over the exercise of power.

At Alexandria, the habits of Greek disputation transferred from physics to theology. Yet these doctrinal questions are not spheres of enquiry that submit to empirical investigation. There could not be any objective test for the truth of Christian doctrine beyond superstitious propitiation: Decius blamed the Christians for the Gothic invasions because they had not honoured the pagan gods at the millennial celebrations of Rome; Diocletian blamed them on the advice of the augurs of Apollo; Constantine's Christian sun god defeated the pagan gods of Maxentius, just as Moses defeated the Amalekites and Elijah the worshippers of Baal, while Julian's defeat in Asia reversed the pagan cause. When the Goths defeated Valens in 378, the pagans took this to show that the Christian god is not the supreme god after all; until Theodosius buttressed the frontiers as well as the argument, and initiated the long purge of pagan and heretic.

Once the Christians gained the ascendancy, all they had to do was live in the imitation of Christ. Despite the obscurity of their metaphysics, they had won converts for 300 years by practising the simple message of the Master. Yet once they gained temporal power and succumbed to factional rivalry, they could not preserve the intellectual freedom of the first three centuries and could not live with divergent interpretations of the faith. The Socratic principle was about rational enquiry through dialogue, and the Delphic principle was 'nothing in excess'. Yet the Christians fought each other and the disputes that split the Church led to the defeats of Yarmouk and Manzikert.

I think back to Father Gregory's insights on the Aventino. If one is raised in the Latin West but cannot cross the 'threshold of hope' into literal belief in the improbable, then seeking a different path through Byzantium as Chatwin and Tavener did, does not help. If anything, the Orthodox Church is more exigent in its insistence on doctrinal purity. Before the Great Schism of 1054, whose trivial pretext was the *filioque* (does the Holy Spirit proceed from the Father or the Father *and the Son*?) the Latin West was as much part of the Orthodox world as Greece is today. Although the doctrinal formulae of homoousis and the hypostatic union were framed within the apparatus of Greek philosophy, Rome was primus inter pares. So Rome and Byzantium were equally to blame: if the Church had tolerated heterodoxy and allowed diverse doctrine, there would have been no schisms, no Latin sack of Constantinople and no Protestant reformation.

Lunch in the refectory is silent in the presence of icons around the walls that give the sense of looking at the viewer: white bean soup with feta and home-made bread, olives, apples and apricots from the garden. On fast days the monks eat lentils and no cheese. The monastery is closed to tourists in the afternoon. So I explore the courtyards and passageways and terraces, delighted to have the place to myself. I discover the staircase that leads to the library roof and look out over the monastery in the warm breeze.

At vespers in the katholikon, the monks sing the office and I absorb the elaborate decoration of the basilica, the silver hanging lamps, mosaics and icons. But it is difficult to still the mind. So I follow the mesmerising light shaft as it picks out the tesserae across the marble floor and the red glass of the lamps. Byzantine chant has eight modes with different patterns of intervals and the vespers have a purifying effect.

The trouble begins when one thinks about doctrine—about miracles and salvation and life after death. Perhaps one should simply not think about these matters and remain content with practice. Father Justin explains, 'There are things in theology and spirituality that defy any attempt to put them into words; they are grasped by each person in his own experience. It is in prayer and in the divine liturgy that they are found.'

It is time to set out for Gebel Musa, the summit of Mount Sinai. From behind the monastery walls, the Path of Moses ascends into the shadow of the rocks above and switches back and forth as it steepens. The route passes out of sight of the monastery into a ravine and up a series of steps carved out of the granite in the sixth century, the physical embodiment of *The Ladder of Divine Ascent*. These Stairs of Repentance pass under two stone arches to reach Farsh Elias, the basin of Elijah's Hollow. In the arid desolation of Sinai this open area, once the refuge of anchorites, has the feeling of a secret world with cypress trees and pools of rainwater. The path leads on to the summit at 2,285 metres, an ascent of 800 metres above the monastery, where there is a spectacular joy of climbing to the peak. The Justinian summit basilica collapsed long ago, probably from seismic activity. Now there is a church from the 1930s and a small mosque. Gebel Musa gives views over the whole peninsula from its gulfs to the deserts of Arabia. The seventeenth-century monk Nektarios reported a beam of light that appears at dusk from the peak, and even in the 1990s magnetic storm effects were observed on the summit: Gebel Musa has a natural air of mystery about it.

Today a throng of tourists clings to the ledges to watch the sunset and rise with the dawn. Historically there was a prohibition against pilgrims sleeping on the summit and even the caretaker of the basilica had to descend to Farsh Elias at sunset. I walk down the Path of the Pasha in the gloom, built in the 1850s for the comfort of the camel's back, and join the archaeologists for supper. They are excavating the site of the Justinian barracks that was dismantled in the eighth century to preserve the peace of the monks, or possibly because the soldiers converted to Islam and there was no longer a frontier to protect. Thankfully, visiting scholars are not restricted to the monks' ascetic regime: over the course of the week we enjoy Red Sea fish, vegetables, steamed rice and monastic versions of Greek specialities.

THURSDAY 5 JUNE | ST CATHERINE'S
Particularity
I sit under the loggia reading Father Justin's article on the earliest Christian papyri. The Huleatt fragments of Matthew (papyri P64), have been re-dated using textual analysis to the late first century. A small fragment known as the Rylands Papyrus (P52) was collected at Fayoum in 1920 and published in 1935. The text is from chapter 18 of *The Gospel of John* and has been dated by palaeography (comparison of handwriting with other manuscripts bearing dates) to the first half of the second century. If John was the last gospel to be written, the synoptic gospels must have been written earlier, possibly from a common source called Q. This tiny fragment is evidence that the gospel had reached Upper Egypt by around the year 125 and supports the traditional history of the early spread of Christianity. Palaeographic analysis of the Alexandrian papyrus sheets of the Epistles of Paul (P46) also dates them to the early second century and suggests that *nomina sacra* (IC for Jesus, XC for Christ and KC for Kyrios) were used at an early date.

After lunch at the guest house, I immerse myself in N.T. Wright's *The New Testament and the People of God*. Wright discusses the historical data points that illuminate the Apostolic Age, including Josephus, other Jewish sects such as the Essenes and the first-century proto-rabbinic books of Ezra and Baruch. Wright criticises F.C. Baur and the Tübingen School of theologians who were influenced by Hegel and situated the early church in the interweaving of Jewish history with Greek philosophy and second-century Gnosticism. Yet the Gospels and Epistles were written in Greek to a mixed audience: Christianity emerged as a Jewish-Hellenic syncretism. Why would an Epicurean or the Emperors Titus and Hadrian accept that the partial Yahweh of the Israelites is the supreme creator of the cosmos? The Christians believe that the Jews were special to the universal god. But to the rational Hellene, the specialness of Yahweh is in need of explanation: the particularity of its Jewish origin makes the universality of Christian doctrine hard to accept.

Wright argues that enlightenment rationalism has caused the modern crisis of faith. Yet as St Thomas recognised, reason and our senses are all we have to go on. Any irrationalities must be confronted to ensure that one has chosen through ongoing free decision to be Christian rather than anything else. In response to the Humean critique of the concept of miracles, C.S. Lewis argued that once the Incarnation is accepted, all the rest follows: the raising of Lazarus, the Resurrection, appearances and so on. But how does one confront the implausibility of the Incarnation itself? If the Word became flesh, then the divine wisdom of our native wit demands that we engage our critical faculties. What conclusions would an unbiased observer draw from the events described in the Gospels?

Ancient minds—from Abraham at Mamre to the mistaking of Barnabas and Paul as Zeus and Hermes in *Acts of the Apostles* —saw the gods as messengers. Like other oriental mystery cults, the Nazarenes lived in a general environment that normalised divine intervention into human affairs, and they combined this with Jewish prophetic traditions. So the Messiah was no mere messenger but rather the Incarnation of the supreme god. The sceptical pagans asked: why *that* man at *that* place at *that* time? Because the transcendent being had to come somewhere? Does not the arbitrary particularity of His having to come *somewhere*, *sometime* make it implausible that He came at all?

At Sinai one feels that the Incarnation is no more mysterious than the cosmos in general. From the Pythagoreans to Philo to Cantor and the puzzle of mathematical fit in modern physics, the inadequacy of the finite has always left a realisation that something lies beyond. But that does not change the fact that as Gilgamesh understood, our mortality is terrifying and unassailable. Sacrificing animals, mummifying the body, Pascal's wager as a passport to the afterlife: all are equally futile. If we are as transient as mosquitoes and lobsters, all we can do is seek paradise in our present experience, in our inner being and the beauty of the world around us. To the believers, the risen Christ represents the conquest of death, not its acceptance. What about the rest of us? No man can tell another how to find the courage to accept death.

Some Christians lament that 'materialistic neo-Epicureanism' is the dominant religion of today. But this is to mischaracterise Epicurus. If Christianity is a tradition of love and the golden rule, then it can be interpreted as a form of humanist Epicureanism. As the Pythagoreans understood, the mechanistic world view has always been limited and Epicurus would have rejected atheistic materialism. So rationalism and mysticism go naturally together in Epicureanism, Sufism, Buddhism and many other traditions. Lossky talks about being 'seized by God'! If only that were commonplace and self-evident then all questions about faith and reason would vanish. Father Justin would bid me to be seized by God as the monks chant vespers and the bright beam of the evening sun picks out the tesserae as it moves across the marble floor.

I walk up the camel path where another path leads to Jethro's Hill, past the chapel of St Theodorus, into the desolate wilderness. At this distance from the monastery all sound dies away and there is complete silence. The monks ruined Scetis but the tourists ruined Sinai, I think to myself. With its stream of visitors, Horeb is too busy to hear the 'voice in the gentle breeze'. But at this spot there is complete isolation; the only intrusion is the autonomic movement of one's own body. If time is the interstitial space between events, then stripping them away leaves only pure existence. God is silent but God is in the silence.

FRIDAY 6 JUNE | ST CATHERINE'S
Platonism
Again I rise too late for matins and take a congenial breakfast with the archaeologists. At the highest point of the monastery on the sun-scorched terrace of the library roof, I find a dusty

armchair and read Louth's history of Christian mysticism in the shade of the cupola, enjoying the breeze and the bright sunlight. After vespers I climb to Gebel Musa, taking various detours to explore the paths and caves around the mountain.

Mysticism is the search for direct experience of the divine or transcendent. Early Christianity used Platonism as its primary form of philosophical expression. Plato himself was initiated as a *hierophant* (priest) into the *mysterion* (secret) and *mystikos* (silence) of the Hellenistic religion. In his *Republic* Plato presents the Allegory of the Cave to argue that the world revealed by our senses is unreal. Reality itself lies in forms such as beauty which are abstractions from material objects. So the soul's quest is to ascend to the eternal realm that transcends the phenomenal world by contemplating these abstract forms. This process of *theoria* leads the psyche (soul) to kinship with the wide ocean of beauty. The highest form is the perfect good or beauty and is the ultimate source of all reality. In *Symposium* Plato identifies this perfect good with divine love that comes upon the soul in a state of ecstasy as it finds 'union with the transcendent'.

For the early Platonists, theoria was a supremely intellectual form of contemplation: the joy of it was akin to Archimedes' Eureka or the delight that Cantor must have felt when he discovered the proof that real and natural numbers are infinite sets of different sizes. Alas for mere mortals this form of 'mystical union' would indeed be rapturous if it were not so unattainable. Perhaps the poor reputation of mystical writing lies in its tendency to pontificate using obscure and grand sounding words? For the mysterion to have meaning it must be intelligible. But the later Platonists and Christian mystics were not playing intellectual games to exercise temporal power: they were concerned with the conquest of internal disturbance, of the malign sources from which flow all the forces of darkness in the world.

To the Christians the mysterion *was* the Incarnation: the highest good of Plato became the logos of Philo and John. The essence of Platonism as reinterpreted by Plotinus, Origen, Evagrius and Denys is the insufficiency of materialism to guide us in our personal journeys to a higher ascent of the soul. Materialists believe that only matter exists and deny the existence of souls. But abstractions like numbers and minds transcend matter and without numbers and minds, matter cannot be understood. For all the success of modern science, at the limit ultimate reality is as obscure to us as it was to Plato. Souls and persons or sentient beings exist but are not material. Souls are not metaphysical serial numbers, cosmic identifiers transferable from one body to another, as materialist monism would lampoon the concept; rather we can interpret the ancient idea of a soul to mean our internal sentience, the subjective experience of our being.

For this reason we can translate what the Platonists and Christian mystics wrote about the soul into our modern concept of ourselves as conscious agents with an interior life. It is in virtue of having a soul—in other words subjective conscious experience—that we can connect with the realm of eternal truth, the realm of the divine or transcendent. In Plato, the soul ascends to God, realising its own true nature. But in Christianity, God descends into the world through the Incarnation. Christianity reinterpreted Platonic hagia sophia, the divine wisdom that lies within all of us, as the logos which is external to us; while theoria, or contemplation of the highest forms, became the experience of the holy spirit and belief in the Incarnation.

The Alexandrian-Roman philosopher Plotinus (205–271) elaborated Plato's ideas. For Plotinus the ascent of the soul is the process of withdrawal into oneself through catharsis, the purificatory pursuit of tranquillity and virtue. But the *nous* (intellectual faculty) is itself an eternal Platonic form, so the process of purification restores the soul to its original state of resemblance to the divine. Meanwhile Plotinus's contemporary Origen (185–254) translated Platonism into a specifically Christian vision focused on the exposition of the Hebrew wisdom books. Proverbs is about the emptiness of transitory things, while Ecclesiastes continues the way of illumination and Song of Songs expresses the ideal form of ecstatic love.

The Christian mystical tradition intersected with the

doctrinal disputes of the post-Constantinian era. After the conversion of Constantine, Christianity transitioned from a social protest movement led by voluntary conversion into the official ideology of the ruling imperial power. To both Plato and the early Christian Platonists, souls are pre-existing and immortal: the soul is already divine and therefore not sinful. But at the Council of Nicaea in 325 the assertion of the doctrine of *creatio ex nihilo*—contra the followers of Arius who believed that logos was created—led to the suppression of Platonism. To preserve the divinity of the logos that entered creation through the Incarnation, Athanasius and the Council rejected the divinity of souls. But if souls are created out of nothing and do not have a divine pre-existence they do not return in the Platonic sense and so, for Athanasius, the only path to divinisation of the soul is belief in the Incarnation.

After Nicaea, mystical writers alternated between Origenist rapture and the *apophatic* way of darkness. The Cappadocian fathers, especially Gregory of Nyssa (335–395), developed Athanasian theology. If the cosmos was created ex-nihilo the divine is of a different order of reality. Since the divine is unknowable and incomprehensible, the journey of the soul is into apophatic nothingness. *Epaktasis* is the longing of the soul; but there is no union, only a deeper penetration into darkness. In the dark night of the soul the divine presence can only be felt in the unknowing. Like Anthony, Evagrius of Pontus (345–399) described hesychia as the withdrawal into silence and solitude to battle against bad thoughts. *Apatheia* is the tranquillity that arises out of freedom from the passions and allows the soul to leave darkness behind: at the mystical summit, the soul does not lose itself in ecstasy but realises itself in continued contemplation.

For the later Platonists, mysticism represents some form of sympathy between the material elements and the divine. Dionysius ('Denys') the Areopagite (lived c.500) expressed a synthesis of these ideas that was brought to the Latin West as *The Cloud of Unknowing*. The soul flees from all created things along the apophatic way, passing through *catharsis* (purification), *photismos* (illumination) and *enosis* (union) with the unknowable in the darkness. At the peak of its ascent, the soul is filled with ecstatic love—as expressed by St Teresa. Denys combines the cataphatic idea of ecstatic revelation with the apophatic path to the unknowable god. Hellenist Platonism is concerned with the divine wisdom within us that enables mankind to interpret the cosmos and allows nature to reveal itself. But in the Christian tradition, following Irenaeus, Jerome, Chrysostom and Benedict, the only real mystery is the love of the Master.

SATURDAY 7 JUNE | ST CATHERINE'S
St Thomas revisited
I finally succeed in waking early enough to join the monks for matins in the katholikon. The dawn is a secret society everywhere but especially in the Levant, where the arrival of Apollo is so dramatic. The ambient light gradually fills the church, and when the sun rises, its rays abruptly burst through the east window above the apse of the Transfiguration—the daily expression of illumination. After the office the monks invite me to join them for coffee and sweets in the salone. Father Ephraim takes me to the museum and I carefully study the books and icons on display. After vespers, I return to Jethro's Hill and sit by the shrine of Theodorus, looking over the barren mountains. Again the silence is truly startling.

Naïvely, each of us believes ourself to be unique, significant and valuable. Belief in communication with the divine reinforces this metaphysical confidence. But when God is silent the shattering of the illusion can be overwhelming. How does one return to faith once the fly has escaped the bottle? There is always the hope of direct encounter, but visions and voices are the province of psychosis. One can hardly expect choirs of angels. The absence of direct experience must lead to metaphysical pessimism: if there is no life after death and no direct communication with the transcendent, then God is irretrievably distant. Still, Christian ethics and practice hold independently of the metaphysics, of the belief in the Resurrection.

So the only path to hesychia is meditation along the

apophatic way, whether its guiding source is divinely inspired or reflects perhaps the interior well of the subconscious. In this way the mystics give a different answer to the riddle of St Thomas: the radical disjunction of our own annihilation takes us to the apophatic darkness and from there to union with the divine which is tranquillity in the soul. To echo Immanuel Kant, there are two routes to the divine: in seeing nature without and in seeing the soul within. Where better for both paths than the desert? The purity of the empty expanse draws us to the transcendent and perhaps that is why the Abrahamic religions came out of the desert?

Sunday 8 June | St Catherine's
Mystical Epicureanism

I rise again in the dark for matins: whether the path to a higher reality is Origenist or apophatic, whether 'mystical union' is the elimination of the self or its realisation, whether one crosses the 'threshold of hope' or languishes in permanent epaktasis, this chanting at dawn is the closest one can get to hagia sophia. I had wanted to climb Gebel Catarina but no Bedou is available to accompany me. So after coffee with the monks in the salone I take notes in the guest house. After vespers, I climb up the steps to Farsh Elias and continue to the deserted peak of Ras Safsafra which has even more dramatic views than Gebel Musa itself. I retrace my steps in the dark with a torch kindly lent by one of the monks and sit on the porch watching the stars.

Since the rationalist enlightenment and the demise of the supernatural as a force in our mind worlds, the prevailing culture has become Deist or neo-Epicurean: the transcendent supreme being exists in a state of perfect blessedness that cannot harm us and makes no difference to our daily lives. But Epicurus could be regarded as a mystic in the tradition of Christian Platonism: the ultimate state of being is one of painlessness, of tranquillity in the soul and freedom from all disturbance or anxiety. This is what the goal of human existence—katastematic pleasure—is all about. From this state to union with the transcendent is a short step, a trivial corollary.

So belief in divine transcendence, detached from the spatio-temporal material cosmos, is compatible with the quest for communion with the divine. As Martin Savage interpreted the parable of the farm workers, we must never give up the search.

The rich often suffer from depression, especially those who inherit wealth and lack the sense of self-respect that comes from making one's way in the world. But in the absence of physical pain, what better condition could one inhabit than having open expanses of time in which to delight in merely being alive? Some people fear the boredom they think would ensue from occupying such a state, and devise activities of varying benefit to give themselves something to do—to distract themselves from silence and nothingness. But the flow state should be like the joy of mere being. Experiential fitness needs training so that we can savour each moment of every day in a permanent state of well-being. The maximally experienced life is shorn of labour, of the pursuit of the ownership of unnecessary objects, of tiredness and disturbance; instead it is filled with the flow state of activities that give joy in themselves, such as the musicians of a string-quartet experience or societies of friends conversing in an Epicurean garden.

Jordan

MONDAY 9 JUNE | NUWEIBA

From the library roof I take a final glimpse of the mountains before walking down to the Desert Fox Camp. The bus to Nuweiba is slow but the wadis are beautiful. We stop for tuna and bread in Dahab and pick up a band of young Israelis who are surprisingly keen to discuss the ongoing Middle East peace process. One of them, Asaf Avnon, talks about an interview that Omri Sharon gave to the *International Herald Tribune*, reproduced in *Ha'aretz*, in which the son of the Israeli Prime Minister said: 'We are not living in a vacuum; there is an international reality. ... Today we are located in the Palestinian areas, we are violating international agreements, but no one is saying anything. The United States is with us. So we talk "Palestinian state, Palestinian state", but in the meantime not even Area A exists. And there is no Orient House, there is no Palestinian representation in Jerusalem ... . Obviously, we all want peace —who does not want peace?'

'Have you considered the situation from the Palestinian point of view?' I ask Asaf. 'After all, it was mostly their country before 1948 and they had nothing to do with the genocide of European Jewry. Should we not try to do to others as we would have them to do us?' And I add, not wanting to sound partisan, 'Isn't that symmetry of action the basis of humanist ethics?' But I need not worry, as Asaf is happy to talk and seems to enjoy presenting the Israeli case. 'Why do you say it was their country? The Jewish people have always had a claim to Judaea and Samaria. But the Arabs tried to drive us into the sea. You British even supported them but we won against all the odds. Do you know about Glubb Pasha?'

Not wanting to haggle over factoids, I try to make the discussion more abstract. 'What justifies a claim to land ownership?' I ask. 'Surely you agree that ancient texts and military conquest do not justify such a claim?' 'They fought a war against us and we defended our land,' Asaf replies. 'The ones who left gave up their land and the ones who stayed became Israeli citizens. Why do you talk about land?' 'This newspaper article talks about land,' I say, pointing at his copy of *Ha'aretz*. 'Aren't these conflicts always about land? Doesn't valid ownership lie in purchase or donation or, where there is no formal title, in continuity back to the original acquisition?'

'Why do Europeans always want to blame Israel for the situation?' Asaf continues. 'If you want to talk about land, look at Sinai. Through the ages the border lay more or less in the middle of the peninsula. Only the western rim of Sinai was part of Egypt and the rest was a part of Palestine, while at times the southern parts belonged to the Wilayat Higaz. The modern border was forced by Britain after rejecting proposals from what was then the Ottoman Empire. Britain needed a hinterland so it annexed the Sinai to Egypt in 1906. The peninsula had switched hands through the ages but before the British occupied Egypt it was a part of the Sanjak of Jerusalem. The Romans called it Palestina Tertia and joined it to Edom and the Negev. After the Arab occupation it was called Falastin al-Jundi (Military Palestine).

'So if history were to decide where to draw the line, it would be somewhere along the al-Arish wadi down to Suez, as the Ottoman Commissioner Ahmed Mukhtar Pasha suggested in 1905. If it were up to the native Bedouin inhabitants of Sinai, they would say it belongs to Israel: they have relatives in the Negev and were loyal to Israel. Nowadays they're left to be guides in the mountains or to grow marijuana for export by smuggling into Israel. Most are bitter but they keep their mouths firmly shut. Most of the businesses you see in Sinai are newcomers from Alexandria or Cairo. So there is more to what I say when I say that we gave it to them and not just gave it back. But it is always hard to liberate Europeans from their convictions of what is right and what is wrong in the Middle East.'

At Nuweiba we part company as Asaf and his friends continue on the bus to Taba. At the al-Bedawi camp I take a grass hut familiar from previous visits to Sinai and swim around the bay, happy to do nothing but eat fuul under the stars in the shadow of the red cliffs and enjoy the tranquillity of this place.

TUESDAY 10 JUNE | AQABA

I board the ferry for Aqaba and fall in with a Lebanese called Nagi Zeidan who works at the Four Seasons Hotel in Sharm el-Sheikh. Nagi asks me if I know about the Sheba'a Farms enclave. Hezbollah and the IDF are presently squaring off in this strip of land at the northern end of the Golan Heights. Nagi proceeds to enumerate the details of Security Council Resolutions 242 and 485 and reminds me that the Balfour Declaration committed to protect the rights of existing non-Jewish communities in Palestine. I tell him that on previous trips I have crossed the Holy Land from Jaffa to Jericho, from Hebron to Nablus, and lament the tragedy of this unresolved conflict.

The ferry has a problem with its engines which fall silent. We are marooned in the Gulf of Aqaba. For two hours the boat turns around and around in the heat as we gaze at the piercing blue water and the red cliffs on either side of the strait. I have little option but to move around the deck from one patch of shade to the next, while Nagi follows me, encouraged by my sympathy to continue talking about Israel. In this region the Arab-Israeli conflict is never far away but it sometimes feels like being Schrödinger's cat trapped in no man's land. Eventually motion is restored, and the ferry reaches Aqaba in the evening.

The world of the Mediterranean basin and Graeco-Roman civilisation is far away. The Gulf of Aqaba is an extension of the Indian Ocean, and the empty wastes of the Arabian deserts are pressed against the town. This is the edge of the Semitic world, of Sheba and the Nabateans, of the wilderness that extends to Mesopotamia in one direction and down to the Horn of Africa in the other. In the First World War this desert was the frontier of a belligerent European power that could not be mentally further from its capital on the Bosphorus, let alone Flanders mud. Aqaba became the emblem of the romance of Arabia, of T.E. Lawrence and Sharif Hussein's Bedouin forces capturing the town and its heavy Turkish guns.

The ferry docks and the foot passengers disembark on to the quay before being ushered into the 1970s terminal building. We stand in line with large photographs of the Hashemite Kings Hussein and Abdullah staring down from the walls. The passage through customs is mercifully quick and soon I am in the melee of the street outside, my senses primed to the best available opportunity that presents itself. I share a taxi to Wadi Musa with two Swiss and bargain a room at the comfortable Alanbat II Hotel.

WEDNESDAY 11 JUNE | PETRA

From the Petra site entrance I walk through the narrow winding Siq, the evocative secret passage to the city of the Nabateans, and imagine the excitement of the early European travellers encountering the façade at the end of the deep rock canyon for the first time. The Siq meanders for a mile until the sandstone red 'Treasury of Pharaoh' (al-Khazneh al-Fira'un) makes its sudden appearance. Despite having become an iconic vista, known all over the world for its stone carved pediments and pillars, al-Khazneh is still thrilling. The remains of the lost city, its fora, gymnasia, baths and colonnades, first-century Roman Theatre and tombs, lie scattered across the sides of the Wadi Musa.

Petra, the capital of biblical Edom, was one of the prehistoric entrepôts of Arabia, rock-hewn out of its mountain wilderness. Nabatean merchants carried bales, spices and ivory in camel caravans from Sheba to the Levant. Petra's heyday followed Trajan's annexation, when the town became the capital of the Roman province of Arabia Petraea and assumed its hybrid Nabatean–Roman splendour. The rise of Palmyra, Persian expansion and the Muslim conquest led to Petra's decline as a permanent settlement. The city was briefly occupied by the Crusaders and then lapsed as the refuge of itinerant Bedou until Burckhardt's visit in 1812 fired the European imagination and Petra became the acme of romantic adventure.

Along the Street of Façades, I meet an American Bible group led by one Isaac Demme and climb with them to al-Madbah, the high place of sacrifice opposite al-Khazneh. After seeing the lion fountain, nymphaeum and triclinium, we take lunch in the museum refectory talking about faith and reason. Isaac tells me that pride is the worst sin and that God speaks to us through dreams and thoughts to make us better people. 'Faith,' says Isaac, 'is as much about loyalty as belief. For those raised as Christians, redemption through faith is very simple: all you have to do is keep true to the tradition. Allegiance is more important than analysis.'

'But,' I counter, 'surely Jesus the humanitarian would not have wanted a single one of his followers to die in his name? If faith is loyalty to God, then is it not a private matter? Is it not better to remain alive and inwardly swear allegiance to Jesus than to die for the refusal to deny that name on the outside as the martyrs did?' 'Faith means acting in good faith,' Isaac explains. 'Christian faith does not mean belief in the improbable, but rather making Jesus one's point of allegiance and holding true to that allegiance. One can pay allegiance to a man whether or not you believe absolutely in what he says.' 'Belonging to a faith community cannot be like membership of a private club,' I reply. 'Surely what matters to a faith is its truth, not the social arrangements afforded to its members? Whether Moses or Zoroaster, Jesus or Muhammad should we not choose our own master based on the rational analysis of all the available options?'

'What is truth?' asks Isaac. 'Ultimate reality just is the way it is,' I riposte, 'but there cannot be any logical distinction between natural and supernatural. We simply observe what is to try and understand that reality. So the question is the reliability and plausibility of descriptions of rare events. If the transcendent Absolute intervenes in the cosmos at one place and point, then why not also at others? No revealed religions can explain why God has intervened at *that* time in *that* place or revealed Himself to *those* people. It is the arbitrariness and particularity of all claims of divine intervention that make them implausible.'

'For the Word to become flesh, He had to come somewhere,' Isaac responds, 'so the particularity of the Incarnation is also irrelevant: those particulars are basic facts.' 'Doesn't the arbitrariness of those facts and their retrogressive justification make the Incarnation implausible?' I reply. 'The writers of the New Testament framed the Incarnation in the context of the Hebrew Messianic tradition, to make the arrival of the "anointed one" believable within that tradition? But from the perspective of the rational Greek standing outside that tradition, those pointers would seem the cryptic nonsense of an oriental mystery religion.'

'If faith means allegiance, not belief, then faith in Christ does not require this barrier to be overcome,' says Isaac. 'Allowing God to guide individual human decision does not require direct exchange with the transcendent Absolute. Rather it requires awareness or wakefulness. The confirmation message, the out of office reply that never comes is simply integrity, the feeling of having made the right decision about who to pay allegiance to.' 'But I want to know the truth—the same truth that extends to all people at all times and places,' I conclude. 'Surely once Christianity is tribalised, it loses its point and the essence of its message, the golden rule? Consider Bachir Gemayel and all those sectarian wars fought in the name of one god over another.' Isaac returns to his group while I walk through the Siq back to Wadi Musa.

THURSDAY 12 JUNE | PETRA
It is suddenly much hotter, so I don my Siwi sirwal undertrousers and pass the time in the canteen opposite the theatre, drinking tea with its owner Khalid. We talk of politics and local life. 'When you look into a woman's eyes,' Khalid tells me, 'you see her soul; the bodies are all the same!' Looking around me I think that perhaps he has a point. We are disturbed by some noisy Antipodeans and I take my cue to continue my wanderings around the ruined city of the Nabateans. The sandstone rocks are the colour of ambrosia and I climb barefoot up the wadi to ad-Deir (monastery), the most splendid building in Petra. In the museum canteen I eat

chicken and rice with two friendly local women and we are joined by a sixteen-year-old girl called Manal who speaks perfect English and gives me a necklace. Manal tells me there are many foreigners living in Petra who arrived as tourists and married local Bedouin. What could be more natural?

I walk up to the rim of the Wadi Araba to watch the sunset in the evening wind, looking west over the rift valley. The light catches the white dome of Aaron's tomb, isolated on its distant jebel above the Negev. This shrine receives visits from Israeli pilgrims who cross the frontier at night, ignored by the Jordanian authorities. For as long as the light permits, I read Lossky who talks about the radical disjuncture of being seized by the transcendent. As at Jethro's Hill, the purity of the landscape and the silent immensity of the empty space put the futility of petty material concerns into the breadth of another perspective.

The internet has enabled the proliferation of noise, while the signal of meanings and ideas worthy of commanding our attention becomes more elusive. Silence itself, the ground bass of contrast, is harder to find: every moment must be filled with information and stimulation, for fear of boredom or falling behind or perhaps the terror of piercing silence itself? To be isolated in nature is glorious. But to be isolated in the noisy metropolis, connected to other urban cells through a computer terminal, is more lonely than anything. As we sever our link to the natural world and our lives become more robotic, we lose our ability to see wonder and stifle the wellsprings of creativity. In the fading dusk, I descend to the nymphaeum and ride Khalid's camel through the Siq to leave that wonderful place in the shadow of the moon.

From hijra to crusade

'There is no god but Allah; Muhammad is the messenger of Allah.' In Arabic: مُحَمَّدٌ رَسُولُ ٱللَّهِ لَا إِلَٰهَ إِلَّا ٱللَّهُ

This statement, the *shahada*, is the first pillar of Islam. The others derive from the *sunnah* (practice) of the Prophet: *salat* (prayers), *sawm* (fasting during the month of Ramadan), *zakat* (alms) and (Hajj) pilgrimage. Muslims believe that Allah gave the final revelation to Muhammad through the Archangel Jibril at that place and time. Islam calls upon the 'umma, the community of believers, to follow divine command as written in the Qur'an and in the hadiths, the attested sayings of the Prophet. Muslims regard Abraham, Moses and Jesus as the most significant preceding messengers of Allah, and distinguish dhimmis (Jews, Christians, Sabians—who may have been Manichaeans—and some others) from mushrikun (idolators, pagans and polytheists). The Qur'an (recitation) reinterprets biblical narratives: Abraham is described as sacrificing Ishmael on Mount Moriah, while Jesus is the prophet, not the son, of God, and is deemed to have descended from the cross.

While Judaism emerged as the voice of a people preserving its identity against dominating empires; while the practices of Zoroaster were adopted across the Iranian plateau through the assent of its native population; while Christianity spread through the Roman world by witness from one house church to another; Islam was indisputably martial in its emergence and propagation as a world force. From its inception in the Prophet's house at Yathrib to its breakneck expansion, the followers of Muhammad spread their creed by force. From the outset of the Islamic 'Apostolic Age', when the Companions of the Prophet were still alive, the caliphs sought to absorb the whole of Christendom into the Dar al-Islam. To the Arabs, their armies brought divine revelation, merciful and compassionate, tolerant of dhimmis, there being 'no compulsion in religion'. But to the Europeans, the Muslim expansion was a force of conquest that overwhelmed their power of self-determination, religious freedom and dignity of indigeneity.

The seventh century opened with the twenty-five-year long war between Byzantium and Ctesiphon (603–628) that began with the Persians overrunning Syria and ended with the Greek invasion of Iraq and defeat of Khosro II, assisted by a military alliance with the Turkic Khaganate. Heraclius won this war but lost the peace. Byzantium had become repressive, forcibly converting Jews and seeking to impose Orthodoxy on the miaphysite communities within the empire. Meanwhile the Persian equestrian aristocracy was more concerned with factional squabbles and disputed successions than with internal reform. Neither state was prepared for the pending assault from the south. When Heraclius died in 641, Byzantium had already lost Syria and Egypt. How did a small group of warrior–merchants from the Hijaz defeat the two empires on the battlefield in just a few years, extinguishing the Sasanians and expelling the Byzantines from the Levant?

Historians have cited the zealous fervour of the Arabian tribes under the banner of Islam, the supreme generalship of Khalid ibn al-Walid and their expert navigation of the desert. Sparked in part by the provocative theory of Hagarism, there has been considerable recent examination of the original sources. The historian James Howard-Johnston has pieced together the most reliable contemporary testimonies—Greek, Syriac, Armenian and Arabic—and synthesised their accounts into a revised chronology of the key events in his *Witnesses to a World Crisis*. The surviving Arabic sources include the Qur'an itself, Ibn Ishaq's *Sirat Rasul Allah* (Biography of Muhammad, c. 760), *Futuh al-Buldan* of al-Baldhuri (c. 875) and the *Annals* of al-Tabari (c. 900). Howard-Johnston argues that the Hagarist hypothesis of a rupture in transmission between the Companions of the Prophet and later historians of Islam's origins is highly unlikely. Chains of isnads (authoritative transmitters) were recorded by the earliest historians of Islam, al-Zubayr (d. 712) al-Zuhri (d. 742) and Ibn Hisham (d. 835) and transmitted into the later surviving texts.

After receiving the first Qur'anic revelation in a cave on Mount Hira, Muhammad began preaching his message. In the face of resistance from the Meccans, the Prophet fled with his followers to Yathrib (Medina) in 622. Known as the *hijra*, this event initiated the Muslim era. The Meccans fought a series of engagements against the nascent Muslim community for control of the Hijaz caravans. The 'umma resisted these assaults and negotiated the peace treaty of Hudaybiya with the Meccans in 628. The polytheistic sanctuary of the Ka'ba and its rites (Hajj) were incorporated into the new monotheist faith and the qibla (direction of prayer) was oriented towards the Ka'ba. Howard-Johnston speculates that Muhammad struck out the other gods in the sanctuary, leaving only Allah behind. This did not mean that Muhammad favoured one factional god over the others venerated at the Ka'ba. Nor is there any evidence that pre-Islamic Allah ('the god') was associated with the moon in the sanctuary as some scholars have suggested. Rather the Prophet identified the supreme god Allah who created the moon along with the rest of the cosmos.

Having won over the nomadic tribes of the Hijaz, Muhammad made a triumphal entry into Mecca in 630 and his opponents had no choice but to submit. Following the Prophet's death in 632, the Rashidun caliphs (rightly guided successors) expanded the writ of the 'umma across the Arabian Peninsula in the wars of *ridda* (apostasy) and then embarked upon the wars of *futuh* (conquest). The leaders of the 'umma harnessed the fractious energy of the Arabs that had previously been channelled into internal tribal conflict and directed it outwards. One Arab army advanced into Palestine and in early 634 defeated a Roman force at Dathin, east of Gaza. In *Seeing Islam as Others Saw It*, Robert Hoyland collates contemporary Christian sources that record how the Arab invaders killed 4,000 villagers and 'ravaged the whole region'. In his synodical letter of 634 Sophronius, the Patriarch of Jerusalem, reported that 'vengeful and God-hating Saracens ... plunder cities, devastate fields, burn down villages and set on fire the holy churches'.

On 23 August 634 the first Caliph Abu Bakr died and was succeeded by Omar ibn al-Khattab. Meanwhile Khalid ibn al-Walid made a legendary crossing of the impassable desert from Hira on the Euphrates to capture Bosra in the Hauran, and converged with the other column from Palestine. The combined Muslim forces then defeated the joint Byzantine-Ghassanid army under the command of the emperor's brother Theodore at the Battle of Yarmouk in 636. Having taken control of Syria by the end of 636, the Caliph Omar made his triumphal entry into Jerusalem in 638. The invasion of Egypt followed in 641. To the east, Muslim forces invaded Lower Mesopotamia from Hira, laying siege to Ctesiphon, and comprehensively defeated the Persian army at Qadisiyya on 6

January 638. The Arabs killed the last Sasanian Shah Yazdgerd III in Kurasan in 651. Initially granted protected (dhimmi) status, the millennium-old Zoroastrian culture of Iran subsequently became the primary casualty of the Arab wars of conquest.

When Jerusalem and Damascus fell to the Caliph Omar, there were some Byzantine commentators who saw the new religion as a form of Arianism. Some miaphysite heterodox Christians as well as the Nabateans and Arab traders of the Syrian deserts, still profiting from the ancient routes, might have seen the invaders as protectors. But when Bishop Sophronius handed over the keys of Jerusalem to the Muslim ruler riding on a white camel, there were tears in his eyes. To the vast majority of Byzantine Christians, there were no rose petals: the Islamic conquest of the Levant was a catastrophe. For centuries after, Copts and Syriacs venerated Heraclius as the final emperor of the lost world of the Christian Levant.

The assassination of the third Caliph 'Uthman in 656 precipitated the first *fitna* (civil war). The governors of Syria and Egypt (Mu'awiya and 'Amr) fought against the supporters of 'Ali, the Prophet's son in law. 'Ali was assassinated in 658, and Howard-Johnston suggests that the Battle of Karbala, at which 'Ali's son Hussein was killed, occurred in 661 (not 680 as per the conventional chronology). Mu'awiya also eliminated the radical purist sect known as the Kharijites that had earlier split from 'Ali. The seed of the conflict lay in whether supreme authority belonged to the Prophet's kin or whether the caliph should be elected by the *shura* (council) of leaders of the Quraysh tribe. Mu'awiya himself was the son of Abu Sufyan, leader of the Quraysh who directed the Meccan forces against the 'umma, and only accepted Islam when Mecca submitted to the Prophet in 630. So the fitna reflected the earlier struggle between the early and late converts, between those who emigrated with the Prophet and the majority Quraysh in Mecca.

Following their victory, the Umayyad dynasty settled down to rule the Dar al-Islam and expand its domains. It won a second civil war establishing its own succession against the principle of shura election (682–692) and continued the war against the Greeks, unsuccessfully besieging Constantinople in 717. Reflecting their origins as the opponents of Muhammad at the inception of Islam, the Umayyads were a warrior-aristocracy, less interested in ascetic purity than in enjoying the fruits of the vast empire they ruled. Politics and pleasure were their primary concerns, and they left the interpretation of Islam to the jurists. The Umayyad caliphs liked to hunt in emulation of Assyrian kings and Achaemenid shahs, and depicted living animals in their mosaics and frescos, from the Great Mosque of Damascus to the palaces of Hisham at Khirbat al-Mafjar near Jericho, Qusayr 'Amra near Amman and Qasr al-Hayr near Palmyra.

But as their non-Muslim subjects experienced it, Allah remained partial to Muslims and discriminatory against dhimmis. In effect Allah was enlisted in the service of one conquering group to extract tribute from the others. As Constantine's victory swung the argument for the Christians in the fourth century, so the rapid expansion of the Arab Empire legitimised their deity too. The Muslims inherited the same proof by demonstration of the validity of their claim that partial Allah of the Ka'aba is the supreme creator god. Reverses to Islamic power implied divine disfavour and were interpreted by such figures as the Persian Sufi theologian Ahmad al-Ghazali as a call to strict piety. As the power of the caliphate ebbed in the tenth century, the *ulema* (clergy) became more strident, leading to the waning of Islamic civilisation.

From hijra to crusade: while the historical facts of the attempts by Latin Christendom to conquer the Levant are well-worn, their interpretation has shifted over the centuries. In the light of recent history, much of the Arab world compares Israel with the Crusader states: Saddam adopted the persona of Salah ad-Din while Hafez al-Assad denounced Sadat as al-Kamil (who ceded Jerusalem to Frederick II in 1229). Yet the proximal cause of the crusades was the Seljuk invasion of Anatolia after the Battle of Manzikert in 1071, for the Abbasid Caliphate had already ceased to be a military power when the Arab House of old Islam fell under Turkish control in the 1050s. By the time Basileus Alexios Komnenos called upon

Pope Urban for assistance in 1095, the Seljuks had already advanced as far as Nicaea on the Sea of Marmara.

In *The Crusades Through Arab Eyes*, Amin Maalouf tells the story from the 'other' side. Maalouf opens his narrative in 1095 with Kilij Arslan as the master of Nicaea, but he does not discuss the Turkish incursions into Anatolia during the preceding decades. Through those 'other' eyes, it is assumed that the Seljuks had the right to conquer Christian Asia Minor, merely because they were Muslim. The Sack of Jerusalem in 1099 has been justly condemned: but the Sasanians achieved the same in 614 and the Muslim conquest of the Levant was no less violent. The contemporary tendency is to denounce past actions by modern standards. By that criterion, should not Tughrul Bey and Alp Arslan have been tending their flocks in Turanian Transoxania? Were the Seljuk leaders, for all the peace in Sufism and all their cultural achievements, not belligerent actors who displaced the indigenes of Anatolia?

Ironically, it was the Western Turkic Khaganate whose support to Heraclius was vital to the Byzantine victory over the Sasanians in 628. Why did the Turks choose Islam when the Franks and Goths converted to Christianity? Why did the Byzantines fail to convert the Turks in the seventh century? Perhaps the cultures around the 'frog pond' were more inclined to disputation and abstraction, the essential preconditions to hypothetico-deductive reasoning, later absorbed and developed by the Arabs? During the dark ages, the western barbarians settled in to defend Christendom with chain mail and stirrup, while the nomadic mounted archers of the steppe kept their simple autocracy. Or perhaps it was due to the path of their migration: would the Turks have become Zoroastrians if the Sasanians had resisted the Arabs?

Steven Runciman, in his seminal *History of the Crusades*, regarded the knights of Outremer as scions of the barbarians who invaded the west during the dark ages. One could argue that the pivotal battle was not Salah ad-Din's triumph at Hattin in 1187, but rather the Seljuk victory at Myriokephalon in 1176 which signalled the permanent Greek loss of Anatolia. The failure of Latin and Greek Christendom to unify in common cause gave the Levant to the Mamluks and Anatolia to the Seljuks. Having used the knights to recover western Asia Minor from Nicaea to Antioch, the Komnenoi could have expelled the Turks or brought them under Greek rule. Instead disunity and strategic failure led to the Latin sack of Constantinople in 1204. It was not until 2001 that Pope John Paul II issued an apology on behalf of the Latins.

Meanwhile the knights of Outremer could have lived in peaceful coexistence with the Muslims as they did for many decades in the 1100s, and as dhimmis in the Dar al-Islam had for the most part since the Muslim conquest. Saladin himself agreed with Richard the division of Jerusalem into the quarters that are preserved to this day. What really mobilised jihad against the Franks were their raids on the Hijaz itself. After the fall of Acre in 1291, Christians continued to outnumber Muslims across the Levant. Following the Ottoman conquest of Syria and Palestine in 1517, relations of mutual respect were maintained between the faiths, even if the Sublime Porte levied discriminatory taxes on her non-Muslim subjects in accordance with the original Islamic system. It was only in the nineteenth century, as other European powers extracted economic concessions from the crumbling Ottoman state, that the position of Christians in the Levant deteriorated.

In the epilogue to his account Maalouf laments that the weakness of the Arabs lay in their inability to build stable political and economic institutions. The Franks had well established feudal rights and judicial procedures: the king could not modify or annul the ruling of a court of knights. But in the Arab east, the arbitrary power of the sultan was unbounded. Maalouf refers to the chronicler Ibn Jubayr who recorded that the Muslims lived in comfort under Frankish rule with their property and dwellings unmolested. But the cultural interchange was mainly one-way: while the Franks learned Arabic, the Muslim Arabs refused to open their society to ideas from the West and remained impervious to their languages.

In the present era the crusades are regarded as the forerunner of European expansion and the division of the former Arab territories of the Ottoman Empire in 1922. Yet the rivalry in the early mediaeval period between what Peter Sarris calls 'empires of faith' in his book of the same name was much like the competition between the later European empires. After all, the original Muslim expansion was only repulsed at Tours, while for the theoretical juridical protection of dhimmis in Islam, al-Hakim destroyed Constantine's Holy Sepulchre at Jerusalem. But the ultimate failure of the knights of Outremer led to the establishment of the Order of Christ at Tomar, to the development of the Caravel and the Portuguese voyages of exploration: indeed the recycled profits of the institutions that operated the crusading venture financed the innovation schemes of Henry the Navigator. It was the very failure of the crusades that precipitated European exploration of the rest of the world beyond the Dar al-Islam, and ultimately, for good or ill, the creation of the global liberal order that sprang from it.

FRIDAY 13 JUNE | DEAD SEA
It is Friday prayers and there are no buses for Amman. But I find another traveller, a Canadian filmmaker called Robert Leger and we share a taxi to the Mövenpick Hotel on the Dead Sea. True to his name, Robert is light-hearted and jolly, and the day is spent visiting the sites along the Royal Road, accompanied by a steady stream of witty remarks. We pass Shoubak Castle, the nature reserve at Dana with its ecotourism display, and Kerak Castle, the imposing Crusader fortress that for lack of manpower surrendered to Muslim forces in 1188. Kerak was operational for barely forty years, yet the structure has a feeling of grandeur and permanence, justifying Frankish power as much by the scale and quality of its construction as by any articles of faith: an inspiration perhaps to the subsequent expansion of Europe, as thwarted Christendom regrouped and the Templars migrated from Outremer to their fortress at Tomar.

At the Mövenpick Hotel, we join Robert's friends Osama Jumean, Seti Farah, Bo and Ayman for lunch. OJ is a flamboyant architect from Madaba with an infectious energy that animates the group. Farah Daghestani is a cousin of the king, and I am abruptly in the company of wealthy and extremely kind Jordanians. Farah talks about her work in development, and we sit like princes looking over the Dead Sea, dipping into the salty water to salve the cracks in our skins. 'It's all about the mind,' says Farah. 'Why do the Bedouin throw their rubbish away, an act we see as polluting the environment? It is because for them, the desert is infinite and the waste will be carried away by the wind. The challenge of development is to change that mind, to adapt it to the mentality of a stable self-sustaining system.' After showering on the beach as the sun sinks, we are entertained by a Russian belly dancer with Amstel beer and nargileh.

We drive into Amman and Farah kindly puts me up at the Bristol Hotel. As I absorb the comfort of this unexpected luxury, I reflect on the Arab tradition of hospitality to strangers, borne of the fragile, arid environment—out of which one may never know quite who the stranger is or when the reciprocal will be vital. To my astonishment, and as I am about to settle in for the night, Farah returns with her friends and the party hauls me off to Madaba for a raucous late dinner at OJ's cousin's place, Haret Jdoudna.

SATURDAY 14 JUNE | JERASH
I use the opportunity of the Bristol's fast internet connection to clear my backlog of emails. In most of the local points the speed is so dire it takes minutes to open a single window. Pyrrha is complaining that I have failed to send any postcards. My grandfather is recovering from an illness and explains that he is worried about the world moving into deflation. England seems very distant. Ayman arrives at the Bristol and drives me to the Fig Tree restaurant, which has the flavour of Knightsbridge-upon-Wadi: charming, but whose prices reflect the steep divide in these societies between the elites and the rest. The others arrive and we set off in two cars for an 'official' visit to Jerash (Roman Gerasa) with Seti Farah.

Gerasa lies in biblical Gilead and is famed for its extensive colonnades. Like the other cities of the Decapolis, its peak of splendour came in the extended economic boom of the Antonine Age. After the Roman conquest, Gerasa retained its

Hellenistic character and was especially devoted to the worship of Artemis. The modern entrance through the south gate bypasses the triumphal Arch of Hadrian and leads directly into the unusual oval shaped forum. The ruins are grand, with fine Corinthian capitals that reflect the prosperity of the region during the second century. Gerasa gives the impression of civic pride one sees at Leptis, although without the maritime position. There is a boisterous atmosphere as we tramp along the cardo past the tetrapylons to the nymphaeum and baths and Temple of Artemis.

From Jerash we proceed north in the little convoy to Salah ad-Din's Ajloun Castle, built on a hill above the Jordan Valley and with views over the West Bank. During the crusades Ajloun functioned primarily as a lookout post and never saw military action. But in 1917 the castle was used by Ottoman forces under Kemal in retreat from the British advance into Palestine. It seems strange to look over the Holy Land and not go up to Jerusalem. More incongruous is the mental dissonance of clambering about the battlements of a Crusader castle at the pleasure of the Jordanians, while fifty kilometres away the Palestinian town of Nablus lies at the centre of the violence engulfing the Occupied Territories.

The party returns to Amman and I bid farewell to Robert. After decamping to the more modest Carlton, I proceed to Book@café, owned by Farah's friend Midian, and read articles in the Arab press about the stalled Israeli-Palestinian peace process. America is a biased mediator, argues the editor of *al-Ahram*, and colludes with Israel in making Arafat seem unwilling to compromise. By refusing to cede control of East Jerusalem, Arafat is asking for what United Nations Resolutions accept, having already *de facto* ceded the territory between the 1947 proposed partition and the 1949 green lines. The so-called 'road map' details milestones in the creation of a Palestinian state by 2005 but does not mention the Israeli 'security fence', a wall arguably designed to cram the new state into fifty-per-cent of today's West Bank. The barrier will coil around four major Israeli settlement blocks and will swallow up areas of Palestinian municipal land.

The Knesset backed Ariel Sharon's decision to dismantle some Jewish outposts. But no peace is possible until Israel agrees to remove most of the settlements: either the 240,000 settlers should return to Israel or they must remain under Palestinian sovereignty. The Oslo Accords outlined a framework to achieve a permanent settlement but each side knows that the other is unwilling to make the necessary concessions. Officially Sharon's so-called 'fence' is intended to keep Palestinian terrorists out of Israel but its real purpose is to maintain Israeli control, while settlements and the barrier create new borders that make a viable Palestinian state impossible. The 145 Israeli settlements in the West Bank are islands in a Palestinian sea but Sharon's Wall will instead make Palestinian towns and villages islands in an Israeli sea.

Katharine Scarfe Beckett arrives with her Palestinian-Ammani boyfriend Yakoub. Katherine is working for the former Crown Prince Hassan bin Talal, promoting the role of interfaith organisations in advocacy and aid: through dialogue they are seeking to improve the conditions and mutual understanding of all communities in the region. Katharine talks about Tarif Khalidi's *Sayings of the Muslim Jesus* but not everyone responds favourably to the idea of ignoring religious differences and focussing on the common elements of humanism and compassion. For those who do, interfaith aid is not so much anti-terrorism as the complete opposite of terrorism. Yakoub is more interested in theories of Islamic social Darwinism and we continue talking about the local music scene over dinner at the Nai Club.

Maimonides and Israel
At the time of the Jubilee in the summer of 2000 an Israeli worshipper spoke to me by the Western Wall in Jerusalem. 'Are you Jewish?' he asked. 'Many mixed Europeans have some Jewish ancestry,' I replied, 'but that does not make them Jewish under Mosaic Law.' 'Forget Halakhah,' the man said, 'live in Israel and find a Jewish bride: you will love it here. Judaism: the first and still the best!' However flattering the invitation to join a society with so many distinguished members, it would feel

false to adopt such membership. Unless the customs and traditions of the community are acculturated early on into the wallpaper of the subconscious, one would always feel an imposter. The Hebrew scriptures may be beautiful but one cannot change one's essence. If one is not born metaphysically into the partiality of the community of Israel, one cannot believe that her partial deity Yahweh is the universal, transcendent creator. Therein lay the seed of the repression of the Jewish people and its evil flowering into jealousy, pogrom and Shoah.

The Tanakh (Hebrew Bible) consists of the Torah (law), Nevi'im (prophets) and Ketuvim (historical writings). Scholars conventionally accept that having formed over centuries of oral tradition, the Torah was written in its present form during the exile which followed the Babylonian conquest of Jerusalem (587 BC). The books of the Nevi'im and Ketuvim were probably completed by the time of the Maccabean revolt against Seleucid rule (167–160 BC). The Torah tells that the land of milk and honey is promised to Israel if the people follow the Law but the rest of the Tanakh is the story of Israel's failure to keep its side of the bargain. The books of *Samuel*, *Kings* and *Chronicles* describe the relationships between one after another corrupt ruler and exasperated prophet. But what is distinctive about Judaism is the continuity of the Hebrew texts and the refusal of Israel to compromise with the demands of pagan rulers, whether Seleucid or Roman, and which led ultimately to the Hadrianic diaspora. Judaism is not the first, for the relationship of a people with its god descends from the Sumerians, if not earlier, but the Israelites claimed that they were the first people to worship a single creator god and that their god spoke to Abraham and the prophets.

The Tanakh is saturated with geography: there are as many place names in these books as there are protagonists. The Jewish people are connected through these texts to that land, but anything specifically Israelitic that pre-dates the sixth century BC is speculation. Contemporary Israeli archaeologists such as Finkelstein suggest that, at its maximum extent, the Davidic state that emerged after the collapse of the late Bronze Age would have been weak and ruled a mixed population of

Canaanites and Israelites. Since the time of the Hadrianic dispersion, Jews retained their link to the Holy Land. While Ashkenazi descent from mediaeval Khazars remains a speculative hypothesis, the Semitic kinship of Arabs and Hebrews across the Mediterranean world is beyond doubt. The irony is that while the Romans periodically excluded Jews from Zion, Muhammad explicitly linked them to the Promised Land. According to the Qur'an, the Holy Land is promised to all the posterity of Abraham, including the Children of Israel.

Moses ben Maimon (known as Maimonides or the Rambam) is widely acknowledged within rabbinical Judaism as the pre-eminent sage of the mediaeval period. Born in 1138 and raised in multi-national Almoravid Cordoba, the Rambam became an exile when the austere neo-Kharijite Almohad dynasty swept to power and forcibly converted or expelled Jews and Christians from their domains in 1159. He then became the head of the Jewish community in Cairo, died in 1204 and was buried at Tiberias, where his tomb remains. The Rambam's primary work, *The Guide of the Perplexed*, written in Arabic, interpreted Jewish scripture within the framework of Aristotelian philosophy. Hence the Rambam provided a rationalist exegesis of the Torah that had parallels with the apophatic theology of the mediaeval Christian mystics and inspired later generations of Jewish philosophers, above all Spinoza. Maimonides identified the faculty of reason or intellect as the constitutive quality of our divine likeness by which man is made in the image of God. Belief does not mean a formula of faith, but the ideas one has in one's mind and the evidence that reality corresponds to those ideas. Maimonides interpreted the purpose of divine law as the quest to attain the highest possible state of perfection; this includes the perfection of ethical virtues, which refer to relations between persons and whose perfection is a prerequisite for the benefit of society as a whole. The writings of Maimonides form part of a universal tradition advocating for individual freedom, rational ethical conduct and mutual respect between groups.

What would Maimonides have thought about the Arab-Israeli conflict? The facts of this long struggle are well-worn.

By 1914 the Ottoman Empire had lost almost all its territory in Europe and there were movements calling for self-determination across the Arab provinces. During the First World War, and as documented in the McMahon-Hussein correspondence, Britain promised Sharif Hussein of Mecca that independent Arab states would be established in these provinces in return for his support in the Great Arab Revolt against Ottoman rule. But in May 1916 Britain also signed the Sazonov-Sykes-Picot agreement in St Petersburg, dividing up control over the residual Ottoman Empire between the Allied Powers.

On 2 November 1917, as British forces were pushing back the Ottomans across multiple fronts, Britain issued the Balfour Declaration, calling for the 'establishment in Palestine of a national home for the Jewish people ... it being clearly understood that nothing shall be done which may prejudice the civil and religious rights of existing non-Jewish communities in Palestine'. At the San Remo conference of the Allied Supreme Council in April 1920, Britain and France divided the former Arab provinces of the Ottoman Empire between them. Two months later, colonial administration of these territories was formalised in the granting of 'mandates' by the nascent League of Nations. With the blessing of Great Britain, Zionist leaders in Europe and America encouraged Jewish migration to Mandatory Palestine but this came to be opposed by the majority of Palestinian Arabs, leading to intercommunal conflict and culminating in the Arab revolt of 1936–1939. Having suppressed the revolt, Britain then sought to limit Jewish migration to Palestine.

The industrialised killing of six million Jews during the Second World War changed the impetus of Zionism. British administrators in Palestine found themselves the target of an insurgency led by Jewish paramilitary groups. The Holocaust perpetrated by Nazi Germany as well as American support for the creation of Israel led to the 1947 United Nations partition, passed as General Assembly Resolution 181. This granted Jews the right to self-determination in the coastal strip, Galilee and Negev, with Jerusalem under international administration. The partition was intended to avoid displacement of any indigenes but the plan was rejected by Arab leaders who implacably opposed the creation of a Jewish State in the region. In the war that followed the British evacuation and Israeli Declaration of Independence on 14 May 1948, 700,000 Arabs were forced to flee from the land that became the territory of Israel, bounded by the 1949 Armistice Green Line. In parallel, between 1948 and 1953, more than 350,000 Mizrahi Jews were forced to leave the surrounding countries. Over the succeeding decades, at least another 500,000 Jews were expelled or chose to emigrate from countries across the Arab world and Iran, where their communities had been established for millennia.

During the Six-Day War in June 1967, Israel captured Gaza, Sinai, the West Bank and Golan Heights. Following another war in 1973, the invasion of Lebanon in 1982 and the First Intifada of 1987–1993, the Israeli Prime Minister Yitzhak Rabin and PLO Chairman Yasser Arafat signed the Oslo Accords and shook hands on the White House lawn on 13 September 1993. The Arab side accepted Israel's existence contingent on withdrawal from the Occupied Territories, which formula had worked for Egypt at Camp David in 1978, but an American-Israeli religious extremist killed twenty-nine Arabs at Hebron and on 4 November 1995 Rabin himself was assassinated. In his final Knesset speech, Rabin noted: '... we did not return to an empty land. There were Palestinians here who struggled against us for a hundred ... bloody years ... . Today, after innumerable wars, we rule more than two million Palestinians through the IDF and run their lives by a Civil Administration. This is not a peaceful solution. We would like this [Palestinian entity] to be less than a state ... . The borders of Israel will be beyond the lines which existed before the Six-Day War. We will not return to the 4 June 1967 lines.'

Tragically, and despite the extraordinary efforts of President Clinton in 2000–2001 to close the gap between the negotiating positions, based on the principle of each side seeking to understand the needs and aspiration of the other side, the Oslo Accords ended without an agreement. Countless accounts have been published analysing the failure of the process but it is widely understood that the most significant obstacles to a final peace deal were the Palestinian refusal to give up the 'right of return' and the Israeli demand to retain settlement blocs in East Jerusalem. In consequence, the Palestinian side returned to violence against Israeli civilians, dispatching suicide bombers into buses and crowded streets, while the new Israeli government under Ariel Sharon sought to apply a *cordon sanitaire* around the West Bank. According to B'Tselem, 3,650 Palestinians and 1,142 Israelis were killed between December 1987 and May 2003.

The building of the Wall stopped the killing but also created a honeycomb of detached Palestinian ghettos in the West Bank, while a new road network integrated new Jewish settlements, called 'development towns', with Israel proper. The International Court of Justice ruled in 2004 that the establishment of those settlements had been in breach of international law: 'After considering certain fears expressed to it that the route of the wall would prejudge the future frontier between Israel and Palestine, the Court observed that the construction of the wall and its associated regime created a *fait accompli* on the ground that could well become permanent, and hence tantamount to a *de facto* annexation.' Since 2004 there has been a steady expansion of Israeli settlements across the West Bank.

What happens now? For nothing is inexorable: each evolving state of the system is freely chosen by the agents with power in that system. Nationalism defines individual identity by reference to a group. There is nothing inherently wrong with national identity, except in so far as some individuals do not wish to be defined by one. What matters is the respect between entities: the golden rule (behave towards others as you would wish them to behave towards you) applies as much to groups as to individuals. The root of the evil is the domination of one group by another, whether Muslim over dhimmi, Latin over Greek, Christian over Jew, 'Aryan' over 'Semite', Arab over Israeli, or Israeli over Palestinian. In a bi-national or federated state, the Jewish character of Israel could be safeguarded through cantonal boundaries and the constitutional mechanism. Davidic Israel was effectively bi-national, and likewise the Cordoba of Maimonides and Averroes.

Israel faces a structural trilemma: negotiate a permanent 'two-state' settlement as envisaged by Oslo with borders close to the 1949 Green Line and shared sovereignty over Jerusalem; or grant Israeli citizenship to the Arab populations conquered in 1967 and undermine the Jewish demographic majority of Israel; or maintain the occupation over the West Bank with the associated continued Palestinian suffering and concomitant threat to Israel's security. Following a series of meetings with the Palestinian Authority leadership between 2006 and 2008, Israeli Prime Minister Ehud Olmert proposed a revised comprehensive plan for peace on 16 September 2008. However, as with the Clinton Parameters in 2001, this offer was rejected by the Palestinian leadership, and since 2008, negotiations to find a permanent resolution have effectively been suspended. Nothing can compensate European Jewry for the Shoah. But Israel will only find itself secure and truly become a 'light unto the nations' when all sides to the conflict recognise the legitimacy of the other sides' aspirations and are therefore able to make sufficient concessions to reach a permanent negotiated settlement.

Sunday 15 June | Madaba

Somewhat fragile from the revelries of the previous evenings, I catch a service taxi back to Madaba. The town is pretty with its limestone houses and open hills, the cousin of Ramallah on the other side of the Jordan. After regulation chicken shawarma on the main square, I find the Greek Orthodox Church of St George with its sixth-century mosaic map on the floor of the apse. Madaba retains a substantial Christian population and preserves the character of what Palestine would have been like before all the trouble began. 1917 was the watershed moment when British forces captured Jerusalem. Yet the Shi'a Druze massacred Christians across the region in 1860, so when did the trouble really begin? The Jumean family restaurant Haret Jdoudna has a stone courtyard with jasmine trees and sparrows—a studied tranquillity that captures the essence of the old Levant. I sip mint tea with my notebook and take a cab to Mount Nebo.

According to the Torah, Mount Nebo is where Moses gazed over the land of milk and honey, and like the high place at Petra, this rocky protuberance has a special quality in the evening light. Was it the collapse of late Bronze Age civilisation that created the movement of peoples that led to the Israelites coming into the mixed land of Canaan? Always the same echoes of history. This land is captivating, and its people have so much shared history and common culture: from the frog pond to the rift valley the same logos has illuminated them. Yet now it seems that the Promised Land flows only with greed and folly.

In Amman I meet Seti Farah for dinner at the Hyatt with her friend Winkie who works at the Jordanian Hashemite Fund. Winkie has been reading the UN Arab Human Development Report and explains that 'higher living standards in the region can only come about from a normalisation to the Western economic model, with greater openness to international trade and investment.' 'Will that not lead to the homogenising of Arab culture into the bland internationalism one sees everywhere?' I reply. 'Is it not possible for Syria to preserve its indigenous skills and domestic goods against the weight of the global machine?' 'You want to come with your clever theories,' Winkie ripostes, 'but competition is the natural order of things and expansionary capitalism is the only viable option.' 'Is that not social Darwinism?' I argue. 'Is the justification through nature not merely a convenient foil for international corporations to gain market share and eliminate the so-called 'uncompetitive' but distinctive and diverse local industries? Do you really want to live in a monolithic world of global widgets dominated by the lowest cost producer?'

Farah thinks that development is mostly futile and refers more to the development industry than to any real process of political economic change. To first worlders, whose basic needs are well supplied, progress means escaping quiet desperation and having a more stimulating life than commuting to a dull office. For the elite of the third world, development is about aspiring to a first-world lifestyle, while pretending that they are working for the greater good or for the benefit of the poor. So the result is the circus of intergovernmental conferences and bureaucratic processes, interspersed with the occasional effective charity. With a few exceptions, nothing much changes: the world creaks on and utopia recedes.

I suggest that once the basic amenities of life are taken care of most rational people would prefer private indulgence to working twelve hours each day. Yet our economies are trapped in the paradox than unless they keep expanding with continuous innovation and the generation of new goods and services, we will collapse into a depression or return to being hunter-gatherers. The question is not how big the cake is or how it should be divided up, but rather what kind of cake it is. That is why culture builds up slowly over many generations: if development for a poor country means fitting in to the global economic machine, this is tantamount to the alienation of an entire country, just as being an expendable resource in the labour market is alienating for the individual. Above all development should be about using what is locally available to supply the basics: attempting to compete in global markets to generate hard currency to buy these basics will for the most part be doomed.

Marxians argue that poor countries cannot develop without replacing their traditional structures with large scale capitalist enterprise, leading ultimately to state capitalism and the triumph of the proletariat. Like Mill, Marx himself saw the British Empire as having the beneficial consequence of spreading capitalism around the world. Development thinking remains influenced by Marxism and we live in a world of competing ideologies. Washington consensus neo-liberals advocate global free markets while Marxians want primitive accumulation and the developmental state. Both groups disparage cultural diversity and place little value on the environment. 'We need new paradigms,' says Farah, and we talk until late in the warm night air, moving from economic theory to the historical legacy that burdens this region, once the heart of the prosperous Arab and Ottoman Empires, now reduced to Balkanised statelets.

A Common Word
When the Emperor Manuel II Palaiologos travelled to the West in 1399, he brought icons, relics and books as gifts, and spoke about theology. A 1330s parchment copy of Dionysius the Areopagite was given to the Abbey of Saint-Denis as a reminder of the common root of Latin and Greek Christendom. On 12 September 2006 Pope Benedict XVI delivered a lecture at Regensburg on science and faith, and quoted from Manuel's dialogue with a Persian scholar: 'Whoever would lead someone to faith needs ... to reason properly without violence and threats. To convince a reasonable soul, one does not need a strong arm or weapons of any kind ... .' Benedict continued: 'Not to act in accordance with reason is contrary to God's nature. For the emperor, as a Byzantine shaped by Greek philosophy, this statement is self-evident. But in Muslim teaching, God is absolutely transcendent. His will is not bound up with any of our categories, even that of rationality. For logos means both reason and word, a reason which is creative and capable of self-communication, precisely as reason ... hence not to act with logos is contrary to God's nature.'

The Pope's remarks sparked condemnation across the Muslim world and led to the publication by the Jordanian al-Bayt Institute of an open letter to Christian leaders. A Common Word was signed by 138 Islamic scholars and stated: 'the basis for peace and understanding ... is part of the foundational principles of both faiths: love of the one God and love of the neighbour.' Alas, both lecture and letter were more political than scholarly for the Pope overlooked the tradition of rationalism within Islamic thought and the scholars merely cited the Decalogue and wasted the opportunity to rebut the Pope's argument. Since inception, tension between arbitrary beliefs versus critical rational enquiry has characterised each religion. As Islam has experienced anti-rationalist movements, from the seventh-century Kharijites to the eighteenth-century Wahhabis, so Christendom has seen an arc of intolerance from the incineration of the Serapeum in 391 to the immolation of Giordano Bruno in 1600. The real task of 'civilisational reconciliation' is to find the common root that leads to universal humanism.

Each Abrahamic faith contains particular, arbitrary doctrines. The Jews have to explain why the creator of the cosmos favours them. The Muslims must explain why Jibril dictated the rules for a utopian society to their prophet in their language. The Christians have to explain why the Word became flesh in those particular circumstances. All revealed religions suffer from the same difficulty. So to achieve reconciliation, each must say, 'We acknowledge the flaw in ourselves and seek the good in the other.' Otherwise there can be no mutual respect and compatibility of coexistence. But there is also a common source in the extra-Abrahamic faiths going back into the ancient world, from the Semitic-Akkadian to the Ptahitic, Hellenic, Zoroastrian and Hindu. Atheistic materialism is logically incoherent, as demonstrated by the riddle of mathematical fit: mind, matter and number are inextricably interwoven. But science owes its debt to all these cultural origins. So the militant atheists should be humble like the ancients and also admit the deficit in themselves. The common source is the impress the cosmos makes upon the rational enquiring mind.

Muslims argue that their religion is more rational than its precursors, that they make no claim on the believer beyond the acceptance of Muhammad as the messenger of Allah. Yet Islam claims that the Qur'an was given to Muhammad by Jibril as the final revelation and it therefore contains the same particularity as any other revealed religion. Claims to Qur'anic metaphysical primacy are as arbitrary as the Christian claim or the Jewish claim that partial Yahweh is the supreme god. But if one is striving for universal humanism, one cannot imagine that the supreme creator could be partial: no tribe can have metaphysical priority. So the path to mutual respect between faiths lies in the acceptance of the absurdity of all claims to partiality. The true 'common word' is the transcultural humanism that each faith sees glimpses of.

In early Islam the options were clear, and purportedly Muhammad wrote them in a letter to the Emperor Heraclius: convert, pay the jizya or die. That means to accept that Muhammad had privileged metaphysical status as the conduit of revelation, and that of all the gods, this one, Allah, is the supreme one. While the historical record does not suggest that the caliphs engaged in any systematic persecutions of dhimmis in the early centuries of Islam—the rules were simple and they were consistently applied—there were Christians and mixed children and others born Muslim who were killed by the caliphate because they apostatised or blasphemed. For some mushrikun (polytheists), the option of jizya was not available: witness the 2014 genocide of Yazidis at Sinjar by the Islamic State group, which reprised earlier massacres from the 1840s.

'Allah the most Compassionate, the most Merciful.' Islamic theology resembles an Arabised Arianism, carrying traces of Platonic abstraction and apophatic Christian theology, blended with Judaic ethics and pre-Islamic traditions of the Hijaz. Islam's declaration that Jesus was a prophet, not divine, dissolved doctrinal problems of the trinity, Christology and miracles. Within Islam, different traditions emerged following the schism between Sunni and Shi'a, just as with the Christians. Protestants and Sunnis eschew saints, while Latins adore Mary and Maghrebis venerate the *zawiyas* (tombs) of *marabouts* (holy men). Likewise, radical movements in Islam have recurred, just as Christianity had iconoclasts and puritans, while Orthodox hesychasm and Sufism share common traditions of interior experience, especially in Anatolia.

The paradox of Islamic civilisation is that a dogmatic element always existed alongside the humane elements that produced the architecture, poetry, music and scientific achievements of the Islamic world. Moreover, much of the culture we admire from the fecund periods of Islamic history came from the syncretic zones: the regions that fell under Islamic rule but which were already fertile societies before the Muslims arrived. The prosperity of Harun al-Rachid's Baghdad, the gentleness of the Sufis and the triumphs of Arab science all had their roots in what preceded Islam. There have always been divergent expressions of thought within Islam but according to the radicals these syncretisms were heretical and the strict sunnah of the Companions of the Prophet was always the only true interpretation of Islam.

During the Islamic golden age, the Mu'tazilites interpreted the Qur'an as placing reason at the forefront of human nature and argued that rational enquiry guides mankind towards knowledge of Allah. Mu'tazilites defended free action over deterministic fatalism and conceptualised Allah as an abstract impersonal being. In echo of the Christian debates over Platonism and the divinity of souls, they argued that the Qur'an is created not pre-existing: written by an inspired man, one might say. So one could interpret Islamic revelation as the illumination of logos. But there can be no final revelation, only the asymptotic approximation to a limit as divine wisdom continues to reveal itself.

During the crusades some mutual respect emerged between the two faiths: Richard cultivated a friendship with Saladin's brother Saphradin, while Frederick II charmed his Muslim interlocutors into ceding the Christian holy places back to the Kingdom of Jerusalem forty years after they had been captured by Saladin. As the inheritors of Byzantium, the Ottomans absorbed the Christian populations of the Levant into their expanding domains and granted them legal autonomy. In the sixteenth and seventeenth centuries, the Sublime Porte was a relative beacon of tolerance compared to the religious conflicts that shattered Western Europe. In the last two centuries, however, the contraction and collapse of the Ottoman Empire, as well as the legacy of European colonial expansion, poisoned that spirit of amity between the mind worlds.

The crusades are now seen through the prism of European imperialism. But what was the expansion of the Rashidun Caliphate if not imperialist? Before the Islamic conquest, the Levant was a focal part of the Christian world of late anquitity that later became Byzantium and the Holy Roman Empire. It could be argued that, in parallel with the Iberian Reconquista, the Crusaders were legitimately seeking to recover the former Eastern Roman Provinces that had been lost in the seventh century. The interpretation of history must be consistent in the application of contemporary norms to the past. One can analyse different historical episodes in the context of the events in question. But one must also judge the actions of historical individuals to an absolute standard.

Together with his friend and fellow writer Mouloud Feraoun, Albert Camus advocated for peaceful coexistence and equal rights between settlers and indigenes in Algeria. Since the Second World War the flow of people has been in both directions and the Camusian imperative applies to almost every society. Integrating immigrant populations in the former imperial power states requires both acceptance by 'indigenes' (descendants of the former colonisers) and respect for a common universal system of institutions and values by 'settlers' (migrants from former colonised states). For there can be no 'other': we are all individuals. Oppression can be conducted by one person over another in the same room—or by a maniac armed with tanks and planes alleging that he is protecting freedom. The kernels of the faiths are what matter as the common source of a transcultural humanism. If all these gods —Marduk, Baal, Yahweh, Ahura Mazda, Christ and Allah—are names for the same principle of logos, then symmetry projects the golden rule of universal humanism to all groups and from one group to another.

Damascus

MONDAY 16 JUNE | RAMTHA

Seti Farah had suggested I should visit Darat al-Funun in the Khalid Shoman Foundation, a home for Arab artists. With its high ceilings and cool stone floor, the Foundation's elegant library has a focussed quality conducive to writing. T.E. Lawrence stayed here after the First World War and must have found inspiration in this space. There is a wide selection of works and I pick out Kenneth Clark's *Civilisation*.

Clark is concerned with Western art history and discusses confidence, stability and momentum as the generative elements of civilisation. Yet it was contact with Byzantium and the Saracens that led to the cultural acceleration of Europe, and the Greater Levant is the source of more than the Gothic arch. Ancient Iraq invented our system of weeks and months, place value representation of numbers, musical scales and astronomy; animal husbandry, crop selection and irrigation; money, financial markets and above all, the foundation for everything else, writing. The Semitic cultures of the Tigris and Euphrates continued unbroken through successive empires until the Mongol destruction of Baghdad in 1258. The concept of the 'West' was first defined by Herodotus as the domain of the free Greeks resisting the oriental despotism of the Achaemenid Empire. But Iraq had been free for millennia before Cyrus the Great and was the earliest source of the cultural elements that laid the foundations for what became Western civilisation.

Yet with its continuous rushing to no end, its intensifying competitive struggle and ever more arcane 'innovations' that add little to human happiness, our present dominant culture squeezes out the mental space required to focus. In this library there are no distractions and I am reluctant to leave its shaded garden. But I must continue my journey to the physical intensity of the Arab transport infrastructure, which is efficient in its way, but always requires a minor ruckus of some kind. At the service taxi terminal, my visa is checked, and I put my rucksack and canvas bag into the boot of the 1970s Mercedes. The taxi fills up quickly but the journey feels slow. It is a short distance to the Ramtha border crossing where there is a queue at the frontier.

My only interlocutor is an energetic Palestinian-American called Alex who sits behind me and insists on educating me about the state of the Arab world. 'Westerners think Islam is about repression and veiled women,' he tells me. 'But true Islam is beautiful—the best system of government ever created. All the theories of science are already present in Islam because the Qur'an is given to us directly by Allah. The problem is that Arab leaders are corrupt: it is the same from Morocco to Iraq. Nothing but hypocrisy and corruption,' he continues. 'That is why we need an Islamic revolution.' My visa is stamped at the border post, and we change taxis from the sleek cream Mercedes to a dilapidated mustard yellow Toyota. As the taxi picks up speed, the wind through the window drowns him out. From my seat in the front, I gaze at the landscape in the breeze as we cross the Yarmouk River not far from the battle site of 636, before passing through Daraa and the Hauran towards Damascus.

Compared to the airy city of Amman, whose low-rise modern buildings fit seamlessly with the older Arabic houses on its limestone hills, Damascus at first glance feels heavy, polluted and chaotic. The louage stops by the busy open area in front of the Hamidiye Souq at the entrance to the old city. I walk through Marja Square towards Souq Sarouja. Baysa Street, the heart of the quarter, has the lively bustle of to-ing and fro-ing, with vines tumbling down over shopfronts and birds chirping away in their cages.

Two Ottoman courtyard townhouses on the street have been converted into hotels. Better quality of the two, al-Haramain has mother of pearl inlaid sofas and courtyard fountain but is full. So I take a room at al-Rabie for 400 Syrian pounds (eight dollars) per night including breakfast. For the next few weeks this charming place will be home. Ahmed the energetic major-domo gives me the only available single room, through the courtyard and up the stairs with a window looking over the modern city centre. Exhausted from the heat, I fall asleep. In the evening I retrace my steps to the Hamidiye Souq. Continuing down Straight Street I find the charming courtyard restaurant of Zeitoun, with a wall fountain and marble tiles on the floor. Nargileh, French onion soup and Barada beer will become the triple leitmotif of these days in the oldest of cities.

TUESDAY 17 JUNE | SOUQ SAROUJA
Unlike the standard anodyne business hotels, al-Rabie is a honey pot for travellers and the courtyard is convivial like a university refectory. Tables are spread under the vaulted *liwan* and around a fountain shaded by trees. The common shower and wash tap lie in one corner while staircases lead to the upper rooms. Guests queue with their towels for the shower and breakfast lends itself to befriending them.

Much of Souq Sarouja has striped pale limestone and dark grey stones similar to the motifs in Genoa. Sadly the cluster around Baysa Street is all that remains from the original mediaeval district. But the residue that has not been bulldozed since the 1950s provides convenient local services. The laundry takes my pile of dirty clothes while the tailor next door applies his sewing machine to my split canvas bag and green linen shirt which is in an advanced state of disrepair. Hani's Zoni Internet operates in a restored building with good connection speed and cool air conditioning. Upon opening the webmail I discover that my emails with their log of this journey have vanished from the server; thankfully they are later recovered.

At the other end of the street, barber's shops groom their clientele with open razors before carved wood framed mirrors. Beside the shawarma stand on the corner with Marja Square I find a juice bar selling litre portions of freshly blended iced raspberry for the equivalent of one dollar. Juice sellers pace the streets in red velvet robes and market gardeners from the countryside sell fruit in large sheets on the ground. Nearby a brass plaque advertises the services of a private neurosurgeon. Marja Square itself is full of cranes and incomplete construction projects, illustrating the malaise of unbridled real estate development. A statue of Youssef al-Azmah, the war minister killed at the Battle of Maysalun in July 1920, stands in front of the Yalbogha Mosque beside an exposed section of the Barada River. The rest of the watercourse has been paved over to make way for the enormous flyover of al-Thawra Street that comes down to the citadel.

Marja (martyrs) Square honours sixteen Syrian and Lebanese public figures who were executed by the Sublime Porte in 1915. It was these high-handed actions of the Young Turk Pashas in Constantinople that fuelled grassroots support for the Arab Revolt. The Society of Young Arabs (Jamiat al-Fatat al-Arabiya) was founded in 1911 and together with a group of Arab Ottoman army officers agitated towards the independence of the Arab provinces. The Arab Revolt was finally launched by Sharif Hussein of Mecca on 10 June 1916. British Commonwealth and Arab Legion forces entered Damascus on 1 October 1918. Promises were made in accordance with the earlier McMahon-Hussein correspondence and on 7 March 1920 the Syrian National Congress proclaimed Emir Faisal King of the Arab Kingdom of Syria. In response the Allied Supreme Council convened the San Remo conference. Arab resistance was crushed by General Gouraud at Maysalun and French forces annexed what became the Mandate for Syria and the Lebanon.

After the Second World War, Syria was the first subject colony of a European empire to gain independence. Free French and British troops liberated Syria from Vichy France in June 1941. But on 17 May 1945 French forces occupied Beirut seeking to restore French administration and on 29 May they shelled the Syrian parliament in Damascus. The British Government issued an ultimatum to France and the last French troops were withdrawn in April 1946. President Shukri al-Quwatli presided over the transition to independence but the new state was unstable and subject to interference by the Cold War superpowers. On 30 March 1949 al-Quwatli was removed in an American-backed coup that became the first of a series.

Following the collapse of the Nasr-dominated United Arab Republic in 1961, the Ba'ath party seized power on 8 March 1963 with Salah Jadid as president and Hafez al-Assad as minister of defence. Assad pushed out Jadid in the 'correctionist movement' of November 1970 and took complete control of the country.

From Marja I walk the length of the bustling Hamidiye Souq and enter the portals of the Umayyad Mosque, emblem of Damascus and legacy of the city's zenith as seat of the Umayyad Caliphate. The Great Mosque was erected between 708 and 715 by Caliph al-Walid I, following the work of his father Abd al-Malik who constructed the Qubbat al-Sakhra (Dome of the Rock) in Jerusalem. The structure was adapted from the basilica of John the Baptist that itself had been built over temples to Roman Jupiter and Amorite Hadad. Walid rotated the axis to enable worshippers to pray south towards Mecca, and opened the north side of the prayer hall to the courtyard. The three bays with double arcade create a sense of expanded space in the forest of columns, interrupted only by the tomb of John the Baptist. The courtyard is famous for its colourful mosaics. Assembled by Byzantine craftsmen in the prevailing style, with gold and piercing green and red, the Barada panel in particular is said to depict the oasis of Damascus as paradise.

I return to Sarouja and read in the courtyard of al-Rabie. William Dalrymple's *From the Holy Mountain* retraces the journeys of two seventh-century monks, John Moschos and Bishop Sophronius, in the twilight of the Byzantine Levant. Sophronius lamented the loss of his own world, and I sense that the world I am now exploring is also vanishing. Over tea I am joined by fellow guests, a wiry smiling faced Canadian journalist called Aydin and his Italian friend Sylvia. They are in Damascus for the week to relax and I am instantly hooked on this charming duo. Later I return to Zeitoun for soup and Barada beer and a smoke. The nargileh is conducive to philosophical reflection but I feel its ill effects as I walk back along deserted Straight Street and look through my notes in the courtyard of al-Rabie Hotel.

Consumption versus craftsmanship

Since our politico-economic arrangements are a matter of free decision, not determined by nature, we should take the Epicurean path of least resistance to maximise aggregate freedom. Reason is the only tool we have to construct our social world. Considered abstractly, an economy is a system for mutual need satisfaction among a group of people. So the aim of economic progress should be to maximise aggregate freedom subject to the constraint that everyone's needs are satisfied. Given our stock of inherited accumulated capital (physical, intellectual and institutional), self-sufficiency is the zero point of the system of exchange that minimises want and increases freedom.

No one should expect someone else to earn their living for them: there is dignity in the private citizen who makes few demands on the public weal—the ideal of the skilled artisan. Techniques are the cultural accumulation of learned behaviours that flow from one generation to the next. But what about those who have become dependent through lack of learned technique? Initiative and will are futile in the absence of practical knowledge. Whether it is the mechanics of transacting business or practising a skill, young people learn by doing through apprenticeship. Being in the flow state means knowing what to do and having mastery because of it. But consider the value of the output: compare Souq Sarouja with Marja Square. One reflects incremental guided accumulation while the other is pure profit-driven dystopia. The aesthetic dimension enters as soon as one asks what is being created by these patterns of flow.

The liberal economic model seeks to maximise utility as assessed by consumption: the guiding force of all activity is end-market consumer demand. But what determines demand and how does consumption relate to freedom? It is evident that accumulation is the basis for wealth. Standard theory states that progress derives from technological innovation that increases productivity and hence the worth of a worked hour. Capital consists of the inherited stock of prior activity and the tools to generate more output. Capital accumulation represents the expansion of the worth of a worked hour: this is the normalised metric of political economy. But which innovations of the last century have advanced aggregate freedom? The automobile represents an improvement over the horse and cart. In rural areas the private automobile makes sense as a transport solution because there are too many routes to serve cost effectively with public transport. But in cities the automobile is pernicious, as the Damascus summer smog attests.

Adam Smith wrote that 'consumption is the sole end and purpose of all production.' Yet since the Renaissance theorists, there has been a parallel tradition: that happiness lies in civilisation, which is craftsmanship. Should not the aim of economic activity be to beautify the built environment and make it a garden of paradise? Art requires commerce but commerce does not guarantee art. A society needs taste and technique to channel profit into beauty. Contemporary capitalism is dissociated from aesthetics because its sole objective is the maximisation of profit to the exclusion of any other consideration. Statistical tables of economic history are standardly taken to show that the eighteenth-century Industrial Revolution represented an abrupt acceleration in the rate of economic growth, and that before this discontinuity, all the regions of the world lay on a similar growth trajectory. Yet there was divergence long before the era of spinning ginnies, steam engines and blast furnaces. The Renaissance theorists revived the classical orders and other lost techniques, while Venice was built centuries before the modern industrial economy emerged.

WEDNESDAY 18 JUNE | BEIT AZEM

I pass the morning drinking coffee in the courtyard, taking notes about heterodox economics. But Aydin is such entertaining company, a veritable Enkidu, a true Sufi, that I abandon my attempts. Aydin is writing a feature article on the Golan Heights and is planning a trip to the area. We talk about the history of the region and head for the new city to meet a contact introduced by Yasmine's aunt Amal Rassam. The Rassams are an Assyrian Chaldean family from Mosul who fled from Saddam's Iraq. One of their forbears, Hormuzd Rassam, discovered the Royal Library of Ashurbanipal at Nineveh with Austen Henry Layard in 1852. Amal suggested that I should look up her friend Atania Kharma. So Aydin and I meet Atania and her colleague Lula at their office and we stroll across the city to the Beit Jabri restaurant talking of life's loves.

On the surface Syria seems more socially liberal than Egypt or Jordan: the only women in chador are Iranian pilgrims visiting the Shi'a shrines. Atania explains that Syrian women wearing Western style clothes are just as likely to be Muslim as Christian, and that Syrian society really is a model of religious tolerance and mutual respect even if there were episodes of sectarian violence in the past. Despite being well-educated and fluent in English and French, they are respectfully conservative in their views and there is a certain awkwardness in speaking with them. Atania is in love with Yasmine's cousin and Lula is about to be married. We pass the Cham Palace Hotel which is notorious for Russian prostitutes, who stand outside the nearby ministries. The contrast between the stated views of well-to-do Syrians such as Atania and the Russian ladies in their characteristic blue jeans, white shirts and black leather jackets could not be more apparent. Damascus retains its Russian links and there are 1970s-style canteens with aluminium framed windows and leather benches that would not have been out of place in the former Soviet Union.

We amble down the Hamidiye Souq, the central promenade of the old city where Shamsis (Damascenes) buy clothes and household products. The terraced double storey shopfronts are surmounted by a corrugated iron roof whose speckled holes illuminate the long thoroughfare and protect it from the heat. From Beit Jabri we explore other sites of the old city: Salah ad-Din's tomb, Assad Pasha Khan and the Beit Azem, built in the 1750s and the former seat of the Ottoman governor of Syria. The palace has distinctive alternating limestone and basalt stones with high recessed liwan similar to the Beiteddine Palace in Lebanon. We end our impromptu tour at al-Nofara coffee shop, below the Umayyad Mosque, where storytellers have given literary recitations for centuries. Later I return to the enchanting gardens of Beit Azem and sit by the rectangular pond, enjoying the spacious esplanade and swaying pine trees.

Economic haecceity

Academic economics distinguishes the 'micro' operation of individual households and firms from the 'macro' organisation of these entities considered as a whole. But on the question of *what* is produced, which reflects the *qualitative* sources of demand and hence what is valued by society, economic theory has little to say. Like the proverbial can opener it is simply assumed that the consumer knows best and propagates demand from the end product through the supply chain. Likewise it is taken that more 'output' in general is good, without any independent evaluation of the quality of that output. Much of the global economy has become oriented to the production of the superfluous, from mobile 'app' machines to disposable goods. But time is a fixed variable: instead of playing computer games, people could learn how to decipher cuneiform tablets, play the piano or study advanced physics. For what is demanded responds to fashion and preference, expressed through marketing, which is the result of the cultural *thisness* or haecceity of particular societies.

Near the Beit Azem in Damascus there is a workshop that uses 200 year old French looms to make the highest quality damask textiles—in sharp contrast to the plastic carpets of Oriental Weavers in Cairo. In an era of mass production and capital returns based on economies of scale, the value of uniqueness has been lost. Well-marketed to an educated consumer, such high-quality traditional products would be commercially viable. Why are resources channelled into the construction of Gothic cathedrals and caravanserais in one era, Renaissance public squares and planned Baroque towns in another, and yet Brutalist housing estates and soulless shopping centres in another? When we have the best surviving examples of thousands of years of architecture to serve as the inspiration for contemporary construction, why have we abandoned the ideal of improving the quality of the built environment as a fundamental social objective?

Despite the excellence of its universities, its scientific, intellectual and artistic achievements, the prevailing culture of America is the world of freeways and sprawl based on fossil fuels and the automobile. More than anything else, the dominance of this culture is to blame for the uglification of the built environment through its having become the aspirational standard for the developing countries. For craftsmanship is not mere handicraft: it is the bedrock of civilisation that determines the quality and value of production. Tools raise up mankind. But tools without technique are blind while products without imagination are empty. It is the cultural interaction between the tool and the product that determines the value of the output. Above a basic threshold of security the nature of production is determined by culture. The division of labour to maximise return on capital without considering the value of its output is the cause of the alienation of labour.

In *The Cunning of Reason* the philosopher Martin Hollis elucidates the indeterminacy of preference within the theory of rationality. Rational choice theory assumes that utility maximising agents have complete and consistent preferences among a set of outcomes, with perfect information and limitless computing power. But the calculus of homo economicus is like a grammar without content: it performs mechanical operations on its inputs without saying anything about what grounds value. This is the deficiency of Smith's 'invisible hand': there is no guarantee that self-interest or the aggregated behaviour of profit-maximising firms can lead to the production of the beautiful or optimise aggregate freedom within the system of exchange.

A person's interests and desires are conceptually independent, so it is not only internal desires that move a person to action. Hollis rejects the Humean analysis of the internal source of desire as the motivation that guides practical reason. As soon as the Humean 'internalist' admits a desire to act rationally, which is itself an internal desire, it must also be accepted that one must have good reasons *for* one's desires. Action requires judging whether one's desires are desirable. On the basis of a Kantian 'external' reason, one can decide rationally against any given set of prior internal desires. So rationality depends on the truth about interests: the manipulation of wants in people is to exercise real power over them. Kantian ethics, the culmination of enlightenment thought, locates the source of value externally in the categorical imperative—in other words, the logos.

The moral of Aesop's fable 'The Ant and the Grasshopper' is that it is not rational within the frame of one's whole life's interests to exclusively pursue present delight. Smithian individual self-interest can lead to sub-optimal outcomes. As Hollis expresses it: 'Covenants without the sword are vain breath, but the sword without a higher principle must become hostage to vested interest.' The Achilles heel of the American Republic lay in the failure of the Founding Fathers to restrain private corporate power. Their concept of divine blessing was directly Abrahamic: more flocks, more cattle, more production in general, regardless of any independent specification of its value by reference to a higher aesthetic. For Winthrop told them that pure material abundance is the metric of their worth and hence of divine blessing upon them. Rousseau's social contract creates the persons who make it, because individuals are reciprocal to the institutions by which they live. Alas, the Pilgrim Fathers forgot to pack Vitruvius.

Marxians hold that value is determined by the quantity of labour input. But as with Smith, the Marxian labour theory of value overlooks the cultural origins of consumer demand. Worked hours sold to produce goods and services can be desired in one culture and abhorred in another. Software developers know how to manipulate symbols on a screen, but who these days knows how to dress stone or work wrought iron? Competitive markets drive excess profit to zero. To maintain margins and growth, business people must innovate. Once the market for any product has saturated and competition has driven down the price, earnings cease to grow. So companies are engaged in an endless struggle to develop new products and find customers for them. But the evaluation of the worth of those products, and hence the sources of demand for them, is culturally bound. Genuine innovations provide benefits that are useful or beautiful, while bogus ones profit from the diminution of value.

THURSDAY 19 JUNE | NATIONAL MUSEUM

Aydin has made friends with a senior official in the Ministry of Information. We take the microbus to the ministry to obtain permission from Munir Ali to visit the Syrian controlled section of the Golan Heights. Sitting in spacious leather chairs at the top of his modern office building, we discuss the Golan and Sheba'a Farms, with Munir explaining by reference to a three-dimensional map of the area. Everything is arranged for the following day. From the ministry I walk along the Barada to the National Museum whose entrance preserves the gateway of the eighth-century Umayyad palace, the Qasr al-Hayr al-Gharbi. The gardens in front contain steles and millstones and funerary monuments arranged in neat rows under the palms.

Inside the entrance is a wall map of the Fertile Crescent with a bewildering array of sites and dynasties, peoples and languages. It all began with the Sumerian cities of Eridu, Ur and Uruk in the alluvial plan that initiated the transition from subsistence farming to urban settlements. Numeracy and literacy on cuneiform clay tablets was invented in these city states sometime between 3200 and 3000 BC. Ebla and Mari, the oldest sites in Syria, emerged circa 2900 BC as satellites of Sumer. Around 2400 BC Sargon founded Akkad in central Iraq and consolidated control over Sumer. Sargonic Akkad was overrun by nomadic Gutians from the Diyala region of the Zagros until the Sumerians expelled them and revived the Third Dynasty of Ur that lasted up until the Elamite sack of Ur around 2004 BC. The isolate Sumerian language, which had coexisted with Semitic Akkadian, fell out of common use after this period.

Around 2000 BC nomadic Amorites emerged in the Khabur River area in modern north-east Syria and began to expand their territory. The Amorite Hammurabi founded Babylon in 1792 BC over the former Akkadian domains and established the earliest codified system of law. Hammurabic Babylon prospered for two centuries, during which the development of mathematics and cuneiform culture reached a new level of achievement and sophistication. Old Babylon was sacked by the Hittite King Mursilis in 1595 BC. Syria and Iraq then declined as the Anatolian Hittites and pharaonic New Kingdom became dominant. Syria was fought over by these rival powers and divided between them at the Treaty of Kadesh in 1274 BC.

Following the collapse of the late Bronze Age world circa 1186 BC, the pastoral Arameans founded a network of oasis city states across the region, making Damascus their capital around 1100 BC. They were subsequently absorbed with their language Aramaic into the resurgent Neo-Assyrian Empire whose warrior King Tiglath-Pileser III conquered Damascus in 732 BC. The Neo-Babylonian Chaldeans and Elamites sacked the Assyrian capital Nineveh in 612 BC, only to be defeated in their turn by the Persians in 539 BC. As the centuries of antiquity come closer, the clarity of dates and events becomes more firmly anchored into more familiar sources that lead from Ashurbanipal to Nebuchadnezzar, from Cyrus to Alexander. Aramaic continued to be the lingua franca of the Levant and Mesopotamia into the Roman and Byzantine periods.

The ninth-century BC Assyrian statue of Hadad, which occupies pride of place in the National Museum, carries Aramaic and Akkadian inscriptions that have been taken to date the emergence of Aramaic as the demotic descendent of the earlier Semitic root. The museum contains statues of Ishtar and other items from ancient Akkad and Sumer as well as finds from the Bronze Age site of Ugarit. Most striking of all are the Roman-period paintings of the stories of Isaac and Moses from the synagogue at Dura Europos on the Euphrates, destroyed by the Sasanians in 254. I return to al-Rabie: my room is open to the sun all day and by the evening is like an oven. But the manager explains that the hotel is full and I resign myself to more nights of dyssomnia. Sylvia rescues me and we meet Atania for supper at the Elissar courtyard restaurant.

The paradox of Zeno's gadget
The concept of value creation in economic theory derives from psychology and culture. Ask 'where have we come from?' and the standard indicators of improvement are cited: life expectancy, diet, healthcare and so on. Ask 'where are we going?' and the answer is: increased annual output ('growth') as a result of technological innovation. Capitalism is a recipe by which retained surpluses are reinvested in high returning projects to generate returns and compound their worth. But there is no end state to this limitless process: the economy is a machine without purpose or objective. Even setting aside aesthetics, the arithmetic of contemporary capital budgeting is astonishingly inefficient when seen in a broader perspective. Consider the Roman sewers of Pavia that have been in continuous use for two thousand years. Depreciated over their life, the annual capitalisation cost of construction would be minuscule. Yet in the modern economy it has become standard practice to depreciate fixed capital such as plant and buildings over thirty years.

The justification for this approach usually takes the form: 'it is not economic to invest over a longer time horizon' (which is circular reasoning) or 'architects cannot anticipate future technological demands' (which is not true, as old buildings have always been adapted to new uses) or 'it is good for employment creation'. But how can it make 'time' sense or 'green' sense to continuously knock down buildings and rebuild them again instead of constructing them to a high standard in the first place? Capital investment decisions are constrained by the technology available at the time. If capital is depreciated durably over a longer time horizon then we are running to gain ground. Schumpeterian creative destruction is a false economy: shorter and shorter depreciation means running to stand still and not accumulating capital.

Find a modern corporation that calculates an internal rate of return on property, plant and equipment with an expected life of 2,000 years! When the Romans constructed the sewers of Pavia, they did not expect the technology to change. Nowadays electronic devices become obsolete in two years as chip processing capacity increases. So the faster rate of technological change shortens the depreciation schedule. But the purpose of technology since the invention of the earliest agricultural implements has been to free up time to be spent elsewhere. Capital-labour substitution is the cornerstone of transmission from idea to higher living standards. The elimination of unpleasant jobs through invention and the accumulation of machines are the primary channels by which economic development is realised.

Technology may be the instrument of progress but at what point does creative destruction become technological enslavement, and *cui bono*? Industrial revolutions are not impersonal forces; they are tools in the hands of one group seeking domination over another. If the providers of the tool become vested interests, their futuristic visions become the accessories to the persistence of unfreedom. The dimension of durability needs to extend from instantaneous consumption to long-term accumulation. Technoscepticism is not technophobia: labour-saving devices do eliminate drudgery. But while some technologies are useful and life-enhancing, disseminating information and capability into formerly blind corners, others are time-consumptive or destructive—mere instruments for the exercise of corporate power.

FRIDAY 20 JUNE | QUNEITRA

Aydin has hired a car for the day's expedition. Sylvia and I wait for him outside the Hamidiye Souq and jump in. We collect our tourist guide, Wa'if, from the Ministry of Information and head south from Damascus. Quneitra is an abandoned town in a slither of land that was lost in the 1967 Six-Day War and recaptured by the Syrian army in 1973. The Yom Kippur (Ramadan) War began on 6 October 1973 as Syria and Egypt assaulted Israel on two fronts, the Golan Heights (Syria) and the Sinai Peninsula (Egypt). After making substantial initial gains, their lack of coordination allowed Israel to hold the Sinai Front, while concentrating its forces with a counter-attack on the Golan. The Syrian Army repulsed Israel with support from the Iraq expeditionary force but Henry

Kissinger, the US National Security Advisor and newly appointed Secretary of State, exploited Arab disunity to force Syria's President Assad to accept a disengagement agreement on 31 May 1974 that recovered the town of Quneitra but left the Golan under Israeli control. Israelis bulldozed Quneitra and left it a ruin before evacuating it. Assad regained some Arab pride but was then able to use the 'Zionist threat' as bogeyman to justify domestic repression and buttress his iron grip.

The ruins of the derelict town have been elaborately constructed as a paean to Hafez al-Assad. Above the entrance to the concrete shell of the bombed out hospital a pale blue sign is written in Arabic with English below: 'Golan Hospital. It was destroyed and changed into a firing target and a training place by Zionists.' We explore the ruined church and the visitor centre and listen to a rambling exegesis from the one remaining resident of the town in the garden of his house. On the road towards Khan Arnabeh we stop at a village taverna down a track off the main road. Wa'if speaks with the patron and we sit outside in the shady garden under breezy trees with vines and creepers and chattering birds. We discuss politics over lunch and think of creative ways to end the conflict. 'It comes back to the same problem,' says Wa'if. 'The Israelis don't want to do a deal and they have no incentive to make one.'

We drive through the countryside to the Shouting Fence below Mount Hermon. There we can see the Israeli gun emplacements around the summit and the stateless Druze villagers of Majdal Shams on the other side. For over thirty years they have been unable to get closer than 100 metres to their family members, stranded over the ceasefire line. Between the lines is a UN watch tower and a minefield. Wa'if takes us to meet the farmer, Nagi Abu Jebel, who grows cherries, apples and plums in the fertile fields along the red line. It is sad to see the idyll of that place ruined by such intransigence. 'If the Israelis had an ounce of goodwill,' says Wa'if, 'they could issue passes for the villagers to cross back and forth over the line.' On the way back to Damascus we stop at the house of a Druze family in the Hauran countryside. They invite us for tea and we sit stiffly trying to understand what they are telling us. Somewhat overwhelmed by the laborious translation, I withdraw to the front garden and finish reading *From the Holy Mountain*. Back in Damascus we join a supper party in the old city and I give Aydin the book.

Later Aydin tells me that the *Holy Mountain* is anti-Islamic. But I suggest that it reaches into the lost world of Byzantium and is no more anti-Islamic than anti-Zoroastrian. The tragedy of the indigenous Levantine Christians is that they were overwhelmed by so many peoples—Persians, Arabs and Turks and later Europeans—and ever since the attacks on Christians in Lebanon and Syria in 1860, supposedly sympathetic Western States have stoked sectarianism while also betraying them. The deficiency of the book is rather that it does not discuss how the Christians reached their present predicament—persecuted for their confessional identity and yet, thinking of the Lebanese Phalangist militia, complicit in oppression. For without insight into the philosophical and historical relationship between Islam and Christianity, one cannot understand the deterioration of the situation of the Christians across these former Ottoman territories.

SATURDAY 21 JUNE | DAMASCUS

The hotel is charming, but the room is uncomfortable. I try to convince the friendly staff that I am becoming a long-term resident: after much discussion, they give me a new room that suffers from the noise of the generator and is no better than the first. But I am absorbed by Brigid Keenan's *Damascus: Hidden Treasures of the Old City* that conveys something of the spirit of the beauty of Ottoman Syria. I collect my shirt and canvas bag from the tailor on Baysa Street and brave the hair cutter next door. Ali takes his open razor to my whiskers and I reflect on the statutory portrait of the president facing me in the mirror. As in most Arab countries, every shop or public building must display a photograph of the autocrat. So there is Bashar, in his Western suit and tie, gazing up and to one side with the Syrian flag behind, the very image of the solid statesman responsible for the security of the state; and there is the whole family in mafia shades: Hafez, Bashar and the deceased brother Bassel, sometimes referred to as 'father, son and holy ghost'.

Directly opposite there is a photograph of the American popular singer Britney Spears looking back at the President. Does Britney know she is 'Big in Syria'? Do the Shamsis know about the tawdry details of her personal life? Or perhaps for them Britney represents Western liberalism, her portrait a silent protest? Britney evokes the romantic ideal as much as any renaissance painting of a nymph. But I am struck that the Shamsis should pick her out from the gallery of Western icons as conforming to their ideal of beauty. I return to the mesmerising Umayyad Mosque whose grandeur still achieves its purpose and shows a different aspect on successive visits. Today there is a group of Iranian pilgrims led by energetic young sheikhs. I am pining for the Wadi Araba and see that the purpose of the white marbled courtyards of these early congregational mosques is to bring the purity and silence of the desert into the heart of the noisy city.

Aydin and Sylvia invite me to join them for dinner in the new city with their friend Naim Zabita. Fine-featured, diminutive and softly-spoken, Naim works as an architect at the Damascus governorate overseeing conservation in the old city. He speaks about Nadia Khoust, former Chair of the Syrian Writers Union who started the movement to preserve the old houses. Souq Sarouja was the first extra-mural district, founded in the 1170s by Salah ad-Din's sister Sitt al-Sham, and named after the Mamluk emir Sarem ad-Din Sarouja. During the 1960s property developers began destroying the areas adjoining the citadel and constructed the flyover. The gardens and orchards along the Barada vanished and the twelfth-century Hammam al-Joset and a mosque were demolished. The wealthier classes abandoned the district for modern houses in the suburbs. Across Sarouja and the old city, Ottoman courtyard houses were divided up for refugees and migrants, sometimes packed ten families to one building. Now some are being restored.

Nadia Khoust reminds me of Nawal Hassan in Cairo. We talk about the economics of conservation and how capital budgeting models cannot in isolation determine economic rationality. Real estate developers will always thrive if left to their own devices to pursue unfettered profit maximisation. But without a guiding force to shape the built environment the result will be dystopian. Naim talks about Solidere, the Lebanese company that reconstructed Central Beirut after the civil war ended in 1990 and built streetscapes that conform to the traditional stone style. With imagination it is possible to marry profitability and aesthetics. The conversation turns to politics. Naim explains that he went to school with Bashar al-Assad and tells us that the President is intelligent and kind. The secular Ba'ath Party protects minorities against the threat posed by the Muslim Brotherhood who want to purge Syria of its diversity and impose fundamentalist Sunni Islam. America demonises Assad because of the politics around Israel. But compared to Saudi Arabia, Syria is culturally closer to the West, and the Christians of Syria are loyal to the Alawite Assads.

SUNDAY 22 JUNE | DAMASCUS

Tariq allows me to move rooms again: this time to the corner above the shower, which has no air flow and smells of drains. But I return to the old city to explore the Christian quarter, which historically extended from the Roman arch along the 'Street called Straight' to the eastern gate (Bab Sharqi). The rectangular grid was laid out by the Macedonians after the Battle of Issus, while the Romans built the seven city gates and widened the Via Recta as a typical decumanus with colonnades. The primary site of interest is the House of Ananias, where according to *Acts of the Apostles* Saul was baptised after his Damascene conversion and became Paul. The stone cave house chapel is some distance north of the Via Recta, while the Jewish quarter was probably to the south where a modern chapel dedicated to Paul was built with stones from the Bab Kisan. But the chapel of Ananias is of Roman vintage and conveys the suitable feeling of antique piety.

In the summer of 1860, conflict between Shi'a Druze and Maronite Christians in Mount Lebanon spilled over into the streets of Damascus as Christian refugees fled massacres.

From 8 to 11 July 1860, Druze and Bedouin militias burned down much of the Christian quarter including the Greek Orthodox Patriarchate, successor to the Antioch church founded by Peter and Paul. According to the contemporary eyewitness Michael Mishaqah, more than 5,000 Christians were killed in Damascus. Many found sanctuary in European consulates as well as in the house of Abd el-Kader, the deposed Emir of Algiers. The configuration of internal instability combined with partisan Ottoman leadership and misguided interventions by external powers widened sectarian divisions and exacerbated the violence—a pattern in microcosm to subsequent events and the backdrop to the professed detribalisation of Ba'athist Syria.

I return to al-Rabie for tea in the courtyard. Aydin has been writing dispatches from Baghdad to a Canadian newspaper and talks about depleted Uranium shells fired twice per minute by American tanks that can pass through 30 metres of concrete before atomising materiel on the other side. The aim of the invasion, he argues, was the elimination of Iraq as a power—to decapitate the posturing Saladin. An influential 1996 policy paper titled *A Clean Break* called for the replacement of Saddam by a pro-Western Hashemite. Why do so many articles in the American press argue that the 'Road to Jerusalem lies through Baghdad'? In part because the Ayatollah Khomeini once said that the 'Road to al-Quds lies through Karbala'. But no weapons of mass destruction will be found in Iraq nor any links with al-Qaeda. All the evidence is that whatever chemical weapons the Iraqis may have previously kept have long since been destroyed. Faulty intelligence was planted, Aydin suggests, which explains why the source was never publicly identified.

From 1979 to 1991 the United States turned a blind eye while Saddam Hussein invaded Iran and perpetrated continuous violence against the Iraqi people, later selling armaments to the dictator. In the First Gulf War, the coalition limited its objectives to liberating Kuwait. Yet the Iraqi army was completely defeated in 1991 and General Schwarzkopf stated that he believed United States forces should have continued to Baghdad. The Americans called on the Kurds and Shi'a Marsh Arabs to rise up against Saddam. Instead Iraqi insurgents were massacred by Saddam's forces in Basra, Najaf and Kirkuk, while Western backed Arab kings and emirs stood silently by. Perhaps the betrayal of 1991 explains why the Americans have received such a different welcome to what they expected, for within days of the toppling of Saddam's statue in Baghdad on 9 April, 'liberation' became 'occupation'.

The United States underestimated the attacks against its forces. Meanwhile, archaeological sites and museums that are the patrimony of all humanity were left unprotected. After twelve years of sanctions and two wars, Iraq needs billions of dollars of investment and there is no indication that the Coalition Provisional Authority has any realistic programme for reconstruction beyond granting oil and gas concessions to American firms. At root there is a lack of consistency in the application of Western ideals. Conventions on international criminal law were established after the Second World War. Yet following the 11 September 2001 attacks, due process became extraordinary rendition and innocent civilians in Afghanistan and Iraq were bombed to oblivion. 'Guantanamo,' Aydin concludes, 'is a mirror to the violence that Arab dictatorships have carried out with the acquiescence of the United States.'

Time and freedom

Above a basic threshold there are diminishing returns of well-being to higher income: happiness lies with friendships, family life and self-realisation. Consumption alone does not increase happiness, although poverty does restrict freedoms and capabilities. Rousseau thought that happiness is obedience to the law we prescribe ourselves, which is similar to the flow state of complete absorption. Aretaic eudaimonism, the realisation of one's potential as virtue, is embedded in culture, beliefs and practices. For most people, happiness consists of raising children with economic security, while balancing the demands of life to enable their talents to flourish. Is this not the ideal of an Epicurean garden applied to the polity as a whole? Perhaps the root of discontent in modern industrialised society is that income generation dominates self-realisation. Yet the essence of Western thought is the mentality of free enquiry that supports adaptability and openness to ideas. So why can we not transition from utilitarian homo economicus to the Epicurean calculus of flow?

Any flow state activity requires time, and time is the scarcest resource. Leisure affords time for private study, conversation, appreciation of the arts and so on. But the means to obtain free time for private pursuits is by selling time and skills—themselves the result of investment through the expenditure of time. A state of real wealth is one in which only a small amount of bound or worked time produces a large amount of free time: that is the fruit of tools, technique and accumulation. Generating real wealth involves reducing the amount of expended time required to satisfy needs, thereby creating the freedom to choose between unbound time and worked time. Aggregate freedom is the summation of this time lever for all individuals. Epicurean economics maximises aggregate freedom.

In *The Affluent Society*, J.K. Galbraith asked how citizens in advanced industrialised economies would use the leisure time made available by technological advances. This question was framed against the deflationary conditions of the Great Depression and the post-war economic boom. The idea that production is demand constrained is the basic response of Keynesianism to macroeconomic dysfunction. Yet, everyone is unique and no one is irreplaceable. Everyone needs to be needed but some people are surplus to requirements. The underlying condition is excess demand for employment that perversely incentivises the creation of new needs to ensure that the creation of new jobs substitutes for the elimination of old ones by technology. But many new products and services are ephemeral. Galbraith's question reflects the cultural attitudes of a society, in which inactivity is a vice and wealth is a sign of providence. Yet the contemporary discussion of 'work-life balance' suggests that, as a society, we work more than we need to.

Intuitively, the value of work is the value of the output it is used to create. Like variables in logic, hours are bound or free. Bound time is captive, hostage to someone else's interest while free time is one's own. The 'marginalist' insight, developed from classical economics as the allocation of scarce resources, is that households optimise the balance between free and bound time. The same principal applies to employees as well as to business owners: entrepreneurship still represents selling hours but with greater uncertainty in their remuneration. The classical labour supply model assumed that households optimise the trade-off between the disutility of giving up time versus the positive utility of consuming the proceeds of compensation. All else equal, economic output is determined by the sum of all these individual titrations between the worth of free time versus the worth of goods and services obtained from selling hours.

But the less we need to consume and the more efficiently we can produce, the fewer hours we need to sell to the market and the more 'time-free' we become. So the path to freedom lies in the reassessment of consumption desire, the maximising of individual productivity and the collective realignment to eliminate perverse incentives and reduce the creation of unnecessary needs. If every citizen were to become a philosopher-king and adopt Epicurean minimalism, immune to the suasion of marketing, the shackles of Mammon would wither. There would be no social pressure to express consumer demand for extra unnecessary objects—there would be no gadget upgrade cycles, no conspicuous consumption of positional status objects, of magpie-shiny chronometers or instantly depreciating over-capacitated automobiles. And yet the daily grind of selling one's time to the world machine rolls on like a Sisyphean cycle of tedium.

So the bedrock of economic freedom is the power of households to supply the optimal quantity of labour or hours. Productivity is the efficiency of conversion of worked hours into valuable output. Technological progress should relax the constraint on the leisure-consumption trade off. But this has not occurred because profit maximising firms are incentivised to create new wants, increasing the intensity of consumption. Apart from the depletion of resource endowments, the only long-term economic variable that changes is technology; otherwise progress is social, cultural and institutional. But the acceleration of technological change has increased the rate of capital depreciation, thereby diminishing the rate of accumulation. Meanwhile households lack the power to determine the optimal amount of labour they supply.

Any system which requires the production of goods and services, not for their intrinsic value but to generate employment, is counter-productive. Keynes's thought experiment about workers digging holes and filling them up again is the *reductio ad absurdum* of the abstraction of 'economic output' disconnected from its cultural environment. It is absurd to create jobs whose output has no value; likewise the willingness of households to borrow to consume, and of the financial institutions that make money out of this folly. If we do not need the disposable tinsel the modern economy produces, we should be richer not poorer. If we accumulate the machines that house, transport, feed and entertain us, then free time should emerge as the path to improved welfare. If the objective of the overall economy is to maximise aggregate freedom, then unnecessary exchanges should be eliminated. Yet this goes against the Keynesian notion: if 'the economy' depends on stimulating demand, which is equivalent to the increasing of needs, then we depend on the diminishment of our freedom for the satisfaction of our needs! A paradox: something must be wrong.

The same surfeit of production for its own sake also afflicts the academy. How many papers did Einstein publish? Does anyone really think they have more to say than Einstein? Yet perverse incentives have resulted in much of science, and especially the social sciences, becoming a production line with papers churned out like widgets. Academics spew out repetitive and irrelevant publications 'peer reviewed' by the coterie that recycles the same jargon. What happened to concision and ontological parsimony and transmitting a clean signal through the noise? Basic research should strive for the ever deeper understanding of ultimate reality. But for all the ideal of the noble quest for truth, of scholars making a contribution to world knowledge, scientists have become an interest group protected by the opaqueness of their field from the need to demonstrate the worth of their activity to the broader society that finances them.

The same perverse incentives apply to defence expenditure, to the 'military-industrial complex'. The first duty of any state is to guarantee the security of its citizens. But if international business buttresses autocratic regimes around the world, global allocative efficiency becomes a false economy. It is not merely a question of allocation within fixed constraint. Rather it is the classical prisoners' dilemma of game theory applied to global security. Consider guns versus butter: all else equal, eliminating the guns generates a total welfare benefit. What is the point in progress through innovation, if there is so much wastage of the fruits of peaceful accumulation? Maximising aggregate freedom cannot be achieved without universalising liberal democracy and hence eliminating the need for military expenditure. But for as long as there is global insecurity, deriving from great power competition or the malign effect of autocratic and corrupt regimes around the world, defence expenditure will consume the surplus that would otherwise go into welfare.

In short: take the programmes of the public sector in creating employment—from ministries to the academy to the armed forces—whose output has no market value, no seal of approval from any final consumer willing to pay for it; take the clever methods of the financial sector to expand leverage, using money to create money regardless of the use of credit in production. Do these activities contribute to the beautification of the environment, to human happiness or to the creation of objects of enduring cultural value? No! Do they contribute to the shortening of labours, to the extension of leisure and the richness of life? No! Commit them then to the flames, for they are nothing more than the instruments of the exercise of power, and the means of the perpetuation of bondage and servitude by one group over another.

MONDAY 23 JUNE | DAMASCUS

My congenial companions Aydin and Sylvia have departed with their tales and I am morose to be alone again with tedious books for company. So I seek solace in routines: visiting museums in the mornings, taking notes in the Umayyad coffee house around the corner from al-Nofara and roaming the streets in the evenings. Of all the quarters in the Old City, I conclude that the most charming is the al-Qaymariyya district that extends east from the Umayyad Mosque with its distinctive streetscapes where Syrian climbing jasmine fills the canopy, dropping tendrils into the shopfronts above the cobbles.

There are more than 2,000 courtyard houses scattered across Damascus that were constructed for merchants and other wealthy classes going back to the seventeenth century. But with the expansion of the city in the twentieth century, the wealthy tended to move into larger modern buildings outside the ancient districts, leaving the old houses to slide into decay. Some have been converted into restaurants and a few into hotels, while the majority have been divided into social housing. The Damascus Historical Museum in Souq Sarouja gives a sense of the way of life of these urban islands, with citrus trees and marble basins, ornate stucco, mashrabiyya balconies and vaulted liwans. The walls are decorated with black and white photographs of Hafez al-Assad with world leaders including Brezhnev, Mao, Nixon and Castro.

Naim meets me at Dar Anbar and we walk around the mansion's elegant courtyards. Dar Anbar was built in the mid-nineteenth century by a Jewish businessman from Iraq. The residence was confiscated by the Ottoman governor after M. Anbar went bankrupt, ostensibly due to the government defaulting on loans he had made. The building was used as a private school attended by many of the Syrian independence leaders during the French period but was later abandoned and fell into disrepair. The Ministry of Culture acquired the building in 1976 and after renovating it converted it into a cultural centre and library. From Dar Anbar, we visit Beit Nizam, the former English Consulate where Richard Burton held literary soirees, as well as some private houses nearby that are being restored with grants from the Ministry of Culture.

After onion soup at Zeitoun, I return to al-Rabie via al-Manakhliya Souq opposite the Barada where there is a large crowd of people from al-Ghouta sitting on the ground dressed in velvet robes typical of the poorest country people, apparently protesting about their marginalisation and the lack of investment in rural areas.

Debt and interest

In 2003 the chief economist of the Bank for International Settlements, William White, warned the Jackson Hole conference of global central bankers that household debt and deregulated American financial markets posed risks to global prosperity. The Great Financial Crisis of 2007 to 2008 was predictable and avoidable. By 2007 the effect of securitisation on overall credit creation dwarfed expansion through bank lending, while mortgage securitisation stimulated unsustainable growth in property prices. Yet policy makers did nothing to deflate these bubbles: rather losses were socialised after the beneficiaries had escaped with their loot. White later observed that zero interest rates and quantitative easing had eliminated any incentive to save while access to leverage privileged institutions closer to the money centres, widening asset inequality.

The root of the problem is a widely propagated piece of bad reasoning: that if borrowing costs fall it is rational to borrow more. But housing in countries with a fixed stock and constrained land supply is more like a Dutch auction than a conventionally equilibrating market. The more people are willing to borrow, the more prices are bid up and the more people are forced to borrow to acquire the housing they need. The overall effect of leverage is that some property investors become extremely wealthy while the majority of owner-occupier households end up holding the same real assets as their forebears but with a larger debt burden. Throughout history bubbles have been caused by households borrowing to finance consumption as well as placing bets on speculative assets whose value cannot be objectively determined. The traditional functions of money include: store of wealth, medium of exchange and unit of account. But the actual numeraire is time: the price of any tradeable entity can be translated into worked hours. To be in debt is to be obliged to supply worked hours to the market, while being in credit gives the power to command them.

Historical usury laws as well as principles of Islamic finance and even Adam Smith himself counselled against the perils of unleashed debt markets. There will always be 'prodigals and projectors' (spendthrifts and fraudsters). So economic justice depends on the ethical behaviour of market participants. The power of the state to issue currency and levy taxes is likewise the power to command worked hours and hence appropriate the fruit of the citizen's labour. The subversion of sound money in this way subordinates the interest of private citizens to collective wastage. When countries incur unsustainable debts, their currencies devalue and in extremis they fall in hock to external agency. International trade is about state power. So national freedom is the mirror to individual freedom: no citizen can be free unless the nation is also free, in control of its capital stock, in mastery of its external balance and in prudence of its public finances.

TUESDAY 24 JUNE | SAIDNAYA

The shrine mosque of Ruqayya bint al-Husayn by the Bab al-Amara in the old city is a focal point on the Shi'a pilgrimage trail. Together with the shrine of Zaynab bint Ali on the outskirts of Damascus, the mosque has recently been renovated by the Iranians. The interior of the prayer hall has Isfahan blue tiles and a dazzling ceiling of cut mirror fragments that creates an effect of shimmering light. Around the tomb itself, devout women tie ribbons to make wishes, and rub the clothes of absent friends and family as they push through the crowd to the front and cling with their fingers to the silver plated ornamental grill. I am astonished by the sight of grown Iranian men breaking into collective hysterical sobbing, immersing themselves into the tragedy of Husayn to frame the adverse events of their own life, and in some way transfer their sorrows, similar perhaps to the emotions of the Trapani Good Friday procession.

From Bab Touma (Thomas Gate) I catch the microbus to Saidnaya. The Greek Orthodox fortress Convent of our Lady was built by Justinian in 547 on the rock above the town and is reached by a series of staircases. There is a legend that Justinian was hunting in the region when the stag he was about slay became an apparition of the Virgin Mary who instructed him to found the convent. As in some Tibetan monasteries the convent is an orphanage, and Saidnaya has a special quality of openness and warmth. For children who do not become nuns, the monastery remains their home and they often return to visit. The convent is venerated for its icon of the Virgin which is the focus of a fertility cult for both Muslims and Christians. Over lunch Sisters Stephanie and Malachi talk about the Assyrian monk Bahira who taught Muhammad. I climb up to the Cherubim Patriarchal Monastery on the flat peak of Mount Qalamoun, and sleep on the divan in the cold still air with the jabbering birds, before returning to the convent for vespers.

Efficiency versus distribution
The discussion of whether the economy is market- or state-led sets the problem within the wrong frame: for the market is merely a mechanism for price discovery and no civilised society can function without an effective state. The underlying intuitions of right versus left (efficiency versus distribution) are consistent with each other. Profit is the criterion for whether an economic activity is worth engaging in: but that depends on end-market demand which is determined by tastes and culture. There is no practical alternative to a free economy: to take from those according to their ability and give to those according to their need incentivises the population to become disabled and needy. But to put an activity in the private sector does not automatically make it more efficient: rather that creates opportunities for profiteering. The economic performance of a nation reflects the motivation and capability of all its citizens.

Whether working in the private or public sectors, people respond to incentives—both carrots and sticks. This action-outcome relationship lies at the root of our psychic structure. But what determines the structure of incentives? Political slogans do not always demonstrate their true sentiments: a certain programme may advertise itself as promoting more freedom or more choice, when in reality it may be supporting the opposite. The fruit of any society is set by the values of the authority that presides over it. And what determines those? Consider the Mafiosi who stole the funds allocated for the reconstruction of Palermo: within the organisation, the members respond to the incentive structure dictated by the bosses, as well as the absence of external punishment for their crimes. In Joseph Conrad's novel *Nostromo*, the Costaguanan silver miners are corrupted by perverse incentives to the cost of the realm and the collective interest.

To maintain social stability in a free economy requires redistribution: but it is better to pay people to acquire skills and education than to do something useless or nothing at all. It is better to redistribute output through a transfer payment to unproductive individuals than to generate employment whose output has no intrinsic value—for then free time is generated and that is the time dividend. The deep problem is how to include non-productive individuals when no one wants to subsidise the indolent. To survive in the global economy, we have to sell something at a competitive price to value in relation to other market participants. What about those who inherit wealth and live off private incomes? It is easy to say 'workers of the world, relax!' when you have inherited a vast fortune. But the goal of maximising aggregate freedom across an entire society should be to make every citizen to a degree a rentier.

Pure laissez-faire capitalism contains within it the seeds of another form of tyranny: skewed asset distribution and the power of private interest. Pareto's Principle is that any economy left to the operation of natural forces will evolve to a condition in which eighty per cent of the wealth is controlled by twenty per cent of the population. Within the model of utility maximisation, skewed distribution generates a purchasing power demand deficit which partly explains median wage stagnation. Such dystopian capitalism is the logical end point of the materialist ideology. But freedom lies in the application of logos to chaos, in imposing order on the Spencerian jungle economy, to move towards the optimal state of political economy. Freedom is power: maximising aggregate freedom is incompatible with skewed power distribution.

On 21 November 2011, an international business newspaper published an article by the Egyptian banker Hassan Heikal arguing that the super-rich should pay capital taxes to the exchequers of their countries of citizenship. Heikal estimated that households with net worth in excess of $10 million represent 0.01 per cent of the world's population, and that a one-off ten per cent wealth levy would raise $5 trillion that could be invested in public sector debt reduction, infrastructure, research and training. Heikal cited the Islamic concept of zakat, a mandatory two-and-a-half-per-cent wealth tax for those who meet certain financial criteria. The Umayyad caliphs deposited the treasury (Bayt al-Mal) in the courtyard of their congregational mosque so that the 'umma could monitor the public finances. Yet the Umayyads lived lavishly: has there ever been a theocratic regime that devoted itself to the service of the community and never used executive power or public office for private gain?

Whenever libertarians are asked about purpose, their stock answer is adaptive fitness: if eyes have been selected on account of conferring the power to see, then eyes have the purpose of seeing. Likewise the purpose of social cooperation is to promote survival: cultural ends cannot be created through acts of will. Yet biological constraint is far from the 'purposes' of societies that have passed through millennia of cultural development. The purposes of any society *are* what its participants choose them to be. Libertarians want to undermine the state in the name of 'liberating' the citizen. It is true that liberal democratic states can fall hostage to dominant corporations and other groups that lobby for their private interest. So the question is the operation of the state, which is one of representation and accountability to the electorate, civil society and free press. But it is no coincidence that libertarians seek funding from autocratic regimes: the logical end point of their position is corporate concentration. Just as totalitarianism can be reached from 'right' or 'left' so the power of oligopolistic technocracy resembles kleptocratic autocracy: in either state the citizen is controlled by dark powers that exert influence through opaque and unaccountable channels.

WEDNESDAY 25 JUNE | DAMASCUS

Naim meets me at Dar Anbar where we embark upon a discussion of what makes actions good or bad. Academic philosophers tend to either deny that moral judgements have truth value (relativism) or assert that a value judgement is true when we are justified in our arguments for holding it true (circular reasoning). The necessity of logic is a force no less binding than electromagnetism. But the axioms of such a framework are as arbitrary as for any axiomatic system. It was obvious that parallel lines do not intersect—until Riemann invented non-Euclidean geometry. Moral axioms must be self-evident, like the golden rule—treating others as we would ourselves—or the principle of virtue ethics: by adopting noble habits we make ourselves noble. Naim poses some ethical dilemmas and concludes, 'You see, reality is complicated and sometimes you have to live with the imperfect solution.' But I counter that these are mind games. Is ethics not very simple: do we not have an obligation to do our best not to cause harm to others?

Naim takes me to the wonderful Hammam of Nur ad-Din that dates from 1160 and has been immaculately maintained. The hammam is one of the most authentic experiences of the mediaeval Islamic world that is accessible to the visitor. But with the institution under threat from social change and the depredations of real-estate developers, only a few mediaeval hammams still operate—in the Maghreb and in Syria. From Orientalist paintings of nymphs reclining in translucent water beside marbled floors, the institution of the hammam has been portrayed as an erotic environment. The warm stones and the steam and the furtiveness are certainly alluring; to the locals however the hammam is simply a place to get washed and massaged and sip tea with friends in front of the television. The fact that a distant sultan might have endowed the building with fine decoration is perhaps a point of pride but taken for granted.

In the relaxed haze, it occurs to me that sections of time suddenly seem detached and inaccessible from each other. The days furthest away were the ones that passed happiest and least weighed down by the action problem—the question of what to do, of how to use time most productively. O the curse of productivity! After the session we dry off in the domed jamekan with tea, speaking in French with Naim's friends about Syria and Iraq. At al-Rabie I meet an affable burly Irishman called Peter who plays chess, and we pass the evening at a popular outdoor place for chess players near Yousef al-Azmeh Square.

Holy Mother Earth
In light of the degradation of the environment, including loss of biodiversity and habitat destruction, no one but the most recalcitrant libertarian ideologue cannot be green. To deny anthropogenic climate change is to commit the elementary error of fitting facts to theory. Yet the tightening of the green noose was unnecessary for it has been self-evident all along. Stewardship of nature has always been intrinsic to the imposing of order on chaos but the ill-equilibrating forces of a sub-optimal capitalism have likewise ignored the green signal transmitted by the cosmos. Ironically it was climate change that caused the flourishing of grasses in the Fertile Crescent: this allowed the cultivation of grain as a higher energy food, which in turn enabled the accumulation of surpluses and the formation of cities.

Rachel Carson's *Silent Spring* is credited as marking the beginning of the rise of the contemporary environmentalist movement. Green arguments about externalities (the true cost of pollution that is not accounted for by corporations) and the depleting resource base are well rehearsed. But throughout history, strong states have run up against environmental constraints that led to their decline, beginning with the salination of the Euphrates valley that extinguished the Sumerian first flowering of civilisation. After eliminating its rivals Carthage and Corinth in 146 BC, the Romans drove salt into the earth around those cities to weaken their productive resource. In 1258 the Mongol Khan Hulagu razed Baghdad and destroyed the irrigation ditches of Iraq that had been maintained for over 4,000 years. Once one of the four alluvial civilisations of the ancient world, Iraq never recovered as an independent power. Mighty Venice declined in the sixteenth century as the Veneto forests became depleted and the cost of ship construction rose.

The global reserve army of labour has driven down wages in developed economies and globalised the environmental footprint of supply chains. But like any trade it works both ways, for individuals respond like iron filings to the paths of least resistance they find themselves bound by in their socialeconomic situation. Economic growth derives from innovation, ideas and technique. 'Green growth' is no different: clean transportation fuels, circularising the production complex and biodegrading consumables will all turn capitalism green. But democratisation matters too: authoritarian regimes have never been green. Central planning failed because of Hayek's 'knowledge problem' or lack of access to decentralised information. 'Greening' the global economy still requires autocratic states to mothball dirty industrial production.

But greening capitalism is not going to change the vast engine of polluting activity which constitutes much of the global economy, for at root is the central principle of consumption itself as the motive force that turns the wheels of commerce. Households presently make small gestures such as recycling glass and cardboard. But the wholesale reduction of consumption across the board, like the curbing of excessively high birth rates, must be part of the green transition. Yvon Chouinard, charismatic founder of outdoor clothing company *Patagonia* and environmental advocate, expressed it thus: 'Don't buy what you don't need'; to which one could add: 'Make sure you need as little as possible above the minimum for a good life'. Above all, the single most destructive human activity to the environment is war. Ultimately nature has no intrinsic value, for what will atoms be worth in a billion years' time? Holy Mother Earth cares not one jot for us and if we fail to secure the environment, she will nod sagely as we make ourselves extinct.

THURSDAY 26 JUNE | DAMASCUS

Rising late due to excessive coffee, nargileh and soft beds I realise that I need exercise, yoga and better sleep. After breakfast at al-Rabie chatting about the perennials, I return to Hani's Zoni Internet. Later I meet Peter for supper at the Elissar courtyard restaurant and we play chess in the new city until the small hours.

Political values and international capital flows

In the absence of any higher power, international law based on the United Nations system is the least bad option to ground international relations. But not all members of the so-called 'international liberal order' are liberal. So without a universal system of ethics, values and law, there is a contradiction between 'liberal' and 'international'. After 1989 it was assumed that the world would be reshaped in the image of the West. But since the incorporation of the former Warsaw Pact countries into Western institutions, the expansion of liberal democracy has stalled. There are notionally democratic states that in reality have weak institutions, limited legal protection of civil liberties and are controlled by rent-seeking oligarchies. Yet liberalism derives from the universality of rights—that all citizens in every polity have natural inalienable rights.

During the period of its overwhelming power advantage the United States allowed trade and industrial policy to be determined by liberal principles on the assumption of an open level playing field. Following the earlier examples of Japan, South Korea and the former European Soviet satellite states, it pursued regime change in Iraq, Libya and Syria, ostensibly to democratise these countries. But in each case American intervention caused or contributed to wars that engulfed these states, creating an 'axis of bloodshed'. Since 2003 it has become clear that 1945 and 1989 were unique moments. Seeking to manufacture political alchemy by force has proved to be extremely difficult and 'liberal interventionism' has largely failed. The sad reality is that, short of invasion, it is difficult to dislodge a well-armed and well-entrenched dictatorship. Meanwhile the open international economy has undermined the unipolarity of American power which is a necessary condition for expanding the writ of the international liberal order.

There is tension between propagating liberal ideals and allocative efficiency in the global capital market. But politics is prior to economics: values must precede profits. Those who argue for growth over rights ignore the welfare gap between liberal democracies and autocratic regimes. Democracy means the primacy of the citizen as the unit of the polity, from which flows equality before the law, representative government and well-regulated capitalism.

Western democracies are not perfect: private networks abound, wealth endowments skew capability and there is a meritocratic deficit in countries with two tier education systems. But democracy is the least imperfect set of political institutions available: households do not receive nocturnal visits from secret police with wire taps and informants; torture is not routine in police detention; minorities are not killed or oppressed by big-brother-big-data-machines; private corporations are not controlled by representatives of the autocrat; and the state, at least in principle, exists to serve the citizen.

In democratic states pro-business parties tend to represent the interests of international business. Theoretical internationalists envisage a fully open globalised world in which anyone can do business anywhere, generate profits and acquire assets. But the weakness of Western foreign policy lies in the 'presumption of regularity'—in assuming symmetry and equivalence of governance. Alas there is not a level playing field in international business and the advantages of capital account openness are not symmetric. In practice global free trade has empowered kleptocratic autocracy and enriched extractive elites. Liberalism has been co-opted by libertarians who genuflect to an ideology of openness that is corrupting Western democracies from within. The background question is *whose rules prevail*: the governance of liberal democracies or of the autocrats? So the principles of symmetry and equivalence should apply to all cross-border capital flows.

The link between wealth extraction in developing countries with weak institutions and its being banked in developed countries is not restricted to direct kleptocracy. It also extends to supposedly legitimate business people who have generated wealth through rent seeking activities. These include acquiring state licenses and other assets at discounted rates, from operating *de facto* monopolies or from directing industrial policies such as subsidies and tariffs to their private advantage. The strict definition of an economic rent is the earning of excess returns from those which would obtain in a perfectly competitive market. That is why economies with developed institutions have competition commissions and anti-trust legislation. But in the developing world, there are few constraints on rent seeking. Every 'emerging' or 'frontier' market has its examples of business people earning super-normal profits via politically protected transfers from the state. As has been amply documented by the International Consortium of Investigative Journalists, a substantial proportion of these directly stolen or unfairly acquired funds end up laundered into offshore accounts.

Within economic theory, 'production functions' map inputs (labour, capital and technique) to outputs (goods, services and capital equipment). In undeveloped economies, the accumulation of physical capital is the primary lever to higher living standards. But in developed economies growth is a function of human capital: investment in education, technical innovation and private sector research. Define 'widget' as any consumable output and 'machine' as any accumulable input. Nations and their citizens thrive when they sell widgets that the rest of the world demands, especially if no other nation produces that widget. Mastery of the machine gives power over production which gives the power to assert values: liberal democracy rests on mastery of the machine. If autocratic powers gain control of the machine, tyranny will defeat liberty.

Selling education services and equity in technology companies is selling machines, not widgets; likewise for any good that can be reverse-engineered and contains within it embedded technology: in effect these are capital flows masquerading as current-account transactions. The flow of capital from the agents of hostile powers into democratic states is like a tide of polluted water flowing into their rivers. Does the foreign investor, whether individual or institution respect democratic laws? Have the funds been generated through the creation of economic value within an equivalent jurisdiction? If not, they are corrupt funds. Western states have become partial enclave economies as wealth managers, lawyers, realtors and other enabling agents legitimise the proceeds of corruption. But democracies cannot impose their ethics and institutions on autocracies. So the only way to preserve the free world from being overrun by autocratic regimes is to restrict capital flows to those democratic states with equivalent or symmetric standards of governance.

FRIDAY 27 JUNE | DAMASCUS

Weary from the heat and the lack of sleep, I read at al-Nofara. Peter meets me at al-Rabie for afternoon chess, followed by supper and Barada beer with Naim in the former Hijaz railway terminus. Opened in 1908, this was the head of the line connecting Damascus with Mecca: now it is a bar called Station One. I ask Naim about rugs and carpets in Syria and he explains that Damascus is one of the cheapest places to buy them, better even than Erzurum and other towns in Türkiye. The annual Daghistani market is one of the primary sources for the Damascene rug merchants. The Daghistanis come en masse from the Caucasus with thousands of kilims and carpets in the weeks before the Hajj and set up a huge market south of the city.

For millennia caravans and camel trains rested in the oasis on the Barada after crossing the desert from Palmyra or taking the incense route north from Arabia Felix (modern Yemen). Damascus used to be the place where pious Muslims started the Hajj, and the official title of the Ottoman governor was 'Protector of the Pilgrims'. In the decades before the First World War, over 2,000 kilometres of rail were laid in Greater Syria and Iraq. But during the Arab Revolt, the Bedouin were only too glad to assist in dynamiting the Hijaz line as they feared the competition. The ultimate cause of the demise of this infrastructure however was the division of the region into small parcels of territory whose rulers were more interested in domestic politics than maintaining trade routes that had flourished for millennia. For all the romance of trade in exotic goods, by far the most significant source of international trade by revenue is tourism, and tourism does not flourish in extractive dictatorships or states that cannot maintain internal security and that slide into civil war.

Thieves of State

In writing about post-colonial African states, the Polish journalist Ryszard Kapuscinski theorised about the *politique du ventre*, the substitution of colonial elites by small cliques that formed around independence movements and that took the opportunity of power to loot the economies they inherited. In *Thieves of State* Sarah Chayes draws the parallel between mediaeval manuals of good governance across the Islamic world—called 'Mirrors to Princes'. The repression and kleptocracy of extractive elites drive populations to despair until ultimately they turn to God or the gun or both. Consider Algeria in the 1990s where the suppression of the Front Islamique du Salut by the FLN government prompted an armed insurrection: more than 150,000 people were killed and many thousands suffered unspeakable torments.

Within the literature of development economics, countless books and articles have diminished the relevance of corruption, citing bribes and asset transfers to 'grease the wheels' of capitalist development. American economists who advised on the transition of the former Soviet Union from central planning to a market system in the 1990s, explicitly called on the transfer of firm equity to company managers to 'resolve disputes between stakeholders' and facilitate the privatisation of state-owned enterprises. Yet their policy prescriptions were contrary to the code of ethics and standard of conduct that applies to listed companies regulated by the US Securities and Exchange Commission. The very same economic advisors who wrote academic papers on corporate governance were complicit in the looting of Russia.

In his 1993 paper *Dictatorship, Democracy and Development* the institutional economist Mancur Olson discussed the effect of external incentives on the behaviour of local dictators. Olson argued that while a stationary bandit has an incentive to reform the domestic economy, a roving bandit can loot and exit. So by allowing the bandits of the world to bank their ill-gotten gains in Western economies, the West gives them a covert free hand to maintain their systems of klepto-repression. If thieves steal with impunity, no one has an incentive to be honest and capitalism becomes delegitimised. Ironically, in the case of Syria, sanctions imposed by the United States in the early 2000s incentivised the dictatorship to invest but the regime responded by pillaging even more. In general, however, giving the elites of developing countries with weak institutions 'golden visas' to a wealthy life in Western economies removes their incentive to reform. Capital flight from autocracies impairs capital accumulation, democratisation and institutional development in those countries. In the case of the former Soviet Union, Karen Dawisha's *Putin's Kleptocracy* traces such flows back to KGB operations in the 1980s.

It is desirable to run an open economic policy that attracts talented individuals to live and work and invest. But capital account openness assumes symmetry or equivalence, and that by allowing foreign capital inflows, domestic business benefits from opportunities in other countries. In reality many jurisdictions of origin for these flows suffer from weak corporate governance, corrupt public officials and ineffective judiciaries that allow tax evasion, fraud and the looting of state resources to go unpunished. Politicians and business people from developing economies with weak institutions are presented with domestic opportunities to make money that are not available to their counterparts in well-regulated jurisdictions. An open capital account without a level playing field results in the transfer of assets to individuals from the developing world who have made money through acts that would be illegal in the developed world.

One should not say that some corruption is the price to pay for an open global system for, eventually, governance standards as a whole will fall to the level of the weakest link. Nor is it right to say that corruption is endemic and merely the 'oxygen of capitalism'. Parallels can be drawn between lobbying as 'legalised corruption' and 'access money' in other systems. But in well-functioning democracies, public procurement and access to state resources are subject to competitive tender and transparent disclosure, while anti-trust regulation limits monopolistic rent extraction. So there is a profound difference between autocratic kleptocracy and even imperfect democratic capitalism. Olson's insight is that if autocratic elites cannot bank stolen money in Western states and offshore tax havens they are more likely to seek domestic reform and improve the quality of governance, else face the sanction of insurgency and revolution.

In a 1990 paper the economist Robert Lucas asked *Why Doesn't Capital Flow from Rich to Poor Countries?* and thereby cause convergence in living standards. From the armchair of the Chicago library one could hypothesise alternative explanations dressed up in the technical language of academic economics. Within the domain of liquid securities markets, capital flows arise from the adjustment of algorithms that arbitrage macro variables such as interest rates, fiscal deficits and trade balances. But in the real economy, capital flows to opportunities that a trained mind has judged on its particular merits. Capital does not flow to projects in countries subject to arbitrariness of government, lack of institutional capacity and insecurity of property claims. The same reasons why the divergence occurred in the first place ensure that it persists.

Since the present era of open capital flows began in 1989 it was widely expected that incomes in the dynamic emerging economies would converge. But now it is apparent that endemic corruption in the developing countries lies at the heart of their politics, and as they become more integrated into the world economy they export their corruption. Political and economic institutions derive from free decision. In a corrupt system, corruption infects everyone, until even the honest man like Conrad's *Nostromo* is drawn into its orbit. In Assad's Syria, the president's family and associates control an enormous share of the economy through the extraction of economic rents. The options facing private citizens in Syria were complicity or immiseration: civil society movements were crushed until eventually the extraction and repression resulted in insurgency and civil war. Is not the case of Syria a parable for the world?

SATURDAY 28 JUNE | DAMASCUS

Tariq organises a third change to a quiet first-floor room on the left of the courtyard, with colourful stained-glass windows and vine creepers that recreate the spirit of old Damascus. After settling in, I visit the magnificent Takiyya al-Suleymaniyya, built in the 1550s by Mimar Sinan, pre-eminent architect of the Ottoman golden age. Sinan was born of Greek or Armenian parents at Agirnas near Kayseri around 1490 and began his career as a military engineer. Sultan Süleyman appointed him Chief of the Imperial Architects in 1538 and more than 300 structures survive from his subsequent fifty years of active work. The Takiyya was built as a dervish lodge for the Mevlevi Order over the ruins of Baibars' Qasr al-Ablaq and is distinguished by its wide portico, domed arcades and prayer hall, surmounted by dome and pencil minarets. The courtyard has a rectangular pool with cypresses and conveys the spirit of Sufism. In sad contrast, the gardens of the Takiyya are occupied by old fighter planes from the Army Museum next door.

At the dilapidated passport office beside the Baradei bus terminal I pass the afternoon extending my visa. Having been warned that the experience with officialdom can be gruelling, in the end I get off lightly. After rigmaroles of photocopying and form filling and meeting different officials, some with their feet up on their desks, others with medals on their lapels who call me Roberto Carlos after the Brazilian footballer, I am despatched with the requisite passport stamp. Another supplicant, a young Somali called Aysha, is likewise bemused by the process and we eat chicken together. I persuade her to visit the National Museum and enjoy explaining the exhibits and especially revisiting the Ugarit tablets. Taking advantage of the new room, I sleep in the evening and play chess until two in the morning: now Peter is winning by six games to three.

Sunday 29 June | Damascus

Despite being pyrexic I am delighted to wake in the bright new room. The streets are empty of the usual throng of Shamsis and I walk down the Via Recta to the Armenian Apostolic Church of St Sarkis beside the Bab Sharqi. The atmosphere is warm and the chanting is beautiful but I have scuttled in late and am reprimanded for inadvertently sitting on the wrong side of the gender-separated aisle. The Bishop of the Armenian Diocese of Damascus gives a sermon in Armenian with translation into Arabic and French, and as these strange syllables pass over my head I examine the chancel with its red velvet banners and paintings of the virgin and saints. After the service I fall in with an expatriate Swiss who invites me for a sandwich and offers a vista into the life of the misfit Europeans and diplomats who live in Damascus.

Dialogues

Dear Rupert, Damascus and her mosques, policemen, scrap yards, music, madrasas, souqs, muezzins, satellite dishes, teahouses, cars, people, pilgrims from Iran and hammams are unforgettable. We lived in Sarouja, where there are some old houses left and chattering old men along the street. Adel at the corner repaired my shoes always giggling and when we left Damascus we had this big new suitcase to carry, the result of dealing behind the Umayyad Mosque where carpets and family silver is for sale to finance Hajj. In Syria at least for you now, it is no longer necessary to buy newspapers in which certain pages are missing and to have water in your mouth and other tortures. The frescos at Mar Musa are beautiful in this dark room of contemplation. But I was not interested in the folks sitting around talking about God and the world, surrounded by their own ego. So we went to Maaloula where Lebanese families come for picnics. Illiana.

Dear Illiana, yes Damascus is fascinating. But the newspapers are not all mutilated: I was given a complete copy of the London *Times* by the head of Public Relations at the Ministry of Information. With its society gossip and sports pages, the newspaper seemed remote from any reality that I could understand: the world's media has moved on from Iraq. The practical mechanics of visiting Syria are simple and cash machines accept European debit cards. I was taken to the hammam of Nur ad-Din by an architect who works for the Damascus governorate. The leaching malaise of the government is visible everywhere, but my new friend insists that Bashar himself cares deeply about the Syrian people. As a tourist I have had no contact with authority apart from the visa extension. On one occasion, I saw the President's sinister convoy of black limousines. But if Bashar signs a Trade and Association Agreement with the EU, Syria could become part of the pan-Mediterranean family of nations. It is hot and I am under the weather. Somehow I must recover my energies to continue my journey. Everyone in Damascus says how beautiful eastern Turkey is: I will certainly be pleased to walk in the mountains of Ararat after four months of sand! Rupert.

Dear Rupert, yes, I know this feeling of being tired of travelling. When I went across Poland during wintertime I was accompanied by this shadow. Now in my memory it is one of the most important experiences I ever made. If you are in Aleppo visit the Armenian school where you will see children learning the wonderful letters of their alphabet. I know Armenia only from the writings of Andrej Bitow. Apart from Kailash, Ararat is one of the mountains I wish to touch during my life. I have seen it only from the perspective of a bird, covered by snow. So for me it is perfect to explore eastern Turkey. Illiana.

Southern Syria

MONDAY 30 JUNE | BOSRA

Still feverish, but longing to escape the Damascus dust, I take the bus to the classical site of Bosra close to the Jordanian border. Bosra is splendid and I float around the quasi-inhabited ruins with that deep sweat one gets from yoga or a visit to the hammam. The local black basalt is extremely durable and the monuments of the Hauran are well-preserved, including the Basilica of Mar Girgis (St George) at Ezra that dates from 515 and whose lintel refers to relics of the third-century martyr—the very same George of the Dragon and Harfleur. Nabatean Bosra prospered in the Roman period from grain production in the fertile Hauran. In 106 the region was annexed by Trajan and Bosra became the capital of the Province of Arabia Petrea. Culturally closer to the desert caravans, Bosra gravitated out of the Byzantine orbit and became the capital of the Ghassanid client state. Along with Lakhmid Hira, these territories would prove to be pivotal in the early phases of the Islamic conquest as Bosra became the first city of the Levant to fall to Khalid al-Walid in July 634. In light of the association with the Nestorian priest Bahira, who is supposed to have taught Christian doctrine to Muhammad, this may have been more than either coincidence or military strategy.

Bosra is dominated by the Roman theatre built during the reign of Trajan and converted into a fortress by Salah ad-Din. Walking through the elaborate passageways, before bursting into the open space of the theatre, all that is needed are flambeaux for the full mediaeval experience. Along the decumanus I pass through the Roman triumphal arch and examine the remains of the third-century basilica that is fancifully associated with Bahira. The ruined octagonal church of SS. Sergius, Bacchus and Leontius from 512 forms a fascinating architectural bridge between Constantine's Golden Church in Antioch and San Vitale in Ravenna. Lastly I visit the al-Omari mosque which carries an echo of the very beginning of Islam. The mosque is thought to have been founded by Omar ibn al-Khattab in 636, possibly after the Muslim victory at Yarmouk, and was completed by the Umayyad Caliph Yazid II in 720. The structure was restored during the Ayyubid period. But the interior preserves the sense of late antiquity with an arcaded courtyard of ionic columns beside the prayer hall strewn about with Persian carpets. The mosque was used by trade caravans and has a square minaret similar to the Umayyad Mosque in Damascus, to which I return for soup and juice.

TUESDAY 1 JULY | MAALOULA

From Bilal Square by Bab Touma I catch an old-style painted bus to Maaloula, bouncing around on sprung leather seats as the road ascends towards the hazy Qalamoun Mountains. The small town of Maaloula is the emblem of the Christian presence in Syria. During the period of the coups from 1946 to 1970 there was a steady exodus of Christians who felt threatened by the Sunni majority and especially the rhetoric of some Islamist politicians. That changed when Hafez al-Assed seized power and the Alawite-dominated government sought alliances with other minority groups. Having fallen from around thirty per cent of the population in 1920 to ten per cent today, Syrian Christians, including Armenians who fled from Anatolia after 1915, have been caught between radical Islamists, who threaten them with extinction like the Turkish Ittihadists, and an extractive and repressive regime. Maaloula is predominantly Christian but the town's inhabitants pride themselves on the non-sectarian nature of their community, which includes many groups.

The town itself is built into ravines that descend from the Qalamoun, and the ancient houses and streets wind around the hillside whose aspect reminds me of the Judaean desert, as if I am once more in the world of the Byzantine Levant.

Maaloula and the surrounding villages are one of the few remaining places where fifty or so families continue to speak Aramaic, the Semitic descendent of Akkadian and antecedent of Syriac. Sometime in the early first millennium BC, Arameans adopted the Phoenician alphabet as more flexible and adaptable than the preceding Akkadian system of pictograms. When Assyria absorbed the Aramean population into its territory after 732 BC, Aramaic and its alphabet became the lingua franca of the region. Assyriologists suggest that this transition led to the obsolescence of cuneiform clay tablets as a writing system, supplanted by alphabetic inscription on much less durable parchment and papyrus.

In the town square a television crew is filming an anti-abortion campaign, a reminder of the traditionalism of Syrian society. Maaloula's primary attraction is the Greek Orthodox shrine of Mar Takla that is approached up stone steps from the square. In Syriac tradition Takla was an early convert from Iconium and companion of Paul who escaped martyrdom and became the subject of voluminous legends. Paths lead through rocks up to a gorge with a grotto, and then on to the Greek Catholic monastery of Mar Sarkis where the Lord's Prayer is recited in Aramaic for tourists. The path continues up to the top of the escarpment and along the crest to the four-star Safir Hotel where I write postcards on the terrace looking over the precipice. Later I return to the capital to meet Somalian Aysha and her girlfriends for cocktails at the Matador club in the Christian Quarter. For them Damascus is the garden of earthly delights.

WEDNESDAY 2 JULY | DAMASCUS

I send the cards from the post office and take an iced raspberry juice under the shadow of an enormous portrait of Hafez al-Assad that covers the entire side wall of the building. I walk through the district of al-Hariqa, formerly known as Sidi Amoud after a local marabout, and renamed 'conflagration' after the French bombarded it in October 1925. In spite of the drabness of the reconstructed district, the authentic Midhat Pasha Souq prompts me to explore the less-well-visited

Damascus museums. Following the Abbasid founding of Baghdad as the new imperial capital in 762, the Bilad al-Shams fell moribund and little was built. In the 1100s Damascus revived as a forward base against the Crusaders who tried three times to capture the city. Nur ad-Din Zengi took control of Damascus in 1154 and initiated a construction boom that continued with his Ayyubid and Mamluk successors. The most interesting legacy of this period is the Bimaristan (hospital) Nur ad-Din that was known for medical research and associated with the polymath Ibn al-Nafis, who theorised about circulation of the blood. Now the Museum of Medicine History, the building has a courtyard with trees around a square pond and a collection of mediaeval instruments.

I wander through the souqs, which preserve their flavour of exotic trade and still supply Iranian textiles, Yemeni carnelian and Afghani lapis from Badakhshan. The markets were ordered by their proximity to the seat of power, usually at the citadel, with the Souq al-Atarin (perfume) having the highest rank. Along the main thoroughfare that threads east from the Umayyad Mosque, two carpet-sellers on opposite sides of al-Qaymariyya street compete for my attention. I descend the steps into the shop that seems to have the finer pieces in the window and promise the other I will return. The rug seller, Abu Jamal Yusuf, offers me tea in time-honoured fashion, and we pass the afternoon discussing religion and history of ideas. Abu Jamal has a good aura and tries his best to convert me to Islam. After two hours, we are going around in circles. Jokingly I tell Abu Jamal that I will convert if he sells me four of his finest silk carpets for $20, and eventually there is some reward in the form of a $10 discount on his Daghestani jajim that I genuinely like.

At that moment a European man arrives in the shop and exchanges familiar greetings with Abu Jamal. Max the Austrian knows his rugs and I observe the scene as more tea is produced and he imparts his carpet-haggling skills. The main thing is not to show that you really want the carpet in question. Equally, you should not buy one unless it calls you first, especially when you sift through so many. Max gives a demonstration of how to negotiate like a wizard, and I am impressed to see the whole performance perfectly executed with false departures, elaborate gestural expostulations and a refusal to budge. Max bargains Abu Jamal down from $1,000 to $500 for two Tabriz rugs, which, he tells me later, would be worth about $2,000 in Europe. We leave the shop and Max invites me to join him for dinner upstairs at the legendary Beit Jabri courtyard restaurant with vine-clad trellises, running fountain and fine home-style Shamsi cuisine.

Max explains that he travels frequently to Damascus to advise the Syrian government on economic reform. As we wait for our *basturma* and *mulukhiyah*, we embark on a political discussion, and Max gives me his pure Austrian vision of the perfect political economy. 'Eliminate tax!' says Max. 'Privatise everything! Break the cartels!' On the latter I can only agree, although he elides the question of how a wholly deregulated private sector would not inevitably consolidate into a system of cartels. Then Max strays into more Hobbesian territory and argues that it is pointless to adopt universal education for the masses. It is self-defeating, Max suggests, to invest in the human capital of the labour force above the point at which the economy can generate opportunities to employ them. The misallocation of capital in education, he says, is why you find disgruntled Egyptian taxi drivers with doctorates.

I counter that in developed societies with high levels of basic education, the economy is normally at full employment. 'You are operating under the consumption paradigm of homo economicus,' I say. 'Are not learning and knowledge ends in themselves? Is there not a fundamental cultural difference between computer games, soap opera and gambling versus science, literature and the arts? Does anyone think that they have reached the limit of enlightenment? Why should not everyone be cognisant of the state of contemporary science, indeed of knowledge in general? The economic question is not about education, which is a good in itself, but about the equilibrium between skills and jobs. Countries such as Egypt have an excess supply of labour that takes the system out of equilibrium. Better universal education is good for the capability of all citizens: is it not better to have an educated unemployed workforce with the wit and capacity to entertain itself than ranks of ignorant angry masses susceptible to extremism and violence?'

THURSDAY 3 JULY | DAMASCUS
The heat and polluted air are becoming more intense. I survive by wearing my thin Siwi sirwal trousers but, like the Cairenes, the Shamsis think they are undergarments and give me peculiar looks. I return to al-Qaymariyya Street and buy a Baluchi kilim from the second rug seller, Yasser Sagherji. In the souqs I find a shop selling damask tablecloths and buy a pair of these beautifully woven textiles to send back to London. At the reception of al-Rabie I run into Kate from 'Stop the War' protest marches in London. Kate has been working for the voluntary organisation 'Project Hope' in Jayyous, a Palestinian village near Qalqilya, and is in Damascus to learn Shamsi Arabic. We had spoken about Syria but not made any plans to meet. Kate is blonde, stylish and vivacious and I give her a tour of the old city with the assumed mastery of an indigene.

Over soup at Zeitoun, Kate tells me about her experiences in Palestine with Project Hope and the International Solidarity Movement. Teenage boys in Nablus are being shot by Israeli soldiers for breaching curfews; ordinary Palestinians feel bitterness towards the internationals who do nothing to stop their suffering and are angry at being labelled 'terrorists' while land appropriation continues and Israeli armour wrecks their cultural heritage. Since the Second Intifada erupted, the historic centre of Nablus with its labyrinthine streets and soap factory has been strafed by F-16 jets while tanks demolish ancient buildings. In Jayyous, the villagers used to enjoy picnics in the olive groves, tilling the crops and selling oil but their way of life has disappeared along with their land: now these people have few options to find work.

Apart from unprovoked incursions into villages such as Jayyous, setting off tear gas and sound bombs, the IDF makes arbitrary detentions of civilians across the West Bank. Teenagers suffer sleeplessness and post-traumatic stress syndrome while much of the population is depressed. The IDF has effectively sealed the West Bank to weapons, so frustrated young boys throw stones, while a network of informants stokes internal conflict as innocent people end up in Israeli gaols. Kate talks about the right of an occupied people to resist under Article 49 of the Fourth Geneva Convention, which outlaws the settlement of civilians in conquered lands. Yet the cycle of violence has ended up with the Palestinians in an ever-worse situation: the logical extension of hardline Israeli claims to Samaria and Judaea that Asaf Avnon cited on the Sinai bus.

We decamp to the convivial Umayyad coffee house and Kate speaks about how the expanding network of Israeli settlements fuels membership of violent groups such as the al-Aqsa and al-Qassam Brigades. In echo of Israel's trilemma, many volunteers working in Jayyous are Jews wanting to understand the situation of the Palestinians. The irony is that after independence the Syrian government wanted to keep its Jewish population. The Jobar synagogue was built on the site where, by tradition, Elijah anointed Elisha, while the Harat al-Yahud district of the old city still preserves its ancient al-Menarsha synagogue. For decades after Jews fled to Israel from across the region, there remained several thousand Jews in Syria who were only allowed to leave in 1992. The Syrian government is said to keep their property in trust, pending resolution of a final settlement with Israel. As night descends, I observe the men laughing over their card games and backgammon against a soundscape of voices without background music, like starlings flocking at dusk.

FRIDAY 4 JULY | SALIHIYE

Kate and I walk up to Salihiye through the new city which is deserted for Friday prayers. Salihiye was founded as a separate city on the slopes of Mount Qasioun to accommodate refugees from the sack of Jerusalem in 1099 and became a centre of Muslim piety in the Ayyubid period. We begin at the monumental Madrasa Maridaniye and continue along the main street which has a lively market and mosques whose custodians invite us in to drink tea on thick rugs. Of greatest interest is the mosque-mausoleum of Muhyiddin ibn al-Arabi, dating from 1516 with an *imaret* (soup kitchen) added by Sinan in 1560. The sheikh, who died in Damascus in 1240, is best known as the author of the Sufi treatise *al-Futuhat al-Makkiyya*. The Ottomans emphasised Sufism as a means of consolidating their rule in Syria and built the complex around the green-domed tomb of al-Arabi.

From Nasib al-Bakri Street we take an old yellow taxi up the hill to Mount Qasioun. The driver leaves us at the restaurant, and we walk along the ridge where people come in the evenings to sit on the rocks and watch the sunset. According to Muslim tradition Cain killed Abel at the Magharat al-Dam (cave of blood) on this peak—a biblical story that mythologises the perennial Khaldunian struggle between settler and nomad. Qasioun is also where Muhammad came as a child in his uncle Abu Talib's caravan to gaze over paradise. Ibn Battuta wrote 'if eternal paradise exists on earth, it is found nowhere else but in Damascus'. The peak certainly has fine views across the dusty grey smog to the anti-Lebanon, with the Umayyad Mosque clearly visible and the trees of the Barada-watered orchard-oasis of Ghouta standing out from the sprawl to the east.

For this land of Bilad al-Shams on the fringe of the Fertile Crescent across the desert from the Bilad al-Nahrayn or Bilad al-Rafidayn (Arabic names for Mesopotamia) is truly the gift of the Barada. Visible across the saddle of another hill is the sinister compound of the Presidential Palace. At the appointed moment, the electrifying cacophony of muezzins fire up for the Maghrib prayer, lighting their green neon strips, and I am taken back to the rock of Siwa, whose clarity of air Damascus once had too. Some boys scramble down the stones and we follow them to the shrine of Maqam al-Arba'in, dedicated to the memory of Abel, from which there is a series of paved concrete steps that lead down to Salihiye at the city's edge.

SATURDAY 5 JULY | DAMASCUS
I pass the morning at al-Rabie with Jerry Valberg's philosophical theory of conscious experience, *Dream, Death and the*

Self. Jerry has given me a pre-publication version of this 1,200-page sequel to his earlier *Puzzle of Experience* and I have carried the printed copy all the way from London. My priority is to extract the content so that I can shed weight, now down to a few books and notepads that still feel heavy in the heat. At the post office I despatch the damask tablecloths to London. Kate joins me for pizza on the corner of Souq Sarouja and I realise that, not being able to post the rugs, weight dictates that I must return the second kilim. So I go back to Abu Jamal's shop on al-Qaymariyya Street, and we talk for two hours about politics and carpets before he agrees to prevail upon Yasser to take back the second kilim. Suitably relieved, I smoke nargileh at the Umayyad coffee house with Valberg and take French onion soup at Station One.

Dream, death and the soul
In seeking to analyse the meaning of words, analytical philosophers tie themselves in linguistic knots and often end up trapped in forests of no-entry signs. Valberg clears this skein of obstructions by describing subjective experience phenomenologically rather mechanistically. He describes interior experience as 'horizonal' and identifies the will as the presence of action in the horizon. Self-originated actions, generated by the will, are only intelligible from the perspective of the agent's horizon and are not the result of any mechanical causal interaction between 'mental states'. Analytical philosophers are concerned to analyse the *concept* of experience but the horizonal frame is of a different subject matter. Experience does not occur 'inside' our heads; it is not part of the world but rather the horizon within which the world is present.

Following Descartes's sceptical dream-challenge to naïve metaphysical realism, Valberg asks: how do I know *this* is not a dream? Which raises the question: what is *this*? For an object in the dream cannot surely *be* the dream. Hence dreams must include objects outside the dream, just as reality includes objects outside experience. *This* being a dream would pre-suppose that there is a wider context into which I can wake up. The dream hypothesis implies that I might emerge from the context of which I am subject, which contains the world of my horizonal experience, into that very same context. But I cannot enter a room by leaving it: I cannot emerge into the context to which I came from my past dreams, for I am already there.

From a standpoint external to the dream, certain propositions are true which do not hold from any standpoint internal to the dream. Likewise with identity. If this were a dream, the date and duration of the dreaming would belong to wider time, not time internal to this. So the dream must be outside time. Different uses of the first person must also be distinguished: the positional use of I picks out which human being is me, while the horizonal use of my means that if this is a dream, you and I are both in my dream. But consider other minds: I am with others in this and we have no common horizon: you have yours and I have mine. So if this is a dream, the dream would be mine and I must regard you as in my dream. Therefore commitment to the existence of other minds makes the dream hypothesis impossible.

What is the relation between the self and the horizon? If I look inside my own horizon I cannot find anything except the objects of experience. One kind of nothingness is the absence of experiential facts within the horizon; but another kind of nothingness is the horizonal property of being nothing-in-itself apart from the entities present within it. So there is a mutual dependency between the horizon and facts of presence within the horizon. This means that if there were no facts of presence there would not be any horizon within which such facts hold, and likewise that if there were no all-containing horizon there could be no facts of presence. If you take away the horizon, the external world would be unchanged and would exist just like it does now. But it would not be present: there would be nothing, the absence of presence.

What makes a subject's horizon his or her own is the fact that it includes all other horizons: what makes my horizon mine is that within my subjective experience, it is the horizon. But in death we face a state of absolute and final nothingness. The meaning of death is its awfulness, and we deceive ourselves to avoid confronting that meaning. We may even admit to self-deception without undeceiving ourselves, as if pretending it will not happen. But as death comes closer, the deception is harder to maintain. The subject matter of death—that which the prospect of my death holds up as ceasing to exist—is this horizon of which I am at the centre, the horizon to which all of the world is internal. Death and the dream hypothesis have the same subject matter. Epicurus was right to assert that we should not fear the death state itself, because we cannot fear what we do not experience. But experience has its own way of making sense to us and the prospect of nothingness is unfathomably disturbing.

The irreducibility of subjective experience grounds the metaphysics of each sentient being as an indivisible atom in the world of experience: this individuation of persons through subjective experience is the source of freedom that anchors the triumph of humanism over mechanism. Any mechanistic totalising theory of society will always lead to worse outcomes as the individual is subsumed into a higher programme— whether that is Spencerian capitalism or fascistic nationalism or the dictatorship of the proletariat. For it is the annihilation in death of the subject of private consciousness that we call persons or souls that anchors the metaphysical and ethical value of an individual life.

The realisation of the existential nothingness of death changes the colour of our attitude to ethics and changes the value we place on existence itself. The individual matters. Scientific materialism is unviable as an ideology because it leads ultimately to the absurdity of positivism, to the stance that any statements that cannot be verified by observation or by direct measurement literally have no meaning, and hence that ethics is purely a matter of taste. A.J. Ayer was surprised by the Holocaust because he had no mental calculus on which to hang ethical judgements. Perhaps this was the response of the interwar generation to the horrors of the trenches? Yet Ayer already had the Armenian case to go on: the latent violence in humankind shorn of any external force to temper naturalism was apparent to anyone with open eyes. Christianity was a social revolution against the brutality and cruelty of the empires that preceded it. Secularised Christianity is the foundation of the modern West. The Sermon on the Mount was a revolution against the Homeric heroic code, against the justification of bad acts by their inevitability as the outcome of impersonal natural forces.

SUNDAY 6 JULY | DAMASCUS
Despite being feverish, I am nostalgic to leave my well-established haunts in this most ancient of cities. Over breakfast I peruse the *Syria Times*, official organ of the regime. An opinion piece by Riad Zein titled 'Democracy and the Market Economy' catches my attention. Zein explains that, of its very nature, the market economy marginalises the individual, plunders his freedom and converts his humanity into a commodity of specifications. In contrast democracy (acceptance of the majority's will by the minority) develops the individual according to sublime values of justice, freedom and humanity and leads to prosperity and progress. But American hegemony is becoming a dictatorship in which sinister forces are subverting the fabric of the polity. Democracy is being replaced by a rich junta in which the minority elite dominates the will and decision of the majority. It occurs to me that perhaps Zein has been reading Qadhafi's *The Green Book*. Like Qadhafi, it seems Bashar al-Assad supports the idea of democracy in theory, so long as he retains control. Yet, in some respects Riad Zein has a point: to what extent are powerful private interests really accountable to the sovereign will of the people in liberal democracies?

I return to al-Qaymariyya Street to collect the money from Abu Jamal for the returned kilim, and promise Yasser Sagherji that I will say a prayer for him at the tomb of Rumi in Konya. Kate joins me at the Umayyad coffee house and we walk to the district of Qanawat, which has old streets with pretty Turkish-style mosques. Kate wants to rent a room in a house with a family and has booked a series of appointments with candidate hosts in the streets around Bab Touma. So we explore the district from house to house, considering the various options before taking an excellent aubergine bake and juice in Souq Sarouja.

Deir Mar Musa

MONDAY 7 JULY TO WEDNESDAY 9 JULY

The Syrian Catholic monastery of Mar Musa al-Habashi lies in a rocky hollow at the eastern outpost of the Qalamoun mountains of the anti-Lebanon range, where the land falls away to the Syrian desert. The monastery was built by order of the Emperor Heraclius over the tomb of the hermit Moses the Abyssinian. Deir Mar Musa lay along two fault lines: the frontier of Byzantium that ran from Dura on the Euphrates to Bosra; and the Greek-speaking zone of Syria that tended to Orthodoxy versus the southern Aramaic-speaking zone that remained Syriac. The monastery was semi-coenobitic, with scattered cells joined to the central set of buildings by stone paths, and may have originally been made up of men and women. Deir Mar Musa was abandoned in the 1830s as Roman Catholic proselytism sapped the Syriac community.

In June 1979 the Muslim Brotherhood assassinated scores of Alawite Syrian Army cadets in the Aleppo Artillery School. In retaliation Rifaat al-Assad's units massacred at least 800 political prisoners in Palmyra prison. This in turn led to the Hama Uprising of February 1982 in which Hafez al-Assad eliminated several thousand Islamist insurgents and destroyed much of the city. The violence secured the regime but was a foretaste of the terrible conflict to come. Later in 1982 a Jesuit seminarian from Rome named Paolo dall'Oglio travelled to the isolated ruins of Deir Mar Musa and began to renovate the monastic buildings. In 1991 Father Paolo was granted a dispensation by Pope John Paul II to dedicate the refounded Deir Mar Musa to the 'love of Jesus for the Islamic world'.

The bus from Abbasiyeen stops at the nondescript town of Nabek, halfway between Damascus and Homs. From Nabek the local taxi passes through a gap in the Qalamoun hills and across the arid plain to the end of the road. I climb up the steep steps to the monastery and arrive in time for lunch with Mikhail, an Austrian philosopher-theologian who explains the unusual offices and shows me around. The various parts of Deir Mar Musa are connected by staircases from the original cave of St Moses to the tower in the centre of the complex and the nuns' quarters across a bridge over a ravine. The monastery church that dates from 1058 is decorated with frescos of the holy family, saints and the last judgement. The frescos are the most complete surviving cycle of Syriac religious art and are in the final stages of restoration.

As at St Catherine's, a routine emerges: chatting in the morning over black tea in metal cups; sitting in the cave of St Moses where a candle is kept lit; volunteering for tasks such as washing-up and drying out the laundry; then wandering around the rocks and dry fields above the monastery. As the sun fades later in the day, everyone gathers for an hour of contemplation in the tent-church on the roof of the main building that looks over the valley. At sunset, the time of the Muslim prayer of Maghrib, the electric lights come on and a mass is celebrated in Arabic, with anyone from any faith or denomination welcome to participate. The service is accompanied by an oud, guitar and chanting, followed by a jovial supper of grilled chicken and falafel.

Mikhail introduces me to Huda who oversees the female quarters and the library. Father Paolo, the abouna himself, imposing and bearded, has all the qualities you might expect from someone who created a place like this, radiating warmth, kindness and limitless energy. He explains that the spirit of the early church continues at Deir Mar Musa, but chaotically bound by living, building and restoring. Over supper we talk syncretism and the parallels between Sufis and the Desert Fathers. Although Islam drew on the Christian mystical tradition, the Sufi way of humility is rooted in the Bedu origins of the Prophet Muhammad. What is in your heart is reflected in your face: if everyone had God in their heart, we would all live in peace. But Sufism is also inherently deterministic: the theologian Muhyiddin ibn al-Arabi argued that God created man's actions and so we should not judge others. If I despise you, I despise God's deeds because everything that happens is divine will. After supper we continue discussing history and religion, before retiring to the dormitory, which feels like a mountain redoubt, guarded by the monastery's red-eyed mongrel dogs.

The wisdom of Father Paolo
'Isn't Christianity about salvation through belief in the Resurrection? Isn't that the magic formula?' I ask. 'You have got it the wrong way around,' says Father Paolo. 'You are reversing the order from the scriptures. First get to know the Jesus of the Gospels and only then do theology, which begins with John. If you start with articles of faith then no wonder you remain blind. Faith is to welcome the call of the divine,' Father Paolo continues. It is all about experience. Does taking the sacrament not leave a different effect from taking just any piece of bread and sip of wine? Far from being an intellectual barrier, other religions corroborate the truths of Christian experience in the elevation from the cross to the opening of the heart. So the heart must witness the lights that shine in different niches but come from a unique and inexhaustible source. Deir Mar Musa participates in the realisation of the Islamic vocation of illumination.

The twentieth century produced an anthropological transformation from subordination, separation and diffidence into the harmony of the human community with equality, solidarity and reciprocity. Faith results from the presence of the divine in the human person: the life of Christ is the design for an all-embracing benevolence. Paul wrote to the Corinthians that, 'The Lord is spirit and the spirit of the Lord is freedom.' But freedom must not be held prisoner to the particularism of different traditions. Faced with scepticism and other religions, we must love in a dynamic of plural identities and common futures. The essence of Christianity is the transformation of our personality through grace and redemption, forgiveness and love.

But the religion has been subverted away from its original message. Some have turned it into a rule book, emphasising judgement and the fear of divine retribution. Some have used Christianity as a means of exploiting weakness and ignorance to preserve unjust hierarchies: consider corruption in the Church and the harnessing of religion to state power. Others have turned Christianity into a metaphysical insurance policy, either for salvation in the putative afterlife or for material success in this life, as a private club for 'the elect'. Lastly there are those who turn the supernatural imagery of the Bible into an aggressive superstition, full of dark powers. These are the most dangerous of all.

'One should not think that the pursuit of individual happiness lies in realising one's talents or even seeking the happiness of others. For one cannot realise oneself unless one gives up superficial happiness for something deeper and more essential. Only then can one achieve the psychological equilibrium that enables all the other things one believes in and seeks to be realised.' I wonder again why Christian mysticism is so insistent on the purification of the spirit through the renunciation of the material world, and especially the sins of the flesh, while also offering the prospect of an ascent to a higher state of being through ecstatic union with the transcendent. 'Read the *Spiritual Exercises of St Ignatius Loyola*,' Father Paolo concludes, and invites me to return to Deir Mar Musa to embark upon the 'living tradition' of St Ignatius.

Alas I am unable to take up his invitation. In the spring of 2011, Father Paolo published an article calling for a peaceful 'consensual' democratic transition in Syria and met with opposition activists. Damascus reacted by issuing an expulsion order. Following the publication of his open letter to the United Nations special envoy in May 2012, he left Syria to join the Deir Maryam al-Adhra community at Sulaymaniyah in Iraqi Kurdistan. In the summer of 2013, Father Paolo entered eastern Syria. On 29 July 2013 he was kidnapped by Islamic State militants in Raqqa with four other priests and has never been seen again.

In August 2011, Father Paolo explained the situation in Syria in a recorded interview that survived his presumed murder:

Muslims and Christians are complex communities with a lot of memory, but the common element of their living together over fourteen centuries is good neighbourhood. Syria has a religious and symbolic pluralism from five thousand years ago ... for Syria is a highway of civilisation between the three valleys—the Hindu, Mesopotamian and Nile Egyptian valley—and this created from Syria the starting point of the other enormous civilisational valley that we call the Mediterranean. Historically Syria worked under the predominance of the Islamic ruler: there was the ruler and the ruled people. This today is in crisis because the idea of the modern state ... goes with the idea of citizenship, so people who go to Europe have the experience of being citizens before being Muslim, Jewish, Christian or whatever.

Today people in the Arabic countries ask to be first of all citizens, without renouncing or putting aside the cultural or religious elements of their identity ... But we have a pole that is the request of Israel to be a Jewish state and to create a Palestinian state where Political Islam is growing, Lebanon that is polarised by religious identities, Iraq that is in danger of sliding into civil war based on religious or ethnic identities ... and Turkey where the ethnic issues are strong between the Turkish and Kurdish populations ... [In Syria] until now there was a system that was able to bring all this together, but now it is at risk of explosion. Perhaps all the people around being afraid that if Syria explodes everything will explode all around, they will say no, don't touch, or touch kindly, handle with care, and probably that is the best thing to do.

THURSDAY 10 JULY | PALMYRA

Reluctant to leave the convivial monastery, I take the bus across the desert to Tadmor and find a room at the Aqfa hotel in the nondescript grid of streets that constitute the modern town. The Archaeological Museum of Palmyra is best known for its collection of stele with Aramaic inscriptions as well as the distinctive funerary reliefs of reclining Palmyrenes that date from the city's zenith in the Antonine Age. The famous ruins themselves are a short distance from the town. I walk to the tetrapylon at the centre of the Great Colonnade, then along its ancient stone paving to the western end of the valley and up the steep hill to the Fakhr al-Din citadel. Built by the Druze emir of Lebanon in the 1620s, the castle affords the best views of Palmyra, picking out the stately limestone ruins against the green of the oasis and the empty wastes beyond.

Palmyra reaches into the Amorite past of the early second millennium BC when Upper Mesopotamia (al-Jazeera) consisted of fertile plains. Even then the springs of Palmyra lay on the desert fringes of the region and formed an oasis along the caravan route from the middle Euphrates to the Orontes and the coastal towns opposite Cyprus. After Trajan annexed Petra Arabia, Palmyra grew wealthy on trade between Syria and Parthia. Following the assassination of Odaenathus, the Roman client ruler of Palmyra, his wife Zenobia revolted against Rome and ruled from 267 to 272 as the 'Queen of the East'. But the Emperor Aurelian defeated Zenobia at the Battle of Emesa in 272, and the glamorous monarch was taken in chains to Rome. Palmyra continued to prosper until the later wars between Rome and Sasanian Persia withered trade across the Euphrates. The city declined but Zenobia survives on the Syrian 500 pound note.

FRIDAY 11 JULY | DEIR EZ-ZOR

The dominant building in the site, the Temple of Bel, is magnificent at dawn. The temple was dedicated in 32 AD over the site of an earlier Hellenistic shrine, and was rebuilt in the second century. The worship of Bel (a title meaning 'Lord' and derived from Akkadian) represented a continuation of the Babylonian supreme deity, Marduk. The nearby temples of Nabu and Baalshamin were also linked to the Babylonian pantheon. After the conversion of Constantine, the Temple of Bel was converted into a church, while other pagan shrines and statues were ransacked by Christian mobs in 385. Sadly all the temples would be dynamited by Daesh (the 'Islamic State' terror group) in 2015. I walk through the Arch of Triumph and back along the cardo maximus, whose Corinthian columns carry inscriptions in Aramean and Greek, and examine the tetrapylon, peristyle and funerary towers. Once again I am impressed by the splendour of late antiquity, with its finely carved public architecture, uncontaminated by the sprawl and detritus of industrial capitalism.

In the town I join an English couple for omelette. Tadmor itself is somewhat devoid of life, and I abandon Palmyra to absorb the conversational comfort of the familiar in the bus, perhaps in the spirit of the caravans of antiquity. At Deir ez-Zor they continue to Aleppo, while I walk into the bustling town which today has a colourful farmers' market. The comfortable 1930s Raghdan Hotel by the Euphrates is full, so I take a room at the uninspiring Damas Funduq. A mile or so along the main street, the museum has an engaging collection of artefacts from the Tells of al-Jazeera and the sites of Dura and Mari. As I walk back along the river, a convoy of blacked out limousines passes by, business executives en route to the nearby oil fields.

In the streets behind the funduq I find the octagonal stone Armenian Martyrs Memorial Church. During the second phase of the Armenian genocide in 1916, hundreds of thousands of Armenian civilians were deported in columns to Aleppo and across the plain of Meskeneh to internment camps near Deir ez-Zor. A substantial number died during the marches, either from lack of food and water or beaten by armed militias that harassed the columns. After Salih Zeki Bey became governor of Deir ez-Zor in the summer of 1916, the camps were liquidated and the prisoners were killed in the wilderness between Deir ez-Zor and Ras al-Ayn. An estimated 80,000 Armenians were executed at Margadeh while 5,000 victims were asphyxiated by smoke in the Shaddadah cave. In recognition of these events, the church in Deir ez-Zor was built with funds raised from the Armenian Apostolic Diocese of Beroea (Aleppo) and consecrated in 1991. In the centre is a column that extends into the upper storey, surrounded by bones in glass cases, with photographs of Armenian priests. The church would subsequently be destroyed by Daesh on 21 September 2014.

Opposite the main square is a pedestrian suspension bridge across the Euphrates, built by the French in the 1920s. I had loosely arranged a rendezvous here with the English friend of the al-Rabie major-domo who teaches at the British Council. But we do not connect, so I sit lonesome at the al-Jisr al-Kabir canteen by the Euphrates Bridge, watching the local boys diving into the Bassel al-Assad open-air swimming pool opposite. The restaurant has separate sections for families to eat on one side and men to smoke nargileh on the other. Oddly it is not possible to order Barada beer in the latter—as if by peculiar writ each intoxicant is frowned upon and cannot be combined. But the languid atmosphere of the river in the sultry air is intoxicating, and it is an extraordinarily enjoyable evening experience to be there.

S<small>ATURDAY</small> 12 J<small>ULY</small> | M<small>ARI</small>
From Deir ez-Zor I take the microbus to the classical site of Dura Europos on the Euphrates. The bus is packed tight and the side door opens at frequent intervals so I am relieved to be dropped by the side of the road some two miles from Dura. I wrap a keffiyeh around my head and walk across the dusty plain towards the imposing Palmyra gate of the ancient city. Crossing the wilderness I am transported to the third century as the bastions rise up against the horizon. Dura was founded circa 300 BC by Seleucus Nicator and prospered from trade between Antioch and Seleucia-on-the-Tigris. In those days the fertile plains of the Dura region generated a rich agricultural surplus. After the incorporation of Roman Syria as a province in 64 BC, the Euphrates became the axis of the frontier zone between the Roman and Parthian Empires. From 165 Dura was fortified as the forward base for the Roman legions until being razed by the Sasanians in 256. After the fall of Dura, the frontier receded upstream to Circessium and a new line of border fortresses was constructed under Diocletian from the Euphrates to Palmyra and Damascus, the Strata Diocletiana.

The ruins are spread across a wide area encircled by a course of walls looking over the green strip of the Euphrates. Since its discovery in 1920 Dura has been extensively excavated and most of the significant artefacts have been removed including the synagogue, whose mural panels were taken to Damascus, and a house church whose paintings are now at Yale. Dura offers a glimpse into the syncretism and exploratory cultic practices on the borderland of empires where one senses there was a free exchange of influences between Mithraism and Zoroastrianism, Christianism and rabbinical

Judaism. Dualist ideas of truth and falsity, and good and evil, would have spread between the followers of Zoroaster and Mani to the Nazarenes. To be good as a normative imperative is the expression of divine wisdom while evil is caused by free acts.

The Achaemenids absorbed the artistic and intellectual legacy of Assyria and Babylon, and Alexander inherited the same. After Pompey extinguished the Seleucid state, the open market in religious ideas continued to flourish. So from around 1000 BC until the fall of Dura there was a continuous axis of cultural interchange that extended from the Levantine shore to the Indus. But after Ardashir made Zoroastrianism the Sasanian state religion in 230 and Rome became Christian after 313, the world moved into confrontation between rival empires of faith and the Euphrates became a frontier. I walk along the decumanus past the agora and outline of the Seleucid Temple of Artemis to the Roman citadel. Here one sees why the location was chosen for its defensive limestone escarpment standing high over the Euphrates, protecting the city from floods and assault while giving access to water for transport and irrigation.

From the highway I catch another microbus along the river to the archaeological site of Mari. This Early Dynastic Period Sumerian city state was razed by Hammurabi of Babylon in 1759 BC. The palace of the city's last ruler Zimri-Lim was originally decorated with frescos but now contains little more than a pile of clay-straw bricks, thirty-eight centuries old. Apart from a series of tunnels and cavities below the plain there is little to see. As at the library at Nineveh, however, the burning of Mari preserved records, and 25,000 cuneiform clay tablets have been excavated from the site. The Mari tablets are written in Akkadian and mostly consist of archives and letters from the period immediately prior to the city's destruction. Tablets dated to circa 2500 BC refer to 'Dimashki', tracing the continuity of Damascus back to this period.

In the direct sun in the middle of the day, the site is fearsomely hot. There is almost no shade except for the cover over the excavated chambers of the palace. At the canteen beside the site, the Bedouin patronne is dressed in flowing garments with a string of pretty children playing around her. From the simplest of ingredients—potato, tomato, onion and herbs—she creates a tastier dish than the mediocre falafel, shawarma and kebab found in most restaurants in the country. Syrian restaurant chefs are all men who eat food cooked at home. But deep in the desert at Mari I eat the first plate of food to be cooked by a woman. As I absorb the spirit of this place, I reflect that Zimri-Lim himself was a gourmet, and tablets have been deciphered that show the elaborate variety of the cuisine of ancient Mari.

Opposite is the low house of the French archaeologist Andre Parrot who excavated Mari for forty years. The solid structure could have been built out of the same sun-baked bricks as its ancient forebear, composed around a triangular courtyard with eucalyptus trees that sway in the wind. In the eternal desert this wind pulses like an ocean current across the barren plains of sun-scorched nothingness where tells and wadis and the languid drift of the Euphrates are indifferent to the aeons. The colour of a thirsty, alien, eucalyptus tree is a beacon in the wilderness, promising the dazzling hues and patterns of a Bedouin's dress, of a jajim or a kilim. Here on these ancient plains, where the sun is the all-seeing, all powerful provider and destroyer, where all colour is bleached to a stupor, what else is there to do but shelter from the heat and *abstract*?

The first advances of civilisation were made in Iraq, where pictures became symbols and writing was born. Deciphered cuneiform tablets suggest that Sumerians and Akkadians and Amorites fretted and gossiped with the same aspirations and anxieties that all people have, building and accumulating, subject to plunder by marauders or extinction from their rival conflicts. For insight is an openness, a receptivity to inspiration: we 'divine' understanding as if the cosmos speaks to us. The Sumerians believed that kingship came down from the heavens and that *meh*—knowledge or technique—was given to Uruk by the messenger god Enki from the supreme deity Enlil. Imagine the constellations in the clear night skies above the plains of ancient Iraq: would it not have seemed obvious that insight and invention are revealed from above?

I continue to Abu Kamal where the Euphrates crosses the frontier into Iraq and wander through the souqs beneath hanging portrait banners of Assad. On discovering that I am British, people ask me if I had crossed from Iraq and how I liked the country. I have to reassure them that I have never been to Iraq but can only express my profound sorrow for the violence and destruction which is engulfing that country. Back in Deir ez-Zor I return to the al-Jisr al-Kabir restaurant and sit by the Euphrates in the warm evening air.

Babylon and Greece
The Sumerians invented cuneiform to record transactions involving quantities of land, livestock and labour and to facilitate the operation of temples and palaces: numeracy predated literacy. The transition from city states into the Sargonic Akkadian and 'Ur-III' Sumerian Empires induced the development of new measuring systems and the abstraction of numerical techniques to enable better integration between them. Originally there were different symbols for different kinds of quantity. But at some point the idea of number emerged as the concept of sameness of quantity. Tabulation, reciprocals and the sexagesimal place value system were invented by the Sumerians during the 'Ur-III' period and used to facilitate trans-territorial accounting. Later in Old Babylon these techniques found new applications and pedagogical curricula were established to train the administrative class. Tablets of numerical exercises have been deciphered that suggest scribes set problems to each other to hone their skills and for the pleasure of playing games.

The same 'y'-shaped imprint from a standard stylus could generate over 600 signs with more than 20,000 variations, and there is a remarkable continuity in their meaning over the 2,500-year period. Ashurbanipal understood both Sumerian and Akkadian and the system of writing cuneiform on clay tablets continued until the Seleucid period. Despite their enormous antiquity, spanning half of human history, cuneiform tablets give a direct vista into the mind world of ancient Iraq which we cannot have for Greek mathematics, with its weaker chain of transmission. Indeed the earliest extant copies of Greek manuscripts date from Byzantine records of the tenth century and the encyclopaedic lexicon of Suidas.

After the Macedonian conquest of Babylon in 331 BC, there was direct interchange between the two cultural traditions. The Greeks looked east and absorbed the Semitic cultures of Assyria and Babylonia. The Antiochus cylinder written in Akkadian in 250 BC shows that Babylonian priests worked with the Seleucids to represent them as heirs to Nebuchadnezzar and to preserve Babylonian cultic practices. Hellenic Babylon was syncretic: Berossus, the astronomer and priest of Bel-Marduk, compiled astronomical tables in Greek. Gradually Greek replaced Akkadian in the public administration and by the time Parthia conquered Babylonia in 141 BC, cuneiform had ceased to be used outside the temples. There is some evidence for cultural exchange with Ptolemaic Alexandria. The writings of the second-century BC astronomers Hypsicles and Hipparchus show a Babylonian influence while *Almagest*, the astronomical treatise of Claudius Ptolemy, used Babylonian observational data and units of measurement for the prediction of lunar eclipses.

The more interesting question is the extent to which Greek mathematics drew on Akkadian and Sumerian sources before the Macedonian conquest. Nothing is known about what Minoan Crete and Mycenae absorbed from Old Babylonia in the Bronze Age. Phoenician commercial tablets written in Aramaic from the early first millennium BC have been deciphered that imply a continuity in numeracy. Their influence on the subsequent development of Greek mathematics is unclear. But the Orientalising Period of Archaic Greece (circa 750–650 BC) coincided with Neo-Assyrian hegemony over Babylonia and the Levant. Although Old Babylon herself was destroyed by the Hittites circa 1595 BC, the cultural line continued unbroken in other southern cities such as Nippur, and Babylon was later rebuilt. The Assyrian heartland remained intact until its destruction in 612 BC and it is likely that there was continuity in the cultural transmission of mathematics and astronomy from Babylonia into Assyria. Indeed Ashurbanipal's library at Nineveh is one of the primary sources for the mathematical innovations of the Old Babylonian period.

Could there have been transmission from Nineveh to Miletus and the Hellenic world? It has long been speculated that epics such as Gilgamesh influenced Homer and Hesiod. Evidence that Greeks learned Babylonian mathematics during the Archaic period derives from a small number of cuneiform tablets that have yet to be systematically collated by Assyriologists. Greeks visited Babylon as well as the Assyrian cities of Assur and Nineveh and some bilingual Greek-Akkadian texts from the early first millennium BC have also been discovered. Plato's *Republic* cites the number 12,960,000 (equals sixty squared squared) as the expression of a great law controlling the universe. Such tantalising references to mystical numbers only make sense within the sexagesimal system and suggest there was some diffusion of mathematical ideas. Theophrastus, Aristotle's successor as head of the Lyceum, referred to 'Chaldean' sages.

In *Mathematics in Ancient Iraq* Eleanor Robson argues that the two traditions developed separately and that cuneiform mathematics is not the precursor to the axiomatic-deductive methods of the Greek tradition. Robson also argues that the Serapeum in Alexandria owed little to the scribal cuneiform culture of ancient Iraq. Logical reasoning about propositions to establish theorems and corollaries of mathematical knowledge seems to have been a uniquely Greek invention, quite different from the methods of the Babylonians who were concerned with systems of calculation to solve practical problems. The Babylonians developed algorithms or numerical recipes as problem-based, concrete lines of argumentation. Applied numeracy was central to administration, and justice ('making straight') was dispensed through precision in calculation.

One can ask to what extent the difference between the two schools inform modern debates within the philosophy of mathematics. Robson suggests that the mathematical systems of ancient Iraq provide an illustration of social constructivism. No Platonic forms or abstract 'truth-making' objects are required to explain the grounds of mathematical knowledge, as the whole system is interactive with the practical demands of the operating environment. But if there is a mutual interaction between cosmos, mind and number, this idea also makes naturalistic sense: the truths of mathematics derive ultimately from the structure of physical reality. Or perhaps we should see modern-day physicists as equivalent to the priests and scribes of ancient Iraq, using mathematics as tools to solve practical problems in the modern temples and palaces, our particle accelerators and deep space observatories?

SUNDAY 13 JULY | RESAFA

From Deir ez-Zor I take the microbus up the Euphrates to Raqqa. Leaving my things at the Hotel Ammar, I continue to al-Mansura and hitch a lift to the ruined shrine town of Resafa. Sergius was a Roman soldier martyred circa 310 and venerated by the Bedouin. Around 500 the Emperor Anastasius built a martyrium over the tomb; Justinian transferred the relics to his new Basilica of St Sergius and erected the ramparts. The town was destroyed by the Abbasids in 750 but the walls and church survived. The square enclosure wall, martyrium and basilica were built using gypsum that contains sparkling quartz crystals and shine out like silver across the dusty plain. The northern gate has fine Corinthian columns with arcaded pediment, leading to the outline of the martyrium and basilica whose walls and arcades are preserved without the roof.

In the ruins of the glistening church in Resafa, rising out of the barren emptiness of the sun-baked wasteland, I think about meditation and solitude, the antidotes to excessive activity. Perhaps reflections on economics are futile: whatever it is, it was ever thus. Of necessity, humans come into conflict and jostle to exercise power. Only the environment, the context and the tools change with time. Should one choose ceaseless feverish rushing, the relentless quest to eliminate silence and empty time, or the ennui of repose and balance in all things? Two Belgians drive me to the drab town of al-

Thawrah. I hitch another lift to the ruined Qalaat Jaber, perched on a rock over Lake Assad, and find a microbus back to Raqqa.

From the Hotel Ammar, I make an evening sight-seeing tour of the monuments of Raqqa. Formerly Roman Callinicum, after Seleucus II Callinicus, the city was refounded in 772 by the Abbasid Caliph al-Mansur, who also constructed the Qasr as-Salam, modelled on his palace in Baghdad. Raqqa was sacked by the Mongols in 1258 and the lavish Abbasid palaces were destroyed. There is little to see beyond the outlines of the Great Mosque and the twelfth-century Qasr al-Banat. But the intact Baghdad gate whose bricks have decorative geometric patterns show the influence of Sasanian palace architecture on the Abbasids. I take supper in a bright restaurant by the clock tower, enjoying the hubbub of Raqqa in the warm evening air.

Aleppo

MONDAY 14 JULY

From Raqqa I continue to Aleppo and take a room at the newly redecorated Tourist Hotel in the Bab al-Faraj district. The hotel has a similar atmosphere to Madame Cressaty's pension in Cairo, a refuge from the bleaching sun that illuminates the pot plants on the landings with a golden hue. Glad to find another charming haven, I set out for new haunts and discover the delightful roof garden of the nearby al-Andalib restaurant. The construction of the hydroelectric Taqba Dam on the Euphrates in the 1970s drastically humidified the climate of Aleppo. By mid-afternoon it is forty degrees in the shade, and I pass the afternoon writing notes in the roof garden with strong Cherry Blend Ceylon tea to sweat out the heat.

As the air cools I visit the famous Baron Hotel next door and order beer on the breezy terrace looking over the street. The al-Shark beer served in Aleppo is less good than the Barada: this may be due to the purity of the water flowing off the anti-Lebanon compared to what the Aleppo brewery extracts from the Euphrates. Founded by the Armenian Mazlumian brothers in 1909, the stone-carved, wrought-iron-balconied Baron Hotel hosted travellers and archaeologists of yore from Gertrude Bell to Agatha Christie and Max Mallowan. In the 1990s the Baron was described by Tewdwr Moss as 'the last outpost of faded splendour in an otherwise rackety and filthy town'. The property remains in the Mazlumian family, but business must be bad as there seem to be hardly any guests. The rooms are less comfortable than the bland modern hotels and the prices too high to compete with back-packer pensions. But the Baron retains the characteristic style of the period that survives in just a few places, most famously at the Palmyra Hotel in Baalbek. The marbled hallways and wood panelled bar have old photographs that show glimpses of a more elegant age.

After a bowl of onion soup at the nondescript restaurant Delta, I walk down to the Antioch gate to the precincts of the mediaeval city and through the al-Medina souqs. Puffing away at my nargileh on the esplanade opposite the floodlit citadel, I am accosted by a certain Abdul, owner of the carpet shop Sebastian, who claims to be the author of the successful West End play *Kicking Oscar's Corpse*. We are joined by his friend Samir and chat until midnight about Oscar Wilde and English letters. These literary Syrians love Wilde's wit and his poignant observation that 'we are all in the gutter but some of us are looking at the stars.' I promise to visit Samir's wool shop and walk back to the Tourist Hotel through the empty souqs.

TUESDAY 15 JULY | ALEPPO

My hopes for a good night's sleep are shredded by the noise of digging machines which go on perpetrating violence against the street until four in the morning. Surfacing at lunch time from the depths of my hard-won slumber, I discover the cosy Abu Nawas canteen up steps off Sharia Bab al-Faraj. After eating aubergines and rice, I drink quantities of hot black tea and make notes. On first appearance Aleppo is sleepless, commercial and brash—stimulating but lacking the charm and softness of Damascus. From the pension I call my only contact in the city, Najim Rifai, who agrees to meet that very evening at the Baron Hotel. Despite the unremitting torrid air, I return to the souqs and explore more of the ancient city.

The cavernous Aleppo souqs are the most expansive covered markets to be found anywhere, preserving the commercial spirit of the mediaeval Islamic world under brick vaulted ceilings with square light shafts. The vast area stretching from the Antioch gate to the citadel mostly dates from the Mamluk and early Ottoman periods. Despite the advance of modernity, the souqs continued to be central to Aleppo's economy but would tragically be burned at the very start of the Syrian Civil War in September 2012. I plunge into the warren of lanes, their carved wooden shopfronts the backdrop to lively conversation, and explore the khans along the primary axis. The first khan on the south side is somewhat cramped and gives an impression of what it must have been like to be locked in these buildings under curfew. Further along is the large Khan al-Jumruk, completed in 1574 with striped stone bands and stalactitic decoration. The khan housed the consulates of the English, French and Dutch merchants until 1791 and is now a textiles depository with merchant stalls.

Most attractive of all is the Khan al-Nahasin that has austerely arcaded courtyards and was formerly the residence of the Venetian consul. Venice opened a trade mission in Aleppo in the early 1200s, signing trade agreements with the Ayyubid emir al-Zahir al-Ghazi that bypassed the Crusader states. The link to Venice is poignant, for the fortunes of both commercial cities declined when the Atlantic trade routes opened up in the 1500s; each mediaeval city state maintained a dislocated suspension in the modern age and did not regain its former power and prestige. Nearby an extension of the souqs admits light from upper-storey windows and gives access to an open area with trees that leads towards the citadel.

The Great Mosque of Aleppo was built by the Umayyad Caliph Walid I but little remains from this period. The structure was rebuilt by Nur ad-Din and forms a dramatic space with arcaded courtyard and three-aisled prayer hall. Its most striking feature is the square minaret built by the Seljuk Sultan Tutush in 1092 with Kufic inscriptions in bands between the registers. Sadly the minaret would collapse in 2013 during the four-year Battle of Aleppo. The austere Madrasa Halawiye nearby was converted in 1124 by Nur ad-Din from the fifth-century Byzantine cathedral, whose apse is preserved. Samir meets me at the madrasa and takes me to his wool shop in the district that belonged to Jews who were forced to flee to Israel and whose rents are given by the Syrian government to the Palestinian Authority. Samir tells me over tea about musical activities in Aleppo and walks me back to the Baron Hotel for my appointment.

His Excellency Dr Najmuddine Rifai is a retired Syrian

diplomat who served in the 1960s as Deputy Permanent Representative to the United Nations and later became Deputy Under–Secretary in the UN Department of Political Affairs. We have been introduced by the former ward of my great uncle and meet for drinks at the Baron Hotel. Najim is interested to hear about my journey and my impressions of Syria. Assad's government may denounce liberal capitalism in official organs such as the *Syria Times*, but slogans rarely correspond to reality. Najim explains that business people can make healthy profits so long as they cooperate with the regime and remain aloof from politics. Indeed the Aleppo economy is flourishing: the proof lies in the many apartment blocks going up around the outskirts of the city and built to a high specification. The general level of education is also high in relation to incomes but there is a significant pool of under-employed skilled labour in Syria. Najim invites me for dinner at his house on Saturday.

WEDNESDAY 16 JULY | ALEPPO MUSEUM
The essence of a place can be elusive: I look for inspiring spots in Aleppo but conclude that the breakfast place Abu Nawas is the most conducive. After taking notes with long hot strong black tea, I visit the Aleppo Museum. Aleppo has a parallel history to Damascus, but is more closely connected to Assyria, which reflects its geography. Two ancient routes passed through Aleppo between Mesopotamia and the Mediterranean ports: one up the Euphrates from Babylon to the great bend at Emar (Meskeneh); the other from the Assyrian Tigris through the plains of the Khabur river basin, not far from the course of the Baghdad-Berlin railway. The name 'Syria' derives from the western part of the Neo-Assyrian Empire.

The earliest reference to the Amorite state of Yamhad derives from tablets recovered from Ebla and dated to 2250 BC. Aleppo emerges into history in the 1800s BC as the capital of Yamhad under King Yarim-Lim, contemporary with Zimri-Lim at Mari. Correspondence between the two rulers survives among the Mari tablets and refers to 'Khalep' as the original Akkadian-Amorite name for the city. The Hittite King Mursilis conquered Yamhad around 1600 BC and overthrew the Old

Babylonian Empire. Meanwhile the Kassites took over Sumer, and Assyria eliminated the Mitanni ruled Hurrian state circa 1400. This configuration of powers (Hittites, Assyrians and Kassites) continued until the collapse of the late Bronze Age world circa 1200 BC. The Arameans emerged from the deserts and settled the region around 1100 BC. Amorite Yamhad became Aramean Bit-Agushi and coexisted with the so-called Syro-Hittite principalities until the Assyrian King Shalmaneser III took control of northern Syria following the Battle of Qarqar in 853 BC.

The Aleppo Museum contains items excavated from several archaeological sites, primarily from tells (mounds) that date from the early first-millennium BC. The most distinctive finds are from Tell Halaf in the Khabur river basin, including giant female statues and the relief panel of Gilgamesh carrying a sun-disc between two bull-men. Basalt panels from Tell Ahmar on the Euphrates south of Carchemish celebrate the victories of the Assyrian King Esarhaddon, while ivory carvings from Tell Arslan Tash depict the birth of Horus and show links to Egypt. There are stone sculptures from Arpad, the capital of Aramean Bit-Agushi, and the temple archives of Ugarit with Akkadian cylinder seals. Most impressive of all are the pieces from Mari, especially the vase decorated with entwined snakes, the statue of King Ishqi-Mari, and a bronze lion with the expression of a loyal lapdog. There are many cuneiform tablets on display and it occurs to me just how difficult it must have been to crack the code of the fine imprint of this script on cracked clay.

From the museum I find a bench in the city park, its lawns long since scorched to dust, and observe the families and children playing. In the cool of the evening, I walk to the citadel: the central districts of Aleppo are compact and easy to walk around despite the heat. Samir meets me at the carpet shop and tells me about the situation of gay men in Syria. Constrained economic opportunities and tight family structures make it difficult for many young men to marry, and some of them channel their frustrations 'unnaturally'. Such activity is officially repressed and used as an excuse by the authorities for arbitrary arrests and beatings. I ask Samir if he knows the kanun player, Julien Weiss. Samir does indeed know Julien, who is at that moment busy entertaining the King of Morocco in his house, and promises to introduce me in the morning.

THURSDAY 17 JULY | JALAL EDDINE WEISS

Next day Samir guides me to Julien Weiss's house near the soap factory in the Bab Qinnesrin district where I am admitted and wait for the celebrated musician in the courtyard. The house is a mediaeval merchant's residence that Julien has lovingly restored. Unlike the Ottoman Damascene houses with their vaulted liwans and rectilinear spaces, this mansion has a wide circular opening with a passageway above the courtyard, a fountain in the centre and irregular spaces on different levels. Julien descends one of the staircases in a white linen suit with a beautiful lady on his arm. He calls for coffee and we recline on the diwan chatting about music and philosophical theories and the cultural life of Syria.

Originally a classical guitarist trained in France, Julien converted to Islam, adopted the name Jalal Eddine after Jalal ad-Din Rumi and founded the Syrian al-Kindi Ensemble. Led by Sheikh Hamza Shakkur, the al-Kindi Ensemble performs and improvises the *nawba*, the specific sacred repertoire of the Umayyad Mosque. Its music has its origins in the Turkish Sufi fraternities which Kemal Atatürk abolished in 1925. In response the Mevlevi Grand Master Abd al-Halim Chelebi Bashi tragically killed himself but many members of the order relocated from the new Turkish Republic to the Takiyya al-Mawlawiyya in Aleppo. Their practices survived here, continuing a tradition of Sufism that reaches back to Ibn 'Amir, the Qur'anic reciter of Damascus who died in 736.

I had met Julien after a concert in Paris in 1997, and despite remembering me only vaguely, he is extremely welcoming. His companion is Dana al-Omari and claims to descend from the Caliph Omar ibn al-Khattab. I do not know whether to believe her but I am transfixed by her slender tanned form, her evident intelligence and the neurotic intensity of her presence. We order kebabs and pass the afternoon talking of music, mathematics and repression, and what Julien describes as his typology of nonsense—above all Marx, Nietzsche and Freud. He takes me on a tour of the mansion and tells me about his concerts across the Arab world from Rabat, Cairo and Amman to Ghardaia in the Algerian desert.

The kanun is the Ottoman boxed zither, plucked with a pick like a weak sounding harp. Julien has constructed a heavier-duty version of the traditional instrument, adding a sounding board and thicker strings to create a more resonant sound and greater dynamic range, reminiscent of Wanda Landowska's harpsichord. Julien leaves for an hour and I put the kanun across my legs, strumming the strings, inventing melodies and trying to accompany them with pedal points. The maestro returns and takes us to a different world of sound. Julien explains that the kanun allows the direct transmission of musical ideas into the strings without any intermediary apparatus such as keys and hammers. A free instrument should be an extension of the voice or the lips: all that machinery inside the piano is an opaque barrier to musical flow and hence to the raw intervals and rhythms themselves. The rigid division of the octave into twelve equal intervals and Rameau's harmonic construction from combinations of thirds are like the marble blocks on the cathedral walls, concealing the transcendent void beyond which is the true music of the celestial spheres.

Julien plays Arabic music written for the kanun. But the instrument is inspirational as a compositional device and one could play Western music on it too from Couperin to Albeniz. We talk about *maqams* and the ensemble's dedicatee, the ninth-century polymath Abu Yusuf ibn Ishaq al-Kindi. Al-Kindi's lost book of music was the historical pivot between the music of the ancient Greeks and the Islamic golden age. Almost nothing survives from al-Kindi's own hand, but we do have later copies and references from other sources. Al-Kindi is believed to have invented the five staves and three clefs of conventional musical notation as well as the representation of note length and rhythm, dividing time from the pearl (brieve) into metrical sub-units. Al-Kindi also wrote about the fabrication of the oud, the Arabic antecedent of the lute that traces an unbroken line back to Sumer and may therefore be the oldest stringed instrument.

Maqams are modes in the sense of being identified by their intervallic pattern (like the Dorian and Ionian) and transposable to different tonics (or resting pitches). But they use quarter tones with rhythmic fluidity and distinctive moods that the performer interprets through improvisation. Each performance is in effect a unique composition. There is a parallel between Arabic maqam and the modes of Byzantine chant that meander continuously around a tonic, relating a narrative and returning to the starting point. But the continuity in the musical tradition of Syria goes back much further than the Seleucids. The Babylonians used maqams as the subgroup of notes within a scale and as groups of notes that formed variations on a series of tonics. Cuneiform tablets have been deciphered from the second millennium BC showing that Hurrian musical intervals are similar to the Greek as well as to the Arabic maqam.

Dana tells me to message her in a few days. I depart the grand mansion and wander through the streets to meet Kate, who has come up from Damascus, for a beer at the Baron and supper at Abu Nawas.

FRIDAY 18 JULY | DEAD CITIES

A young Basque couple is staying at the pension and together we negotiate a taxi tour to the historic sites of the Belus massif west of Aleppo. The Dead Cities consist of more than 700 abandoned settlements across the primary area of Greek colonisation in north-west Syria and date back to the Seleucid, Roman and Byzantine periods. Scattered over the desolate limestone upland, reddish-hued dressed blocks, stone towers and fragments of carved lintels emerge from under the occasional pistachio and almond tree. In some areas there are porticoed villas with stone presses for olive oil and wine. This was a wealthy rural economy in the hinterland of Antioch that prospered for centuries on the export of olive oil. Some of the structures such as the fourth-century pyramid tombs at al-Bara tell a fascinating story about Christian-pagan syncretism. There is no single explanation for why these towns were abandoned but some have speculated that demographic decline, excess production and an olive-oil glut may have led to a sudden drop in incomes to the region.

But this vanished Eden is a poignant emblem of the disappearance of the Syrian late-antique world following Sasanian invasions, Antioch earthquakes and the Arab conquest. We set out for the Jebel Sheikh Barakat and visit the churches of Qalb Lozeh and Qirqbize near the Reyhanli frontier crossing. Built in 460, the Qalb Lozeh basilica is roofless but otherwise substantially intact with twin towers and semi-domed stone roof above the altar. This church may represent the earliest known projection of an apse beyond the rectangular form of the Roman basilica that influenced the later development of the Romanesque style. Nearby there are houses built with blocks taken from the ruins. The sun-exposed local Druze villagers wear colourful velvet clothes, and some have fierce dogs. The driver takes us past olive groves and fish farms to the idyllic village of Harim which is surmounted by a Byzantine castle captured by Baibars after the fall of Antioch in 1268. We continue through the countryside with its red hills and olive trees to see the solitary ruined church at Baqirha. After stopping for a shawarma in Sarmada we visit Qalaat Semaan, the monumental ruins of the four basilicas dedicated to St Simeon Stylites.

The case of Simeon who lived on a high pillar for three decades until his death in 459 shows the peculiar tendency of humans to suggestibility, like the craze for tulips or the South Sea Bubble. As the Desert Fathers rejected worldly wisdom, so the ascetic Stylites called for the renunciation of selfhood. Simeon and his followers dispensed sermons and healings from their pillars to the pious Antiochenes who venerated their virtuous ideal. One imagines stern matrons sending wayward sons to be hectored by these mad monks, enforcing Pauline sexual ethics in a still mixed Christian-pagan society. For if it makes sense to adopt purity as preparation for the day of judgement, in the absence of such sanction one might as well enjoy the natural pleasures of the body. The Simeon memorial complex was completed by 491 but damaged in the earthquake of 526 and later abandoned. Now the site is an atmospheric ruin where the wind sighs in the pines as visitors examine the acanthus capitals and courting couples cavort in its further-flung corners.

We take tea in the gardens and continue in the evening to the fifth-century church of al-Mushabak. This austere three-aisled basilica has distinctive clerestory windows and is thought to have been used as a chapel for pilgrims walking from Aleppo to St Simeon. A group of Bedouin dressed in velvet robes lives beside the isolated building and we chat to them in broken syllables as they use the church font to water their goats. Back in Aleppo, Kate and I find the superb Beit Yasmeen restaurant in the Jdeydeh district (Christian quarter). We settle into a lavish meze of plates for which Syrian cuisine is famous —mutabbal and tabbouleh, with kibbeh, maqloobeh and yalanje —and talk away the warm night until the restaurant closes.

SATURDAY 19 JULY | ALEPPO CITADEL

We are joined over omelette and black tea at Abu Nawas by Kate's friend Juliette from the British Council. While they visit the Hammam al-Nasri in the ladies' time slot, I send emails from Abdul's air conditioned carpet shop and read a special feature in *Newsweek* about 'sustainable development technologies'. For all the good intentions of the purveyors of water pumps and smokeless stoves, I wonder if a simple programme of universal education and healthcare of the kind espoused by Habib Bourguiba in Tunisia would not have more effect: it all goes back to responsible demography, good governance and a political elite that cares about raising up their own people instead of extracting rents and exporting the proceeds. Kate and her friend return, talking excitedly about lesbianism in the hammam, and we make a tour of the citadel.

The Aleppo citadel is built across a large earthwork that dates back to the Amorite period and was fortified by the Seleucids as well as by the Byzantines during the Sasanian wars. The present structures were initiated by Salah ad-Din's son al-Zahir al-Ghazi between 1186 and 1216 when Aleppo became the base of Muslim power in northern Syria. Al-Ghazi deepened the encircling ditch, faced the steep glacis with stone, raised the upper ramparts and built the ring of walls around the hill. Following the Mongol destruction of the Ayyubid fortress in 1260, the iconic portals of the citadel that appear on tourist brochures were rebuilt by the Bahri Mamluk Sultan Qalawun, and again by Sayf al-Din Jakam in 1415 after the Timurid sack of Aleppo. The bridge tower carries an inscription celebrating the victories of Sultan al-Ashraf Khalil over the Franks in the early 1290s, capturing Acre and the last remaining Crusader fortresses at Atlit and Tartous.

Inside the monumental gateway, the route traces six right angle bends before leading to the courtyard. We walk around the remains of the Ayyubid palace, impressed by the monumental liwans of the hammam, and sit beside Nur ad-Din's mosque of Abraham, built in 1167. It was around this time that Halep became associated in Muslim tradition with the Patriarch, who is said to have milked his goats on the hill, a pun perhaps on the city's ancient name with the Arabic word for milk (halib). Beyond is the mosque of al-Ghazi whose terrace has fine views over the city. At the Bimaristan al-Arghuni near Julien's house, we are given a tour by a friendly guide called Mashaf who talks about creationism versus Darwinism. Originally a private mansion the building was converted from a mansion into an asylum and hospital by the Mamluk governor Arghun al-Kamili in 1354. The bimaristan is associated with the physician Ibn Abi Usaybi'a, who pioneered music cures for melancholia, and was in use until the nineteenth century.

We wait outside the Amir Palace Hotel for Najim who drives us to his apartment near the university. The Rifai residence is on the second floor with fine carpets on the marble floors and comfortable furnishing. Najim is kindly and seems pleased to introduce us to his family. But I can see him looking at my Siwi sirwal trousers thinking there is an odd disjunction between his guest and the impeccable introduction. The younger teenage grand-daughters Nagla and

Zayn are delightfully vivacious and soon we are chatting about their lives and plans for the future. The conversation turns to regional politics: Najim had been involved in the drafting of the UN Resolutions concerning Israel and the Palestinians, yet so many decades later, those efforts seem to him doubly futile. Concerning internal politics he is reluctant to say anything at all, and although we tell stories until late, there is a certain awkwardness when we talk more about Palestine and Syria.

SUNDAY 20 JULY | JDEYDEH

Kate and I share thoughts about the quest for lost idylls, and set out to explore the Christian quarter of Aleppo. Following the Timurid sack of Aleppo in 1400, the Jdeydeh (new) district was constructed immediately to the north of the Ayyubid walls. The small quarter has five cathedrals and winding narrow streets of stone houses dating from the Ottoman period. The Syrian Catholic church of Mar Assia al-Hakim was consecrated around 1500 while the Syrian Orthodox church of St George was built by Syriacs expelled from Edessa (Urfa) in 1924. Sadly the district would be severely damaged in the most intense phase of the Syrian civil war: on 28 April 2015 the Free Syria Army and Islamist Ahrar al-Sham rebel group would detonate bombs in tunnels under Jdeydeh's central al-Hitab square, devastating the surrounding buildings.

The Armenian Cathedral of the Forty Martyrs dates from 1491. We walk around the precinct and stand in the back of the church to enjoy the singing. The Beit Ajiqbash nearby was built by a merchant family in 1757 and is now the Museum of Folk Traditions. The house has a double-storey, stone-carved courtyard with trees and a fountain in the centre that makes me think of John Frederick Lewis's colourful painting of the House of the Coptic Patriarch. We look over the city from the upper terrace and chat to a Tunisian–American documentary maker who talks about how development must evolve from within the culture of the country in question. Kate and Juliette return to Damascus and I wander in search of the Madrasa al-Firdaws in the al-Maqamat district. The monument is closed but these poorer areas give a sense of the less touristic side of Aleppo.

Northern Syria

MONDAY 21 JULY | CYRRHUS

A fresh group from the pension joins me for breakfast at Abu Nawas. Maggie has recently completed a doctorate in comparative literature at Harvard but is feeling worn out by the exertion and has come to Syria in search of a parallel reality to pass time with her Spanish girlfriends, Laura and Christina. 'Big Schools will not bring you any happiness,' Maggie tells me over omelette and tea. 'All they do is enmesh you in the academic machine with its fixation on citations and pointless content generation.' Ah yes, I agree, these universities can be oppressive with their manufactured competition and endless intellectual point-scoring. Modern life in general is too complicated. I reflect that misfits come to Syria to escape their domestic societies, to be somewhere 'other' and find dissenters like themselves. But once the thrill of discovery has worn off, they find a country whose background reality is even more dystopian than where they came from. Where do misfits go now when so many 'other' places have disintegrated too?

They are a relaxing group to travel with for the day and we discuss places to visit in the countryside around Aleppo. Maggie has a dog-eared copy of Ross Burns's *Monuments of Syria* and as they organise themselves for the day's expedition, I leaf through this encyclopaedic trove of information about the less visited sites in Syria. We head north from Aleppo in the taxi and pass once again through the distinctive landscape of the karst with its red soil and ancient walls between orchards of pomegranate and pistachio.

Ain Dara lies on a prominent green mound rising out of the fertile plain looking over the Afrin valley. The ancient site contains several Bronze Age layers and on the summit are the ruins of an early first millennium BC Syro-Hittite temple dedicated to the fertility goddess Ishtar. Ain Dara is known for its bas-relief winged lions and sphinxes carved on basalt orthostats. The site is being excavated by a team of archaeologists who explain that the temple has two enclosures. The dead would be brought to the first room which is surrounded by basalt-carved figures of mythical lions who would judge them to decide if they could pass to the second room which represents heaven. In front of the temple is a paved courtyard and the gateway stones bear the imprint of giant footsteps thought to signify a single omnipresent chief deity. Along with the other Syro-Hittite cities, Ain Dara was destroyed by the Assyrian Tiglath-Pileser III in the 740s BC.

We head north and stop to examine a fine Roman bridge over the dried-up Afrin River before continuing to the ruined city of Cyrrhus close to the Turkish border. Cyrrhus was founded by Seleucus Nicator circa 300 BC, flourished in the Roman period as the capital of the province of Euphratenses, was refortified by Justinian, briefly occupied by the Crusaders and then disappeared from history. The site contains a Roman hexagonal tomb tower and a third-century theatre laid out across the hillside in black stone. From the theatre we climb up to the citadel which has open views across Anatolia towards the Taurus Mountains. As we lean against the walls to eat our picnic, I reflect on the similarity with Segesta and the remarkable continuity of a thousand years of Graeco-Roman civilisation. We return to Aleppo across another Roman bridge for lamb pot and mulukhiyah at the Beit Sissy restaurant.

TUESDAY 22 JULY | APAMEA

After breakfast at Abu Nawas, I set off on the bus for Hama. From there I take the microbus to Skailabeyeh downstream from Hama on the Orontes and continue to the ruined classical site of Apamea. Like Antioch and Cyrrhus, Apamea was founded by Seleucus Nicator on a hill above the Orontes and named in honour of the ruler's Persian wife Apama. The city was laid out by the Macedonians and used as a military base and breeding centre for Seleucid cavalry horses. Following an earthquake in 115, the city flourished in the Antonine

Age and was embellished with temples, baths, villas and a theatre. Apamea became a bishopric in the fifth century and continued to thrive unbroken throughout the Byzantine period despite being extensively damaged by the Sasanian Khosro I in 540. The town acquired a small Ayyubid fortress in the 1160s but ceased to be a major city as economic activity migrated to the Homs-Hama-Aleppo axis.

The museum occupies an Ottoman caravanserai below the ruins and has a collection of Roman mosaics as well as an enthusiastic custodian. Apamea itself is the loveliest classical site in the Levant, with views over the Ghab Plain and the Jebel al-Ansariyyah beyond. Its most striking feature is the north-south cardo maximus, which is the longest colonnaded street in the Roman East. The mile-long rows of spiral fluted columns with their high entablature dress the landscape in a fine raiment that surpasses Jerash or Palmyra. I take tea with an old lady and lie in the shade of a column to dream in the breeze. In the evening I fall in with a French couple and we walk to the Arab citadel. This fortress of Qalaat Mudiq was built by Nur ad-Din to defend against the Crusaders across the Orontes. After earthquakes destroyed Apamea in 1157 and 1170 the population migrated there. The citadel has expansive views over the landscape and light that shines from a different epoch, with friendly local people whose goats and chickens nestle into its walls.

The French couple drive me back to a Hama that is incongruously clogged with traffic jams and drop me by the clock tower. I take a room at the Cairo Hotel and walk to the Four Norias restaurant, beside the wide sluggish Orontes, bordered with eucalyptus trees. This stretch of the river is famous for the seventeen mediaeval norias or giant wooden waterwheels used to irrigate the surrounding fields and divert channels along stone viaducts into Hama. When the wheels turn they generate a distinctive creaking sound resembling a 'groaning lament'. I sit by these enchanted gardens with my poulet roti watching local boys climb to the top of the noria from the aqueduct and dive into the green waters below. Hama reaches back to Aramean Hamath and Seleucid Epiphania and the city's ancient streets that escaped the depredations of the Syrian Army in 1982 are beautiful, their cobbles and organic structures softened by the patina of age.

WEDNESDAY 23 JULY | CRAC

I call Dana from the hotel and she agrees to meet me for lunch at Crac des Chevaliers. I take the microbus to Homs and continue to Qalaat al-Hosn. From there I walk up the hill to the Round Table Hotel where Dana greets me warmly through the open window, having hired a driver for the day from Damascus. We eat at the recently opened restaurant before exploring the enormous fortress on its windswept bluff.

Crac des Chevaliers is the apogee of Crusader architecture and was the leading Latin forward position until its fall in 1271. After the Second Crusade failed, the knights realised that they could not hold their positions in the Levant without building a series of castles to dominate the passes from the Muslim hinterland to the coast. The Crac was positioned on a hill at the southern end of the Jebel al-Ansariyyah to control the Homs Gap to Tortosa as well as the northern entrance to the Beka'a valley. Combining Frankish, Byzantine and Arab elements it was more formidable than anything that had come before, transplanting the architectural genius of mediaeval France to the alien surroundings of Outremer. The original castle belonged to the County of Tripoli but was transferred in 1142 to the Order of Knights of the Hospital of St John of Jerusalem. The military orders of the Templars and Hospitallers built and defended the great castles, the former taking Tortosa, Areimeh and Beaufort and the latter Marqab, Banias and Crac.

The Hospitallers expanded Crac in the 1170s, building the circuit of outer enceinte walls and towers. The great hall and loggia of the inner fortress were completed around 1250 and reflect the High Gothic style. The craftsmanship of the stonework is the peer of Carcassonne, with perfectly executed details from the ribbed vaulting to the Warden's chambers. The fortress was cunningly laid out and victualled with stores and cisterns to withstand a five-year siege. One has to imagine the knights chanting the Latin mass and celebrating banquets while waiting endlessly for a potential assault. The Crac has never given up all its secrets: the window ledge at the top of the Warden's Tower bears the cryptic inscription: 'Ceso: LT:Bor...' and the fortress was lost by ruse not storm. After the fall of Antioch in 1268, Latin power in the Levant began to wither and by 1271 the garrison of Crac had fallen from 2,000 to 300 knights. Sultan Baibars pierced the outer enceintes after a four-year siege. But the Saracens could not breach the inner fortress that fell instead to subterfuge, as Baibars forged a document from the Count of Tripoli ordering its surrender.

The perfectly preserved massive castle seems oddly out of place on these misty hills that can feel cold even in high summer. As we clamber over the battlements of the enceinte walls of the Crac, Dana speaks about her life and loves. Dana works in Beirut for an advertising agency promoting Pepsi International. Her job is to change peoples' habits so they start drinking Pepsi, and it gives her dignity and financial independence. But she dislikes being used as a tool in a cultural invasion by a multinational corporation that not only squeezes out local producers, but also repatriates its profits and does not invest in Syria. I suggest that perhaps Dana could sabotage Pepsi's operations by comparing their filthy soda with the thirst-quenching fresh squeezed natural fruit juices one sees on every street corner and asking Syrians to make their choice.

I argue that the Pepsi analogy extends to other sectors such as construction where foreign competition degrades the indigenous traditions as the international technology does not fit the local environment: this was the view of Hassan Fathy. Equally if wealth is a function of productivity and ideas and accumulation, it is a false economy to work sixty hours a week instead of thirty. We talk about my theories of Epicurean economics and discuss the idea that international competition in the tradeable sectors has lengthened working hours across the board because of the global reserve army of labour. If political economy is a game, I say, it is the powerful who determine the rules and indeed which game is being played. But it was not foreign competition that induced the Sumerians to invent writing, geometry and astronomy.

What Dana really loves to do is tell stories and she has several filmscripts on the back burner. I tell Dana that storytelling is in her blood and that she should fill her scripts with narrative, for the life path of every one of us is like the *Thousand and One Nights*—full of stories within stories. Dana believes in the total liberation of the body, which is perhaps an expression of the existentialist detachment of sensuality and love from social and familial duty. Julien is just a friend, Dana explains, adding undiplomatically that she finds him uninspiring. Really she is in love with an absent Danish film-maker called Jasper. As we climb up to the top of the Warden's Tower, Dana explains that the relationship makes her try to distinguish between actions driven by her own demons and what she truly believes in. A parallel perhaps with the Pepsi.

I suggest to Dana that if she can use the proceeds of her marketing job to write good filmscripts and find backing to make them, it will have been worth it. Syria is the historical heart of the Levant and has been less exposed to the more pernicious aspects of Western culture. Bar catastrophe Syria will gradually open up and join the international business world. So Dana has an opportunity to show the Syria of today before it is homogenised and the old cultures are lost. Dana suggests that we visit the nearby town of Safita. We bundle into the car that takes us past the sixth-century Greek Orthodox monastery of St George and over the hills of the Wadi al-Nasara. The stone-built hilltop town of Safita is busy and a little claustrophobic. We eat supper in a square at the top of an alley staircase and make speed in the dark to Damascus. Dana drops me at Marja and I walk to Sarouja. Both Rabie and Haramain are full and I settle for the charmless Ridwan.

Thursday 24 July | Hama

I surprise Naim at Dar Anbar and we take a coffee at the Umayyad. Dana meets me for lunch at Zeitoun and we talk about the Epic of Gilgamesh. I tell her that Enkidu represents the archetypal Platonic other half. Gilgamesh cannot find his peer among the people of Uruk, so he brutalises them out of contempt. But he recognises his equal in the wild man sent by the gods and falls in love with him, as Rumi did with Shams-e-Tabrizi. When Enkidu is killed, Gilgamesh is stricken by grief, crushed by the realisation of his own mortality. His search for eternal life leads him to Utanapishtim who teaches him to accept his mortality, return to Uruk, and serve his own people. So we need to be solo but not alone, with a library and a congenial companion to indulge wanderlust and the migratory life of the adventurer, the restless seeker.

Dana tells me that Jasper torments her: he says he loves her but wants to be alone, while Dana wants to be with him and feels rejected. I reply that the sources of our torments are not our own actions, or even those of other people, but the rules of the cosmos. The best way to live is to be good to people who are good to us and avoid those who treat us badly. We live in our own bone boxes and cannot depend on anyone else for our own happiness and equilibrium. We walk through Bab Touma, buy some discs of the Iraqi oud master Munir Bashir, who inspired Julien Weiss, and drink a farewell lemonade beside the Harasta bus station. I tell her that I adored her immediately and that she will always have a friend on the other side of the world. But as the bus makes its way to Hama, I look out at the anti-Lebanon glowing orange in the evening light and realise that I will never see her again. I am enthralled by her presence but feel dejected to have lost her.

From the bus station I walk around Hama and admire the distinctive stone textures of the narrow streets, designed for foot and hoof. In the late 1970s, Hama was dominated by the Muslim Brotherhood who made a stand against the government, calling for a more democratic system and eventually leading an uprising against Hafez al-Assad. In February 1982 the president's brother Rifaat al-Assad besieged Hama for four weeks and moved into the city with heavy armour, eliminating the insurgents and killing thousands of civilians. Much of the old city was destroyed, including an eighth-century mosque. The districts on the north side of the Orontes were reconstructed with characterless hotels and apartment blocks; many of the surviving buildings in central Hama still carry pockmarks left by the bullets—a warning of the violence to come.

By the ancient bridge over the Orontes I sit in the mosque of Nur ad-Din where the last rays of the sun shine across the river and through the window down the prayer hall. As night falls, I move to the pillar at the front by the mihrab, with only a small electric light in the corner to illuminate the darkness, and think about everything I have experienced these last weeks. The Western liberal commentariat has become indifferent to the effects of corruption and autocracy, but the situation in Syria is an allegory for the world of its consequences: neither bread nor freedom. And who will reconstruct the world? I return to the Four Norias for supper and watch international news channels at the Riad Hotel to distract myself from the loss of Dana.

Homage to an Ancient Poet

> Pain is running through my veins
> These cords are tying my existence
> Rivers of sorrow are reshaping my landscape
> Creating a delta of sadness
> In the heart of my being.
>
> The foundations of my city are trembling
> My castle is shaking
> In fear of an ugly black terror
> That speaks a barbarian language
> A language that was not taught in my land.
>
> The capital is pounding in resistance
> Each pulse is an ancient song
> United with a beating heart
> A final plea for life
> Asking the holy moon for wisdom.
>
> Exhausted I walk in empty streets
> But cannot recognise my own kingdom
> I cannot recognise my own face
> I weep on every majestic wall
> Hoping that the stone would utter a word.
> Alas the rocks are speechless

Just like my enemy is faceless
I am drunk of tasteless wine
Vulnerable but cannot comprehend my weakness
The danger is surrounding me.

Breathless, I shout with my last gasp of life
'Show me your face!'
But my enemy is mute and coward
I am doomed to face the profane
I don't know the ways to save my kingdom.

What is life if it is lifeless?
What is existence if you are not being?
I look up to the sky and ask
Is this my mortality?
To float in existence but not be?

In the depth of night the wise moon sends a word
'Surrender' the twinkling messengers say
'Patience' is your only weapon to fight
Against a coward enemy that will leave your kingdom
Because it cannot defeat the underlying breath of life.

They promise that the deluge will not sweep my
    small kingdom
That light will shine again on my land
And wine will be full of flavour
My kingdom will dance under the mother sun
Music will sound in the rivers of my land.

Laughter will conquer grief
Sorrow will be ostracised and shall leave my city
And sex will never be as delicious
My veins will flood with the deep red
And I shall see life again.
Dana al-Omari

Friday 25 July | Latakia

After breakfast of yoghurt and tea, I take the local bus over the mountains to Baniyas and Latakia. The brightly decorated bus has sprung seats and fresh air from wide-open windows. We pass the ruined castle of the Assassins at Masyaf that was unsuccessfully besieged by Salah ad-Din and captured by Baibars in 1270, before beginning the ascent to the 1,000-metre pass above Qadmous. The Jebel al-Ansariyyah is the northern extension of the anti-Lebanon and divides the Orontes valley from the coastal plain. The vegetation reminds me of the Maritime Alps, green with pines and ilex, while the fresh air is intermittently misty and hot in the direct sun. As the road steepens, the bus slows almost to a walk before gaining the pass and rolling down the other side to Qadmous. But the glacial pace gives me time to absorb these low coastal mountains whose scenic beauty is the most compelling of my entire journey around the Levant.

From Baniyas the bus continues along the coast road to the port city of Latakia. I walk along palm lined boulevards with the smell of *merazea* in the breezy salty air and I am excited to see once again the waters of the frog pond for the first time since Alexandria. I take a room at the Riyadh Hotel and pass the afternoon exploring the city. There is not much to see but the guidebook mentions a well-preserved Roman tetraporticus and I duly walk back to Port Said Street by the train station to examine it. The settlement at Latakia was originally Punic then Assyrian and was developed into a port metropolis by the Greeks, who renamed her Laodicea in honour of the mother of Seleucus Nicator. The city prospered on the export of wine to the Hellenistic world and continued to flourish into the Roman and Byzantine periods.

After the Muslim conquest, Latakia found itself part of a shifting border zone between the Byzantine and Arab empires. During the crusades the city belonged to the Principality of Antioch and the Venetians established a trading colony here from 1229 to 1436. Latakia declined with the silting of the harbour and the Ottomans expanded Alexandretta as a better-positioned port for supplying al-Jazeera and central Anatolia. During the French mandate, Latakia was the capital of the Alawite State from 1920 to 1936 when the French dredged the harbour and expanded the facilities. Latakia became Syria's principal port following the loss of Alexandretta to Kemal's

Turkish Republic in 1938. The city has a pan-Mediterranean atmosphere, with people promenading beside coffee houses and brasseries, and I eat fish at the Petra restaurant near the harbour.

SATURDAY 26 JULY | UGARIT

Directly opposite the pension I take a microbus past the glitzy Blue Beach hotels to the headland of Ras Shamra. Already known about from references in the Mari tablets, the archaeological site of Ugarit was discovered at Ras Shamra in 1928. Dating back to the Neolithic period, Ugarit prospered in the third millennium BC as the trade conduit from the copper-producing island of Cyprus to Akkad and Sumer, and then became part of the Amorite network of city states. In the late Bronze Age, Canaanite Ugarit flourished under Hurrian rule, and maintained friendly trading relations with both the Hittites and the Egyptian New Kingdom. Around 1200 BC Ugarit was destroyed and burned: the famous letter from the city's last ruler Ammurapi to the King of Cyprus shows the sudden nature of the collapse.

The site itself consists of a series of stone walls, with the outline of the palace visible alongside the temples of Dagan and Bel-Marduk.

Ugarit is best known for the discovery of Bronze Age cuneiform tablets bearing a thirty-symbol alphabet. This writing system was based on the phonetic alphabetic principle of one sound per symbol and was a significant innovation in the representation of ideas beyond pictograms and ideograms. It is not clear whether the Ugaritic alphabet is the actual precursor of the Aramean–Phoenician system that later became established in the early first millennium BC. Whether branch line or not, the Ugaritic alphabet is certainly one of the earliest such systems, along with parallel second millennium BC Semitic alphabets discovered in Sinai and in Upper Egypt. The historical importance of the alphabet is not just the expansion of the malleability of representation, but also in the eventual supplanting of cuneiform as the primary medium of written record in ancient Syria and Iraq. The names of the letters derived from the objects used in the earlier pictograms: aleph came from ox and beta from house. In modern Arabic the word for house is still *beit*.

Some of the tablets excavated from the royal palace at Ras Shamra contain the earliest known musical compositions dating from circa 1400 BC. The Hurrian songs are a set of musical fragments that were deciphered by Anne Kilmer and Marcelle Duchesne-Guillemin in the 1970s. The intact H6 tablet records the Hurrian cult hymn to the goddess Nikkal and is the oldest surviving complete work of notated music yet discovered, pre-dating the Greek Delphic hymns by a millennium. Old and Neo-Babylonian texts were later found to contain tuning methods for the Babylonian nine-stringed lyre. Other Babylonian musical treatise tablets have also been analysed, their text category as musical works encoded along their spine or colophon. Tablets interpreted by the archaeo-musicologist Richard Dumbrill describe a system of hepta-tonic and enneatonic scales for the lyre and imply that the intervallic patterns we know as the church modes (from Glarean's *Dodecachordon*) were already present in Old Babylon circa 1750 BC.

I return to Latakia and take the microbus to the village of Hafah in the Jebel al-Ansariyyah. From there I walk through the pine forest to the Qalaat Salah ad-Din, enjoying the cool air of the hills. Formerly known as Sahyun, this Crusader fortress was built on a tongue of rock between two ravines and guarded the passes from the Orontes valley to the coast. The site had been fortified in 975 by the Byzantine Emperor John Tzimisces, who dug the ditch separating the castle from the hillside, with a drawbridge across the 100-feet-high stone pinnacle. Knights from Antioch led by Robert of Saone later enlarged the ditch and built the present structures. Incredibly, Salah ad-Din captured the fortress in 1188 after heavy bombardment and stormed the breached defences up the hill. As Sahyun was not recaptured and never belonged to the military orders who remodelled the Levantine castles, the fortress is the outstanding example of early Crusader architecture. After wandering around the splendid donjon and ramparts of

Sahyun, I walk down to Hafah in the evening sun and catch the microbus back to Latakia. It is three hours by bus to Aleppo where I reach the Tourist Hotel in the small hours.

S̲u̲n̲d̲a̲y̲ ̲2̲7̲ ̲J̲u̲l̲y̲ | A̲l̲e̲p̲p̲o̲

On my last day in Syria I return to the Jdeydeh district and attend mass at the Armenian Cathedral of the Forty Martyrs. There is an elaborate procession in progress that seems like a spectacle of theatre for the small congregation. Under the gaze of a large icon representing Judgement Day, the priests chant and counter-chant across the nave while robes are donned, incense is swung and the sacred texts are covered and uncovered. The chanting takes me back to the Armenian cathedral in Jerusalem and the distinctive melodies of that tradition. At the Beit Ajiqbash nearby I meet an English couple and we drink tea in the courtyard of the Beit Wikal, talking of the history of the Christians of the Ottoman Empire.

During the Armenian genocide, Aleppo was the primary deportation hub between Anatolia and Deir ez-Zor, and from May 1915 convoys of survivors began pouring into the city. Led by the churches, and especially Sahak II, Catholicos of Cilicia, the 10,000-strong Aleppo Armenian community, opened their homes and formed a council to assist thousands of destitute refugees. The council appealed to the Ottoman authorities in Constantinople to change their deportation policies, writing to senior ministers including the pashas Enver, Talaat and Cemal, and even Sultan Mehmed V himself.

But no word came. The Ottoman government responded to the relief efforts of the Aleppo Armenian community by imprisoning or exiling the leaders and sending the Catholicos to Jerusalem. Over the summer of 1915, the majority of the refugees were re-deported to internment camps around Deir ez-Zor and later massacred. Supported by missionaries and other foreign nationals, the Aleppo Armenians enabled thousands of deportees to disappear into the fabric of the metropolis and escape re-deportation by employing them in factories, military hospitals and orphanages. After 1923 many more Ottoman Armenians migrated to Syria under French protection and of the 100,000 or so Armenians in Syria, more than half live in Aleppo.

From Jdeydeh I wander again through the souqs exploring other routes beyond the primary axis. The ancient districts of Aleppo are mostly filthy with rubbish blowing about in the streets. But the city has a special quality and I admire the old mansions in the Bab Qinnesrin district before meeting the Basque couple for dinner on the terrace of the Martini Hotel which has fine views over the floodlit Aleppo citadel.

Dialogues
Rupert, there is a man singing *habibi* behind me and it sounds amazing. I moved to the boarding house of Um Michelle, which means being set up with her son Zuhair. Everyone is excited about getting married: love is all they talk about. Weddings are lavish but it feels as though men and women are so divided in this society that when they marry they do not know how to live together as friends. I see the division between the sexes and the lack of understanding of the other as a person. Although there is sex outside marriage behind closed doors, everyone acts as if it does not happen. Words are spoken about the *ajaneb* (foreigners) and their forbidden liaisons. But while preaching against it, people are doing it, like Zuhair creeping out late last night, or like my first landlord, constantly asking me to his place, even though he has a wife. I believe that gender separation explains this division, which comes in many forms, from the hijab to voluntary public segregation and causes the general harassment one receives as a single female: I am often asked if I am Russian, which is a thinly veiled question for whether I am a prostitute.

Yesterday I went to the hills to escape the dusty streets. On my return Um Michelle told me a man had called for me five times and they feared he was from the *mukhabarat*. It seems the family does not pay tax on the rooms they rent and Um Michelle was paranoid that the authorities might discover the tenants. So I made peace with them by going for pizza with Zuhair, who admitted that he has been secretly sleeping with a married woman for the past three years, sneaking out to her house at night. I asked if he climbs up the balcony like Romeo but Um Michelle rebukes Zuhair for being a man about town and they are always at war. Um Michelle is clearly the boss in this troublesome household and certainly a character.

If a man has his own place, he tells me within a matter of minutes: this means he will take girls there. It is unlikely to happen at night, but during the day. These girls are considered to be of a certain 'type' although that depends what the girl wants from the man. If she considers him to be marriage material, she will create barriers for the future husband. In one case a 'relationship' like this happened for two years almost entirely by telephone. They might find a place, go there once and never talk again, or sometimes they talk for two years and never go to a place. In this case the barrier meant that they did not trust each other. When I asked my friend where he found these people, he told me that it is easy to exchange numbers with girls at the nargileh bars. It all explains why strange men ask me to their place. People want to keep up appearances in the eyes of family and neighbours, hence the underground relations with all the guilt and deceit it involves.

Government censorship is omnipresent and pushes activists underground. People do not like to discuss politics and any groups that challenge the state meet with the harshest response. So opposition groups chase their tails, knowing that they are powerless to change the situation. Repression under Bashar is less severe than it was under Hafez. But the memory of what did happen and what could happen again keeps people in line. The dictatorship permits some freedom of speech. I have been watching a Syrian television series called *Spotlight*. In one episode a man was arrested by the mukhabarat on suspicion of dreaming about creating a political party: so they put him to sleep to monitor his dreams. An embassy official told me that the series is part of regime control and that censorship has in fact been tightened.

My house mate and I laugh at the daily drama in Um Michelle's house. But so much is depressing about Damascus. From the language exchanges at the British Council I learned that Shamsis are frustrated by Western perceptions of Syria. I was photographed for the *Syria Times* as a foreigner coming to live in a 'rogue state'. But the next Arabic course has been cancelled and I am looking for a private teacher while I give an English class at the Al Khayyam Language Institute. It is beautiful and never short on character in the old city. But for the majority of Syrians there is 'neither bread nor freedom'. Kate.

Dear Kate, your descriptions of Um Michelle's menagerie are hilarious: is not the basic human material constant all over the world? Do we not all feel the same desires and emotions? Sorry to hear that your course was not as rewarding as you had hoped. But congratulations for making it into the *Syrian Times*: I suppose that next time I go to Syria, I will see your photo in the Sarouja barbers' shops next to Bashar and Britney! Rupert.

Syrian Civil War

2003 was the year in which the world was shaken out of its post-Cold War 'end of history' stupor: the United States disposed of the velvet glove of international law and Russia turned its back on the West. Since the global financial crisis of 2008, the Levant has witnessed the Arab spring, the disintegration of Libya, repression in Egypt, authoritarianism in Türkiye and in Syria one of the longest, bloodiest and most destructive wars since 1648. Meanwhile economic globalism has intensified as developed countries feel the impact of capital flight from kleptocracies around the world and asset distribution has become ever more concentrated. The free flow of capital has allowed extractive elites to export their ill-gotten gains, eliminating incentives to reform, while Western foreign policy has become entirely transactional. The Syrian Civil War has been one of the most tragic consequences of this configuration of circumstances.

In a plural society, the only path to peaceful coexistence is a set of governance institutions that all groups can agree is consistent with their particular traditions and the superstructure of a well-functioning state. Ironically this was the aspiration of the secular Syrian Ba'ath party founded by Michel Aflaq and Salah ad-Din al-Bitar in 1941. Since Hafez al-Assad seized power in 1970 however, the sole purpose of the Assad regime has been its own preservation and the extraction of economic rents. Hopes for reform upon Bashar's accession in 2000 were dashed. Initially the new President tolerated the 'Damascus Spring' civil society movement of 2001 and canvassed external advisors.

But reforms rapidly proved to be illusory and economic liberalisation promoted by Abdullah Dardari became a cover for rampant corruption: the President's cousins Rami and Hafez Makhlouf controlled access to state contracts, import permits and telecom as well as other licenses. Protectionist industrial policies had worked during the 1970s and 1980s to build domestic productive capacity. But the new programmes merely entrenched the extraction of economic value by the small group around the Presidency. Meanwhile high birth rates, drought and rural underdevelopment led to the degradation of service provision and worsening living conditions in areas such as Hauran and Idlib, which had formerly been bulwarks of Ba'athism.

In *The Story of Syria*, Ghayth Armanazi locates the causes of the civil war in lack of economic opportunity and anger towards the venal and repressive ruling clique. The 2011 'Arab Spring' began with the self-immolation of the young Tunisian Muhammad Bouazizi and spread across North Africa. When protests broke out in Syria in February 2011, the regime could have brought representatives of all groups into the government and begun to address their legitimate grievances. Instead the authorities shot and tortured teenage protestors in Daraa on 15 March, and Bashar blamed foreign conspirators for the disturbances. The aggressive military response to peaceful protests pushed demonstrators and disaffected elements within the state towards armed insurrection and the first full scale battle occurred at Baba Amr in Homs.

Despite the public hand-wringing and stated outrage at Assad's brutality in the early stages of the spiralling catastrophe, Western governments never put the interests of the Syrian people at the centre of their policy. Through various channels fair and foul, Western states supplied weapons to rebel groups such as the Free Syrian Army which stoked the revolution and perpetuated the conflict. But the West failed to create no-fly zones or provide sufficient military support to challenge the regime, which retained control of the Damascus–Aleppo corridor, coast and mountains. The insurgency suffered from disunity, lack of materiel and inconsistent support, and the ensuing void became a proxy theatre for malevolent external actors.

Later the focus lay on Special Forces operations and assistance to the Kurds to eliminate Daesh, Jabhat al-Nusra and other resurgent terror groups. But there was never any concerted action by the United Nations to compel Bashar to negotiate a settlement with legitimate opposition groups. The Arab League referred Syria to the United Nations Security Council, which sent envoys to Syria to navigate a transition of power. All international mediation assumed Bashar's resignation as the prerequisite condition. But Damascus believed it would prevail in the conflict and had no need to compromise or seek a negotiated transfer of power.

The failure to intervene in Syria was put down to the 'lessons of Iraq'. So the practical effect was to destroy Iraq through commission and Syria through omission. Yet for decades the common thread of Western policy in the region was to buttress 'friendly dictators' while seeking commercial interests, above all arms sales. What is the point of preaching democratic 'values' only to subordinate them to the particular objectives of special-interest groups? Leila Mustafa, Mayor of Raqqa, expressed it thus to French journalist Marine de Tilly in 2021: '[despite all that happened here]… there was no genuine initiative on the part of the United Nations Security Council or so-called human rights organisations. When you listen to these organisations founded on humanism and observe their work out in the field, what they say has nothing to do with reality: on the contrary, humanity itself is trampled on.'

Meanwhile Russia took the opportunity of Western posturing to reassert its strategic interest in Syria, securing its naval base at Tartous and tilting the war in Bashar's favour. While Russian snipers shot civilians from the roofs of government buildings in Aleppo, while Russian jets supported regime forces to barrel bomb rebel held districts in Aleppo, Homs and Ghouta, Western states continued to prevaricate. The civil war was not defined by sectarianism, as Bashar initially appealed to the Sunni as well as Christian urban middle class. The Ba'athist regime was dominated by Alawis but also supportive to other minorities. In contrast to Lebanon or the prior Ottoman administration, there had been no formal representation of groups defined by confessional identity since independence in 1946.

But community identity came to be used as a tool by the regime: the Sunni majority absorbed the most violence inflicted against any single group, while many Christians fled to Lebanon, and Alawites formed militias in their mountain fastness. As the conflict morphed from a general uprising against tyranny into a sectarian struggle, security guarantees proposed in international conferences lacked credibility. There was no will in the United Nations to garrison blue helmets to protect Syria's minorities who feared reprisals from the opposition Syrian National Coalition and came to view the regime as a lesser evil than the prospect of Sunni domination. Radical Islamic groups such as Jabhat al-Nusra stated their intention to eliminate the Christians of Syria. The Ba'athists had historically protected Syrian Christians against the Islamists. Bashar told a group of Christian leaders in 2011: 'Support me or your churches will burn.' So many of them did.

The Kremlin reached back to the historical role of Tsarist Russia as the protector of Christians in the Ottoman Empire and backed Bashar al-Assad. After recovering the rebel held cities with Russian military assistance, the regime settled into a partial post-conflict equilibrium of status quo ante, placing a *cordon sanitaire* around the remaining rebel province of Idlib. But according to the United Nations, 350,000 Syrians have been killed and 10 million out of 22 million displaced as internal or external refugees over the duration of the war. Meanwhile per capita income has fallen from $3,000 before the conflict to non-quantifiable subsistence as the country's housing stock, industrial capacity and infrastructure have been devastated. Syria's glittering cultural inheritance has been irreparably harmed, with between one third and one half of her historical artefacts, archaeological and architectural monuments damaged or destroyed.

In *Aleppo: Notes from the Dark*, filmed in the summer of 2013, Michal Przedlacki and Wojciech Szumowski interviewed an eight-year-old girl who had lost her entire family in regime raids and barrel-bomb attacks on civilian residential areas. A rebel fighter tells her: 'We are going to kill the men who killed your parents.' 'No, no, you must not do that,' says the girl. 'That is wrong; you must forgive them.' The girl's humanity, born of the clarity of anguish, is an inspiration. Yet how does one forgive people who accept no responsibility for any wrongdoing and continue to perpetrate the very same bad acts with impunity, one after another? How does one reverse the cycle and incentivise political reforms that move towards representative government, accountability and equality before the law? Or perhaps Western states have abandoned the attempt to spread these values while happily receiving 'donations' and 'investment flows' into corrupted Western institutions? For if evil is anywhere, eventually its effects will be felt everywhere.

Antioch

MONDAY 28 JULY | İSKENDERUN

James Hector Mackay is a family friend who worked for *The Economist* magazine in Istanbul in the 1970s. His grandfather Joseph Mackay had been a British officer at Gallipoli in 1915. The story goes that against the rules of engagement, Joseph had been taken prisoner by the Ottomans while recovering bodies in no man's land, so he demanded to be taken to the commanding officer and found himself in front of Mustafa Kemal. After agreeing to return him to Allied lines, Kemal asked Mackay what he did in civilian life. Joseph explained that he managed his family's estate in Sutherland, in the Scottish Highlands. As they talked, they warmed to one another and Kemal told Mackay that after the war Türkiye would need expert agronomists. Joseph returned to Republican Türkiye in 1922 and advised the government on agricultural development.

Inspired by his grandfather's adventures, James learned Turkish during his years as a journalist and made friends with Bülent Ecevit as well as other members of the political and commercial elite. Now in his sixties and having exchanged his apartment in London for an annuity with a friend, James has retired to Hatay to indulge his penchant for long cheap whisky and even cheaper, filthier Turkish cigarettes. James has a heart of gold. But a bottle of whisky a day would make anyone cantankerous.

There is no bus to Antakya, so the hotel orders a taxi which travels at speed across the limestone karst, passing the Turkish frontier without incident. A *dolmuş* (minibus) takes me over the Belen Pass, known in antiquity as the Syrian Gates, to İskenderun, the ancient port of Aleppo. James meets me at Koç on the edge of the town and bundles me into a taxi to a beach restaurant on the road to the town of Arsuz. Back once more on the shores of the great sea at the centre of the world, I drink Efes beer and gaze at the lapping waves as the weather turns and thunderclouds approach. A windstorm whips up the sand and we retreat inside with our meze. We take a taxi to the village of Höyük up the hill behind Arsuz, stopping on the way to buy food at Migros, the local supermarket. James's house is on the corner of two country lanes under the shadow of the Amanus Mountains that run along the spine of Hatay, with a garden and fields beyond. James has been restoring it, treating the wooden rafters, plastering the walls and adding modern windows.

We smoke cigarettes in the shady garden while the dogs soak off in the irrigation ditches on the edge of the fields. James's conversation consists of a peculiar mixture of deep knowledge of early Christianity and an avowedly 'pro-Turkish' stance on all matters relating to regional politics. We talk about the Gnostic Gospels and the repressive bishops who stamped out heterodoxy in the early centuries. Then James explains that Greeks let the Turks into Constantinople in 1453 by opening a postern gate in the Theodosian walls, that Archbishop Makarios provoked the Turks into invading Cyprus in 1974 and that the Greeks deserved to be thrown out of Istanbul in the 1950s after dismantling the mosques in Salonica. We are joined by Ali, son of Keskin, the local aga who sold James the house, and pass the evening looking at maps of the classical sites around Syria and Anatolia. James puts me in the guest room under the roof. But my sleep is disturbed by a mysterious itching. I switch on the light to discover cockroaches in the bed, one of which is just inches from my face. I leap up and wake James who agrees to swap rooms.

TUESDAY 29 JULY | ARSUZ
'All these months in Arabian budget hotels and I haven't seen a single cockroach! Not even in that mosquito nest in Mersa Matrough! Not one of the foul creatures until chez Mackay! Of course the house is squalid,' I tell him; 'you never empty the bins. No wonder you have cockroaches picking through all that rubbish, rotting away in the heat!' I spend the morning boiling

tea, cleaning up the kitchen and spraying insect repellent into every dark corner, while James talks about the archaeology of Hatay. We amble down to Höyük village for ayran (salted fermented milk) and börek (spiced pastries) under the shade of an awning. Cockroaches aside, the place is charming, and the villagers consider James one of their own.

'Is Türkiye culturally so different from the Arab world?' I ask. 'Unlike the Arabs,' says James, 'Turks are clean, hardworking and organised: the Latinised script reflects how Türkiye is more European than "Oriental". Türkiye may not be perfect but it is a democracy, while the Arab countries are all corrupt monarchies or dictatorships.' Nationalist Türkiye needed the port of İskenderun to protect its southern borders and Ankara regarded French control of the province under the Syrian mandate as unfinished business from 1923. France offered the Sanjak of Alexandretta to Türkiye in 1938 as an inducement to neutrality in the impending war. Ankara relocated Turks from elsewhere to achieve an electoral majority in the Hatay Assembly which voted to cede from French Syria in 1939. Although the province was Turkified, many of the indigenes identify as Arab and take advantage of the free education available in Assad's Syria. 'But when they return,' James explains, 'they are relieved to escape the tentacles of the mukhabarat and are glad to be Turkish citizens.' How true this would become when Syria plunged into the abyss.

Back at the house we pass the afternoon jabbering on about history and politics, from the Byzantine Empire to the PKK (Kurdistan Workers' Party). James talks about the alliance of rural *agas* (landlords) and imams in Turkish politics and how the AK Parti will ruin secular liberal Türkiye. 'I love this country,' he says, exhaling his cigarette with a flourish as one might have gestured *effendi* in Ottoman days. 'But under the Islamists, it will slide into incompetent dictatorship.' We talk about the collapse of the Ottoman Empire and the Turkish War of Independence that lies in the background of all contemporary regional politics.

'Yes, the fire of Smyrna was terrible,' James continues. 'But what did that Cretan pirate expect? The Greeks landed troops in Anatolia in May 1919 and began to massacre Turks in their own country. It was a fight to the death that was imposed on Türkiye by the Allies, who reneged on the terms of the Armistice of Mudros. The Turks had no option but to regroup their forces and expel the invaders from their territory. If Smyrna burned, it was because of the folly of Lloyd George and Venizelos. The Greeks deserved their own fate: Venizelos' so-called 'megali' was just that—megalomaniacal hubris. The situation in Cyprus was the same: in the 1950s the EOKA terror group sought Enosis (union) with Greece. When Britain granted independence to Cyprus in 1960, a well-balanced settlement was negotiated between the two communities. But the Greeks abused their position of numerical advantage. If Ecevit had not invaded to protect the Turkish Cypriots, Archbishop Makarios would have ethnically cleansed them like the fanatical Serbs did at Srebrenica.' What clearer statement could one have of the Turkish view: and what about the Armenians?

We take a cab to the steak restaurant on the road to İskenderun, which feels almost Californian with the cicadas chirping away in the warm evening air, and walk under the moon to Arsuz along the sea, talking of James's love for a beautiful thirty-five year old called Marianne Sadek. I wonder if by the time I get to James's age, I will not have equally hopeless dreams. We take a drink at the deserted bar of the Arsuz Hotel where there are three grand pianos that were once fine instruments but are now utterly ruined, and retreat up the hill to James's garden to drink whisky and smoke in the effulgent air of the Levantine summer night.

WEDNESDAY 30 JULY | RHOSSUS

I pass the morning boiling tea in the kitchen while browsing through Philip Carrington's 1950s history of *The Early Christian Church*. James's friend Christina arrives and we picnic on cold meat and beer by the stream with her children and dogs. It is hot and James sits in a pool of water complaining about his itching skin. Christina drives me to Rhossus beach to swim and tells me that James is ill and becoming increasingly dependent on the expatriate community. Even so, I am impressed by the beauty of the Hatay countryside.

James had explained that Rhossus was the ancient port of Antioch, and that after exploring the ruins, I could walk along the coast to the town and meet him in the Arsuz Hotel. In fact the port of ancient Seleucia Pieria is at Samandağ to the south where the main channel of the Orontes flows into the Mediterranean. But at the northern end of Rhossus beach, beyond the umbrellas and deck chairs, there is a cluster of fallen Classical columns, scattered over the rocky promontory. There seem to be no references in guidebooks or historical accounts, and I wonder if this is not a forgotten site, the location of a subsidiary port along a former minor watercourse off the Amanus? After photographing the columns, I walk towards Arsuz by the water and see ahead of me what appears to be the town rubbish dump. There is a high fence that extends across to the rocks by the sea, and there seems to be no way around it, but the gates are wide open and there are no signs.

I walk along the gravel track past the piles of rubbish and continue through the gate. It is hot and sultry, and I find myself heading towards a boy standing beside a concrete pillbox. I am walking uphill directly into the afternoon sun while the boy is staring out to sea. So I fail to notice that he is carrying a machine gun until the next thing I know, he is pointing it at me, shouting in Turkish, apparently to get down on the ground. I say to him 'I am English, Turkish yok,' and make a hand to the heart gesture. The boy shouts louder and more rapidly and is joined by a group of young soldiers who point their guns at my head. Unable to communicate with them and not knowing if they are going to shoot, I am terrified but try to guess what they want me to do. As I lie face down on the gravel, one of them puts his boot on my shoulders and uses the muzzle of his gun to peel off the canvas bag I am carrying with my towel, swimming trunks and camera, and to fling it away beyond my reach.

I have inadvertently strayed into a military installation whose location is kept secret because it is used for storing illegal landmines—hence the absence of any signs. It is in fact a divisional site of the İskenderun Naval Base. Later I am told that the soldiers think my backpack may have contained a bomb, which is why they threw it safely out of range with their guns, to be retrieved after questioning. I am handcuffed and blindfolded and walked into the base headquarters. Three English-speaking officers, Lufti, Ilhan and Enver, interrogate me separately to corroborate my story. Thankfully they are friendlier than the conscripts. After a couple of hours, during which time they give me dinner and copious cups of tea, the officers explain that if I can ask Mr James to please bring my passport, they can verify my identity and release me. James has no functioning telephone but luckily Christina had given me her own number. Eventually James and Christina arrive with my passport and drive me into Arsuz.

Rattled by my near-death experience, I write to Pyrrha from the Arsuz internet point, recounting what happened. Atatürk put two letter I-s into the Latinised Turkish script, one with and one without a dot. Tapping away with the letters in unfamiliar locations on the Turkish keyboard as well as the poor connection speed is not easy. 'James is argumentative and full of nonsense,' I write. 'He says his contacts with the Turkish Admiralty got me out of the Naval Base or I would have been taken to prison in Ankara. But in fact the lieutenants told me they only needed to see my passport to verify my story. He must be completely deracinated, as he made no mention of the military base and told the English lady who lives here that I was his son!' James has appeared and is standing over my shoulder reading my words. He charges off in a huff, and I close my session to follow him. James has taken the only taxi and no one is going to Höyük. So I walk the four miles up the hill in the warm night air, which is in a way a relief, and find James smoking in the garden. 'How dare you?' he yells at me. 'Take your things and leave at once!'

THURSDAY 31 JULY | HÖYÜK
Having ignored his temper, I patch things up with James. I do not want to part on bad terms and am glad to wash my clothes

before setting off for the east. I begin reading Czesław Miłosz's *The Captive Mind* and we continue our conversations about the history of the region over ham and eggs. James suggests I should explore the paths up the hill behind the house. 'Ask the Keskin boys to take you to the top of the ridge which has fine views over Hatay. You can walk up to Kisil Dağı, the highest point of the southern end of the Amanus.' Kisil Dağı rises to 1,700 metres and of course James has never been up there. But the ridge looks dramatic from below and I set off to explore it. The boys are not cooperative: they take me to a path leading off one of the lanes and then laugh and run away. The path leads into a watercourse full of boulders, and after trying to find another way up the hillside in my flip-flops, I end up with my feet full of thorns.

But the natural beauty of Hatay is astounding, and I am struck by the lush variety of the trees: banana, magnolia, olive and fig. These villages are an idyll of rural purity watered by the streams off the Amanus, and wandering along the lanes, I notice how many pregnant women there are. Somewhat bothered, I find a place to swim and cool off my feet, enchanted by the Arcadian simplicity of this natural verdant garden. Later we sit by the river in Arsuz, eating meze with Christina and a German called Max, and I understand why this small group of expatriates has independently discovered Hatay, and despite the challenges of language and local bureaucracy, loves living here in this halcyon environment.

FRIDAY 1 AUGUST | ANTAKYA

Loathe to leave the garden of Arsuz, I retrace my steps to İskenderun and over the Belen pass to Antakya. Drained from three days chez Mackay, I find a quiet room in Hotel Gurey and sleep until mid-afternoon. The air is beginning to cool and I explore the compact city centre, looking for the scant traces of its immense history. What would E.M. Forster have written about Antioch if he had lived here?

In Siwa I encountered Stark's thesis that Rome's victory at Magnesia in 190 BC severed Alexander's bridge between East and West, marking the Euphrates as the permanent frontier of the Levantine world. Walking along the Orontes embankment ones feels the sense of dislocation that this Turkish provincial town was once the eastern epicentre of Hellas. Following the wars of the Diodachi, Seleucid Antioch became the capital of the larger part of Alexander's Empire, stretching from the Levant to the Oxus. From 312 to 64 BC the Seleucid kings presided over this vast region, substituting the Greek administration for the Persian, transmitting Babylonian culture into the Hellenic world and vice versa. Antiochus III the Great fought an ill-advised war against the Roman Republic and its allies, Rhodes and Pergamum. The Latin Cohort under Lucius Scipio obliterated the Macedonian Phalanx of Antiochus, and Greek power was irretrievably broken. The Seleucids continued to hold territories east of the Cilician Taurus until the wars of Pompey the Great, who extinguished the dynasty and absorbed their vestigial domains into the Roman Empire in 64 BC.

As the capital of the Roman province of Syria, Antioch retained its Hellenic character but became the military springboard for Roman campaigns against Parthia and Sasanian Persia. Hadrian was proclaimed imperator at Antioch in August 117 when the Roman Empire was at its maximum extent, having incorporated Armenia and Babylonia under Trajan. Meanwhile Antioch became a centre for rabbinical Judaism and the magnet for apostolic proselytisation. Peter and Paul lived in Antioch circa 47 to 54 and expanded the appeal of the new faith from obscure Jewish sect to the wider gentile audience. In the early second century, Ignatius of Antioch was a leading church father together with Clement of Rome and Polycarp; in late antiquity Antioch became the intellectual battleground between pagans and Christians. It is thought that Constantine delivered his *Oration to the Saints* in Antioch on Good Friday 325, the prelude to the Council of Nicaea, and built the Golden Church next to the imperial palace on an island in the Orontes.

Antioch was captured by the Persians in the years 260, 540 and 613 and was severely damaged by earthquakes in 526 and 588. Following the Byzantine loss of Syria and the emergence of Damascus as the Umayyad capital, the former metropolis became a frontier town. Heraclius surrendered Antioch in 637 and it remained under Muslim control until recovered by Nikephoros II Phokas in 969. The Byzantines rebuilt part of the city and erected a fortress on the saddle of Mount Silpius. Antioch flourished once more until it fell to the Seljuks in 1084 and was then captured by the Latin knights in 1098, becoming the capital of the eponymous Crusader principality. Between 637 and 1098 the population contracted from 250,000 to 40,000. The city was sacked again by Sultan Baibars in 1268 and Antioch was never re-established as a metropolis.

The city's founder Seleucus I Nicator (the Victor) dedicated Antioch, fair crown of the Orient, to Tyche, goddess of fortune; her streets were oriented to catch the afternoon breezes off the Orontes. The Romans laid out new walls that enclosed the summits of Mounts Silpius and Staurinus together with the palace island. The wide central thoroughfare, preserved in the modern street layout as Kurtuluş ('liberation') Caddesi, was paved by Tiberius in the first century and beautified with covered marble colonnades. Nothing remains of Seleucid Antioch; indeed not much remains from antiquity at all, except for outlines of the stadium and circus maximus on the island, downstream from the modern town, as well as the mosaics and other artefacts in the museum. The successive layers of ancient Antioch, from the Seleucid city with Tychaion and temples, to the Roman imperial palace, baths and theatre, to Constantine's octagonal Golden Church, that some scholars believe was the model for San Vitale in Ravenna—all were destroyed in the earthquakes. Over the centuries, following invasions and the Byzantine retreat, the stones were taken away.

Generations of travellers have lamented the loss. But like modern Alexandria, her sister city of nostalgia, Antakya has a special atmosphere and, with some imagination, one can sense her glorious past. For Alexander chose the location himself, a day's march from the mouth of the Orontes, protected by a ring of hills and with the cool breezes of a gentle microclimate. The setting remains and the town is charming with its covered bazaar and well-proportioned houses. The features of the buildings—wrought-iron balconies, carved wooden lintels on stone corbels, cornices and shutters—reflect the nineteenth-century style that one sees traces of across the former Ottoman world: a good period for construction, when aesthetics and durability were more important considerations than return on capital and convenience for the automobile.

Antakya is relaxing: the townspeople wear the same clothes as across the Syrian border and old men play tric-trac on the raised terraces of courtyard houses, under trellises with vines. The Hatay Archaeological Museum is a good introduction to Anatolian archaeology and displays Hittite reliefs from tells on the Amuk plain north of Antioch. The museum is famous for its collection of Roman mosaics excavated in the 1930s. The pieces are comparable to those in the Bardo or at Naples, and suggest a comfortable world of private wealth built up through steady accretion. The fifth-century *Yakto Mosaic* depicts megalopsychia (the clemency of a just ruler) and the springs of Daphne with a background thought to show the Golden Church.

Most of the mosaics date from the second and third centuries. Like the Pompeiians, the Antiochenes admired pavements of animals and sea creatures woven into the representation of mythological scenes. Their recurring theme is the tribulation of unrequited love. In *The Seasons* Meleager gives a boar's head to Atalanta as Adonis sets off on a hunt; Hippolytus is killed after being falsely accused by Phaedra; while Echo wastes away as Narcissus falls in love with himself in a bucolic landscape. Orpheus plays a *kithara* to an audience of wild animals, while Cupid and Psyche, excavated at Seleucia, shows Psyche stealing Cupid's bow and quiver as he sleeps beneath a tree to avenge the tortures inflicted by love. The depiction of these fables reflects the stability and security of the Antonine Levant, a world in which there is nothing more to worry about than intrigue and trysts, antecedents perhaps of Elizabethan romances?

Yet the Antonine Age passed into the crisis of the mid-third century that led to militarisation of the state, persecution and civil wars, then Christianisation of the state and reprisals against the Hellenes. Is not the recurring theme of history that Arcadian episodes are overtaken by diverse forces of unfreedom that repress the individual in different ways in different epochs? I think of the unnecessary cluttering of our lives in the post-industrial economy: of analogue alienation in the age of software and electronic devices, and the tyranny of big brother, big data and big tech. We need to return to the spirit of the Antonine Age—of white marbled gymnasia and bath houses, of triclinia and open air theatre at dawn. One can imagine a scenario in which Hellenism had survived across the Seleucid territories, in which the syncretic metropolitan culture of that world had continued unbroken and absorbed the liberation theology of the Nazarenes without the repression of the state-backed church that Christianity became after the Constantinian moment.

Opposite the museum, in a building looking over the river that formerly housed the Hatay Parliament, a pornographic cinema advertises itself in large letters. Perhaps the carefree sybarism for which the city was famous survives in Antioch after all? As Cavafy observed in his Julian poems: 'the notorious life of Antioch' was 'delectably sensual in absolute good taste'. Near the central crossroads of the ancient city, I observe prayers in the Habibi Neccar Camii (mosque), and admire its Ottoman dome, rebuilt on pendentives over Crusader buttresses. In the evening light, I walk through the warren of streets on the east side of the Orontes, and up the slopes of Mount Silpius to watch the sunset. The hill dominates the Orontes valley downstream from Antioch, and traces of the Roman wall are visible, together with sections of the viaduct that brought water from Daphne. One can see the modern city spread around the west bank of the Orontes and the eastern spur of the Amanus up to the Belen pass. In the fading light I return through the souq for çorbası (lentil soup) and aubergines at the Sultan Sofrası restaurant by the river.

Pagans and Christians

In the 250s Decius imposed compulsory emperor worship: Christians faced the dilemma of renouncing their beliefs or being killed if they refused to sacrifice to the emperor. Epicurean philosophy was a theory, and the doctrine of salvation through belief in the Resurrection was likewise another theory. So the Christians were one of many sects who sold their ideological wares in the intellectual marketplace of late antiquity. But the Roman state religion was essentially institutionalised superstition: the failure of Christians to honour the millennial anniversary of the foundation of Rome was blamed for the Sasanian invasions. Epicureans, Cynics and other Greek philosophical schools are now seen as antecedents of Enlightenment thought. But in the third century they were also marginalised by the Roman state religion which revolved around the power of the Principate. Why did the Christians prevail?

Robin Lane Fox's masterpiece *Pagans and Christians* takes the reader into the mind world of the period. Before the fourth century, the vast majority of the inhabitants of the Mediterranean coastal cities followed the old religions. Their civic life consisted of the gymnasium, public office, games and circuses, processions to shrines and embassies to other cities. The wealthy classes left inscriptions of their careers, benefactions and oracles. Oriental mystery cults dedicated to Mithras or Dionysus were accepted so long as other deities were not excluded. The Hellenic religion was based on propitiation of the gods in fear of natural disasters and invasions: they sought divine wisdom through oracles at Delphi, Didyma and Claros and believed the gods spoke in visions. Consultation of oracles would be preceded by fasting and lamp-lit ceremonies. For it was the Hellenic mind that gave rise to much of Christian philosophy: rapture and ecstasy derived from the mystical sects such as the Hermetists whose ethics were close to the Christians.

By the time of the Edict of Milan in 313, Christians represented less than ten per cent of the population, mostly from the humbler classes, and conversion required a two year novitiate before baptism. They offered a vision of society based on equality achieved through an attitude of mutual support and love. In the mid-third century the state targeted church leaders and sought to destroy Christian property, especially books. Later on, between the reigns of Decius and Diocletian, Christians were normalised in Roman society, taking office as magistrates, serving in the army and participating in the literary culture. The new religion spread by witness and voluntary conversion. Why would the Hellenes abandon their prosperous comfort for the rigours of this peculiar Messianic cult? Perhaps the old religion failed to satisfy its adherents? Propitiation no longer worked, while Epicureanism lacked the inspiration to lend colour to life. The contemporary historian Ammianus Marcellinus described Christianity as a just and gentle religion.

Following the conversion of Constantine, the Church came to enjoy legal privileges, endowments and a budget for ecclesiastical architecture. But the Great Persecution left a legacy of division in the Christian community. Those who handed over their scriptures to the authorities were called *traditores* (traitors) by the Donatists who argued that collaborators had dishonoured the blood of the martyrs—those perfectionists who stood for the ideal. Factionalism led to conflict between groups who competed in their piety, and galvanised attacks on non-Christians. Western unbelievers were called pagans and those in the east were called Hellenes. The Christians attacked the propitiation that Epicureans themselves had derided, but also classical writers such as Democritus who were not considered proto-Christian. The humanism of the Master became subordinate to power politics and factionalism: free enquiry and natural philosophy were the casualties.

Antioch had been the bridgehead of Hellenic rationalism into the Semitic world. But while the Ptolemies encouraged syncretism, the Seleucids were less tolerant. In the Christian era Antioch continued to be the crucible of Hellenic resistance against the followers of the Nazarene. Libanius (314–393) was a classical rhetor and teacher of the apostate Emperor Julian who lamented that the civilised Hellenistic world had been captured by the 'Galilean madness'. Reflective of the atmosphere of fear that had taken root in the Byzantine court,

Libanius destroyed his own library, although a substantial body of his orations and declamations survive. About the Christians he wrote: 'If they wished to free themselves from earthly passions, why undo the very education that provided them with the means to do so? Was not classical Greek literature mankind's most precious possession, its study the most effective means of moral training? Was not rhetorical education the main ingredient of civilisation?'

Perhaps Libanius would have said that in relation to violent societies driven by brute power and primitive superstition, Christianity represents the illuminating ideals of forgiveness, love and peace: but in relation to a millennium of Hellenic reflection, might he also have said that the Galilean claims were a step back into unreason and darkness? Likewise in consideration of Islam as Arabised Christianity, its impact is framed by context: on the one side the messenger of order and reason to regions still carrying the imprint of savagery, but on the other an obstacle to the liberation of the mind as imagined by the Greeks. Or perhaps the antecedents of Christianity continued to extend their influence? By the time of the Muslim conquest, Zoroastrianism was a millennium old: Constantine absorbed Appolline sun worship while the Armenian cross has a sunburst at its centre.

Libanius's finest pupil was John Chrysostom (347–407), Patriarch of Constantinople, whose liturgy is standardly used in the Greek Orthodox Church, and who wrote a series of orations defending Christian doctrines. The best known of these is the Easter Sermon (circa 400) that foreshadows Rumi in its focus on the intensity of joy experienced by devout lovers of God. To the contemporary rationalist ear the sermon sounds saccharine, exhorting its listeners to believe in the conquest of death, but it is also strangely ecstatic, almost trance-like. If the kingdom of heaven is in this world, if the teaching of the Master is the basis for an ongoing revolution in human conduct, if the meaning of grace is the ongoing illumination that calls all of humanity to come to its senses and seek divine wisdom, is that not a cause for joy?

Lane Fox discusses church propaganda that exaggerated

the extent of the prior Roman persecution. Victors write history and we have an obscured view of the preceding epoch. So one can regard Christianity after the Constantinean moment as repressive in the hands of state power, smashing temples, closing the philosophical schools and burning the Serapeum. But what else tamed the brutality of the classical world, in which the body was praised but life was cheap, in which violence was normalised and the suffering of another was of little consequence? Inevitably the Church became corrupt after it was absorbed into the state and left behind its origins as social protest movement. But this does not change the essence of the Christian religion, which is the message of love and forgiveness, tolerance and charity.

Jesus was the successor to Zoroaster, Plato and Epicurus. What else but hagia sophia, in its parallel streams of illumination to different cultures at different times, restrains the descent of humanity into the law of the jungle, the tyranny of Mammon and the elemental forces of savagery unbound? The European Enlightenment secularised the central Christian values. For when the mind world of antiquity with its superstition and propitiation is stripped away, the meaning of Christianity is the illumination of humanism, true to its root of logos, as the precursor to the enlightenment ideals of 'liberté, égalité, fraternité'. So today we need a new syncretism between Christian ethics and Hellenistic philosophy: between the phlegmatic Epicurean rationalism and the transcendence that was inherited by the Christian mystics from the Platonists.

SATURDAY 2 AUGUST | SAMANDAĞ

I take the dolmuş past Karaçay towards Samandağ and disembark in the village of Uzunbağ. The road to the ruined monastery of Simeon Stylites the Younger (Aziz Simon Tepesi) is initially uninspiring. But as the track begins to ascend to the 450 metre summit, I sense its other worldliness as the Hill of Wonders or Magic Mountain of Byzantine Antioch. Simeon established himself on the crest of this hill, and for four decades dispensed sermons, exhortations and healings to visiting Antiochenes. Following his death in 592, the Stylite's devotees built a monastery complex dedicated to the Holy Trinity that was abandoned after the sack of Antioch in 1268. An old man called Isi, who stands guard with a shotgun and a horse, offers me a sandwich and sells me a small black chlorite soapstone cross. Isi guides me around the complex where an octagonal outline is visible around the location of the pillar. But the monastery is essentially a pile of old stones on a windy hill, with only the upturned Byzantine floral capitals to indicate their provenance.

The hills are exposed, and waiting for the dolmuş to Samandağ, I drink cherry juice from a stand in a lush grove to escape the sun. Seleucia Pieria was founded as the harbour of Antioch at the northern end of the coastal plain, where the flank of the Amanus descends into the sheltered inlet. The lower city lay around the harbour while the upper city stretched from the beach up to Mount Cassius and a long wall enclosed both districts. Excavations have shown evidence of trading settlements going back to the pre-Achaemenid era, with the outlines of houses from the Seleucid period. It is too hot to explore the Doric temple and Titus tunnel at Çevlik. So I walk along the beach to the wide mouth of the languid Orontes, having followed its course from Hama to Antioch, and observe the local people taking their weekend picnics on the strand.

Sunday 3 August | Daphne

After the service in the Greek Orthodox Church, I walk along the cardo, Kurtuluş Caddesi, to Sen Piyer Kilisesi (St Peter's Church). According to *Acts of the Apostles*, the followers of the preacher from Nazareth were first called Christians at Antioch. The unusual three-doored stone façade to the shrine church was built by the Crusaders in the 1200s before a wide esplanade with white painted olive trees. On the floor of the damp mossy grotto lie broken sections of mosaics from before the Muslim conquest, while passages lead into Mount Staurinus above. The cave-church attracts pilgrims on the apostolic trail but is particularly sacred to the Syrian Orthodox Church, non-Chalcedonian inheritors of the original Patriarchy of Antioch.

There is no firm evidence linking the cave-church with the early Christian community and the knights may have followed a local tradition or sanctified this spot for lack of any other. Near the church is the monumental rock carving known as the Charonion, believed to have been erected to protect against the plague (hence Charon the ferryman to the underworld) and dated to the reign of Antiochus IV (175–163 BC). The figure is weathered and indistinct, and scholars have suggested that it may also have been a representation of the Aramean or Assyrian hearth goddess Atargatis, equivalent to Anatolian Cybele or Greek Demeter. So it would make sense that a small vulnerable community would congregate at a sacred place on the outskirts of the city, as in the catacombs outside Rome. It was the same Antiochus IV who precipitated the revolt of the Maccabees by installing a statue of Zeus in the Temple of Jerusalem.

I sit below the church and reflect on the continuity between Hellenism and Christian thought, and the recurring theme of domination of one group by another, of how rare it is 'to live and let live'. Antioch lay on the linguistic divide between the Hellenistic and Semitic worlds: Christianity is intrinsically syncretic. But syncretism is also part of Hellenism, for the Seleucids absorbed Mesopotamian knowledge, from mathematics to astronomy, and were receptive to the cults they encountered in the east. Christianity in its Constantinian phase became authoritarian and dogmatic, defining Orthodoxy by the decisions of successive ecumenical councils. Yet pagan Libanius was admired for the clarity of his thought. Back along Kurtuluş Caddesi, I find the Muti Baba café, haunt of old men playing cards on tables with red velvet tablecloths and take notes from *The Captive Mind* with ayran and tea.

I take a dolmuş to the gorge at Harbiye, where in Greek legend Daphne became a laurel to escape the advances of Apollo. Following Pompey's conquest of Syria, Daphne was built as a colony of private villas around the springs of Pallas and Castalia, and it was here that Anthony courted Cleopatra. The villas have been excavated and little remains of the Roman resort. But the cascades from pool to pool down the hillside are profoundly charming and I take a place in the canteen to enjoy the tranquillity of the warm breeze, the trees and the running water. Surely the aim of life is to find beautiful places and stay in them? Mostly doing nothing is the best solution. A discarded copy of *Time* magazine has an article about American missionaries undermining indigenous Christian cultures in the name of their narrow interpretation of the faith.

On the next table is a group of quiet and serious young men. One of them speaks good English and invites me to join them. They have been exploring the Crusader fortress of Koz Kalesi, former residence of the Latin patriarch that was abandoned in 1275. Ali explains that they are Alevis and is open to talking about the place of Alevism in modern Türkiye. Alevis, like their Syrian Alawite cousins, are a branch of Shi'ism that venerates the Trinity of Ali, Muhammad and Allah; they have secret rites and can drink alcohol. I wonder if they are not crypto-Christians. Ali does not know. But he explains that despite being ethnic Turks, numbering ten per cent of the population and staunch Kemalists, Alevis feel marginalised in nationalist Türkiye and fear the rising Sunni AK Parti.

Within Hatay province, west of Antakya, is the hill of Musa Dağı that was scattered with hermitages during the Byzantine period. In 1915 the villages around its slopes became famous for the heroic resistance of Armenians against Ottoman death squads and deportations. One of the villages called Teknepinar (Vakıflı Köyü) retains a small Armenian population. Ali explains that Alevis feel sympathy with all the oppressed minorities in modern Türkiye. Back in Antakya I wander again through the streets below Mount Silpius, admiring the old houses before returning to Sultan Sofrası for lamb stew and ayran.

Ketman and the Pill of Murti-Bing

Czesław Miłosz is the Eastern Bloc equivalent of Orwell or Huxley, writing in 1951 from inside the Soviet Imperium about the repression of individual freedom. *The Captive Mind* could be read as an intellectual history of the twentieth century. But the predicament Miłosz describes is just as relevant today.

Sartrean *Nausea*, disgust with determination by absurd laws and slaughter on the Western Front motivated the New Faith of dialectical materialism to break those shackles and raise man by his bootstraps. But the New Faith, propagated as the pill of Murti-Bing, the Sino-Mongolian Asiatic cure to Western 'decadence', destroys the inner life, creating subjective impotence. The New Faith eliminates creativity or free expression, branding such longings 'bourgeois sentimentality' and absorbing the artist into the machine of socialist realism. The mind world becomes determined by collective suggestion not by personal conviction. The individual becomes a social monkey and is forced to take refuge in an inner sanctuary.

Miłosz refers to Ketman, a concept which grew out of Zoroastrian resistance to Islam, and which involves hiding one's true beliefs in the face of persecution. In Ketman, the concealing of one's thoughts and feelings is something everyone performs while being fully aware that everyone else is doing the same. Professional Ketman is the retreat into private study: scientists deliver reports adhering to the party line, but make their life goal private discoveries made in the name of a disinterested search for the truth. In the absence of any joyous immersion in the stream of life, the individual creates internal works of art to replace the drabness of the public architecture and the stiff, institutional spaces outside. There is also ethical Ketman which results from opposition to the party's definition of good or evil solely in terms of service or harm to the interests of the revolution. Ketman creates an inner core of comfort, without which there would only be a void.

Historically the Imperium failed because it created material poverty: the instinct for barter, trade and speculation was ineliminable. Intellectually the New Faith failed because it made human nature its enemy, and because science and the arts were subordinated to the method of dialectical materialism: creative enquiry conformed to the dictates of the Party instead of searching for objective truth and beauty. The motive force of insight became fixed and never renewed by observation. When external reality brings the realisation that everything is senseless, dialectical materialism falls apart.

Likewise those who romanticise the steppe nomads as noble savages do so from the security of their liberal democratic fastness: if they actually had to live under the khaganate, when would their optimism expire? For Asiatic autocracy has been the same for millennia: the Great Khan is all-powerful and the dissenter submits or dies.

But the mechanism of our new world machine is just as destructive to individual freedom as Asiatic-Stalinism. The New Faith created the conditions whereby work is worthless: is this not where post-capitalism is taking us? The writer's task is to look at the world from his independent viewpoint, to tell the truth as he sees it, and keep watch over the interest of society as a whole. Miłosz warns against seduction by socio-political doctrines that accept totalitarian control for the sake of a hypothetical future. But isn't the dictatorship of our hyper-technologicised global economy just as destructive to the individual? Without something external to guide it, the will of the Market becomes as totalitarian as the will of the Party. Miłosz writes that the creative act is associated with a feeling of freedom born in the struggle against an apparently invincible resistance. The creative individual must trust the inner voice and express what seems to be true. But this inner voice is absurd if it is not supported by a belief in an order of values that exists beyond mere human affairs, that derives from an external source of inspiration.

In *Veritatis Splendor* Pope John Paul II criticised theories of freedom that reduce humans to the sum of their immediate desires. Instead freedom is the habit of freely choosing the good. The free society has three interlocking parts: a democratic political community, a free or market-based economy and a public moral culture. Political and economic freedom liberate energies that are frustrated under authoritarian rule. But politics is downstream from culture. The cultural civilization of the West was born from the interaction of Jerusalem, Athens and Rome, or pilgrimage, reason and law. A loss of faith in reason is lethal to the democratic project, for argument based on reason and moral truths is the lifeblood of democracy.

John Paul II continues that pluralism means tolerance between groups seeking the common good, and engaging difference within the bounds of civility. Whereas nationalism involves pursuing the good of one's own nation without regard for the rights of others, patriotism is a love of one's native land that accords symmetric respect to other nations. What matters is the respect between groups. The openness of a free society must be comprehensive. But if one group believes that their ideology is above the superstructure—for example because they believe it is God's word or because some natural law gives them the power and hence the right to dominate—then the overarching structure will fail. To maintain peace and freedom in a liberal society requires that all individuals and groups and nations accept the liberal axiom as self-evident and prior in its force over the particular requirements of their own group.

Christianity inherited from Hellenism the metaphysics of the individual as the social unit and the practice of analytical disputation as the source of knowledge. So what used to be called Christendom has become the liberal-secular-humanist world order, based on the values of individual freedom, equality before the law and representative government. The liberal axiom is that individuals should be free to behave as they wish so long as they do not infringe the liberties of others. This derives from the golden rule: symmetry and reciprocity are inherent to liberal humanism. The challenge of our era is to defend this order against rival ideologies, including radical religious dogmatism, dictatorship of the proletariat, authoritarian nationalism of whatever colour, as well as a libertarian capitalism that subverts democratic accountability over the corporation. Yet how does one wish universal humanism on the rest of the world if the rest of the world does not want it? For in practice, universal humanism is unviable unless it receives universal assent.

Edessa

MONDAY 4 AUGUST | ADANA

After breakfast I return to Sen Piyer Kilisesi before taking the bus to Adana. The route retraces the Belen pass to İskenderun and crosses the Sarus River into Adana along the main highway. On one side is the second-century Ponte Sarus, once a vital artery in the Roman road network connecting Iconium with Antioch and Zeugma, and still open to heavy traffic; on the other is an enormous modern mosque in the high Ottoman style with embanked gardens beside the river. Adana lies on the fertile plain of Cilicia and has long been a centre for agricultural production especially of cotton and textiles. Adana was once part of the Armenian Kingdom of Cilicia that was governed from the fortress of Sis in the Taurus Mountains and was extinguished by the Mamluks in 1375. The city retained a significant Armenian population with extensive industrial and commercial interests until the Adana riots of 1909 in which more than 20,000 Armenians were killed, to be followed by the *Medz Yeghern* (Great Crime) of the First World War.

Taxi fares in the *otogar* (bus station) are exorbitant so I walk the hour's distance to the airport. By the perimeter fence a local family invites me to join their picnic, curious to see this strange tourist walking along the road. Politely declining, I ponder the next section of my journey from the frog pond to the spectacular Armenian Highland. Having shed most of the books since setting off in March, and James having kindly sent on the overflow canvas bag to Konya, I am at last travelling light. But it is too hot for the walking boots, bought at Nice in the cool spring. So I abandon them beside the picnickers—someone will pick them up—and trust to my leather flip-flops from Jerusalem. Will they hold out in the mountains, I wonder? But I am glad to be unencumbered. As I wait in the uninspiring restaurant of the International Terminal, I begin reading *Nausea* and wonder what new discoveries Illiana will bring.

Illiana arrives wearing a headscarf and clutching a large suitcase made out of chequered laminated cotton, more commonly used to carry sacks of potatoes than one's things. After greeting her warmly I ask: 'Do you think Alexander would have conquered Asia lugging around a deadweight like that? We need to be light, agile and mobile!' Illiana is nonplussed. We take a taxi back to the otogar and get to know one another again. Illiana produces the guidebook I had asked her to bring and we look through the entry for Adana. The guide explains that the Sabancı Merkez Camii was completed in 1998 and is the largest mosque in Türkiye, modelled on Sinan's 1574 masterpiece, the Selimiye Camii in Edirne, although with two minarets added to the courtyard. The Adana mosque was built by subscription with donations from the Sabancı family, whose wealth derives from the industrial conglomerate founded by Hacı Ömer Sabancı in the 1920s: 'local boys made good'. Still ill at ease we take the bus to Gaziantep and a room at the Evin Hotel.

Annihilation of the Ottoman Armenians
To explore eastern Türkiye is to travel through a ravaged ancient land that carries only traces of its long history. Like the Copts in Egypt, the indigenous Christians of Anatolia were the inheritors of the classical civilisation, extending in an unbroken line from the Homeric period into the Roman and Byzantine Empires. From the headwaters of the Tigris and Euphrates to the 'Seven Churches of Asia', late antique Asia Minor was the wealthy heartland of the Christian east. Following the Turkic invasions of the eleventh to the fourteenth centuries the Christians were ruled by one Muslim polity after another and eventually absorbed into the Ottoman domains. From the time of Süleyman the Magnificent until the mid-nineteenth century the Armenians had the status of most favoured *millet* (autonomous community) within the empire. At the beginning of the nineteenth century, Christians represented over twenty-five per cent of the population of 'Turkey-in-

Asia' while Armenians constituted over forty per cent in the six eastern *vilayets* (provinces). Yet by 1924 the Christian presence in the entire peninsula had been reduced to less than two per cent of the total population.

Between them, the scholars David Landes, Patrick Kinross, Christopher J. Walker and Mark Mazower give as good an account of the history as any. The Ottoman Empire began to shrink from its maximum extent after the second siege of Vienna in 1683 and the ensuing Treaty of Karlowitz (1699). As economic historian Landes describes it, the empire was plural on the Porte's terms, which represented the Turkish overlay to the original Islamic system, and whose purpose was to extract tribute from the subject populations under cover of the caliphate. Economic stagnation and an obstructive corrupt bureaucracy caused military weakness that led to territorial contraction as provinces broke away or were annexed by European powers. By 1830, the Greeks had successfully revolted to form their own state, while by the 1833 Treaty of Hünkâr İskelesi, Russia temporarily extracted control of passage through the Bosphorus.

Partly to address problems of competitiveness and partly in response to external pressure from the Great Powers, in 1839 Sultan Abdulmejid I issued the Edict of Gülhane. Together with subsequent decrees up to the *Islahat Fermani* (Imperial Reform Edict) of 1856, these became known as the *Tanzimat* (reorganisation) reforms. Like other minority communities within the empire, the Armenians were previously protected as a self-governing millet in exchange for paying additional taxes, and could not serve in the armed forces. Tanzimat aimed to abolish the dhimmi system of Islamic law with a concept of citizenship that granted non-Muslims constitutional equality under the pan-confessional Osmanli Legal Code. It also allowed them to serve in the public administration and armed forces.

One could see Tanzimat as the philosophical reconciliation between Islam and Christianity, as the logical conclusion of Ottoman syncretism in the spirit of the European enlightenment. But although the Porte issued decrees, there was no mechanism to overcome the vested interests opposed to their enactment or develop new institutions to implement them. In effect they remained dead letters as nothing changed in the army, ulema and bureaucracy that held power in conjunction with the Porte. In addition, some aspects of dhimmi status were retained even under the decrees: Christian testimony against Muslims was not accepted in courts, which granted Muslims effective immunity for offenses conducted against Christians. Meanwhile Muslims continued to dominate the public service and armed forces.

As the nineteenth century progressed, the millets were torn between Ottoman and national identities, a division that was hastened by resentment towards them from the Muslim majority. How did the sectarian hatred develop so aggressively? Since the early 1600s the Armenians had operated a trading and financing network that extended from the Balkans to Bengal. Armenian *amiras* in Constantinople were highly regarded for their enterprise and trusted by the Porte to hold tax revenues before remitting them to the Ottoman treasury. As the empire weakened economically their situation changed. By the 1870s adverse economic factors undermined the social fabric of Anatolia. Commercial concessions to European agents (known as 'capitulations') and technological backwardness led to the undercutting of domestic production by imported manufactures. Meanwhile balance of payments problems and external debts increased the domestic tax burden, while famines in the early 1870s undermined living conditions. Armenians in the eastern provinces faced intermittent violence, extortion and land appropriation from their Muslim overlords.

Some historians cite anger towards the Christian 'bourgeoisie' in cities such as Adana to explain this trend. But in fact the vast majority of the Armenians in the eastern vilayets were rural peasants, working the land and improving themselves through a long established tradition of education. The Porte systematically failed to provide security to the Armenians, allowing Kurdish chieftains in the east to oppress them. From 1876 onwards the court system and police punished Armenians for resisting Kurdish raids and extortion, prompting them to make more assertive demands for equality and autonomy. The Armenians in Erzurum, Bitlis and Van called for autonomy under a Christian governor following the precedent of Mount Lebanon. In 1877 Tsar Alexander II invaded the Ottoman Empire from Russian Transcaucasia ostensibly to protect the Christians. The ensuing 1878 Treaty of Berlin, by which the Porte ceded Kars and Ardahan to Russia, also contained provisions to guarantee their protection. But the Porte used troops to quash tax rebellions, delayed reform and reneged on promises to the Great Powers.

Since the sixteenth century, the eastern Ottoman provinces had effectively been ruled by Kurdish amirs who levied taxes and maintained security. Efforts by the Porte to centralise control from 1826 onwards largely failed, as local sheikhs asserted power. Armenians were scattered across the region where they had lived alongside the Kurds for centuries. As their situation deteriorated some Armenians were inspired by the Greeks and others to seek national self-determination. The Armenians had every claim to carve out an independent state from the shifting borderlands of the Ottoman and Tsarist empires. But the fatal weakness of their position was to be fragmented instead of concentrated with clear regional majorities like the Balkan nations. In response to Ottoman atrocities the Great Powers pressured the Porte to preserve their security. Gladstone in particular championed their cause, in echo of the Philhellenes who supported Greek independence, although Bismarck was circumspect. American missionaries operated schools and health clinics in towns such as Harput and kept the 'Armenian question' present in American political discourse.

In the early 1890s Sultan Abdul Hamid II responded to unrest in the eastern provinces by inviting leading Kurdish families to form auxiliary cavalry regiments that would be directly loyal to him, with the aim of reasserting control over potentially separatist elements in the east. Between January 1894 and July 1896, the sultan unleashed these paramilitary 'Hamidiye Light Cavalry Regiments' on Christian civilians across the eastern provinces. Most historians estimate that more than 200,000 Armenians were killed during this period of the Hamidian Massacres. Local qadis and muftis issued fatwas authorising the killing of Christians and the seizing of their property.

On 17 October 1895 Abdul Hamid issued another reform decree promising to honour the earlier commitments to protect his Christian subjects. But once again this turned out to be a hollow gesture to assuage the Great Powers as the Porte's objective became to stop the creation of an independent Armenian state in the eastern provinces. The sultan and the state institutions around the Porte feared that the new Armenian Hunchakian ('clarion') and Dashnaktsutyun ('federation') parties would lead secessionist movements. But the Ottoman state had breached its obligation to protect its citizens regardless of ethnicity or creed, thereby stoking Armenian aspirations for independence. The Ottoman Bank Raid of 1896 and attempted assassination of the sultan in 1905 inflamed the Ottoman Muslim elite against the Armenians. The adoption of the ideology of Turkish Nationalism within the elite that controlled the state would result in the annihilation and dispossession of the Ottoman Armenians between 1915 and 1923.

Why were the Armenians and other Christians of Anatolia targeted for elimination? The answer lies partly in Salonica, *de facto* nerve centre of the late Ottoman Empire until being lost in the First Balkan War of 1912. Salonica was the most cosmopolitan city of the empire and the most influenced by progressive European ideas. The *Ittihad ve Terakki Cemiyeti* (Committee of Union and Progress or CUP) was founded in Salonica to seek the revival of the liberal constitution that had been suspended by the sultan following the Russo–Turkish war of 1877 to 1878. As nationalist tensions rose in Ottoman Rumelia ('Turkey-in-Europe'), the Salonica branch of the CUP joined forces with officers from the Third Army Corps stationed in the city as well as members of masonic lodges and some senior officials in the administration to plot revolution against the *ancien régime*. Even Hilmi Pasha, Inspector-General of the Balkan Provinces from 1902, was linked to the movement that became the Young Turk Revolution.

In the spring of 1908 sectarian killings between Greeks and Bulgarians in Salonica provided the spark that triggered the Ittihadists to act. On 24 July the sultan acceded to CUP demands and restored the 1876 liberal constitution. In early April 1909 the sultan attempted a counter-revolution led by loyal elements in the armed forces. The Ittihadist commander of the Third Army Corp, General Shevket Pasha, formed the 'Action Army' and on 24 April 1909 marched on Constantinople deposing Abdul Hamid in favour of Mehmed V. Even as the counter-coup was launched and then crushed, Muslim mobs in Adana killed an estimated 20,000 Armenians, destroying their homes and looting their property. To assuage the Armenians, the CUP ostensibly worked with the Dashnaks to bring the perpetrators to trial and later in the summer signed a cooperation agreement with them in Erzurum. But this rapprochement proved to be illusory.

The Ittihadists framed their revolution in terms of liberalism and representative government under the banner of fraternity between all Ottoman citizens. Initially the new government carried the support of the substantial Salonica Jewish community, the Greek Orthodox and Armenian Patriarchates as well as Hunchaks and Dashnaks. But in reality the CUP was a proto-Turkish Nationalist conspiratorial organisation whose aim was to retain control. As centripetal forces of the Balkan nationalities accelerated, so too did the transition in ideology from Ottomanism to Turkish Nationalism. Taking inspiration from Namik Kemal's 1872 nationalist play *Vatan Yahut Silistre*, writers such as Ziya Gökalp and Halide Edib sought to construct a new Turkish Muslim identity in a homeland that would stretch from the Bosphorus to Baku.

It soon became clear that the Young Turks could not stop the disintegration of the empire as the Porte lost Crete to Greece and Bulgaria declared complete independence. In the autumn of 1912, Greece, Serbia and Bulgaria coordinated their forces to expel the Ottomans from the whole Balkan Peninsula except for part of Thrace. The First Balkan War concluded in April 1913 and was succeeded by the Second Balkan War as the disgruntled Bulgarians attacked their former allies and allowed the Ottomans to recover Edirne (Adrianople). But the final failure of Ottomanism and the loss of Rumelia prompted the Ittihadist leaders to abandon reform. On 23 January 1913 Ismail Enver led a coup in the fledgling parliament, ousting the ruling liberal party under Kamil Pasha. Following the assassination of General Shevket Pasha in June 1913, the Three Pashas (Enver, Talaat and Cemal) formally assumed power and installed a one-party dictatorship. If Macedonia was to be Hellenized, Anatolia was to be Turkified.

Meanwhile land disputes between Kurds and Armenians in the eastern provinces induced a fresh Russian intervention, compelling the Porte to sign a new reform proposal on 8 February 1914 that was seen by the Ittihadists as paving the way to an independent Armenian state. The agreement was immediately revoked upon the entry of the Ottoman Empire into the First World War on 31 October 1914. Sometime over the next five months, the Ottoman administration under the Pashas took the decision to eliminate the Christians of Anatolia. Following the earlier precedent from 1877, on 14 November 1914 Sultan Mehmed V, acting as a figurehead for the Ittihad regime, declared a jihad or holy war 'against the enemies of Islam, who have proven their hostility by their attacks on the caliphate'. The declaration of jihad was an appropriation of the concept because the Porte was now allied with other non-Muslim powers, while the use of Islam to construct a Turkish national identity was contrary to the universal principle of the 'umma.

Amid the chaos of the war, the Ittihadist government began the systematic destruction of the Ottoman Armenians, forming a *Teshkilat-i Makhsusiye* (Special Organisation) to execute the killings. In towns and villages across the six eastern vilayets, Armenians were detained by Ottoman gendarmes with the assistance of Kurdish irregulars and executed by firing squad, thrown into mass graves or marched into the Syrian Desert for 'resettlement' where they died in transit or upon arrival. Ottoman death squads were observed by German military advisors led by Franz von Papen, as well as other German officials such as Scheubner-Richter, vice-consul in Erzurum, who compiled their own reports of the massacres, even as they did nothing to intervene. On 24 May 1915, Britain, France and Russia issued a joint declaration of Ottoman atrocities as 'crimes against humanity and civilisation', the first use of these terms by any government.

Viscount Bryce and Arnold J. Toynbee's *The Treatment of Armenians in the Ottoman Empire 1915–1916* runs to over 700 pages of eyewitness accounts of the killings, including from the United States's Ambassador Henry Morthenthau, as well as other American diplomats, missionaries and business people. Talaat Pasha told Morgenthau in August 1915 that the vilayets of Erzurum, Bitlis and Van had been emptied of Armenians. On 15 September 1915 Talaat cabled the prefect in Aleppo, 'You have already been informed that the government has decided to destroy completely all the indicated persons living in Turkey ... their existence must be terminated however tragic the measures taken may be and no regard must be paid to either age or sex or to any scruples of conscience.' British intelligence reports confirmed the killings from sources across the lines. The international press gave them considerable prominence: on 7 October 1915 the *New York Times* carried the headline '800,000 Armenians counted destroyed'.

Most historians estimate the number of Armenian civilians killed between 1915 and 1923 at between one and one-and-a-half million. The Armenian genocide has traditionally been dated from 24 April 1915, when the regime instructed the detention of all Armenians in Constantinople. But it was always known that deportations started in Zeytin and Marash on 8 April 1915 and possibly earlier in Cilicia and Erzurum. In recent years, considerable effort has been dedicated to the analysis of Ottoman archives and especially the encrypted telegrams of the Ministry of the Interior. Scholarly debate persists concerning the exact sequence of events in the early stages of the genocide. Critical documents were destroyed by the Ittihadists and the authenticity of some surviving documents such as the so-called 'Ten Commandments' remains unproven.

In the last twenty years there has been a proliferation of research scrutinising the primary sources by such scholars as

Raymond Kévorkian, Ronald Suny and Hans-Lukas Kieser. Historians from outside Türkiye were not previously granted access to the Ottoman archives. But the Turkish-German scholar Taner Akçam uncovered the secret ciphers that were used to pass instructions by telegram from the Ministry of the Interior to local officials in the provinces, and published his research in 2012 as *The Young Turks' Crime Against Humanity*. Akçam's discoveries in the Ottoman archives show categorically that the CUP formulated a detailed and premeditated plan to eliminate the Christian population of Anatolia. They also explain how, in an era when it took three weeks to travel from Constantinople to Van, the genocide was executed so quickly. Akçam's work has become the standard reference quoted by historians.

Analysis of the letters of members of the Special Organisation by Akçam suggests that the first explicitly genocidal killings of Armenians began in Erzurum on 1 December 1914, before the Ottoman defeat at Sarikamish; and that the decision to eliminate all the Ottoman Armenians was taken in early March 1915, before the Allied landings at Gallipoli or the Van uprising. As early as mid-November 1914 Armenian Ottoman soldiers were being killed with impunity in the Ottoman Third Army. The Erzurum decision was taken by Bahaeddin Shakir, head of the Special Organisation and CUP committee member. Akçam discovered telegrams from local governors in which the term 'extermination' of Armenians was openly used. This evidence disproves the argument that the Armenian deportations occurred in response to Ottoman military setbacks but rather were premeditated. Sources such as Talaat's private notebook from 1917, published in 2008, show that the aim of the killings was the demographic re-engineering of Anatolia, hence the target to reduce the Christian population of every district to less than ten per cent.

There were some Armenian deserters who welcomed the Russians as protectors, but there were also many thousands of Armenians fighting in the Ottoman armies, and the civilian population remained loyal to the sultan. As Eugene Rogan relates in *The Fall of the Ottomans*, Hunchaks and Dashnaks each argued to the CUP that Armenians should remain loyal to the governments under which they lived on both sides of the frontier. There were also many Turks and Kurds who disobeyed the CUP orders such as Cemal Bey, governor of Konya until October 1915, and others who sheltered Armenians in their homes. The Turkish governor of Deir ez-Zor Ali Suad Bey set up orphanages for Armenian children but was recalled by Talaat Pasha and replaced by Zeki Bey who turned the town into a concentration camp. Other officials were particularly brutal, such as the Circassian governor of Diyarbakir Mehmed Rashid, who had himself been ethnically cleansed from the Russian Caucasus, in which repression the Armenians had no part.

Armenians later carried out reprisals that the Turks emphasise in their version of events. But the Turkish narrative conflates the War of Independence and the aspiration of the National Pact with the rights of the indigenous population, regardless of creed or language. Nothing in the 1907 Hague Convention, to which Ottoman Türkiye was a signatory, implies that military expediency can justify the unilateral removal, whether by ethnic cleansing or killing, of populations whose presence is inconvenient. When Kemal held the Congress of Erzurum to draft the National Pact from 23 July to 4 August 1919, it was in the same city that the detailed plans to eliminate the Armenians had begun to be put into effect in December 1914.

The Turkish Nationalists had the right to claim the eastern provinces which had historically formed part of the Ottoman Empire. But they extended that claim after having killed the Christian inhabitants of those territories. If the Ottoman Government failed to honour its obligation to provide security to Armenians, the latter had the right of self-determination to seek their security in an independent state. Turkish denialism obfuscates the competing rights in order to hide Turkish crimes against humanity and avoid reparations. Nowhere else during the First World War was the desire for self-determination answered with the destruction of the wider community from which those nations came: consider Poland under the Tsars or the constituent nations of the Habsburg Empire whose demands for self-determination were honoured in 1919.

The Ottoman elimination of the Christians is pre-figured in earlier episodes, from the Roman conquest of Gaul to the slaughter of the North American indigenes to the Zulu expansion in southern Africa. By American political scientist Rudolph Rummel's broader concept of 'democide', and proportional to the population, the annihilation of the Ottoman Armenians is comparable to the most destructive known mass killings in history. Yet today the Turkish government decries the United States for having no business to lecture Türkiye about her own history. American settlers primarily killed indigenes inadvertently through germs such as smallpox, as well as through the destruction of the pre-colonial habitat, and now have ongoing legal processes to address the claims of Native Americans. But Türkiye continues to deny the genocide of its Christian subjects.

Since the 1920s exiled and refugee Armenians experienced great difficulty in getting their story believed in the West. History is told by the victors: had the Third Reich prevailed in the 1940s, doubtless we would know very little about the extinguished Jewish culture of Central and Eastern Europe. The ultimate victory of the Turkish Nationalists and the place of the Turkish Republic in the new dispensation allowed their narrative to prevail and prevented justice ever being served to the victims of the genocide. Yet the historical record is incontrovertible. The Ottoman Military Tribunals of 1919 passed death sentences on eighteen defendants, including the three Pashas, Bahaeddin Shakir and Mehmed Nazim. The records of these trials show that following the earlier massacres instigated by Abdul Hamid in the 1890s, the Ittihadist government deliberately set out to eliminate the Christian population of Anatolia and seize its property.

All of this has been recorded and yet also forgotten, for the protagonists are shadows. All that remains are borders fixed in the wrong place and vestigial indigenes cognisant of their identity and ancestry but alien to their cousins across the closed frontier. Article Twelve of Wilson's 'Fourteen Points' called for protection of the non-Turkish minorities in the former Ottoman territories. In 1922 Viscount Bryce asked in public lectures why the Turkish Government had been treated with such leniency despite massacring more than one million of its Christian subjects, and why the Armenians who suffered more than any other people in the 1914 to 1918 war, were so 'cruelly abandoned'. One answer is that following the US Senate vote in 1919 that emasculated the League of Nations, Britain and France needed Kemalist Türkiye as an ally to counter the new Bolshevik threat.

The First World War was the cataclysm that catalysed the transition from dynastic empires to nation states. Nineteenth-century nationalism destroyed the polyglot, multi-confessional empires, and the Christians of Anatolia were the casualties of that process. Yet nationhood through language and religion is a natural clinging-together of people with their own kind, finding security and solace in shared tradition and identity. *Acts of the Apostles* speaks of taking the Christian message to all nations: that was the meaning of the Christian Pentecost. Likewise with the 'umma: from Berbers to Baluchis, group identities flourish within the Dar al-Islam. So there is nothing inherently contradictory about the interaction of universalism, humanism and nationalism. The trouble starts with relations between nations, whether inside a polity or between states.

Commentators sometimes ask: what do the Armenians want? The answer is clear: recognition and reparation. After a century of cupidity it is the duty of Western democracies to seek to persuade Türkiye to accede to those demands. But it is also in the interest of Türkiye to make this history right. Taner Akçam wrote in the conclusion to his book that Türkiye has a moral responsibility to acknowledge the injustice of what the Ottoman regime perpetrated against the Armenians and undo as much as possible of the damage it created through indemnification. To return to Hacı Ömer Sabancı, the 'local boy made good', whose eponymous mosque in Adana was constructed over the site of an Armenian cemetery: the purpose of the Ittihadist programme was not only to eliminate the Christian population, but also to recycle their capital and create a Muslim Turkish bourgeoisie. Examining the paper trail of confiscated Armenian property is an ongoing subject of research both inside and outside Türkiye: the historians Uğur Üngör and Mehmet Polatel have written about how the proceeds of genocide capitalised Turkish conglomerates such as Sabancı.

TUESDAY 5 AUGUST | ANTEP
Breakfast is amusing. The name Antep derives from *ayn teb*, meaning good spring, and the city is known for its well-watered pistachio orchards. The hotel is located in the warren of streets near the former Armenian Cathedral of St Mary, built in 1892 and later converted into the Kurtuluş Camii (Liberation Mosque). We explore the Gaziantep Archaeological Museum, a division of the Museum of Anatolian Civilisations in Ankara. The museum is well laid out with a spacious arcade around first- and second-century mosaics from the nearby Roman town of Zeugma. In the side corridors are cabinets with artefacts from local Bronze Age sites, basalt Hittite reliefs, pottery, seals, stele and other fragments, as well as a collection of Urartian artefacts. Oddly, the bell from the Armenian cathedral is also on display.

Despite its extensive Neolithic settlements such as at Nevalı Çori and Göbekli Tepe, Anatolia lay on the periphery of the later Bronze Age centres of technological invention and cultural development. Hattian and Hurrian Kingdoms emerged at around the time of Sargon, and the archaeological record is sparse until the arrival of the Hittites into central Anatolia in the seventeenth century BC. Speaking one of the earliest Indo-European languages, the Hittites may have originated from the steppe north of the Caucasus and became a power of the later second millennium BC until their capital Hattusas was destroyed around 1180 BC.

The Urartians emerged as a distinct identity in the early first millennium BC and may have descended from the Hurrians. They ruled the Lake Van basin from their capital at Tushpa (Van) and built a series of fortresses that survive on high rocky bluffs, including Çavuştepe, Toprakkale and Van itself. King Menua developed a system of irrigation channels, and their culture was distinguished by ornate metal work and viniculture. The Urartians were rivals to the Assyrians until their defeat by King Tiglath-Pileser III in 745 BC, and used cuneiform, which is suggestive of cultural interchange along a North-South axis. The destruction of Nineveh in 612 BC heralded the decline of Urartu, which is thought to have succumbed to Scythian and Medean invaders around 590 to 585 BC. Shortly after, in 550 BC, the Lake Van region was absorbed into the Achaemenid Empire as the heart of the Satrapy of Armenia whose capital was at Tushpa.

As the heat mounts we climb up to the citadel. Smaller and with less ornate stonework than its cousin in Aleppo, there is not much to appreciate except the dominance of its position, with views from the turret openings over the ancient landscape and the sprawling modern city. We take the coach from Antep's palatial otogar across the baking plain to the shrine city of Şanlıurfa. A short distance upstream from the Assyrian city of Carchemish, we cross the Euphrates at Zeugma, the Roman frontier town and custom post that was destroyed by the Sasanians in 256. The languid flow of this long wide river is Nile-like in the strip of green it carves through the plains: for millennia this section was the junction of trade from comfortable boat on the navigable Euphrates to arduous mule and foot across Asia Minor.

When we reach Şanlıurfa at tea time, it is over forty degrees and the oven-like air rises up in every direction. Illiana had called ahead to book a room in the boutique Gülpalas Hotel, located in an Ottoman mansion some distance from the otogar. We settle into a charming subterranean cave *locanda* by the Ulu Camii (Great Mosque) to shelter from the heat and drink cool fresh watery ayran. The cave has wooden tables under an arched stone ceiling. With the only light entering from the top of the wide stone steps, it reminds me of the Tomb of the Virgin in Jerusalem. As the air cools, we wander through the streets and enjoy music and meze on the terrace of the Gülizar Konuk Evi with its arcade and wrought-iron railings.

WEDNESDAY 6 AUGUST | URFA

At the apex of the fertile crescent, and as ancient as Haleb, Urfa is where in the Semitic traditions Abraham tended his flocks before setting off to Mount Moriah. Archaeologists have located biblical 'Ur of the Chaldees' in Sumer. But the Genesis story also mentions Harran, south of Urfa, to which city Abraham despatched a servant to find a wife for his son Isaac 'from among his own people'. It would seem easier to travel from Urfa to Canaan via Aleppo than across nearly a thousand miles of open desert from Sumer to Judaea. To date the quasi-mythical Abraham historically would be impossible. But it is known from the Assyrian king lists that the pastoral Arameans emerged as a distinct group across the region sometime after 1200 BC. By the time the Assyrian King Tiglath-Pileser III conquered Damascus in 732 BC, Aramaic had become the lingua franca of Greater Syria: perhaps one should consider Abraham the Aramean as the representative linguistic ancestor of the wider Semitic Levant?

The name Urfa derives from the Hurrian or possibly Hittite name Orhoi, while Edessa is the Greek name for the city. Out of the fragments of Alexander's Empire, Edessa was refounded by Seleucus Nicator circa 300 BC and became the capital of the small independent Kingdom of Osroëne, ruled by the Aramaic speaking Agbarid dynasty. From 64 BC the Agbarids were clients of Rome until Osroëne was absorbed as a Roman province by Caracalla in 216. Edessa was proselytised from Antioch and was associated with the Gnostic philosopher Bardaisan who was born in the city in 154. Agbar VIII the Great formally adopted Christianity as the official religion around the year 200. Osroëne was most likely the first Christian polity, before even Armenia, and Edessa thus became the legendary early centre of Syriac Christianity. The Agbarids maintained a palace on the citadel, from which twin columns survive that stand out above its walls.

Urfa was conquered by the Arabs in 639 and the province became a self-governing territory under the Abbasids in 812. The Crusaders captured Edessa with a diversionary force in 1098. There is little trace of their presence apart from an inscription on the Bey gate from 1123 that refers to Count Joscelin being taken hostage. The County of Edessa formed the short-lived fourth Crusader state until its capture in 1144 by Zengi, atabeg of Aleppo. Given the remoteness and indefensibility of Edessa, one wonders if Christendom considered it part of the Holy Land because of the link with Abraham or with the Christian Agbarids. Sacked by the Mongols in 1260, Urfa was abandoned until the arrival of the Turkoman Ak Koyunlu, whose most notable ruler, Uzun Hasan (1452–1487), repaired the citadel and constructed the Hasan Pasha Camii. Urfa retained a substantial Armenian and Syriac population into the Ottoman period. But from 1915 to 1923 most of the Christians were killed or expelled and the last Syriac families fled to Aleppo in 1924.

After breakfast in the cave, we explore the souqs with their incense, pop music and considerable banging, from squatting cobblers to metal workers turning out copper trays. Urfa feels distinctly Arab, and it is an immense pleasure to wander through the hubbub of these ancient streets, one's eye caught by one distraction after another. The Hasan Pasha Camii has three large domes supported by an octagon of arches with a portico, while the Gümrük Hanı is a splendid sixteenth-century caravanserai built with two storeys around a shaded square courtyard. Geography, history and culture do not fit the modern borders: this is not Anatolia but al-Jazeera, the hybrid upper reaches of Mesopotamia.

Below the citadel is the sacred rectangular pool, the Birket Ibrahim. In Islamic tradition this pond is where the patriarch kept carp and the waters still bristle thick with these dark fish. Pilgrims wander along the stone embankments by the pool, replenished by its freshwater spring, and throw chickpeas to the fish. The pool has been a shrine for millennia, reinterpreted by successive religions, and may have its roots in the fertility cult of the Akkadian goddess Ishtar. The legend that Abraham had been born in the nearby cave is thought to have developed during the Umayyad period. Adjacent to the pool is a series of stone arcades and the Rizaniye Camii, built by the Ottoman governor in 1736. Between the sanctuary and the citadel is the immaculate Gölbaşı Park which has lawns, fountains, plane trees and kiosks. Set against the dusty plain, the sanctuary gives a glimpse of paradise, with the dew rising off the water under the breezy trees. We walk up to the kale, returning for çay (Turkish tea) and dark cherry juice beside the Ayn-i-Zeliha lake in the gardens.

Illiana reads Osip Mandelstam's 1930 'Acmeist' prose-poem *Journey to Armenia*, reciting excerpts in English from the German translation of the Russian, talking about the love affair of that vast cold nation for the ochre landscapes and sunlit uplands of the Shangri-La that was Soviet Armenia. Illiana sees Mandelstam as the quintessential Jewish social philosopher. Osip idolised Armenia as the ancient land of a proud and indestructible people with luscious thick hair and eyes 'drilled straight into their skulls', maximally alive, hewing their new capital from arid wilderness in its remote mountain fastness, pioneers out of the ashes of genocide and the greatest hope for International Socialism.

Journey to Armenia pays homage to an antique wisdom, reclaiming man's connection with the natural world, broken by modernity. Mandelstam's descriptions of the 'Japhetic' Armenians are John Galtian in their description of the brute will of enduring determination, of an oppressed people whose historic elements, like John-Paul II's, define Western civilisation in a constant state of evolution as 'an event, a happening, an arrow'. But the 'anchor-like stubs of oak-trees of a wild and legendary Christianity' sounds poetically disconnected from what happened between 1894 and 1924. For the Armenians were destroyed, and the Turks rooted out the tree stumps, looting their culture, property and capital accumulated over millennia. Armenians constituted a third of the population of Urfa up until the Hamidian Massacres of 1894 to 1896 and almost nothing remains of their presence. The Armenian Cathedral of John the Baptist was built in 1842 when Urfa was going through a period of revival and expansion. In 1993 it was converted into a mosque and named after Salah ad-Din; the Church of the Twelve Apostles is now the Fırfırlı Camii.

In *Rebel Land*, his 2009 account of Turkish minorities, Christopher de Bellaigue tells the story of an Armenian from Yerevan who visited a village in the province of Erzurum and bought an antique silver belt from a Kurd. The Kurd had been using the belt as a holster for his revolver. But it was inscribed in Armenian on the inside and had embossed detached sections and a date: 1902. For the belt was a traditional marriage belt that Armenian women wore, adding and removing sections as they became pregnant and slim again after giving birth, and had been plundered from the corpse of a murdered woman. Yet here in this eighteenth-century Ottoman shrine complex, one cannot help but be impressed by the magnificence of the gardens and mosques and the carp pool of Abraham, while wondering wherein lie the seeds of such violence. At dusk we walk up to the citadel which has fine views over the town and return for çorbası in the cave.

THURSDAY 7 AUGUST | HARRAN

We take the dolmuş to Harran, tracking the irrigated fields along roads lined with trees for shade. It is forty-five degrees, and even in my Siwi sirwal under-trousers, walking the short distance to the archaeological site feels like being crushed in a furnace. We are mobbed by a group of children and stop for chicken kebab at the canteen by the entrance to the site of old Harran.

The Harranians worshipped the moon deity Sin at a temple that dates to the early first millennium BC and may have been reconstructed by Ashurbanipal. To the Romans, Carrhae (Harran) was the location of their defeat in 53 BC to the Parthians who poured molten gold into the throat of Crassus. Harran was Christianised early but the Emperor Julian visited the Temple of Sin in the fourth century, implying that the old religion still flourished. Following the Arab Conquest, Islam was slow to take root, and it was not until the 740s that the Great Mosque was built over the temple by the last Umayyad Caliph Marwan II. In 830 Caliph al-Ma'mun visited Harran on a campaign against Byzantium. Arab historians relate that the Harranians continued to worship Sin, calling themselves

Sabians to gain dhimmi status. Harran flourished over the next century and was a centre for the Hanbali School of Sunni jurisprudence. During the Crusader period, Harran rotated between Muslim rulers before falling to Zengi in 1127. The Ayyubids rebuilt the citadel but the city was abandoned in 1271 following the Mongol invasion.

We clamber over the mound, retreating to the shade of the ruined Ulu Camii, which once had a courtyard and a four-aisled prayer hall. These blocks, the square minaret and a few traces of the Ayyubid University are all that remain. But Harran was for millennia a prosperous city along the trade routes connecting Asia Minor with Lower Mesopotamia. We are joined by some pretty children who gather around Illiana in the mihrab, juggling stones and peddling dolls and other objects. As the heat dissipates, we wander around the mud-brick beehive-domed houses below, continuation of a style that developed millennia ago in al-Jazeera for lack of timber, and chat to striking-looking women in velvet robes, smoking cigarettes. At the friendly Kultur House, we eat vegetables and ayran on a brass tray and sleep on the roof in the warm open air.

Friday 8 August | Urfa

The preindustrial simplicity of the Kultur House is charming and we rise with the cockerels and absorb the primaeval tranquillity of Harran at dawn, as local people take advantage of the cool air to work in the fields. By the time we walk back over the hill and return to Urfa for lunch in the cave, it is already getting hot. Urfa's Ulu Camii was built by Nur ad-Din and modelled on the Great Mosque of Aleppo with five arches in the courtyard, possibly an arcade from a prior church, and an octagonal minaret. According to an inscription on the ablution fountain, the medrese was constructed in 1191. The texture of the stone esplanade and the pines rising above the courtyard remind me of the Haram al-Sharif in Jerusalem. I lean my back against the wall beside the window adjoining the street and think of taqwa and the tranquillity of this pre-modern way of life: in an environment of simple daily routines, uncomplicated by the continuous quest for innovation in a competitive industrial economy, the diurnal rhythms of Islam fit perfectly.

There is a parallel in this static routine with the prehistoric life of the beehive society in Harran. Attending mosque five times a day, feeling the cooling water on one's limbs by the fountain, chanting from the holy book, stretching one's body in the punctuated movement of the prayers, to be reminded always of the ultimate triumph of the absolute over the futility of mortal strivings, makes sense in an unchanging world. Is the muezzin's call in the Muslim world so different from church bells or the reassuring chatter of bat and ball on an English village green? My flip-flops are wearing out and I find a shop to repair them: the same techniques of leatherworking extend from here to Jerusalem. Illiana and I climb to the rocks above the kale in the sunset. At Gülizar we argue over a bad kebab: Illiana is annoyed that I would send it back. If the aim of life's quest is hesychia in the soul and chantilleuse in the heart, the briefest glimpses are all we seem to get.

SATURDAY 9 AUGUST | URFA

From the Gölbaşı Park beside the carp pool of Abraham, the Ottoman interpretation of a sacred enclosure: this is the puzzle of the subjective experience of the passing of time. Jerry Valberg's concept of 'horizonal' experience resembles the image of consciousness as a pool reflecting the sky. But the pulse of the mind's internal rhythm does not match the external time in which it beats. In calm waters the internal pulse can be controlled so that extra time, even the most irksome delay, represents an opportunity to introspect, to recollect and advance one's understanding of the deeper meaning of things. In this state the open expanse of empty time is entirely benign: time never hangs. But this state of internal calm is only an ideal: the waters are never flat. Ripples on the surface respond to the breeze of external irritation and may harmlessly drain away. But if there is inner anxiety, its energy magnifies the ripples into waves of agitation.

Negative thoughts disturb the water's surface: trivial

problems are not problems at all while the difficult ones seem to be intractable. Or could it be the associativity of the mind that makes it so difficult to still the waves and maintain a permanent state of internal tranquillity, impervious to external sources of disturbance? Where is total silence except in the empty reddish desertscape of Jethro's Hill on Sinai? *For the ultimate source of all the evil in the world is mental disturbance.* The realisation of peace between all groups and the optimal state of political economy cannot be achieved without the internal revolution that eliminates all disturbance from the soul. Does the solution not lie in hesychasm or Sufism or or any form of meditation that calms the waves across the internal pool of the horizon until their negative energy subsides?

Sad to leave this inspiring place, we take the evening bus to Mardin. The flat expanse of nothing with the red sun setting behind us reminds me of the journey from Tripoli to Benghazi. We take a room at the Başak Otel and eat dinner at the only open locanda looking over the plains of Upper Mesopotamia.

SUNDAY 10 AUGUST | DEIR AL-ZA'FARAAN

Having slept badly, we are revived with cardamom coffee opposite Mardin's stone carved nineteenth-century post office and walk down the hill admiring the old houses. From the edge of the town it is an hour's walk across the rocky Tur Abdin plateau to the monastery of Mar Hananyo (St Ananias). Known as Deir al-Za'faraan, the Saffron monastery, this magnificent fortress was the seat of the Syrian Orthodox Patriarchate from 1160 until 1924 when it relocated to Damascus. The indigenous people of these well-watered green hills descend from the Arameans and lived in an unbroken line until the twentieth century.

The Tur Abdin or 'Mountain of the Servants of God', which spreads across the long ridge of Mount Izla, became a haven of refuge to the non-Chalcedonian Syrian Orthodox Church in the fifth and sixth centuries. The miaphysite Syriac or 'Jacobite' Church emerged as a distinct entity under the leadership of Jacob Baradaeus in the 550s following repression by the Emperor Justinian. For the next 200 years the region prospered as a Syriac Athos, with many monasteries and thousands of monks. After the Islamic conquest and the imposition of the usual taxes, surplus funds for construction dried up, and from the 770s Syriac architecture declined. In addition to the major monasteries of Mar Gabriel and Mar Hananyo, several other churches remain intact across the Tur Abdin, most famously the seventh-century Yoldath Aloho (Church of the Virgin) in the village of Hah and the unusual transverse-naved Mar Yakoub at Salah (Baristepe). Despite the loss of life, land and livelihoods, Tur Abdin remains the centre of the Syrian Orthodox tradition.

The monastery of Mar Gabriel is the seat of the Archbishop of the Syriac diocese of Tur Abdin and the focus for the Syriac community in Türkiye. But Mar Hananyo is known for its architecture and its outstanding position under a rocky outcrop facing south across the open expanse of al-Jazeera. We enter the courtyard through a fine carved portal and admire its arcades. Below the first floor terraces are low relief friezes of deer and birds. The monastery contains a mausoleum chapel whose ribbed dome is modelled on the Artuqid Sultan İsa Medresesi in Mardin, showing the peculiar interchange that characterises this region. Deir al-Za'faraan welcomes visitors and we are taken on a tour by a young Australian Syriac called Gabriel.

In the foundations of the monastery there is a pagan temple that captures the rays of the rising sun on certain days of the year, and a nearby chamber for animal sacrifice. The temple was dedicated to the Assyrian sun god Shamash around 2000 BC and later became Zoroastrian. The complex was re-established as the Syrian Orthodox monastery in the year 493. The principal church, dedicated to the eighth-century Bishop Hananyo, is broadly square with high apses on three sides. Behind the altar are inscribed the names of the Syrian Orthodox Patriarchs going back to St Peter. I am reminded of Trinacria, of how the ancients selected temple sites for their position and how these were subsequently Christianised. Gabriel shows us the deep well in the courtyard. But as he releases the mechanism, the spokes hit my wrist causing a painful bruise. In sympathy the abbot (the Syriac Metropolitan of Mardin) invites us for lunch in the refectory.

The abbot explains that Armenians have captured international attention because of their sizable diaspora communities in America. But the Syriac and Assyrian Christians were also victims of the genocide. Kemal is in some ways seen as a protector by the Syriacs for having secularised the Turkish Republic. But Kurdish raids continued after the 1923 Treaty of Lausanne. In 1984, the Turkish Army fought battles in the region against the PKK, and the majority of the 50,000-strong residual Syriac population was forced to flee to the city of Qamishli just over the Syrian border. Community leaders promote good relations with the Kurds, while the children of the villages learn Syriac and the traditional sacred chanting but as recently as 1992 the Syriac community in Tur Abdin suffered attacks, with little protection from the state. The monastery receives many visitors and has good relations with the authorities. Following the purges of the twentieth century and recent emigration, however, the Anatolian Syriac community has dwindled to tens of thousands.

The abbot suggests that we should look for the ruins of the Church of Mar Shimun at Qudshanis (Koçanes) near Hakkâri. In the mid-sixteenth century the Chaldean branch of the Assyrian Church entered into communion with Rome while the Nestorian Assyrian Patriarchate migrated from Amida to remote Hakkâri in 1662. From their seat at Koçanes the quasi-hereditary Patriarchate represented the Assyrian millet to the Porte and to the local Ottoman beys at Başkale. The church and residence at Koçanes were destroyed in 1915 as part of the broader Ittihadist campaign. It is unknown how many Assyrians and Chaldeans were killed by Ottoman troops and Kurdish irregulars during the First World War, but contemporary reports estimated the number at 250,000. More than 25,000 Assyrians escaped into Iran. Some of them later returned to Hakkâri but were expelled by the Turkish Nationalist government in 1924. Unlike Koçanes, the fourth-century Syriac Orthodox monastery of St Matthew near Mosul has survived intact despite the wars.

Illiana takes a siesta on the terrace while I explore the monastery, admiring the fine stonework and the views from the terrace above the central courtyard. In the shade of the entrance portal, I chat to some Turkish tourists from Ankara. They have come from Mar Gabriel and talk about the ruined Temple of Heracles at the eastern edge of Tur Abdin that was destroyed by monks in the fourth century and is mentioned in one of the orations of Libanius. Vespers follow in the monastery church, beautifully sung in Aramaic, and the abbot dramatically raises his arms to extend his guidance and love to his flock.

We walk back to Mardin in the evening, carrying something of the abbot's spirit and return to the same locanda. Christian Anatolia was culturally European, the stranded outpost of the pre-Islamic and pre-Turkish civilisation. Ibn Khaldun had a notion that settled urban societies were cleansed of corruption by nomadic incursions who brought 'purity' with them from the desert or steppe. Or perhaps the distinction gains expression in the creative destruction of nomadic risk takers who disrupt the habits of settled conservatives. Western societies have had periods of corruption, but internal 'awakening' or conscience led to the purification. Accumulation is the essence of civilisation while plunder and pillage are the opposite. Over the centuries marauding nomads achieved more destruction than purification, the Mongol sack of Baghdad being the *reductio* of the Khaldunian thesis. The settler Armenians had lived side by side with the nomadic Kurds and Tartars for centuries yet they ended up being annihilated. The situation continues today as demonstrated by the ongoing problems the settler Syriacs continue to face from the pastoral Kurds.

Diyarbakir

MONDAY 11 AUGUST | NISIBIS

After another hot night in the Başak Otel, we are once again restored by cardamom coffee at the Yusuf Ustanın Yeri opposite the post office, with melon, ayran and egg on toast. Mardin is distinguished by its fourteenth-century Turkoman Artuqid architecture that bridges the periods between the original Seljuk and later Ottoman styles. We walk up to the Sultan İsa Medresesi on the hillside below the kale that looks over the plain. Built in 1385, this complex has carved portals and fluted domes reminiscent of the Mamluk style.

The bus to Nusaybin (Nisibis) on the Syrian frontier carries us along the dusty plain past the ruins of Byzantine Daras and some destroyed Kurdish villages, marked out by barbed wire flapping in the breeze. We explore the old railway station which has German telephone equipment and maps from the 1910s. The section of the Berlin–Baghdad railway between Nusaybin and Kirkuk was completed in 1940. But owing to the Kurdish conflict and Iraqi politics, the line remained in active service for only a few decades. What better reminder of how the arbitrary modern borders have cut the natural flow of goods and people across a region that was an integrated geographical region for millennia until the collapse of the Ottoman Empire? Nisibis was a significant urban centre on the Seleucid road network which developed from the earlier Babylonian and Persian trade routes. Maps of the ancient roads show their density across this zone between Antioch and Assyria before the vestigial Seleucid territories were absorbed into the Roman Empire.

The Assyrian Church of the East traces its apostolic foundation to St Thomas. In 325 the Syriac poet-theologian St Ephrem founded the Nisibis School that taught philosophy, theology, law and astronomy—a veritable quadrivium that predates Boethius. Syriac was the literary language descending from Aramaic that became the medium of intellectual life across the Eastern Roman and Persian Empires. At the Council of Ephesus in 431, the Assyrian Church followed the doctrines of Nestorius, the heterodox Patriarch of Constantinople, and came to be called Nestorian. In 489 the renowned theological school, called the 'Athens of Syria' by Gibbon, was closed by the militantly Chalcedonian Byzantine emperor and many Nestorians migrated into Persian territory. The Church of the East was the community of Christians who lay beyond the frontiers of Byzantium; until the Arab conquest, Assyrians administered the Sasanian court at Ctesiphon. Nestorians from Nisibis and Edessa later took ancient Greek manuscripts to Abbasid Baghdad and initiated the translation movement that led to the flowering of science and mathematics in the Islamic golden age.

Little remains of ancient Nisibis beyond the Syrian Orthodox church of Mar Yakoub, constructed around 360. Given how little survives in general, not to mention the travails of the Syriac Christians over seventeen centuries, the church is the well-preserved rare trace of this lost world. The stone apse and large blocks give the interior a sense of the unbroken connection to the deep past, and the quality of the carving in the lintels with Syriac inscriptions over the portals testify to the refined craftsmanship of the period. Oppressed by the intense heat as we wander through the modern town, we are invited by a young man called Zeki to take ayran in his airconditioned and immaculately clean café. Zeki explains that Nusaybin does not receive many tourists and so the few that pass through are all the more special, even if they only visit the church and drink çay.

Proceeding across the arid landscape to Midyat, the dolmuş passes through beautiful valleys lined with poplars, sacred to the Arewortik, the Armenian Zoroastrians. The man next to us on the bus tells us proudly about his work in Midyat prison where he extracts information from Kurdish political prisoners. As we enter Midyat, he points out the prison on the edge of the town—known for its use of torture and the shocking condition of its inmates—and offers to give us a tour of Midyat. Strangely, the man seems intent on adopting us as his charges, whether to monitor our movements or for pecuniary reasons we cannot tell. Hungry on our arrival, we take ayran and soup in the surprisingly good restaurant near the otogar, while the prison warder loiters outside. To get him off our trail, we make vague promises about meeting the next day, before taking what turns out to be a comfortable room in the only available hotel, Otel Demir.

From the modern district of Estel it is a short taxi journey to old Midyat, where we explore the multiple levels of the town and enjoy the colourful carpets left hanging to air in the late afternoon sun. The expulsion of the Syriac community broke the ancient fabric of the town, and many elegant stones houses with carved portals were taken over by Kurds who moved in with goats and large families. At the Church of Mor Barsawmo we meet a returning Syriac businessman from Sweden, who introduces himself as Debasso, and we speak about the history of Tur Abdin. Debasso explains that the Syriacs descend from Hurrians and Arameans who had lived continuously in this region since the Bronze Age. After the killings and expulsions of the 1915 to 1924 period, a significant Syriac population remained until the 1980s when the intensification of conflict with the PKK led to further emigration. Now wealthy Syriac communities across Europe are finding ways to return to their ancestral lands, investing in Tur Abdin, building houses and buying land.

The problem is the animosity of the Kurds who live in the villages, and Debasso speaks bitterly about the ongoing disputes with the 'cucumbers' as he calls them. The monasteries depend on the cultivation of local land holdings. But the Kurds are challenging their title, filing lawsuits with the help of the Turkish authorities and claiming infringement on their pastures. 'The Kurds want to take land that has been demised by the monastery of Mar Gabriel and say they have Allah on their side. The Syriacs are productive,' he tells us, 'and always knew how to build and make the land fertile. But these illiterate Kurds—all they know how to do is herd flocks and sprout like cucumbers. That is why our people were murdered and deported.'

The same Khaldunian theme runs through the millennia: the pastoralists remain free but never advance and then plunder what the civilised have created. The solution is to empower them to change their habits and become self-sustaining: 'teach a man to fish'. But then I wonder if, long after our hyper-technologicised global economy has self-destructed, the Kurds will survive in their remote mountain pastures. If the mountain is the source of wisdom, we must still come down and apply it to the world. Just as one cannot have peace between two communities if they cannot agree on the legitimate grievances that each side has against the other, so one cannot move towards a unified political economy if there is not a common understanding of what would represent the optimal set of arrangements. Nothing can change in behaviour unless the mind changes. We exchange details with Debasso and promise to keep in contact. But we are cheated by the cabby who drives us back to the hotel and there is nowhere open in Estel to eat dinner.

Tuesday 12 August | Midyat

Illiana and I are woken by the patron knocking insistently at the door to tell us that our 'guide' has arrived. We ask him to explain to the guide that we are on our honeymoon, and we are sure he will understand why we intend to pass the day in our hotel room. Thankfully this ruse works and we avoid having to meet our friendly jailer again. Over lunch at the Saffron monastery we had been told about a village whose Syriac population took refuge in a fortress church during the First World War, and which is still populated by a dozen Syriac families. Illiana agrees to walk there, and we set off across the countryside from Old Midyat to Ayn Wardo. Alas we take the wrong road, walking instead towards Idib to the south-east. A passing shepherd gives us melons and we leave the road, heading into the scrub, looking for the correct road to the north-east. After an hour or so we are rescued by two more shepherds who lead us to a well. My feet are full of thorns but the water is elixir and they guide us to the narrow asphalt road that leads to Ayn Wardo.

Even so the heat is overwhelming and we carry no water. Illiana objects to the whiteness of my linen shirt and Siwi sirwal trousers, which to her parched eyes seem overwhelming in the bright light. So I am instructed to walk a few hundred metres behind her and regard her sinewy figure in the distance advancing across the landscape. After another ninety minutes we reach the village, hot and thirsty. We are rescued for a second time by a Syriac family who invite us into their house. They have all modern conveniences in their kitchen and explain over tea how, despite the hostile state, they maintain their presence in Ayn Wardo. One is left with a sense of futility that in such a remote place, these hostilities persist, as well as admiration for the Syriac determination to maintain their association to these ancient places. We wander through the desolate remains of the village and the fortress church that sheltered Syriacs in 1915.

The family take us back to Midyat in their car and we enjoy the silence of the plateau as the driver stops to pick melons from his field. On reaching the edge of Midyat, we find a locanda on the main road opposite the post office, with pictures of Proust's house and Swiss mountains on the wall. We take a table on the street in the shade of some jacaranda trees, and enjoy excellent lamb and aubergine stew. About halfway through the meal a group of extremely agitated Turkish soldiers jump out of their military vehicles pointing their guns at everybody as they visit the post office. Apparently a few months previously some soldiers had been killed in a hit-and-run attack by Kurdish militants sitting outside this same place. After leaving the post office some of the soldiers come into the restaurant and stand around while others order çay.

Without any warning one of the soldiers abruptly takes the third chair at our table and addresses us in English. The man ignores Illiana and without so much as a 'would you mind awfully' subjects me to a rapid-fire interrogation about our movements, leaning forward closely towards me as he speaks.

The questions come so quickly that I hardly complete my answer before another one is interjected. After about ten uncomfortable minutes the man stands up and just as abruptly leaves with the other soldiers. Flustered by the episode, we leave the locanda and walk again around Old Midyat. We climb to the roof of the town 'museum' which has fine views over the old stone mansions in the evening breeze.

Wednesday 13 August | Hasankeyf

From Midyat we continue to Hasankeyf whose low-lying districts would subsequently be flooded by the Ilısu Dam on the Tigris. From the bridge we climb the steep hill above the village and scale the walls of the fortress palace. This stronghold illustrates the pattern of Asiatic nomadic dynasties that invaded Anatolia, bringing with them successive ideas into the architectural style. After the Mongol Ilkhanids drove out the Kurdish Ayyubids and Turkic Danishmenids they left behind the Turkoman Artuqids in Mardin and Hasankeyf, who themselves fell suzerain to the Timurids. We look over the Tigris where the Zeynel Bey Türbesi stands out with ribbed onion dome and inlaid turquoise bricks. Built in 1473 the tomb tower traces its elements to the polyhedral brick Alaviyan Gumbad in Hamadan (1300). The Timurids added turquoise glazed bricks to the Goharshad Mosque in Mashhad (1420) and spread this distinctive style across their domains. The contrast between the brick texture and glazed turquoise is timeless, but I wonder how this play of pattern and colour relates to the authoritarian mind that ordered it?

We take the dolmuş to Diyarbakir along the sunlit Tigris valley, past the oil donkeys of Batman and the distant shadow of Mount Judi, associated with Noah's Ark in Syriac tradition. The dolmuş passes through the ramshackle outlying districts of Diyarbakir, the largest city of the south-east, before reaching the black basalt walls of Roman Amida that ring the city centre. Disoriented to be in such a hot crowded place we sip çay under the massive Harput gate before taking a room at the Otel Gap on İnönü Street. The pension has an internal courtyard with green-painted walls and sparrow-sized parakeets chirping away. We rest in the late afternoon heat and explore the ancient streets which are lively in the evening like a Spanish town. A brightly lit locanda near to the pension has a cauldron in the window on which there is a plank with five lamb's skulls neatly arranged along it. We are told that they are goats, not sheep, and that the soup is a delicious Kurdish staple. So we eat beans with the goat's-head soup before browsing a music shop selling compact disks of local popular artists. The music is fun, but the Kurdish stew is a mistake and I retreat to the hotel courtyard with severe diarrhoea that intermittently attacks me for the next several days.

THURSDAY 14 AUGUST | DIYARBAKIR

All morning I am prostrate, with hardly the energy to read a single page, while the kind patron offers me glasses of ayran and overpowering cigarettes that I decline. Illiana returns and we explore the fifteenth-century Nebî Camii which has pretty Iznik tiles. We climb up the steps by the Harput gate and walk around the high city walls built by Byzantines and Artuqids over Roman foundations. The citadel contains an Artuqid mosque from the 1160s. But of the sixth-century Assyrian church, recorded by nineteenth-century travellers to be of handsome construction with fine brick domes, nothing remains. The eastern section of the walls perches dramatically above the Tigris and shows the significance of ancient Amida, located where the plains of al-Jazeera meet the Anatolian plateau. The evening sunlight over the Hevsel kitchen gardens picks out giant watermelons growing beside the Tigris as well as the sprawling *gecekondu* slums below the walls.

From the Mardin gate we proceed to the Deliller Hanı, renovated as the Hotel Büyük Kervansaray, for a pricey supper of which I can eat little. Now we are back in the world of Ottoman civilisation, of khans and mosques and tekkes, of hammams and mansions. Following the destruction of the Mongol and Timurid invasions, Diyarbakir prospered under Turkoman amirs and later the Ottomans who constructed many fine buildings. Ottoman khans were built around courtyards with two or three storeys, the lower chambers used as stables and the upper ones as guest rooms. Such khans were self-sufficient institutions, with a *darüşşifa* (hospital) and *imaret* (public kitchen). The Deliller Hanı was built around 1530 with striped stone arcades that resemble the motifs of Genoa and Damascus and has trees and a running fountain.

Friday 15 August | Diyarbakır

We take çay and yoghurt in the Hasan Paşa Hanı, the haunt of old men in leather jackets, and pass the morning in the khan examining carpets with a rug seller called Sait Sanik. The guidebook refers to the house of the Turkish Nationalist intellectual Ziya Gökalp but we cannot find it in the narrow streets. Instead we discover the Mesopotamian Cultural Centre in a stone building set around a spacious courtyard where classical guitarists practise and perform. Despite the name it is in fact a Kurdish community centre. Some boys offer us çay and we are joined by a group of young students who ask us about life in Europe. They want to talk about the situation of Kurds in Türkiye now that the PKK leader Abdullah Öcalan has been taken prisoner and the active insurgency has become dormant. Soon they begin raising Kurdish grievances. 'It is always the same pattern: we protest and they respond aggressively; we want autonomy to manage our own affairs and freedom to speak our own language but they provoke our people and retaliate with force.'

The origin of the Kurds has been difficult to trace because, while speaking an Indo-European language, they were never literate and being pastoral, lacked any civic culture. A variety of groups from the Zagros may have been their antecedents. Nomadic 'Guti' from the Upper Diyala near Halabja extinguished Sargon's Akkadian Empire, while Seleucid sources mention 'Cyrti' as pastoral tribes in the northern Zagros. Some have speculated that Kurds descend from the Medes. But Media was absorbed into the Achaemenid Empire and their continuity with mediaeval Kurds is unclear.

In the seventh century Kurdish chieftains submitted to the Arabs and converted to Islam. They provided auxiliary troops to the Seljuks in their conquest of the Armenian Highland.

Kurds who rendered service to Turkish rulers were granted land and became local amirs. Imad ad-Din Zengi and Nur ad-Din recruited mercenary Kurdish warriors to fight the Crusaders: one of them, Asad al-Din Shirkah, took control of Egypt in the 1160s and was succeeded by his nephew Yusuf ibn Ayyub (Salah ad-Din). Following the Mongol invasions, Kurds migrated north from the Zagros into Hakkâri and the Upper Tigris basin. Kurdish amirs mixed with the Turkoman Koyunlu dynasties that were overthrown by the Safavid Shah Ismail in 1507 and then came under Ottoman suzerainty.

The clan-based pastoral Kurds continued to practise brigandage and exploit the Armenian peasantry until the twentieth century. Allied with the Porte in its repression of the Christians, core constituents of the Hamidiye Regiments and an instrument of the paramilitary Special Organisation in 1915, the Kurds might have expected to be favoured by the Kemalist regime but the Nationalists saw a distinct Kurdish identity as a threat to their interests and above all to the borders of the Turkish Republic. In 1925 Atatürk's assimilationist 'Turkification' policies provoked a Kurdish uprising in Diyarbakir led by Sheikh Said. This was suppressed and in 1927 a Kurdish Republic of Ararat was proclaimed that led to a four-year conflict. Since then repression has led to intermittent Kurdish revolts, culminating in the ongoing PKK insurgency.

One of the students, called Hadice, wants to show us more of Diyarbakir whose streets are crowded with Kurdish children. Near the fifth-century Syrian Orthodox church of St Mary we encounter Jeremiah Mattix, an American evangelical missionary who is proud to introduce us to his young flock of recent converts. The Turkish state does not allow them to proselytise to Muslims, so these missionaries seek instead to convert the few remaining Syriacs to Protestantism. The nineteenth-century American missions drew international attention to the situation of the Ottoman Armenians, and Euphrates College, their mission school at Harput (Elazığ), was attacked by Hamidiye Regiments in 1895. Yet despite being well-intentioned, their presence has been a mixed blessing to the vulnerable minority communities. For the history of

Diyarbakir from 1894 to 1924 reflects the overall situation: Christian property was expropriated and many Armenian monuments suffered further destruction, although the Church of St Giragos in Diyarbakir would later be restored.

Jeremiah talks about Ignazio Maloyan, Armenian Catholic Bishop of Mardin, who was arrested on 3 June 1915 along with his thousand-strong flock. Maloyan was tortured, tried on trumped-up charges and ordered by the judge to convert to Islam. One week later Ottoman soldiers slaughtered the Christian community in front of him and again insisted that he convert to Islam, finally shooting him when he refused. Bishop Maloyan was beatified by Pope John Paul II in 2001. Yet speaking with Jeremiah, I conclude that proselytisation is inappropriate here in the former heartlands of Christendom, and that American missions undermine these ancient churches with their particular interpretation of the Christian religion.

We retreat from the heat to the spacious basalt stoned Ulu Camii that is probably the oldest mosque in Türkiye, founded by the Arabs who captured Amida in 638 and renamed the city Diyarbakir. The building was reconstructed in the 1090s and again in the 1160s. It preserves the original design that resembles the Umayyad Mosque in Damascus with a three-aisled prayer hall along the principal axis. We sit on the carpets observing some young medrese students memorising the Qur'an. In Western societies children are initiated into the contemporary hyper-technologicised culture, but should they not be memorising Shakespeare and Beethoven too?

SATURDAY 16 AUGUST | DIYARBAKIR
Stiff from sleeping for so long, I can do nothing after breakfast at the Hasan Paşa Hanı except return to bed. Somewhat recovered by lunchtime, my Ferrari flip-flops have become loose again after the repairs in Urfa. I find a cobbler at the corner of Nebî Camii who this time fixes them with a machine, twine and glue. The Behram Paşa Camii is closed and I am too weak to wander around. But I return to the Mesopotamian Cultural Centre to drink ayran with Hadice and we talk about Islam and Kurdish politics.

'Why do you wear a headscarf when you have such beautiful hair?' I ask her. 'My brother's wife Yasemin wears a headscarf, and my mother too,' she answers; 'it is because we are Muslim. It is according to our religion that we should do, because a woman's privacy is like jewellery. We think that's not true of everyone to see it: some things should happen only between those who will get married. Can you understand me? You know, it is a difficult thing because everyone wants to dress comfortably, especially in the summer. But Allah wants this from us. Allah created us and knows everything about us. We Muslims believe in this way.

'Unfortunately, Türkiye is not a very free country. Girls cannot go to school with the headscarf! Some people think the threat to secularism is head-covering. The government wants to remove the ban but it does not allow it in YÖK (the Council of Higher Education). This is a matter of conscience. There are people in Türkiye who are not head-covered, because in the Qur'an there is "no compulsion in religion". People should respect each other. But some people, unfortunately, do not. We should be tolerant against each other, not so? Maybe you think it is absurd. But this is the situation in Türkiye. It bothers me. It is a matter of conscience, yes, but it is also a matter of personality. And if not wear the headscarf, then why not drink alcohol? There are many Muslims who drink alcohol—to enjoy the taste of wine and to relax.'

'... and to stimulate their creativity!' I add. 'Turkish Cypriots drink Commandaria. In Morocco there is a thriving wine and beer industry.' 'I do not intend to drink,' Hadice replies. 'This is a matter of preference. I prefer not. Some Muslims drink. Maybe I also handle other sins. After all, one cannot judge anyone. But to drink, we are forbidden in our religion. Damage is greater than the benefits. I want to marry a Muslim, yes, because it is my religion and to me that is required.'

'Do you think Beethoven could have written the late string quartets and piano sonatas, the zenith of all music, if he hadn't been inebriated?' I ask. But Hadice has never heard this music. This young woman has a natural sweetness and openness, but the horizons of her world are limited by her experience of being raised a Kurdish Muslim in eastern Türkiye.

Sunday 17 August | Tatvan

Diyarbakir is oddly deserted on the Sunday morning. Our patron arranges a taxi to the otogar, and I continue reading Sartre's *Nausea*, enjoying its studied flavour of time suspended in words. The bus to Tatvan passes through Silvan, the most likely location of Tigranakert, the long-vanished capital city of the first-century BC Armenian potentate Tigran the Great. We stop to eat at Bitlis and examine the familiar set of Ottoman public buildings: Şerefiye Camii, İhlasiye Medresesi, hospital and imaret. Above the town is a fortress whose position commanded the caravan route to Iran. For a thousand years in Anatolia, there were parallel traditions of Muslim and Christian architecture that existed side by side until the First World War. But power resided with Turkic and Kurdish amirs who dominated the trade routes and extracted rents from local communities of farmers, artisans and merchants—standing conditions for the events of 1915.

The road from Bitlis to Tatvan ascends between rocky crags and woodland giving a sense of verdure and three dimensionality. At the Tatvan otogar, situated near to the railhead for the ferries across Lake Van, there is a military presence with soldiers all around. It is a short walk to the town where we explore the accommodation options, choosing the Artilar Otel which has quasi-Alpine wooden style decor. Until the nineteenth century Tatvan was a cluster of buildings around a jetty by the lake. But with the new roads and railway, the settlement took its present form along the wide main street, and Tatvan has a distinctive upland quality with pines and corrugated-iron roofs that could be colonial-pioneer in far-flung frontier outposts. Once again I experience the peculiar combination of European familiarity—reminiscent of the upper shores of Como or Garda—alongside the ghostly sense of lost worlds from the Urartians to the Armenians.

Along the lakeshore we find a makeshift wooden stand and drink çay on the pebble beach with a group of young Kurdish men. One of them, called Aukat, speaks some English, and Illiana engages the others in fragments of broken Kurmanji that she has learned from her friend Uli. After talking about football and their plans to move to Istanbul, I ask about the Armenians and the history of this region. But they say that Ermenistan is in Russia and there have never been Armenians here. 'Who then built the monasteries of Vaspurakan?' I ask, and Illiana is annoyed that I should challenge them. After the çay we walk along the lakeside path, and Illiana rebukes me for engaging so directly with the local people instead of smiling and acquiescing in what they say. At the hotel, the patron arranges a tour to the dormant volcano Nemrut Dağı. We find the Koşem restaurant, which is hot in the static air but serves good kebabs, and stumble back to the hotel in the dark, clambering over the high curbs, designed to protect the street from floodwaters.

Ararat

MONDAY 18 AUGUST | NEMRUT DAĞI

The patron's driver takes us to the mountain whose peak is 2,900 metres above sea level. According to local legend the name Nemrut derives from a king who tried to usurp the power of God. The road leads over a declivity in the volcano's edge and into the crater, past cliffs that rise in parts almost one thousand metres to the rim. We descend to the crescent-shaped freshwater lake on the crater's floor, where Illiana is frightened by some fierce dogs who follow the taxi. We walk down and swim naked in the warm water, with fish that radiate intense colours. Some Turkish tourists disturb our solitude, and we play rummy stones with them by the lake before sleeping under the trees by the hot springs in perfect silence for two hours.

To gain the best views, we climb up to the rim of the crater: it is hard work but worth every step. From the top we can see across the wide expanse of the Lake Van basin: visible in the foreground are the outlines of the Urartian fortress that guarded the western edge of the lake, and the remains of the mediaeval village. We walk back to Tatvan past a creep of coupling tortoises in the corn fields and more ferocious dogs. I tell Illiana, 'You see, this is the elemental rawness of Armenia that Osip talks about: these tortoises have no qualms but to live!' But Illiana has become distant from me and does not want to dance in the wild places.

TUESDAY 19 AUGUST | LAKE VAN

After breakfast in the tea shop on the main street of Tatvan, we walk to the ferry terminal and wait by the rails for two hours in the sunshine. I continue to read *Nausea* as the trains load on and off the boat. An inland sea surrounded by mountains,

Lake Van has a Patagonian quality, mysterious and primaeval. The soda lake is plugged by an eruption from Nemrut Dağı and the water is so alkaline that local people use it to clean their clothes. The feribot, *The Orhan*, departs one hour late, but it could have been ten and we would not have minded. The journey across Lake Van is lovely, with views over the other dormant volcanoes Süphan and Artos and the promontories on the southern shore. We are the only tourists on a fairly empty four-hour passage and so the ship's captain Abdullah invites us into the command room. We smoke the last fragments of my Sicilian Amphora tobacco in his pipe and he tells us about his wife and six 'arkadeshes' scattered around the region.

At Van port the captain accidentally crashes the ferry into the harbour wall but it seems no harm is done. We sit on the mole drinking cherry juice under the shadow of Van Castle high above us on its rock and watch the sun sink over the lake. From 840 to 590 BC the Urartians ruled the Lake Van basin from their capital Tushpa, centred on this dramatic fortress. In the mediaeval period the region around Van became the Armenian Kingdom of Vaspurakan. Nothing remains of the original town that lay north of the rock and was relocated to the south by the Ottomans in the sixteenth century. As darkness falls we catch a bus to the featureless breezeblock town of modern Van up the hill from the lake and a room at the Otel İpek.

WEDNESDAY 20 AUGUST | VAN

We rise early to visit the famous Armenian church of Aghtamar. The driver stops first at 'Yedi Kilise', the ruined monastery of Varagavank on the road to Hakkâri. The last Vaspurakan King Senekerim Hovhannes founded the monastery of Varagavank in 1005 to house a relic of the True Cross. But the site is closed and there is little to see of this once-magnificent complex except for part of the ruined façade. We continue to Gevaş (Vostan in Armenian), formerly the principal settlement of mediaeval Vaspurakan. Nothing survives apart from a Turkoman tomb tower built in 1358 and surrounded by poplars. From the lakeshore jetty we take the short passage across to Aghtamar Island.

Vaspurakan was one of the provinces of Greater Armenia that became a kingdom during the mediaeval period. The territory was ruled by the Artsruni dynasty from 800 until it passed under Byzantine control in 1021 and fell to the Seljuks in the 1060s. The Mongol invasion of the 1240s led to the relatively benign Ilkhanid overlordship from Tabriz that disintegrated after 1291. Over the following centuries the Armenians toiled under Kurdish amirs, Timurids and Turkoman Kara Koyunlu, who subjected them to exorbitant taxes, land sequestration and religious persecution. Despite the oppression, the Armenian monasteries continued to flourish, producing manuscripts, preserving stone carving and developing their skills in miniature painting, metalwork, textiles and music. After the region was incorporated into the Ottoman Empire in the mid-1500s, they received dhimmi protection that constrained the arbitrary abuses of local beys. Aghtamar has become emblematic of the lost legacy of western Armenia but all over Vaspurakan stand the ruins of beautifully situated Armenian monasteries constructed between the fifth and eighteenth centuries and in active use until the First World War.

In 1914 the Armenian Patriarchate of Constantinople documented more than 200 monasteries and 1,600 churches across the Ottoman Empire. After 1923 the Turkish government confiscated Armenian property under the 'Law of Abandoned Properties', keeping them as public buildings, selling them at auction or giving them to refugees from Rumelia. By 1973 almost all Armenian historical monuments not kept or got rid of had vanished or were in ruins, while most religious buildings had been dynamited or dismantled. In *Eastern Turkey: An Architectural and Archaeological Survey* T.A. Sinclair compiled detailed histories, ground plans and descriptions of these monuments. Likewise, Jean-Michel Thierry's *Monuments arméniens du Vaspurakan* contains exhaustive documentation of the cultural heritage of western Armenia. The Turkish authorities continued to allow the pillaging of Armenian monuments until the 1980s, when they realised that historical sites such as Aghtamar and Ani could be the source of tourism revenues. Since the 1990s the major surviving structures have been monitored by the World Monuments Fund.

The most important Armenian Apostolic monasteries in western Armenia were the fourth-century Surb Karapet (John the Baptist) and eleventh-century Surb Arakelots (Holy Apostles), both located in the Mush district. But the architectural focus of the region was Lake Van, and the monasteries formed a glittering necklace of pearls around the dazzling sapphire sea. Arterivank on Arter Island, Karmravank and Surb Thovmas near the Deveboynu peninsula have all fallen into irreparable ruin. Likewise Surb Hovhannes on Ktuts Island and Surb Kevork on Lim Island: the latter was in good condition in 1956 but has now been destroyed; Surb Kevork at Goms was preserved intact as at 1972 but was subsequently ransacked. South of Lake Van, Armenian churches in varying states of ruin include: Kchavavank, Aparank, Narekavank, Hogots, Baridzorivank and, most dramatically, St Bartholomew near Albayrak on the Great Zab, which was restored in the nineteenth century but whose roof and dome collapsed in 1966.

These monasteries should not be thought of as the haunt of gaunt men in cowls chanting rites in solitude but rather as vibrant cultural hubs that provided guidance, education and shelter to the Armenian communities of Vaspurakan. Quite apart from their political significance, they are exemplars of a lost indigenous culture. For the Armenians achieved a high level of craftsmanship and made a pivotal contribution to world architecture. They were obsessed with the precise function that each element served in the stability of the edifice, with the aesthetic effect of the ensemble and with finishing their work to perfection. The quality of architecture was higher than anything achieved in Western Europe before the 1200s as the Armenians developed stereotomy, the technique of using freestone with perfectly fitting joints. They translated all preceding forms of construction into stone, introducing rib-vaults and the conical dome above a clerestory drum. Together with the use of the circular ambulatory, exterior stone decoration and blind arcades, these elements created the distinctive verticality of Armenian ecclesiastical architecture.

The Cathedral of the Holy Cross (Surb Khach) on Aghtamar itself was designed by Bishop Manuel and built by King Gagik Artsruni between 915 and 921. Aghtamar was the residence of the Armenian Catholicos from 928 to 943, and originally had a palace complex in addition to the church and *zhamatun* (chapter house). The monastery was renowned for the production of manuscripts and remained in continuous use until 1917. The cathedral has a symmetric design of four-apsed recesses around a central square. Low-relief friezes encircle the exterior with vine branches around figures of the evangelists and sculptures of other biblical characters. In the south-east niche are figures of Sahak and Hamazasp, Artsruni princes killed by the Arabs in 786 for refusing to renounce their faith. On the west wall is a relief of King Gagik presenting a model of the cathedral to Christ, while the interior shows scenes from the life of Christ and of the apostles in paintings.

We climb the hill behind the church for its views over the lake. The beauty of the desolate landscape is overwhelming. The historian Richard Hovannisian wrote on a 2014 visit to the region: 'We see the ruins of what was, imagine what could have been and have a difficult time coming to terms with what is. You have to hold on to dreams for as long as you can. The reality is that ... we are in a vanishing Armenian landscape. Increasingly as years go by, less is to be seen as the cities expand, populations increase and memories fade.' There is a party of South Koreans who sing harmoniously in the church and continue with worship songs in the open motorboat back to Gevaş. I am struck by the strangeness of these Pentecostalist converts celebrating the faith of their lost co-religionists through pilgrimage to Aghtamar.

Back in Van we find our way to the museum. The most prominent items in the collection are pieces of Urartian jewellery, shields, belts and bowls. Looking at these skant remains, one realises how little we know about our ancient forbears. There are also skulls on display, apparently from 'disturbances' during the First World War, and a letter from a Turkish professor in the 1990s claiming that the skulls are of Turkish racial type, killed by Armenians. In twentieth-century politics, archaeology has been put to the service of belonging. Despite being invaders into a land with an indigenous population, Kemal's Nationalists promoted the theory of the Hittites as antecedents of the Turks. Meanwhile the Urartians were de-emphasised as forebears of the Armenians and are presented as merely the rival to Assyria. Yet there is no evidence for the Armenian conquest of any pre-existing culture; rather that external elements mixed with the Urartian population. The relation might be similar to that between Etruscans and modern Tuscany.

We hitch a lift to Old Van with a pharmacist who tells us that most people in Van have Armenian ancestry, whether mixed with Turkish, Kurdish or other roots. Old Van adjoins the lake south of the kale and was abandoned following a series of earthquakes between the 1920s and 1950s. From the road we climb up the path to the kale. The famous trilingual inscription of Xerxes is visible from below, and further along are cuneiform blocks recording the foundation of Tushpa by the first Urartian King Sarduri. From this vantage point one can see over the whole of Old Van that had over 80,000 inhabitants before 1915. It is a strange earthquake that reduces a city to green fields across which there are no traces of any buildings at all except for three mosques that rise out of the lush grass. For Old Van was dismantled after 1923, beginning a systematic purging of any Armenian presence in eastern Türkiye, from monasteries and graves to their distinctive stone carved *khachkar* memorial crosses.

Sitting on the edge of the kale looking down over the ruins of Old Van on one side and the shimmering lake on the other, I imagine the events of April 1915. I think of the Armenian Patriarchate in Jerusalem and the wall maps whose variously sized red circles indicate the numbers of Armenians deported and killed in 1915. 'Where does one hide a leaf?' asked Father Brown. In a forest. Where does one hide a murder? In a battle.

Where does one hide the annihilation of a people in their ancient homeland?

In the spring of 1915, Ottoman forces under Enver Pasha's uncle Halil Bey advanced into Russian controlled Iranian territory. On 15 April they were repulsed at the Battle of Dilman by Russian troops and Armenian volunteer units under General Nazarbekian, and retreated towards Van. On 19 April Armenian Dashnaks under Aram Manukian led an uprising in Van, taking control of the city but not of the citadel, whose Ottoman garrison fired down on them from these stones. The 30,000-strong Armenian residents of Van barricaded themselves in the garden city while the conflict raged about them. The Dashnaks could not have known of Talaat's system of encrypted telegrams or of the plan to eliminate the Christian population, but they must have known that Armenians were already being massacred by agents of the Ottoman state and took matters into their hands instead of being slaughtered as they had been in 1894.

The Armenian people recognise 24 April 1915 as the Genocide Remembrance Day on which the Ottoman administration detained 240 leading Armenian Ottoman citizens in Constantinople. But deportations from Dörtyol and İskenderun began in February 1915 and pogroms in Van under the provincial governor Cevdet Pasha were already being prosecuted in March. The Venezuelan mercenary Rafael de Nogales later reported in his memoirs that Ottoman officials had explained to him that they were carrying out orders received directly from Constantinople to exterminate all Armenian males of twelve years of age and over. On 2 May 1915 Enver Pasha ordered the removal of the entire Armenian population of the Lake Van region.

Meanwhile a Russian column advanced from Persia into the Başkale plain, forcing the Ottomans to evacuate Van Castle, which was then taken over by Dashnaks on 19 May. The Turks responded to the Russian advance by accelerating the massacres of Armenians in the districts of Mush and Bitlis in June and July of 1915. After a two-month siege by Turkish forces and Kurdish irregulars, the monastery of Surb Karapet was sacked and according to eyewitnesses, three thousand men, women, and children were killed in its courtyard. Ottoman forces recaptured Van and the surrounding districts on 31 July, causing an estimated 100,000 Armenians to retreat with the Russian army. In August 1915 Talaat Pasha communicated to Morgenthau that, 'we have already disposed of three quarters of the Armenians; there are none at all left in Bitlis, Van, and Erzeroum.' The Russians recaptured Van in November 1915 and held the province until March 1918. But the Armenian civilian population were never to return to their historic Vaspurakan.

Thursday 21 August | Doğubeyazit

It is the second hot night in the concrete box that passes for our hotel in Van. Illiana and I argue over whether to leave the window open and be eaten by mosquitoes or to close it and lie in a dank sweat. Morning comes and in a fit of mutual loathing we abruptly bid farewell to each other with the same intensity that Sartre describes in the denouement of *Nausea*. After seventeen tempestuous days and nights with Illiana I am suddenly alone. Still intermittently queasy from the goat's-head soup, I find the dolmuş station and wait for the minibus to fill up. The pause gives me time to reflect: despite being sick and an alien in a dangerous region, I feel free again, detached and happy to be on my own. Shortly the bus sets off. I rest my arm on the ledge of the open window, calmed by the breeze, and gaze in wonder at the mountains. The route proceeds along the east side of Lake Van into a deforested pale green landscape.

From the northern end of the lake, the dolmuş passes across the plain of Chaldiran where the Ottomans overcame their Safavid adversaries with superior materiel in 1514. Ismail Shah founded the Safavid dynasty in 1501, made Shi'ism the official religion of the state, and proselytised Shi'ism within Anatolia. Having deposed his father the previous year, Sultan Selim advanced east, massacring an estimated 40,000 Shi'a Alevis along the way, and comprehensively defeated Ismail's forces on this plain. Sultan Süleyman extended his father's conquests into Iraq and established the frontier with Safavid Iran in the 1555 Amasya Treaty. Minor adjustments followed a further war in the 1620s and the present border was agreed in 1639. Today these desolate upland pastures are dotted with pretty houses made of bright reflective corrugated iron. At intervals off the single lane tarred road, tracks disappear into the distance. Due west of Chaldiran lies Malazgirt (Manzikert), originally a Urartian fortress, later a walled city that changed hands between Arabs and Byzantines and was the location of the epochal battle of 1071.

From the plain of Chaldiran the road passes across marshy ground before ascending through basalt strewn grassland towards the shoulder of Mount Tendürek which rises up to 3,200 metres. The road ascends to the pass close to the Iranian frontier, and as the dolmuş rumbles along, suddenly, in the distance, Ararat rises up, ringed against the piercing blue sky by a crown of light white clouds, towering over the surrounding plains and peaks, massive and unmistakable. If we measure mountains not by their absolute altitude but by the vertical distance from the base where the land begins to rise up to their peak, then volcanic Ararat, rising more than 4,000 metres above the Arax, is among the highest one can experience. No wonder Ararat has always been sacred to the Armenians, their Masis at the heart of the Armenian Highland.

After meandering for another hour down to the foot of the mountain, the dolmuş arrives at the border town of Doğubeyazıt, popular with travellers on the overland route to India. Although Ararat is in a closed military zone and officially one needs a permit from Ankara, the local army officers take expeditions up the mountain for five thousand dollars. It is the best time of year to make the ascent but I have neither money nor boots, so after finding a room in the Hotel Sarunan and eating stew in one of the locandas along the town's main street, I take my own route to see Mount Ararat from the hills opposite.

Heading south-east from Doğubeyazıt I pass a military base with a brigade of tanks and walk up to İshak Paşa Sarayı. This ornate palace fortress carved in pink-hued stone with courtyards, domes and minarets, was built in the eighteenth century by Kurdish beys. The complex gives the impression of a romantic ruin perched on a rock above the remains of mediaeval Bayazit looking over Ararat. An English-speaking guide is giving a tour to a party of bikers from Hamburg. The guide explains that the office of Pasha of the Sanjak of Bayazit was inherited, much like central-European castellans, and one member of the family became Grand Vizier in 1723. His great-grandson Ishak Pasha completed the present palace by 1784. Officially the beys represented the Sublime Porte in this remote region, closer as it is to Isfahan than to Constantinople but in practice they were semi-autonomous tribesmen who became rich from piracy and extortion. After Russia captured Bayazit in 1828, the palace was abandoned and then damaged by an earthquake in 1840.

Retracing my steps to the junction, I climb up the valley below the rocky ridge on the south side of the ruined palace. After an hour or so I encounter a Kurdish shepherdess sitting cross legged on the grass with a lamb in her lap. Her son is standing nearby, dignified in a grey tailored suit jacket, and calling to some large and ferocious sheep dogs. The woman is killing the lamb in the halal fashion, gently cutting its throat while whispering in its ear so that it hardly makes a sound as the blood drains away over the grass. The man is interested in my wristwatch and I exchange it for the right to take photographs of them, but also in the hope they will protect me from the fierce dogs.

Leaving the dogs behind, and with Turkish soldiers patrolling their outposts in the distance, I continue to the end of the path and walk through the scrub, progressing up the valley until it broadens out. Regretting that I had abandoned my boots in Adana but trusting in my Palestinian Ferraris, I continue under the ridge towards the frontier. By this point the weather has turned and a storm is brewing. I trudge up the grassy valley, looking north over the volcano of Ararat, rising above its lava strewn plain. On one side the valley south of the mountain extends into the distance while on the other the col atop the valley marks the Iranian frontier. Like Alexander, I pine to continue to the edge of the known world and beyond. Alas, the road of freedom eventually dissolves into the quicksand of age and I know that I must return. At the point where the crest descends to the col, an overhang offers some shelter from the elements and I half-sit, half-crouch, in the hollow of the rock.

The storm becomes more severe and I am suddenly drenched. The sky turns a sombre maroon red and in the distance the peaks above the plain are brightly lit up by silent flashes of lightning. With the dogs and the soldiers and the tanks, and the spectacular mountains and the snow-capped volcano, and the electricity in the air and the heavy rain and the dark clouds in the red sky, I am suddenly overwhelmed by a feeling of the fragility and precariousness of human life. Gazing in a stupor at the bulk of Ararat and beginning to shiver, I realise that I have reached my destination and that, in spite of everything, the strongest and most intense of all human experiences is simply the primaeval desire to survive. Despite the defeats and disappointments of life, not to mention the tedium and toil, the greatest success is to continue *being*, to reach tomorrow, to listen to the elements, to experience for one more time the joy of birds singing, of the wind in the trees, of the smell of the earth after rain and the feeling of the sun on one's face.

After a while the storm passes and in the twilight I descend to the İshak Paşa Sarayı. As I walk down the road towards the town, I pass a picnic spot where a car stops and offers me a lift. Inside are squeezed a kindly Kurdish family of nine, who somehow make space for me in the front. I try to tell them about my experience of the storm over Ararat but they look at me blankly. To make conversation, I ask about the family and discover that the woman has had eighteen children in total. 'Why so many,' I ask? The man explains that it is the Kurdish way—God's will. I thank them profusely for the lift.

Friday 22 August | Iğdır
Still weak from the goat's-head soup, I eat an omelette and amble around Doğubeyazıt to see if anyone is visiting the

supposed site of Noah's Ark. Since Fernand Navarra discovered pieces of ancient plank embedded in ice on the mountain in 1955, there has been a tradition of amateur archaeology in the vicinity of Ararat, claiming to prove that this was the resting place of the Ark. The Genesis story of Noah was written down during the Babylonian captivity in the sixth century BC and was presumably therefore adapted from stories of local epics, particularly the flood story of Assyrian Gilgamesh. In the earliest surviving versions of Gilgamesh, on glazed cuneiform tablets retrieved from Ashurbanipal's burnt library at Nineveh, the Ark came to rest on Mount Nishir or Nimush in the northern Zagros. If the Ark had set off from the lower Euphrates plain, this theory would make sense, given that the prevailing winds are from the west.

The Assyriologist Irving Finkel deciphered the eighteenth-century BC Old Babylonian Ark Tablet in which the god Enki advises the sage Atrahasis to destroy his house, build a boat, spurn property and save his life. The tablet contains detailed instructions for how to construct an ark in the event of a deluge, and suggests that the boat was a giant circular coracle, constructed from ribbed palm branches surfaced with reeds and sealed with bitumen in the style that persisted in Iraq until modern times. In view of the speed with which the flat plains of Akkad would have flooded in the event of excess rainfall pouring off the Taurus and Zagros Mountains, and with tidal waves coming up from the Gulf, one wonders what the forewarning would have been to put the 'ark plan' into effect. Did the Akkadians develop a system of advance signals based on rainfall patterns or astronomical observation? Or was the ark plan only ever fanciful, a literary device whose purpose was to immortalise the wisdom of Utanapishtim, mythical survivor of the deluge?

None of the Old Babylonian tablets or second-millennium flood stories identifies any resting place for the ark. But considering the Ark Tablet jointly with the sixth-century BC World Map tablet, whose *nagus* indicate mountains at the rim of the world radiating out from Babylon, Finkel speculates that the 'mountains of Ararat', 'somewhere beyond Urartu', could have been the Ark's final location as related in Genesis. Then again, unless the waters rose above 1,000 metres, there would have been many other peaks before the ark reached this Mount Ararat. That leaves open the question of why the geographical associations of the story would have changed from the earlier Epic of Gilgamesh. In the Assyrian Christian and Muslim traditions, Mount Judi (or Qardu in Aramaic), where the Tigris crosses the modern border of Türkiye, was long associated with Noah's Ark. The site was visited in 1909 by Gertrude Bell, who reported that a Nestorian monastery, the Cloister of the Ark, had been constructed on its summit but was destroyed by lightning in the year 766.

No one is going to Ararat so I take a dolmuş north to Iğdır over a low pass around the side of the mountain. Iğdır is a small provincial capital with few amenities and a rustic feeling. On the edge of the town, where tractors and horse-drawn carts carry freshly-cut timber along a small road that runs towards the Arax, I see a man sitting on a log, reading some papers. As I approach, he rises and addresses me in English. After enquiring where I am from and why I am in Iğdır, the man explains that, like much of the population in these eastern frontier districts, he is descended from survivors of the Medz Yeghern who were forced to convert to Islam. His given name is Muslim but he prefers to be called Kevork. 'I am Armenian,' he tells me—and points to post-Soviet Armenia, visible in the distance across the closed frontier. Many Armenians who survived the genocide were assimilated as Muslims with Turkish names, or were adopted by Turks and only discovered their true identity late into their adult lives. Some of them practise Armenian traditions behind closed doors, while some seek baptism in the Armenian Apostolic Church.

Kevork explains that before the First World War the province of Iğdır corresponded to the district of Surmali that was part of the Erivan governorate of Russian Transcaucasia. The name derived from the ruined Armenian town of Surmari meaning Surb Mari, or St Mary, and whose castle still stands on the border near Tuzluca. Directly east of Ararat on the northern side lies a slither of territory known as the Araks corridor which extends between Armenia and Iran to the Azerbaijani exclave of Nakhijevan. By the 1639 Treaty of Zuhab, Surmali lay within Persian territory as part of the Erivan Khanate. Surmali was then annexed by Russia during the Russo-Persian War of 1826 to 1828. Under the ensuing Treaty of Turkmenchay, most of the Plain of Ararat, including the northern slopes and peak of Greater Ararat, passed under Russian control while Iran retained administration over Lesser Ararat, and the Ottoman Empire kept the southern slopes of Greater Ararat within the Sanjak of Bayazit. Surmali was part of the First Republic of Armenia before being ceded to Türkiye by the Soviet Union in the treaties of Moscow and Kars.

Since Surmali had been part of the Yerevan governorate, Kevork continues, Lenin had no authority to sign it away to Kemal. But Surmali and the Araks corridor were both transferred to Turkish control under the 1921 Treaty of Kars. Against the backdrop of the genocide and the Turkish invasion of 1920, the First Republic of Armenia had no choice but to accept its terms as well as the allocation of Nakhijevan and Karabakh to the Azerbaijan Soviet Republic. Kemal fixed the border at the Arax for military convenience and to preserve a corridor into Nakhijevan in line with Ittihadist pan-Turanist aspirations. Iran was not a signatory to the Treaty of Kars and the status of Surmali and the Araks corridor remained disputed until the 1932 Tehran Convention determined that 'the whole of Mount Ararat would be within the boundaries of Turkey.' Reza Shah and Kemal finalised the borders of the Araks corridor in the 1937 Treaty of Sa'dabad.

Kevork suggests that he might show me something. Later I wonder if he did not have in mind some Armenian ruins or secret khachkar crosses. But something in his manner makes me uncomfortable. Bidding him farewell, I set out from Iğdır along the narrow road shaded with lime trees to a village called Arahk near the closed border crossing into Armenia. There I wait beside a pile of newly cut sweet-smelling logs for the bus to Aralık, with the intention of exploring Ararat from the north. On the bus I fall in with one Sayyid Mehdi Hosseyin Mehdad.

Hosseyin explains that he was formerly a junior minister for tourism in Iran but having advocated that tourists be allowed to drink alcohol, he is now on the run from the Iranian security forces, accompanied by his Turkish friend, Ferhat. They have a plan to visit Nakhijevan, the Azerbaijani exclave bordered by Armenia and Iran that has a single point of entry from Türkiye. Hosseyin is free to live in Türkiye but needs to renew his visa every ninety days by entering a friendly country.

Having left my passport at the hotel, I return to Doğubeyazıt, where I collect my things and make my way back to Aralık to join Hosseyin and Ferhat for kebab. Hosseyin is hilarious and I am glad to have made the effort to meet him. Although devout, he explains that it is acceptable for a Muslim to believe that the Qur'an was written by a man and not dictated by Allah through Jibril. In fact, he argues, Islam exhorts the faithful to use their God-given faculties of reason to reflect on their total experience of the world. Arbitrary non-rational dogma is the means by which the clergy maintain temporal power and keep their grip on the superstitious minds of the uneducated. Up to this point, I am in agreement with the Sayyid, but Hosseyin continues with an elaborate theory of telepathy and six degrees of parapsychology, and I wonder why, if he is in possession of such powers, he has been unable to arrange the renewal of his Turkish tourist visa. Still, he wants me to be part of his mission, to translate his theories into English and help him disseminate them to an expectant worldwide audience.

SATURDAY 23 AUGUST | ARALIK

We share a small room with three beds in the one hotel in Aralık but the mosquitoes are vicious and, with recurring bouts of diarrhoea, I hardly sleep. In the bright morning sunshine we eat breakfast of yoghurt and çay under the shadow of the volcano. We catch the bus to Nakhijevan but the authorities refuse to grant us entry at the border and we have to turn back. In the first place I do not have the required visa and, in any case, they explain to Hosseyin, the Azerbaijani police are in cooperation with the Iranians—so he must try another frontier, ideally Georgia. We return to Iğdır in an Azerbaijani coach full of boisterous Turks from Erzurum who have been on a tax-free shopping trip to Nakhijevan.

Parting from the Sayyid, I take lunch on the edge of Iğdır and catch the bus to Kars via Tuzluca and Digor, the first stage of my journey home from Ararat. The route passes through the most extraordinary landscape: the wilderness of Türkiye's closed eastern border with Armenia, strewn with lava, volcanic peaks and empty steppe, the treeless lost homeland of an exterminated people. In the distance, north of Ağrı, one mountain has an astonishing shape, turned and twisted over itself like an ancient tree. From Tuzluca the road continues to Akçakale where the Akhurian (Arpa) flows into the Arax and continues along the Armenian frontier close to the hamlet of Pakran (Bagran), the former capital of Bagratuni Armenia.

North of Pakran along the Akhurian lies Mren Cathedral. Ancient Armenia ceased to exist as an independent state after the Sasanian dethronement of the last Arsacid king in 428. According to the Armenian chronicler Sebeos, Mren was erected by David Saharuni in thanksgiving for the triumph of Byzantium and Armenia in the twenty-five-year war against Sasanian Persia that concluded in 628. Yet by the time Mren Cathedral was completed in 640 the Arabs had already conquered the Levant and were soon to reach the Caucasus. Armenia fell suzerain to the Umayyad and Abbasid caliphs until regaining independence in 855. Mren Cathedral is an early instance of the Armenian nine-chambered principle of architecture, with four interior piers supporting the dome on an octagonal drum—a design repeated at Ani Cathedral more than three centuries later. The west lintel is carved with figures of Christ, Peter and Paul while the north lintel depicts the return of the True Cross to Jerusalem by Heraclius in 630. Mren was abandoned during the Ilkhanid period. Sadly I am unable to visit Mren for lack of transport from Tuzluca.

The dolmuş continues to the village of Digor where we stop for tea. The café has a rustic quality with painted floral patterns around the cornices and weather-beaten old men dressed in ancient grey suits who smoke and play cards at square wooden tables. On the bus is a group of young Hungarian architects who comment that our setting would not be out of place in rural Hungary. Near to the village above a gorge formed by the Digor River lies the ruined complex of Khtzkonk. The five churches of the ensemble were still intact when photographed by the Armenian archaeologist Ashkharbek Kalantar in August 1920. But in 1959 the art historian Jean-Michel Thierry visited the site and found that four of the five churches had been destroyed, with only the Church of St Sargis surviving. The testimony of local people suggested that the buildings were destroyed with explosives by the Turkish army. From Digor, the route passes below Alaca Dağı, the piebald mountain, and across a wide expanse of grassland to reach the provincial capital of Kars.

Kars feels like Turkish Siberia, isolated and remote, with crumbling Russian buildings from the late nineteenth century. After decamping to Hotel Ahmet Yilmaz, an old tailor stiches my sweater while I explore the streets. In Harran it was almost fifty degrees in the middle of the day. Two weeks later and 1,800 metres up on the plateau it is hardly touching fifteen. The hotel has hot radiators and thick pile carpets that have probably never been cleaned but exude a comforting warmth: it is still August and the Karsians are already preparing for the long hibernation. I set off to visit the well-preserved former Armenian Cathedral of the Holy Apostles whose foundation stone was laid in 930 and was later converted into a mosque. The building is known for its geometric design, although the friezes are relatively crude compared to Aghtamar. The twelve-sided drum contains low-relief figures of the twelve apostles in blind arcades and there are sculptures of the four evangelists in the keystones of the squinches. Above the oculus in the north side is a figure thought to be Gregory the Illuminator, who converted Armenia to Christianity.

Beyond the cathedral lies the fortress rock that rises high above the upland plateau. Kars controlled the passage between the Kur River, which from the eighth century marked the frontier with Georgia, and Theodosiopolis (Erzurum). An American lady is following in the footsteps of her late son, prematurely taken, leaving her in a blizzard of grief. We spend the evening together with the Hungarians.

First Armenian Republic
Ashot I the Great (855–890) founded the Bagratuni dynasty and established the independence of Armenia from the Abbasid Caliphate. Ashot ruled from Bagaran on the Akhurian; his successor Smbat I moved the capital upstream to Shirakavan in 890. Kars became the capital under Abas (930–952) until Ashot III (952–977) moved the court to Ani. From the 1010s Armenia lay on the frontline of the Turkish incursions. Bagratuni Armenia was absorbed into the Byzantine Empire in 1045, captured by the Seljuks in 1065, and then ruled by a succession of Kurdish, Ilkhanid and Turkoman amirs. Following the Ottoman–Safavid wars of the sixteenth century, the Ottomans took control of Kars in 1579 and governed through semi-autonomous pashas. Russia expanded into Transcaucasia in 1828 and acquired Kars, Ardahan and Batum under the Treaty of Berlin in 1878. During the First World War, Kars was far from the frontlines until the Russian collapse in 1917 allowed Ottoman forces to reoccupy the three north-east provinces.

Having lost three-quarters of their population during the First World War, the Ottoman Armenians were to be further dispossessed in its aftermath. At the Brest–Litovsk peace negotiations in February 1918, and flush with the anticipation of victory by the Central Powers, the Ittihadist delegates to the conference threatened to complete the annihilation of the Amenians if the Transcaucasian Armenian delegates did not cede Kars, Ardahan and Van. Having gained these provinces, and in pursuit of the pan-Turanist dream of a Nationalist Türkiye extending from the Bosphorus to Baku, Enver's Third Army under Vehip Pasha then advanced across the Akhurian into Transcaucasia. But in late May 1918, while the Ottoman Empire and the Transcaucasian Republic were engaged in a peace conference at Batumi, General Nazarbekian repulsed the Ottoman army at the Battle of Sardarapat, saving Armenian refugees from further massacres. Following the battle, the Armenian National Council led by Hovhannes Katchaznouni and Aram Manukian declared the independence of the First Republic of Armenia on 30 May. Six months later, Lenin annulled the Treaty of Brest–Litovsk that had been agreed in February and the demarcation of the eastern border of the residual Turkish state became an open question.

The previous month, on 30 October 1918, the Armistice of Mudros was signed between the Ottoman Government and Britain as the occupying power and representative of the Allied Supreme Council. In the eastern provinces, Ottoman troops withdrew to the 1914 borders in accordance with the terms of the Armistice, and Armenian forces took control of Kars and Ardahan, but Britain violated the terms of the Armistice, occupying Mosul and Alexandretta after Ottoman forces had withdrawn. More egregious still, the Greeks began landing troops into Smyrna on 15 May 1919 with British support. These aggressive acts precipitated resistance, under the leadership of Mustafa Kemal, to the Allied occupation and the declaration of the Turkish National Pact by the Ottoman Parliament on 17 February 1920.

In the negotiations of the Allied Supreme Council, lines were drawn on maps in accordance with principles of self-determination that applied to the European nations of the defeated Central Powers. Woodrow Wilson sought an American mandate under the League of Nations to protect an Armenian state that would have included the districts of Kars and Ardahan. But a fact-finding mission led by the American General James Harbord in August 1919 concluded that only an Allied Mandate and military guarantees of protection could prevent the Turkish reoccupation of these eastern districts. Following the Senate's rejection of the Treaty of Versailles on 19 November 1919 the United States never joined the League, and on 1 June 1920 the Senate formally rejected President Wilson's request for an American mandate in Armenia.

In the absence of defensible borders and without American intervention the mandatory maps became dreams. Despite Allied promises of salvation, Armenia was abandoned to her fate. From 1918 to 1920 the ruling Armenian Dashnak party had allied itself with the Whites in the Russian Civil War. But the withdrawal of Allied support to White forces and their collapse in the spring of 1920 meant that the Armenians found themselves fighting both the Turkish Nationalists and the Bolsheviks. Piłsudski's victory against the Red Army outside Warsaw on 25 August obviated the need of the Allies to confront the nascent Soviet Union. Meanwhile the Turkish Nationalists settled their differences with France and on 24 August 1920 agreed a Treaty of Cooperation with Russia that provided them with arms and bullion.

With their slender resources and lack of manpower the Armenians were no match for Kemal's resurgent Turkish army. On 20 September 1920, he ordered Kâzım Karabekir's XV Corps in Erzurum to advance towards Kars. Karabekir captured the citadel and took 2,000 Armenian prisoners on 30 October. The Turks continued to advance, occupying Alexandropol on 7 November and threatening to march on Yerevan. Meanwhile, the Central Committee of the Russian Communist Party ordered the invasion of the Republic of Armenia from the Azerbaijan Soviet Republic and Bolshevik forces entered the country on 29 October. Under duress, and even as the government of the residual territory of Armenia had already been transferred to Soviet control, Armenian representatives signed the Treaty of Alexandropol on 3 December, ceding the districts of Kars and Ardahan. Kemal and Lenin extinguished the First Armenian Republic and divided the Armenian heartland between them. The borders were fixed in the Treaty of Moscow, signed on 16 March 1921, between the government of the Soviet Union and the Grand National Assembly of Türkiye. On 13 October 1921 the Armenian Soviet Republic acquiesced to the Treaty of Kars that cut off the Armenians from their ancestral homelands including, most poignantly, their sacred Masis (Ararat).

SUNDAY 24 AUGUST | ANI

After yoghurt and çay I take a trip to the ruined city of Ani. Celil Ersozoğlu—a middle-aged dark-faced half-Georgian marked by alcohol and winters on the steppe—collects the Hungarians and me from outside the Ahmet Yilmaz and drives us briskly across the grasslands to Ani. While Celil takes the others back to Kars after their cursory tour, I have a few hours until he returns with another group to inspect these exquisite ruins of mediaeval Armenian architecture, alone in the desolate landscape.

The city of Ani was built in a dramatic position between the Akhurian gorge and the Tsaghkotsadzor ravine. The Bagratuni capital from 961, Ani reached its zenith under King Gagik I, who built the cathedral between 989 and 1010. As a result of internal factional conflicts and Byzantine pressure, Gagik's successor King Hovhannes-Smbat bequeathed the kingdom to Constantinople upon his death in 1040. The Seljuk Alp Arslan captured Ani in 1064 and handed it over to the Kurdish Shaddadid dynasty that already controlled Dvin east of the Arax. From 1201 to the 1350s, Ani was ruled by the Zakarian dynasty, under first Georgian and then Ilkhanid suzerainty, before being taken over by Turkoman Koyunlu. Ani owed its commercial position to the trade route from Trebizond to Baghdad but by the 1400s the primary route had moved south to Bayazit and Ani declined.

From the Lion entrance gate, paths lead across the grassy expanse to the widely spaced ruins. The churches lack the exuberant carving of Aghtamar but are distinguished by their geometry. The circular church of the Redeemer was completed in 1036 and survived until 1957 when it was struck by lightning and half of the building collapsed. The church has a dome over an eight-apsed interior with traces of paintings dating from 1291. Over recent decades the masonry and carvings have been hacked away. The most impressive structure at Ani is the cathedral, designed by Trdat Mendet. The dome and drum have fallen down but the remainder of the building is intact, with blind arcades and a texture of reddish tufa. Four piers divide the interior into nine spaces, the foremost of which is continuous with the apse of the chancel. The cathedral's height is accentuated by the creation of levels according to the principles of Armenian architectural theory that reflect the trinity in the thrice-tripartite division of the interior.

The domed monastery church of Tigran Honents was completed in 1215 and is the only church at Ani whose frescos survive. The paintings show scenes from the life of Gregory the Illuminator, from his being tortured by King Trdat III to the baptism of the Armenians following their conversion, with the Ascension in the dome and Christ Pantocrator in the apse. The round church of Gregory Abughamrents was built in the 960s and has six interior niches below a drum. Nearby is the outline of the Church of Gregory of Gagik, also designed by Trdat, and the Shaddadid Menüçehr Camii. Visible in the ravine below are the surviving abutments of the mediaeval bridge across the Akhurian River, whose thirty-metre single-arch span fell down long ago. Further up the Akhurian is the monastery of Horomos that dates from 1038 and became a burial place of Armenian nobility. Little else remains of the Armenian heritage on the Turkish side of the frontier.

Stumbling over the ruins of Ani, one cannot help but feel the weight of history in this forlorn place, where the reverberations of the past still sound. From the edge of the site, I can see the fence running along the Akhurian that marks the closed Turkish-Armenian border. During the taxi journey Celil had suggested that the livelihoods of the people on both sides would improve if diplomatic relations were normalised. Having opened the border following the collapse of the Soviet Union in 1991, Türkiye closed the frontier crossings in April 1993. This was in response to the Armenian occupation of the Azerbaijani district of Kalbajar during the First Nagorno-Karabakh War, a conflict in which 30,000 people were killed. The ruins of Ani feel like a dream at the edge of the known world, and it seems that reopening the border remains a remote possibility. As I stand on the citadel looking beyond the Akhurian, Armenia seems irretrievably distant. While the Turkish soldier looks the other way I take photographs of the ruins.

Celil returns and after helping him find his lost petrol cap on the way back to Kars, I explore the town art gallery, which has some delightful kilims. Kars glows in the warm evening light, its belle époque Russian buildings giving the flavour of the twilight of the Tsars. But at the Karisma internet point, fateful news reaches me. Pyrrha has written to say that the plants on the balcony have all died in the heat wave and that she is moving out of the apartment. Neither Calypso nor Penelope for this Odysseus. As I grapple with the Turkish keyboard to compose a measured reply, I become aware that my digital camera has been stolen from the outer pocket of my leather jacket. Leaping up, I run after Celil, who takes me to the police station and patiently interprets. But it is pointless: all the photographs I have taken since leaving Tripoli sixteen weeks earlier, documenting the central sections of my journey, are lost. The police advise me to return later, and when I do, they give me back the camera without the memory card.

Anatolia

MONDAY 25 AUGUST | KARS

Summer in Kars is short and an autumnal chill bites the air, but the town is bright with concerted activity as shepherds make the most of the breezy light before the long, deep cold sets in. I am determined to recover the memory card. Returning to the fray, I am required to repeat my story several times, first to the tourist police, then to the 'children's police' as apparently the thief was a minor, then to the district police, and eventually to the public prosecutor Sinan Tür, emphasising the enormous value of these photographs.

As we stand in front of the customary memorial to Atatürk that one finds in government buildings all over Türkiye, Sinan tells me that the British have always been anti-Turkish and that I must be a spy. No, I explain, I have no links to the British state and nor am I 'anti-Turkish'. Since the Elizabethan age, England was allied with Türkiye against the Catholic Central powers, propping up the Ottoman Empire throughout the long nineteenth century. In the Crimean war Britain fought alongside Türkiye against the Russians. It was only on the eve of the First World War that the alliance was broken, due to the intervention of Wilhelmine Germany. One should not to be 'pro-' or 'anti-' any particular group but rather evaluate the past in the light of reason and defend what one justly believes.

Sinan replies that Britain acts for itself, making alliances expediently, depending on the circumstances. I concede he has a point, except that in 1914 the Young Turks sought alliances with all the major powers, right up until the last minute. It was the British decision to impound the warships *Osman* and *Rashadieh* that tilted the balance but it was a German admiral's disobeying orders from Constantinople that led Russia to declare war on the Ottoman Empire. These were fast-moving events, with cascading poor decisions leading from one catastrophe to another. There is an affinity between our two nations, I say: your country is beautiful and for all their love of eccentricity, the English share the Turkish clubbishness. In any case, Britain is no longer top country and my lost photographs are more important than international politics.

'So why did you photograph the monuments in Ani when you know it is not allowed?' Sinan asks. He looks at me knowingly but I sidestep his question and suggest that if we can recover the memory card, I could show him the photographs of my journey from Cyrene to Kars. Judicial procedures are set in motion and I pass the day between police stations, offices and law courts, each bearing portraits of Kemal Atatürk wearing tail suit and white starched wing collar, with piercing blue eyes looking directly at the viewer or slightly up to the heavens, the embodiment of the Turkish state. Such photographs capture the spirit of a vanished era when military dictators were polite companions at fashionable dinner parties: one senses that Kemal would have been more engaging than Cromwell.

Although the official procedure started with the children's police, it moves to the court room and a man in his forties is produced as the defendant, looking like a local tramp scrubbed up for the purpose. I am called on to give my testimony via a translator. I state that an unknown person took the camera from my pocket in the internet point the previous evening and that it was subsequently returned to me by the police without the memory card. At this point, the man rushes towards me, kneels at my feet and pleads with me in Turkish. The translator tells me that he is saying he did not do it and that I must retract the charges or he will face three years in prison. 'But I only want the memory card back,' I say. 'I never accused this man of anything, and have never seen him before he entered this room.'

After leaving the court, the police take me back to the station and produce the memory card, cut into two pieces, saying that they found it in a dustbin. 'Why would the thief take the card and cut it in half?' I ask. Contradicting the earlier statement that the tramp was the thief, the police now explain that two boys stole the camera, used it to take photographs of themselves and, not wanting to give themselves away, cut the memory card into pieces. I leave the police station to wander around the town in the evening, reconciling myself to the loss and concluding that the authorities must have engineered to have the camera stolen in order to destroy the photographs I took of the Armenian ruins at Ani.

I can only reflect that photographs never capture the most interesting moments: that memories are always more reliable, if less easily communicable. Having previously reviewed my photographs after taking them, I am able to bring many of them back into my mind's eye. But Mahmoud Shennib, Martin Savage, Naim Zabita, Jalal Eddine Weiss, Dana al-Omari, Paolo dall'Oglio and James Mackay, not to mention Mari, Dura and Palmyra, are all gone: precious friends hid in the past's dateless night. And my only record of them cut in two by the clumsiness of the authoritarian Turkish state. Levant Lost twice over; twice over Lost Levant.

Tuesday 26 August | Erzurum

When I call on him in the morning, Sinan suggests that I apply for civil damages. Sinan is from İzmir and has been posted to Kars by the Justice Department. He would far prefer to be in his home town on the warm Aegean than in these wild highlands of brigands and bone-crushing winters. There is not much to do in the public administration of a small town on the edge of a closed border and Sinan is pleased to have the company of a foreigner. He introduces me to his legal advisor and takes me to speak with officials in the tourism department. There is a lot of discussion in Turkish about the lost photographs and I wonder if it is not all an elaborate act for my benefit. Over tea in the sunshine I ask him why the Turkish government will not open the Armenian frontier. 'Why are you here in these sensitive border regions of Türkiye?' he asks. 'It is not to find Noah's Ark! How do we know you are not spying for the British or the Americans? What were you doing in Syria?' Türkiye fears an American-backed independent Kurdish state in Erbil and declined the American request to use its bases to invade Iraq from the North.

'These lands are beautiful,' I reply. 'It is understandable that Türkiye fought to recover them from Russia. But with its indigenous people destroyed, they are desolate and poor: of what use is it to hold these barren borderlands as a badge of national pride? Would it not be in the best interests of Türkiye to make friends with the Armenians and begin a new chapter of warm relations through a process of truth and reconciliation? Would that not be more consistent with the ideals of Süleyman and the Ottoman golden age? Türkiye continues to suffer from not recognising these historical facts and making compensation. The Armenians were the 'most favoured millet' within the Ottoman Empire. Your greatest architect Mimar Sinan may have been Armenian, like the Balyans who designed Sultan Abdulmejid's Dolmabahçe Palace. Even the mother of Sultan Abdul Hamid himself may have been Armenian. That is the tragedy of it.'

'The Armenians wanted to establish an independent state on these territories,' explains Sinan. 'By 1913 the Porte had lost almost all of Rumelia and the Armenians conspired with Russia to dispossess the Turks of what was left of their country. At the end of the First World War, Britain supported the Greek invasion of 1919 and imposed the humiliating Treaty of Sèvres. But Mustafa Kemal saved the Turkish nation and restored our pride: that is why these borders are so sensitive. Events took their course and all sides committed atrocities in these wars but they occurred long ago so why do you care about them now? Leave the past in the past.' Impressed by Sinan's candour, I am left at an impasse except to say that until the past is resolved Türkiye will be shackled by it. Yet I wonder where lay the irrevocable inflection point in all this tragic history. 'There is nothing more you can do here,' Sinan concludes. 'If you want to claim damages for your photographs, write to the British Ambassador in Ankara.' Then he warns me that there is renewed concern about militant Kurdish activity, with disturbances expected in the coming week.

Having lost these days, I cannot continue to Ardahan and the Black Sea coast. Sad not to visit Pontus, especially the Sumela Monastery at Karadağ and the church of Hagia Sophia at Trebizond, I realise that it is time to head west. From Kars the bus proceeds across the high plateau. I am hurtling towards the sea like Xenophon's men, but having followed their path from Van to Kars, now my passage leads across the peninsula to Marmaris. The driver's assistant walks up the aisle dispensing pungent green aftershave from a plastic bottle into the cupped hands of the passengers. The bus drives through the Sarikamish defile, where Urartian fortresses cling to the ridges above. Sarikamish is known for the battle in December 1914 at which the Ottomans lost 80,000 troops to the cold and which contributed to the scapegoating of the Armenians as a fifth column. From Horasan the bus passes the Ilkhanid Çobandede Bridge and continues to Erzurum. There is a room at Akçay Otel which has red velvet curtains and four-poster beds and I take it.

Formerly Elegeia and then Byzantine Theodosiopolis, Erzurum (Gates of Rome) is a busy provincial capital. Located at the watershed of the plateau between the Arax and Euphrates, Erzurum has the feeling of the last days on the marches of a decaying empire whose enemies are on the move. The city was fortified by the Romans as the military base for their north-eastern frontier and this region became a peripheral zone in the confrontation between empires. But the Seljuks brought fresh energy into Anatolia and left behind some fine monuments. The Çifte Minareli Medresesi is particularly impressive with its twin towers and carved portals that illustrate the quest for perfect balance and proportion. Erzurum was absorbed into the Ottoman Empire in 1515. The Rüstem Paşa Kervansarayı, endowed by Süleyman's grand vizier in 1561, was probably designed by Mimar Sinan, who also constructed the vizier's mausoleum in Constantinople.

Along the lane leading to the citadel there are some charming old shops and in one of them, I buy a pair of kilims. I also find batteries for the digital camera into which I return the first memory card, intact despite its misadventures in Cyrene.

But it is sad to see the wooden houses in this district scheduled for demolition. The citadel itself was originally constructed by the Romans, and its high ramparts give wide vistas over the upland landscape and distant mountains. According to Dio Cassius, the Armenian client King Parthamasiris was summoned to Elegeia by the Emperor Trajan in 114 and then 'disappeared' prior to the short-lived Roman annexation of Armenia. Was this the precedent for their misfortune, I wonder?

Over dinner at a canteen I meet a student called Racip, who describes himself as Kemalist but appears to be Islamist: with or without Allah, it seems that Turkish Nationalism is much the same. We end up in a fierce discussion about Türkiye's bid for EU membership. Racip wants to feel European and be accepted as such, as well as to have visa-free travel across the EU and access to Erasmus schemes, and so forth. He does not see any obstacles to EU membership beyond prejudice and anti-Islamism. I suggest that Türkiye is too large for Europe to absorb and that perhaps its cultures and mind worlds are too different. The benefit of the accession process to Türkiye is to drive internal reforms but given the reluctance of the authoritarian state to relinquish control and Europeanise the institutional fabric of Türkiye, membership is probably unattainable.

Wednesday 27 August | Sivas

The journey to Sivas takes seven hours along a primary route travelled as much for invasion as well as trade. The bus crosses the high rolling tableland of plains and pasture, past railway gorges and Ottoman stone bridges. This beautiful country of mountains and valleys and rivers has seen everything since the beginning. As salination rendered Sumerian soil infertile, deforestation and overgrazing left the landscape barren. Over the millennia the trees were cut down for fuel and building material while goats eroded the topsoil and gullied the hillsides. All these Edens ruined by human disequilibrium for, once, these uplands where the great rivers rise were covered in trees. The forests must have seemed infinite until they were cleared. Was the first Fall a parable for the felling of the forests —for the wanton consumption of natural capital?

At Sivas I take a room near the central square before exploring the town, known for its collection of fine Seljuk monuments. The nearby ensemble of medreses mostly dates from 1271, a period of resurgence for the Sultanate of Rum after the earlier Mongol invasion. Seljuk medreses were built around an arcaded courtyard and taught a curriculum that included theology, law and medicine. In the Ottoman period the medreses were joined with *vakıf* (religious foundations) to form *külliyes* (integrated dispensaries of social services). The Ulu Camii is fine, and the stalactitic portals and minarets of the Gök Medresesi are particularly striking, but the most delightful complex is the Şifaiye Medresesi from 1217, which contains the tomb of the Seljuk Sultan Kaykaus and a fine arcaded courtyard around a rectangular pond. Something of the quest to replicate paradise on earth seized these Islamified Turkic peoples, and sipping çay by the rose bushes in the geometric tranquillity of the courtyard, the sense of it survives.

THURSDAY 28 AUGUST | KONYA

I take the dawn bus to Kayseri, city of Mimar Sinan, and continue to Ereğli and Konya. The nine-hour journey crosses central Anatolia through steppe and agricultural land towards the hinterland of the Aegean coast. The bus proceeds snail-like through Konya's sprawling suburbs but the tram into the city centre is fast and comfortable. I find a room at the Otel Tur off Konya's principal thoroughfare that looks over the Mevlânâ Müzesi, the mausoleum of Jalal ad-Din Rumi. As the light fades, I explore the Alaeddin Hill, focus of ancient Iconium, and whose Seljuk monuments have stalactitic decoration with ceramic tiles in turquoise, aubergine and white. After the Seljuks were driven out of Nicaea by the Crusaders in 1097 they established the Sultanate of Rum at Konya and ruled central Anatolia for the next three centuries. The sultanate reached its zenith under Alâeddin Keykûbad I (1220–1237), who initiated a construction boom across his domains, building caravanserais, mosques, medreses, hospitals, palaces and bridges.

The Mongol irruption through Central Asia into Persia and Iraq in the 1220s and 1230s led to the westard flight of imams, scholars and jurists, such as the sage Haji Bektashi and Baha ud-Din Walad, the father of Jalal ad-Din Rumi. Konya became a leading cultural centre of the Islamic world and exerted a lasting influence. The Mongols broke Seljuk military power at the Battle of Köse Dağ in 1243 but the Sultanate of Rum survived and prospered between the Ilkhanids and Byzantines. The Seljuk rulers encouraged the founding of medreses and Sufi lodges, to assert Sunnism against Shi'a influence from Iran, while also preserving the shamanistic influences they had brought with them from Central Asia. Together with the Galata Mevlevihanesi that was founded in 1491, Konya continued to be a leading centre for the Sufi brotherhoods until shut down by Kemal Atatürk in 1925. Over lamb-shank stew at the Sifa restaurant opposite the bazaar, I read Wilfred Thesiger's obituary in *The Guardian*, puzzled by this adventurer of a lost era who venerated the archetype of the noble savage.

FRIDAY 29 AUGUST | KONYA

The Mevlânâ Müzesi is built around the mausoleum of Jalal ad-Din Rumi, founder of the Mevlevi Sufi order and author of the mystical poem *Masnavi*, written in Konya in the 1260s. In 1231 Sultan Keykûbad offered his rose garden as the burial site for Rumi's father, which then became the first Mevlevi tekke. When Rumi died on 17 December 1273, he was buried next to his father and the mausoleum was built by Husamettin Chelebi, his successor as master of the order, with funds from the sultan's family. Under its striking conical green dome, the tomb shrine became a centre of pilgrimage. The other buildings in the complex were built by successive Ottoman sultans. Next to the mausoleum is the semahane, the hall in which the dervish dance ceremony was performed, with examples of the instruments used—ney (flute), kanun (zither), oud, rabab (fiddle) and tanbur (lutes)—and the original illuminated copy of *Masnavi*.

Over the centuries, lavish gifts were bestowed on the foundation, including instruments and silk carpets, and the museum has a library of over five thousand volumes on Sufism and the Mevlevi order. In *Mystical Islam*, Julian Baldick relates that the word Sufi may derive from 'wool', as in sackcloth, or 'sophos', meaning wise. Sufism emerged as a set of mystical practices drawing elements from multiple sources, including Zoroastrianism and Orthodox Christianity. Sufis followed the path of the Christian mystics, seeking virtue through contrition on a path to illumination. Some Sufis practised sama to seek joy in music and dance. Other traditions advocated for strict austerity similar to the fourth-century Egyptian hermits. *Zikr* is divine remembrance, chanted by repetition of the names of God, leading to the loss of awareness of the self.

The eleventh-century Persian Sufi Ahmad al-Ghazali, who taught at the Madrasa al-Nizamiyya in Baghdad, wrote a treatise linking love to the divine spirit that transcends worldly attachments, intellectualism and fame, arguing that one-upmanship and word trickery are mere props to social status when we should strive instead to be pure-hearted and good. The *Sawanih*, written in quatrains like the *Rubaiyat of Omar Khayyam*, influenced Persian Islamic mystical literature and can be seen as the antecedent to Rumi's *Masnavi*. Ahmad al-Ghazali believed that all created beauty is an emanation of divine beauty: since the transcendent is both absolute beauty and the lover of all phenomenal beauty, to adore any object of beauty is to participate in divine love.

Sufi practice seeks the liberation of the divine spark in man apart from the darkness of matter, a parallel tradition to the hesychasm of Byzantine spirituality. The Seljuk Sultanate of Rum was religiously syncretic as the sultans married into the Byzantine noble families: most of them had Greek wives and Orthodox Christianity was practised in the harem. In this environment it was natural that Jalal ad-Din Rumi would link the Hellenic concepts of logos and hesychasm with Sufi theology and practice. Rumi thought that mankind must accept mortality in order to affirm the existence of the divine. In 1244, by which time he was established as a sheikh at Konya, he met a wandering dervish, Shams-e-Tabrizi, and became devoted to him as a mentor. For several years the two were inseparable, until Rumi's students engineered the disappearance of Shams. The ensuing shock of separation was the trigger that prompted Rumi to begin writing the 26,000 rhyming couplets of the *Masnavi*, the name of which refers to its poetic form.

The purpose of the dervish dance is to rise above the Ptolemaic celestial spheres and have direct experience of the divine from the vantage point of universal intelligence. 'I dance in the glow of the sun so that the dancing speck of dust remembers me.' In that statement one can sense the tantalising link between Rumi, the mediaeval Sufi, and apophatic theology on one side, and the antinomy of mathematical fit on the other—for the Sufis were not just influenced by Platonist ideas about souls and the stages of ascent towards the ecstasy of union with the divine but also absorbed Pythagorean numerology. As elaborated by Alan Wenham-Prosser in his book *The Music of Rumi*, the Mevlani musical system of maqams derives from the Pythagorean melodic system of naturally occurring intervals with exact mathematical ratios.

In *The Song of the Reed*, the exordium at the beginning of *Masnavi*, Rumi gives a poetic explanation of the joy that dervishes experience in the dance ceremony. The lament of the reed that has been cut from its bed to make a flute represents the anguish of separation from God: the reed-flute sings to express the sorrow of being apart, of being a soul in solitude. The poem is about the joy that lies hidden within each one of us. Rumi exhorts us to be consumed like the reed by the fire of divine love, for not to live in a state of ecstatic joy is to subsist in a deathly shadow world. Love is the force that intensifies the yearning to return to the state of union with the transcendent divinity. 'Falling in love' includes within itself the possibility of abandonment. The tension between spirit and material is fierce but love will triumph in the end.

The monastic orders emphasised brotherliness and friendship. Muhammad himself seems to have regarded monasteries as contrary to the commonwealth of the 'umma, their mysticism a substitute for living. But the Mevlânâ Rumi showed how members of Sufi orders could achieve the opposite by raising themselves, through the example of love and wisdom. The purpose of the Sufi path is to become better as an individual and then radiate the spirit of peace into broader society and ultimately the body politic of the entire world. Perhaps that explains the long-lasting devotion of many Muslims to Sufism and especially to Jalal ad-Din Rumi. I say a prayer for Yasser Sagherji, the Damascus rug seller, and buy an English translation of *Masnavi*.

From the museum I visit the Ottoman Selimiye Camii, completed in 1570. While the Seljuks used single domes or a row of triple domes, fifteenth-century Ottoman architects developed methods to contain large spaces with minimal vertical supports. In the classical Ottoman style, associated especially with Sinan and following the inspiration of Hagia Sofia, a central dome is supported by semi-domes, while eliminating internal divisions by pushing the dome supports against the walls. On the roof terrace of the Turistik Otel next door, I eat peaches with the sunset before returning to Sifa for more lamb-shank stew.

SATURDAY 30 AUGUST | AFYON
I rise early to visit the Koyunoğlu Müzesi down a quiet lane and admire its collection of eighteenth-century kilims. Collecting my things, I take the tram to the otogar. On the bus to Afyon there is a man from Catania. He has some medical training and, over lunch, he diagnoses my intermittent Diyarbakir bug as giardiasis and recommends that I should eat lots of garlic to kill it off. On reaching Afyon, I climb to the kale, the 250-metre-high rocky outcrop above the city that carries fragments of fortification from Hittites and Phrygians to Byzantines. It is striking how attractive Afyon is, distinguished by Ottoman-era wooden houses, and above all by its twelfth-century Seljuk Ulu Camii. As I eat supper my reverie is interrupted by an extended military parade through the town. There are military vehicles and troop carriers with soldiers sitting or standing to attention as smoke machines and coloured light beams create a sound-and-light show with loud martial rock music.

I discover that it is a national holiday parade to celebrate the Battle of Dumlupınar in which, between 26 and 30 August 1922, near to Afyon, Atatürk and İnönü completed the shattering defeat of the Greek army. Following the battle, the Turkish Nationalists pursued fugitive Greek forces to Smyrna, entering the city on 9 September. What followed was the final denouement of the Turkish War of Independence: in revenge for atrocities committed by Greek troops in 1919, advance Turkish units began massacring Greeks and Armenians in the streets of Smyrna. The Turks dowsed cloths in petroleum and set alight houses in the Christian districts of the city. The ensuing Fire of Smyrna between 13 and 22 September destroyed the Greek and Armenian quarters, killing 50,000 civilians before an estimated 300,000 refugees were evacuated on British and American ships. The war formally ended the following year with the departure of all the Anatolian Greeks in population exchanges agreed in the Treaty of Lausanne.

Kemalism and modernism
Turks venerate Kemal Atatürk as military commander and founder of the modern state. Kemal believed that Ottoman weakness had its roots in Islam and traditional ways of life—in conservatism and resistance to modernisation. Hence his replacing Osmanli with modern Turkish, Latinising the script, closing down Sufi brotherhoods, vesting constitutional power in the army and launching a dirigiste industrialisation programme. But the command-and-control economy the Kemalists created from 1923 to 1938 was against the pluralist spirit of the Ottoman administration. From the time of Elizabeth I, England had admired the tolerance of the Ottoman Empire, in stark contrast to the sectarian conflicts of Western Europe.

Today, however, the historical monuments of Türkiye's golden age under Süleyman the Magnificent feel like relics of a vanished polity, for much of the aesthetic fabric of Türkiye has been destroyed by the ideology of latterday industrial state capitalism. This can be seen in the old neighbourhoods around Beyoğlu in Istanbul, where Ottoman wooden houses have been pulled down and replaced with concrete apartment blocks—making fortunes for real-estate developers but eliminating the cultural essence of the inhabitants, as portrayed in the 1998 Turkish-Italian film *Hammam*. The same has happened all over Türkiye and it is only in a few areas such as Afyon and Konya where the pre-modern Ottoman urban fabric has been preserved. The beauty of the built environment is an allegorical reflection of its cultural ambition and whereas developed economies have planning regimes to protect the urban fabric, modern Türkiye, like so many so-called emerging markets, has allowed these to fall victim to the commercial imperative of the construction sector and investors.

To be sure, the process of uglification is not unique to Türkiye. The spread of Western techniques of mass production in the twentieth century and the destruction of craftsmanship as a way of life can be blamed for destroying the aesthetic elegance of the pre-1914 European civilisation all over the world. What once distinguished Türkiye from other powers was the depth of its artisanship and craftsmanship, which survived for a while, due to its resistance to change. Perhaps the rise of the Islamist AK Parti lies partly in the belief among Turkish voters that Kemalism may have made Türkiye a stronger country but cost it its soul.

Twentieth-century Islamic intellectuals such as the Iranian Seyyed Jalal al-e-Ahmad denounced Western materialism as the pivot for Islamic complaint against the evils of imperialism and colonialism. Yet Political Islam operated expansionary regimes from the Umayyads to the Ottomans, while the complaint of materialism is a Christian one that Islam inherited. Islam has many interpretations and there are many ways of being a 'good Muslim', just as there are many ways of living faithfully to the New Testament. Secular Kemalists fear Wahhabism and the Ayatollahs: for them the 'revolution of Atatürk' must be protected against Türkiye's descent into an Islamic republic. The battle over the headscarf is symbolic of this conflict. But perhaps they would do better to invest in the re-beautification of Turkish cities, the revival of traditional skills and craftsmanship, and the renewal of the Sufi brotherhoods.

Despite its supposed tolerance, the enduring condition of

the Ottoman Empire was the domination of Christians and other minority groups. As caliphs (from 1517 to 1922) the Ottoman sultans perpetuated the legalised superiority of Muslims over dhimmis. Despite the Tanzimat reforms, it was always clear where power lay in the later Ottoman Empire. Much contemporary narrative blames the problems of the Middle East on the colonial powers. It is true that Anglo-French expansion into North Africa and the Sazonov-Sykes-Picot agreement represented an opportunistic carve-up of former Ottoman possessions. But Ottoman Türkiye was itself an imperial state and other defeated powers ceded territory after 1919. The Habsburgs administered a diverse empire that succumbed to nationalism and was broken into pieces in 1918: the Ottoman Empire could have done the same without eliminating its minority communities.

Moreover, since 1923, Nationalist Türkiye has continued to persecute and maltreat its domestic minorities. The root of the problem was the failure of the United States to join the League of Nations after the Senate voted against Wilson's policy, hence the inconsistent application of the principle of self-determination of peoples and nation states. Far from granting equality of rights to minorities after 1923, Kemal and his successors continued the same policies, vindicating the centrifugal instincts over the preceding century of Greeks and Rumelians, and of Arabs and Armenians, who saw that the supposed equality of national rights decreed by the Porte were never more than token gestures to mollify European Great Powers. The Turkish Nationalists then sought to absorb all minorities into a manufactured monolithic national identity.

From 1945 to 1989 the West considered Türkiye to be secular, liberal and capitalist—an extension of Europe and America and a strategic bulwark against the Soviet Presidium —but the Turkish Republic was never fully democratic or liberal and since 2003 has become an increasingly rogue member of NATO. While post-war Germany admitted responsibility for the Holocaust and has paid reparations, Türkiye continues to deny the Armenian genocide. The Turkish government disputes both the number of Armenians killed as well as the systematic nature of the killings—that is to say, it denies that there was pre-meditated intent or that orders were ever issued by the CUP government. Turkish writers and journalists who call for recognition and reparation are routinely denounced. On 19 January 2007 the Turkish-Armenian journalist Hrant Dink, the 'bird of Istanbul', was gunned down in the street outside the offices of *Agos*, the newspaper he edited. Yet even Atatürk declared on 23 April 1920 that the annihilation of the Armenians was a 'shameful act', although this admission has also been seen by historians as a negotiating gesture with the Western Allies.

For a century the Atlantic Powers have made declarations to the victims, yet the annihilation of the indigenous Christians of Anatolia remains unpunished. The path to justice for Armenia is a process of 'truth and reconciliation', which would enable all Turks to address their country's toxic legacy and benefit from having done so. Türkiye's enduring political ideology derives from the suspension of its liberal constitution in 1878. Since 2018, the ruling AK Parti has made a pact with the extreme nationalist MH Parti, as well as other hardline elements. As documented by the non-profit organisation Freedom House, opposition leaders face harassment, while freedom of expression in the media is curtailed and reporters are routinely jailed. Cengiz Çandar, former adviser to President Turgut Özal, explained in 2020 to the Swedish Institute for International Affairs that despite its democratic, parliamentary façade, Türkiye has in reality been a security state since the time of Sultan Abdul Hamid II and that to change this autocratic Türkiye would require a paradigm shift.

Aegean

SUNDAY 31 AUGUST TO TUESDAY 2 SEPTEMBER | RHODES

The dawn bus takes me from Afyon to Marmaris. The town is charming, if touristic. After inspecting pricey and lacklustre rugs, I buy some compact disks of classical Ottoman music on the Taksimleri label with ney, oud and kanun to mark my farewell to Anatolia. The sea passage to the ancient island of roses is short and breezy, and I am once more in Hellas. On disembarking, an entertaining Greek called Nassos takes me pillion on his scooter to his eponymous pension inside the mediaeval walls of Rhodes Town.

In 408 BC the settlements of Lindos, Cameirus and Ialysos pooled their resources and founded the city of Rhodes on its present site. They constructed the harbour with dry docks, thereby providing the island with the most advanced port facilities in the Mediterranean. The city was laid out in blocks faced with white marble and its streets were decorated with 3,000 statues. During the wars of the Diodachi, Rhodes resisted the siege of Demetrius Poliorcetes, and in 290 BC erected the thirty-five-metre-high bronze statue of Helios. According to legend this was the famous Colossus that stood astride the harbour entrance, although more likely beside it. Rhodes, the maritime city state, prospered on Levantine trade, pioneering the first body of sea law, and remained a distinct polity until destroyed by Cassius in 42 BC. Sadly, nothing remains of Hellenistic Rhodes except for the few artefacts discovered in the harbour and exhibited in the museum.

Today Rhodes Town is dominated by the Gothic walls and palaces of the Hospitaller Knights of St John, who governed this island for three centuries until being removed to Malta by the Ottomans in 1522. After leaving my things, I swim off the shingle west beach and celebrate my new freedom by drinking a full litre of fresh Makedonikos red wine with kleftiko on the strand. Somewhat inebriated I am unable to find my way back to the pension but I walk to Mandraki harbour, watching Mars and the boats in the twilight and the wind on the stormy waves, before retracing Nassos's steps through the gap in the walls by the port.

Next day I take breakfast of yoghurt and honey, iced coffee and spinach pastry at Ganymede, run by a Dutch couple who have migrated in search of simplicity and a beautiful environment. The coffee house is in a quiet square with the same paving of small brown flint stones that one sees in Merton Street in Oxford and in Avignon, vestiges of a common architectural vocabulary, but with bougainvillea and fig trees swaying in the breeze. In the *International Herald Tribune* I read about the early life in Bulgaria of Elias Canetti, literary champion of humanism and student of how the behaviour of crowds can descend into mob violence.

I catch the bus to Lindos and walk through the well-preserved mediaeval town to explore the archaeological site. The Lindos acropolis has a fine propylaeum, stoa and Doric temple, with views of St Paul's Bay where the saint is supposed to have landed. I return to Rhodes town and find a taverna in one of the quiet squares, enjoying wine and calamari. Later I wander past the knights' palace to the harbour and shipyard. Sitting at the end of the mole looking towards Asia Minor with the night wind on the stormy waves, I reflect on the vast difference in mind world this small channel of water represents between the island and the peninsula.

In the morning Nassos prepares pekoe tea and we discuss politics with Zeinab, a Europhile Turkish lady staying at the pension. Zeinab explains that European societies are mature and that Türkiye's problems would be solved if it could become more like France. I tell her that de Gaulle once said no one can govern a country that produces 246 varieties of cheese and that Kemalism and Islamism are two sides of the same authoritarian coin. The future of the Levant must lie in the renaissance of a pan-Mediterranean civilisation, a revival of the Antonine Age—diverse and with a common purpose to a prosperous humanism. European maturity is the fruit of the freedom of the European mind, with its root in Hellenism and hypothetico-deductive reasoning, and its willingness to challenge authority and engage in free discussion. It goes back to Herodotus and the Persian Wars, to the struggle between the free Greeks and Asiatic despotism. It is the same conflict we see today between liberal democratic freedom and all forms of collectivist-authoritarianism that are equal in their subordination of the individual to the brute power of Leviathan.

I roam the charming streets and discover the Minos roof garden at the highest point along the landward walls, with views over the old town. The fortress Palace of the Grand Master below casts a spell, with its Gothic tracery and dressed-stone halls. For six months in 1522, the 600 knights of the Order of St John repulsed the 100,000 strong Ottoman forces under Sultan Süleyman. Eventually the knights capitulated and were given safe passage to Malta. The palace was reconstructed during the inter-war period when Italy held the Dodecanese, and the floors and furniture of the interior reflect the fascistic style. But the space is captivating and there is a good exhibition about the knights and ancient Rhodes. Later I return to the mole beside the shipyard where the evening wind is blowing up stormy waves, and embark on the ferry to Kos which traces the sea lane through the waters of the Sporades, passing Symi under the light of the moon.

Wednesday 3 September | Kos

From the white sandy beach of Cape Skandari around the coast from Kos town, Bodrum and the western edge of Anatolia are visible across the water. There is not much to prevent a Turkish invasion of these islands. But the Hellenic Republic still maintains National Service and at the end of the beach there is a small military outpost where young conscripts sit with their radios, hanging out their washing. The soldiers welcome the distraction of passing tourists: they seem unconcerned as I walk through the military zone—quite a contrast with the Turkish bases. I swim in the warm sunshine and rent a moto to speed over the island.

The archaeological site of the Asclepeion lies open on its ridge: the cypress trees and partially rebuilt stoa are extremely evocative. The site of this three-levelled sanatorium was chosen by the doctor-priests of Kos for its airs and waters, much like an eighteenth-century spa town, with hospital below and temple above. As in Agrigento, one imagines the ancients arriving with their complaints, hoping that offerings to the gods might offer respite, while enjoying the comforts of the spa and its views over the sea. As in many classical sites, the transition from propitiation of many deities to the worship of one god is evident. For the Hellenic mind is at once sceptically rational while also attuned to the religious element of the transcendent. At the village of Zia in the hills above, the local honey and yoghurt could be nectar and ambrosia. I zoom down to Tigaki to swim in the shallow waters and return to Kos town along the green littoral of the north coast.

THURSDAY 4 SEPTEMBER | PATMOS
At first light I walk to the port, past the plane tree of Hippocrates that spreads its tendrils ficus-like over the dewy soil, admiring the Ottoman buildings whose stones glow golden in the dawn and remind me of the governor's house in Acre. The Babylonian-Hellenistic priest and astronomer Berossus founded a school here at the time of Epicurus. Sultan Abdulmejid I, promulgator of the Tanzimat, built a mosque in Kos to the memory of Tirimüjgan Kadın, his beloved second wife and the mother of Sultan Abdul Hamid II.

It is a short journey to Patmos past the treeless islands of Leros and Leipsoi. I stow my bags at the port before walking up to the Sanctuary of the Apocalypse. By tradition this hillside cave is where the apostle John dictated Apocalypse (Revelation) to his disciple Prochorus. From the window I look across the sea below and think back to my reflections at Sinai about Epicurus, apophatic theology and Platonism. As at Sinai the island has a natural peculiarity, with electrical storms sometimes visible from as far away as Samos. I open the pocket New Testament that I bought in Jerusalem at the time of the Jubilee and read Apocalypse from beginning to end. The book is disconcerting in its imagery as it prophesises the opening of seven seals, the battle of celestial powers, the thousand-year rule of the beast and the casting of the beast into the lake of fiery sulphur, culminating in the day of judgement and the New Jerusalem. From the cave, the path continues up to the town on the crest of the hill.

The hill is dominated by the fortified Monastery of John the Theologian. The land and funds for its construction were granted to the Bithynian monk Christodoulos by the Emperor Alexios Komnenos in the year 1088, even as the Seljuks had overrun Smyrna and disrupted navigation in the Aegean; but it was not until the Byzantines recovered control of western Asia Minor with the help of the Latin knights that the monastic community took root at Patmos. The monastery has an extensive collection of books and icons, and I am taken back to the sunlit afternoons at Sinai on the library roof. The Patmos library has several hundred codices, the most famous of which, the fifth-century Codex Porphyrianus of the Epistles was, like the Codex Sinaiticus, taken to St Petersburg and never returned. The courtyard has a mural depicting John's defeat of the magician Cynops in an emblematic struggle of light against darkness.

The town, with its white houses and pale-blue window frames, is deserted but one taverna is open for lunch. At three o'clock I return to the monastery for vespers and stand in the stalls, resting my weight on the wooden frames. As I follow the chanting, I study the gilded figures on the iconostasis and am transported once more to the time-suspending light of Sinai that picks out the red glass of the incense burners and silver hanging lamps as it passes across the floor. Once again I conclude that practice is more important than doctrine: if you subject the propositions of arbitrary belief to the logical scrutiny of formal argument, their spirit of transcendence vanishes. The essence of the tradition lies in the stillness of the present moment.

I think of the looming prospect of *fuma Londra*—the limp grey of leaden skies and diesel exhaust. How to capture the spirit of the sunlit Levant with its traditions of hesychasm and

Sufism, and live with the humanist ideal of Jesus the Master as companion to philosophise with over wine in an Epicurean garden? Equally, I think of the Orthodoxy of post-Soviet Russia that operates in league with the Kremlin. Of what use is the Church as the custodian of universal ideals, of the divine light of reason, if its officials become handmaidens to the criminal classes? At the close of the office, Father Antipas, the abbot, invites me to return and stay in the monastery. Glad to be included I walk down the hill to swim and eat kleftiko before attending a concert at the open-air theatre beside the holy cave. The performance is an homage to the Greek poet Odysseas Elytis, with piano, baritone and spoken voice. Lit with candles under the stars, the songs and Byzantine hymns are evocative of the natural maritime beauty of the Aegean. After the concert I descend the stone steps to the beach and lie on the sand, looking up at the night sky before taking the overnight boat to Piraeus.

Parousia

What does 'Apocalypse' mean? Despite two centuries of modern critical analysis, scholars remain divided about the book's authorship, date and interpretation. The Orthodox tradition holds that the same 'disciple whom Jesus loved' wrote the Gospel of John, letters and Apocalypse. John had settled in Ephesus but was exiled during the reign of the Emperor Domitian (81–96) to Patmos where he had the visions of the 'Parousia' or Second Coming. John was said to have escaped martyrdom and lived to an extreme old age. This tradition is anchored historically by the second-century writer Irenaeus, who relates that Polycarp had known John as an old man at Ephesus. If the apostles believed that the Incarnation was the beginning of the End Time, by the end of John's life the first generation of the Church had passed away and there had been no Parousia. Some New Testament scholars argue that John's prophetic poem dates from the period of the Jewish War that was initiated by Nero in 66 and ended with the sack of Jerusalem in 70. Against this backdrop of ongoing political events, Apocalypse was written in the style of the earlier

Hebrew texts such as Daniel and Ezra that prophesy the return to Zion.

While the literal interpretation focuses on the book's description of the Parousia, many scholars have suggested that the text would have been understood at the time as an allegory of the struggles confronting the nascent Christian community as it sought to achieve a social and political revolution. John describes the struggle between the 'ocean of love' in opposition to the beast and the dragon as the embodiments of earthly principalities and supernatural powers of evil. In that vein Apocalypse can be viewed as continuing the passion of the Gospels into an imagined political philosophy: the New Jerusalem as the reign of perfection, the kingdom of God as the Christian revolution that was inaugurated with the First Coming.

How does this relate to logos? Consider why the physical universe was in its lowest state of entropy at the point of inception: it means that it was in its highest state of order or perfection in the beginning, which is also the limit state. The unrealisable infinite, the completed totality, was present at the moment of inception: logos stands for the original perfection of the cosmos and for redemption from its necessarily ever-deteriorating condition. One can therefore reinterpret the allegorical poem of Apocalypse as a parable of the continuous human quest for freedom and social perfection. Equally there is a warning: that Mammon—the subordination of ethics to profit—will ruin our happiness and that everything awry with politics has its source in the malign decisions of bad actors.

One can see Epicurus liberating humanity from fear of the gods, the celestial bodies, as a step on the road to the human-historical kingdom of God. One can view the Kantian reassessment of rationality as the continuation of the Christian revolution in political economy that forms the basis of liberal democracy and theories of the ideal state—for the kingdom of God is the domain of freedom and justice in this world of atoms and neurons, of nations and states, of pay cheques and taxes, not the supernatural world of angels and harps, of demons and sulphurous fiery lakes. Just as there is no final revelation but the continuous unfolding of logos, so the Christian revolution is the seed of the continuous improvement of the human condition.

Those who attack Christianity overlook its historical significance. They are right that the religion has been repressive of sexuality and imposes unfeasible demands of credulity: these are its twin Achilles heels. But if Christ died for every soul, then every soul is precious. The Christian revolution defined the individual as the metaphysical unit and advocated for the equality of every individual before universal law. Since its inception as a social movement in the Roman world, the Christian message has been to love one's neighbour and see the humanity in the other. The 1952 Amsterdam Declaration of the World Humanist Congress declared 'the worth, dignity and autonomy of the individual and the right of every human being to the greatest possible freedom compatible with the rights of others'. All known alternatives to humanism must lapse into tyranny, venality and brutality. The humanist tenet, 'that morality is an intrinsic part of human nature based on understanding and a concern for others' descends in part from Christianity.

If God is apophatic—the infinite extension of the unknowable—then logos is the ongoing revelation of divine wisdom. Christianity reinterpreted as universal humanism represents the flowering vine of logos set against the violence inherent in nature and against the competitive struggle and the power of Mammon. There is a tension between humanist ideals and the compromises necessary for them to prevail: that is the root of global politics. The ideal of a transnational kingdom of God means the universal extension of democratic values, representative government and self-determination for all nations: it does not mean the elimination of the democratic nation state. The imperative of logos is to 'be decent people', love others, be good for its own sake, and work hard for the fruit of the work itself. Equally it is simply wrong willingly and deliberately to cause harm to another person: all the evil in the world flows from that.

God is silent and silence is God. About that which we

cannot speak, we must remain silent. The ancients understood the limits of finitude and knew that what lies beyond is unknowable. The apostles believed in the reality of miracles and in the Resurrection. But the ancient mind was different from the modern one. For them, reason had not yet sought to master nature and deities were as real as men: visitations of Hermes were normal to the Hellenes, while Yahweh spoke to the prophets of Israel. St Paul wrote that all humanity is 'saved by grace through faith in Christ'. Even today some Christians say that we should welcome death as the bridge to eternal life. But what happens if no faith is given? To the modern mind, literal belief in life after death is an intellectual impossibility: as Gilgamesh understood, our mortality in unassailable and the best we can hope for is the consoling illumination of the apophatic darkness.

Hellenism is the spirit of reason, truth and beauty, set against the countervailing forces of destruction, dogmatism and plutonism. Yet Hellenism was eastward-looking and syncretism was part of its spirit. The Judaeo-Hellenic fusion which became Christianity is the foundation of Western values. If there is no life after death, then life is sacrosanct in a different way, for the infinitude of annihilation colours every aspect of our brief incarnation. The logos that illuminated Pythagoras and Archimedes, Philo and John, still lights the natural and moral sciences whatever the cultural wallpaper—whether Buddhist, Confucian or Hindu, whether Zoroastrian, Muslim, Sikh or Bahai.

For we are not mechanistic beings: our subjective conscious experience is the foundation of our metaphysical freedom. We are not the 'throwaway survival machines' of our genes: rather the machinery of heredity is the vestigial path in natural history of how we came to have our individual humanity. Our very mortality entails that values, rights and political freedom have primacy over purely economic considerations. Laissez-faire capitalism cannot on its own be the agent of human freedom. Despite being advocated as an optimal system that maximises aggregate utility, the competitive struggle of the world machine compresses our freedom as individuals.

Beyond a basic level, happiness does not lie in material things or worldly success, but in music and sunlight and salty air and the wind on the waves and in the trees; and in love and companionship, for solitude is hard to endure. If we are as transient as mosquitoes, our salvation lies in *chantilleuse imperator*, seeking paradise in our present experience, in our imagination and in the beauty of the world around us. We can only live to enjoy each successive moment until the last. But if we believe in freedom, we must grasp it and shape the world to its image. Our social and economic fabric can be recalibrated from the utilitarian homo economicus to the Epicurean calculus of flow. We are the result of our imaginings, and the imagination is more powerful than the will. But if we put our soul in a straitjacket to conform to the wishes of others, our imaginings must die and our paradise will be extinguished along with them.

PATMOS TO PIMLICO

I sleep well in the lifeboat box on the top deck. Dawn comes with rosy fingers as the ferry cruises up the Saronic Gulf to Piraeus, where the Parthenon stands out above the Athens haze. After an English breakfast at the port, I take the train over the Corinth canal to Patras and board the evening boat to Ancona. The Adriatic is cooler than the Aegean. But the crew give me a blanket and I find a place sheltered from the wind by the buttresses of the ship's funnel. Soon after I wake, the boat rounds a windy headland and there is Ancona on its promontory, looking splendid across the green sea with the hills above. At Bologna I explore the squares and the towers, the arcades and the churches. Milan is already northern Europe under grey skies but there is fine dining near the station. The overnight train to Paris reaches Gare d'Austerlitz in the fresh dawn of a clear autumn morning. From Gare du Nord I take the local train through northern France. At Calais I walk across the tarmac to the ferry terminal in my Siwi sirwal trousers and leather flip-flops, carrying the few books that remain, with the jajim from Damascus and kilims from Erzurum.

The ferry canteen serves cheese toasties in greasy white-bread triangles and superheated tea in polystyrene cups. I sit on the deck in the sunshine, thinking of my journey, travelling light to Ararat and back, in flight from tedium, in quest for epiphanies. As the white cliffs loom, I long to set off again for Trinacria clothed in temples and theatres; to climb the walls that Archimedes built as the last stand of youthful Hellenism; to reach Africa and the grandeur of Leptis; to find writer's heaven among the palm trees of Siwa as the warm desert wind casts the chatter of donkeys into the night; to admire the mosques of Cairo and vespers at Sinai; to explore the old houses of Damascus; to cross the Syrian plains and the Euphrates valley through commercial Aleppo, charming Antakya and baking Urfa, and across Lake Van to the desolate Armenian Highland and see Ararat rising above its plain and the ruins of a people dispossessed.

To leave the wild places will be a shock, for the regret of return is the loss of freedom. Freedom means the state of time suspended, where obligations and conventions make no demands, for the diversions of modern civilisation quickly fade: wanderlust returns and longing for the empty spaces comes back again. Suddenly those simple delicacies of the 'mysterious' Orient, from mint tea to strong black tea in curved glasses, from ayran to cardamom coffee, from the sweet lemons of Scetis and pulped sugar cane of Misr to the cherries of Damascus and lamb shanks of Konya—all seem far away. White cliffs, Trinacria, passport control, Saharan sands, Dover Priory, Siwa Oasis, no trains, Sinai sunset, slow coach through green hills, the indolent Euphrates, iridescent light of late summer, London traffic, disorientation, Anatolian peaks, Victoria Station, Aegean blue, inotic dislocation, never the same again, the parapet of Pimlico beach, alone but home.

Afterword

Following the completion of Lost Levant in 2022, events across the eastern Mediterranean region have continued to unfold. In particular, many of the places described here have continued to suffer from wars, political instability and natural disasters.

The Türkiye-Syria earthquakes of 6 February 2023 killed over 60,000 people and caused widespread destruction, especially in Antakya, with the loss of some of the historical monuments referred to in the book. Corruption and shoddy construction drastically worsened the earthquakes' toll.

Libya remains insecure, divided into three regions under the control of different factions, and without effective government that could begin to reconstruct the country and normalise the economy. Floods in Derna on 10 September 2023, washed almost the entire city into the sea after heavy rainfall and lack of maintenance caused dams to burst.

In the South Caucasus, following the 2020 Second Nagorno-Karabakh War, Azerbaijan attacked the residual disputed enclave of Karabakh on 20 September 2023, resulting in the forced displacement of the entire population of over 120,000 Karabakh Armenians whose forebears had lived in that territory for millennia.

The 7 October 2023 attacks that killed over 1,200 Israelis led to widespread destruction in Gaza and Lebanon, killing tens of thousands of civilians and leading to the displacement of millions.

At the end of 2024, the Syrian Civil War, effectively frozen for eight years, abruptly reignited as rebel forces from Idlib province seized Damascus and overthrew the Assad regime, even as much of the country remains in ruins. At the time of writing it is unknown whether this will bring peace to Syria.

The government of the Republic of Türkiye has opened

fresh negotiations with Kurdish groups, including the PKK and the semi-autonomous Kurdistan Region of Northern Iraq. There is even the possibly of rapprochement, albeit potentially a compromised one, between Ankara and Yerevan.

In facing the facts of history, as well as confronting the present, one can only hope that the divine light of reason will illuminate the minds of all people, everywhere.

Mount Ararat

Bibliography

Akçam, Taner (2012). *The Young Turks' Crime Against Humanity*. Princeton University Press.

al-Ghazali, Ahmad (1114). *Sawanih*. (Translated by N. Pourjavady, 1986.) Routledge, London.

al-Khalili, Jim (2010). *Pathfinders: The Golden Age of Arabic Science*. Allen Lane (Penguin Books), London.

al-Qadhafi, Mu'ammar (1976). *The Green Book*. People's Committee, Tripoli, Libya.

Archimedes. *Measurement of a Circle*. (Translated by T.L. Heath, 1897.) Republished (2002), Dover, New York.

Armanazi, Ghayth (2017). *The Story of Syria*. Gilgamesh Publishing, England.

Ayliffe, Rosie et al (2003). *The Rough Guide to Turkey*. Rough Guides, NY.

Baldick, Julian (1989). *Mystical Islam: An Introduction to Sufism*. I.B. Tauris & Co, London.

Belgrave, C. Dalrymple (1923). *Siwa, the Oasis of Jupiter Ammon*. John Lane, London.

Bryce, J.J. and Toynbee, A.J. (1916). *The Treatment of Armenians in the Ottoman Empire 1915–1916*. H.M. Stationery Office, London. Republished (2000), Gomidas Institute, Princeton, N.J.

Burns, Ross (1999). *Monuments of Syria: A Historical Guide*. I.B. Tauris & Co, London and New York.

Carson, Rachel (1962). *Silent Spring*. Houghton Mifflin Harcourt, Boston, MA.

Cavafy, C.P. *Poems*. (Translated by John Mavrogordato, 1951.) Chatto & Windus, London.

Chatwin, Bruce (1987). *The Songlines*. Jonathan Cape, London.

Chayes, Sarah (2015). *Thieves of State*. W.W. Norton & Company, New York.

Chitty, Derwas J. (1966). *The Desert a City*. Basil Blackwell and Mott Ltd, Oxford, Great Britain.

Clark, Kenneth (1969). *Civilisation*. John Murray, London.

Conrad, Joseph (1904). *Nostromo: A Tale of the Seaboard*. Harper & Brothers, New York.

Csíkszentmihályi, Mihály (1975). *Beyond Boredom and Anxiety*. Jossey-Bass Inc, San Francisco, CA.

Dalrymple, William (1997). *From the Holy Mountain*. HarperCollins, London.

Dawisha, Karen (2014). *Putin's Kleptocracy*. Simon & Schuster, New York, NY.

de Bellaigue, Christopher (2009). *Rebel Land*. Bloomsbury Publishing, London.

di Lampedusa, Guiseppe (1958). *The Leopard*. (Translated by Archibald Colquhoun, 1960.) Collins, London.

Dobrowolska, Agnieszka (2005). *The Building Crafts of Cairo*. AUC Press, Cairo, Egypt.

Duchesne-Guillemin, M. (1980). *Sur la restitution de la musique hourrite*. Revue de Musicologie 66 (1), p.5–26.

Dumbrill, Richard (2018). *A Treatise on Sumerian and Babylonian Music Theory*. Iconea Publications, London.

Durrell, Lawrence (1957). *Justine*. Faber & Faber, London.

Epicurus. *Letter to Menoeceus*. (In *The Epicurus Reader* translated by Brad Inwood, 1994.) Hackett, Indiana.

Fathy, Hassan (1973). *Architecture for the Poor*. University of Chicago Press, Chicago.

Finkel, Irving (2014). *The Ark before Noah*. Hodder & Stoughton, London.

Forster, E.M. (1918). *Alexandria: A History and a Guide*. Republished (1974), Overlook Press, New York.

France, Anatole (1890). *Thaïs*. (Translated by Robert B. Douglas, 1929). J. Lane, The Bodley Head, London.

Fromm, Erich (1957). *The Art of Loving*. George Allen & Unwin, London.

Galbraith, John Kenneth (1958). *The Affluent Society*. Houghton Mifflin Harcourt, Boston, MA.

Hall, Edward T. (1966). *The Hidden Dimension*. Doubleday & Co., Garden City, N.Y.

Hegel, G. W. F. (1823). *Lectures on the Philosophy of World History*. (Translated by H. B. Nisbet, 1975.) Cambridge University Press.

Heilbroner, Robert L. and Milberg, William S. (1996). *The Crisis of Vision in Modern Economic Thought*. Cambridge University Press.

Herodotus. *The Histories*. (Translated by Robert Waterfield, 1998.) Oxford University Press.

Hollis, Martin (1987). *The Cunning of Reason*. Cambridge University Press.

Hourani, Albert (1991). *A History of the Arab Peoples*. Faber & Faber, London.

Howard-Johnston, James (2010). *Witnesses to a World Crisis*. Oxford University Press.

Hoyland, Robert G. (1997). *Seeing Islam as Others Saw It*. The Darwin Press Inc. Princeton, NJ.

Hume, David (1748). *An Enquiry Concerning Human Understanding*. Ed. E. Steinberg, 1977. Hackett, Indiana.

Ibn al-Arabi, Muhyiddin (1231). (In *Sufis of Andalusia*, transl. by R.J. Austin, 1971.) Allen & Unwin, London.

Ibn Khaldun (1377). *The Muqaddimah*. (Translated by Franz Rosenthal, 1958.) Princeton University Press.

John Paul II (1993). *Veritatis Splendor*. Libreria Editrice Vaticana.

John Paul II (1998). *Fides et Ratio*. Libreria Editrice Vaticana.

Kapuscinksi, Ryszard (2002). *The Shadow of the Sun*. Penguin Books, London.

Keenan, Brigid (2000). *Damascus: Hidden Treasures of the Old City*. Thames & Hudson, London.

Kévorkian, Raymond (2011). *The Armenian Genocide: A Complete History*. I.B. Tauris & Co, London.

Kieser, H-L. (2018). *Talaat Pasha: Father of Modern Turkey, Architect of Genocide*. Princeton University Press.

Kilmer, Anne Draffkorn (1971). *The Discovery of an Ancient Mesopotamian Theory of Music*. Proceedings of the American Philosophical Society, 115 (2), p. 131–149

Kinross, P.B. (1977). *Ottoman Centuries: The Rise and Fall of the Turkish Empire*. Jonathan Cape, London.

Landes, David (1998). *The Wealth and Poverty of Nations*. W.W. Norton & Company, New York.

Lane Fox, Robin (1986). *Pagans and Christians*. Penguin Books, London

Lawrence, T.E. (1926). *Seven Pillars of Wisdom*. Republished (2000), Penguin Books, London.

Lossky, Vladimir (1978). *Orthodox Theology: An Introduction*. (Translated by Kesarcodi-Watson, 1989). St. Vladimir's Seminary Press, Crestwood, New York.

Louth, Andrew (1981). *The Origins of the Christian Mystical Tradition*. Oxford University Press.

Lucas, Robert E. (1990). *Why Doesn't Capital Flow from Rich to Poor Countries?* American Economic Review, 80(2), p. 92–96.

Maalouf, Amin (1984). *The Crusades Through Arab Eyes*. (Translated by Jon Rothschild.) Al Saqi, London.

Mahfouz, Naguib (1967). *Miramar*. (Translated by Fatma Moussa-Mahmoud, 1978.) AUC Press, Egypt.

Mandelstam, Osip (1930). *Journey to Armenia*. (Translated by Sidney Monas, 1977.) Notting Hill Editions.

Manginis, George (2006). *Mount Sinai: A History of Travellers and Pilgrims*. Haus Publishing, London.

Marcuse, Herbert (1964). *One-Dimensional Man*. Beacon Press, Boston, MA.

Mazower, Mark (2004). *Salonica, City of Ghosts*. Harper Perennial, London and New York.

Meinardus, Otto F.A. (1961). *Monks and Monasteries of the Egyptian Deserts*. AUC Press, Egypt.

Merton, Thomas (1960). *The Wisdom of the Desert*. New Directions, New York.

Miłosz, Czesław (1953). *The Captive Mind*. (Translated by Jane Zielonko, 2001.) Penguin Books, London.

Moore, A.W. (1990). *The Infinite*. Routledge, London.

Moses ben Maimon (1190). *The Guide of the Perplexed*. (Translated by Chaim Rabin, 1995.) Hackett, Indiana.

Moss, Robert Tewdwr (2008). *Cleopatra's Wedding Present: Travels through Syria*. Duckworth, London.

Olson, M. (1993). *Dictatorship, Democracy and Development*. American Pol. Sci. Review, 87(3), p. 567–576.

Robson, Eleanor (2008). *Mathematics in Ancient Iraq: A Social History*. Princeton University Press.

Rodenbeck, Max (1998). *Cairo: The City Victorious*. Picador (Macmillan Publishers), London.

Rogan, Eugene (2015). *The Fall of the Ottomans*. Penguin Books, London.

Rumi, Jalal ad-Din. *The Masnavi*. (Translated by J. A. Mojaddedi, 2004.) Oxford University Press.

Rummel, R.J. (1998). *Statistics of Democide*. Transaction Publishers, Rutgers University. NJ.

Runciman, Steven (1951–4). *A History of the Crusades*. Cambridge University Press.

Russell, Bertrand (1946). *A History of Western Philosophy*. George Allen & Unwin, Great Britain.

Sarris, Peter (2011). *Empires of Faith: The fall of Rome to the Rise of Islam 500–700*. Oxford University Press.

Sen, Amartya K. (1992). *Inequality Reexamined*. Russell Sage Foundation. Harvard University Press.

Sinclair, T.A. (1990). *Eastern Turkey: An Architectural and Archaeological Survey*. Pindar Press, London.

Stark, Freya (1966). *Rome on the Euphrates*. John Murray, London.

Suny, Ronald Grigor (2015). *They Can Live in the Desert but Nowhere Else.* Princeton University Press.

Temple, William (1959). *Readings in St. John's Gospel.* Macmillan, London; St. Martin's Press, New York.

Teresa of Avila (1567). *Autobiography.* (Translated by E. Allison Peers, 1991.) Doubleday, NY.

The Bible. New International Version, 1978. International Bible Society, East Brunswick, New Jersey.

The Epic of Gilgamesh. (Translated by Benjamin R. Foster, 2001.) W.W. Norton & Company, New York.

The Qur'an. (Translated by J.M. Rodwell, 1909.) Republished (1957), J.M. Dent & Sons, United Kingdom.

Thierry, Jean-Michel (1989). *Monuments arméniens du Vaspurakan.* Librairie orientaliste Paul Geuthner, Paris.

Todd, Olivier (1996). *Albert Camus: A Life.* (Translated by Benjamin Ivry, 1997.) Chatto & Windus, London.

Üngör, Uğur and Polatel, Mehmet (2011). *Confiscation and Destruction.* Continuum Books, New York.

Valberg, J.J. (2007). *Dream, Death and the Self.* Princeton University Press.

Walker, Christopher J. (1990). *Armenia: The Survival of a Nation.* Second Edition. Routledge, London.

Ware, Timothy (1963). *The Orthodox Church.* Penguin Books, London.

Warnock, Mary (1970). *Existentialism.* Oxford University Press.

Wenham-Prosser, Alan (2012). *The Music of Rumi.* Saraswati Society, Sutton, Surrey, United Kingdom.

Williams, Bernard (1973). *Problems of the Self.* Cambridge University Press.

Wright, N.T. (1992). *The New Testament and the People of God.* SPCK, London.

Index

Abbasid Caliphate 170, 216, 415
Abbasiya Coptic Cathedral 168
Abduh, Sheikh 172
Abraham 212, 223, 224, 317, 375–6, 378, 380
Abrahamic 95, 203, 232, 246
Achaemenid Empire 236, 374, 392
Acts of the Apostles 39, 40, 197, 254, 354, 372
Adana 360–61, 363, 366, 372, 407
ad-Din, Nur 267, 279, 283, 309, 321, 326, 379, 393
ad-Din, Salah (Saladin) 159, 168, 178, 216, 218, 234, 255, 280, 328, 330, 335, 377, 393
Aegean 436–41
Affluent Society, The 257
Afyon 431–2, 433, 436
Aga Khan Foundation 172, 184
Against Heresies 192
Agati, Ali 92, 93
aggregate freedom 241, 242, 245, 257, 259, 260, 265, 266
Aghurmi 119–22, 125–8, 133
Agrigento 75–8, 439
Ahtiname (Covenant of Peace) 188, 189
Ain Dara 319, 320
Ajloun castle 221
Akçam, Taner 369, 372
Akhenaten 154
Akragas 77, 78, 79
al-Assad, Bashar 252–4, 279, 291, 333, 335–7

al-Assad, Hafez 216, 240, 251–3, 261, 281, 282, 292, 325, 333, 335
al-Assad, Rifaat 292, 325
Al-Azhar 153, 158, 159, 169–73
Al-Bayda 104, 105–7, 109
Albert Camus: A Life 76, 81
Aleppo 298, 307–38, 339, 376
    Armenians 331
    Battle of 309
    citadel 316–18
    Great Mosque of 309, 379
    Museum 310–12
Alevis/Alevism 356, 405
Alexander (the Great) 33, 48, 91, 119, 128–30, 132, 136, 137, 139, 345–7, 375
Alexander II, Tsar 364
Alexandretta 328, 341, 416
Alexandria 128, 131–52, 167, 193, 303, 347
Alexandropol, Treaty of 417
Al-Fitouri, Suleyman Omar 104–5, 108, 109
Algeria 74, 235, 274
al-Hakim 172, 219, 318
Al-Husseini, Hajj Amin 117
Ali Baitro, Salem 89–91, 93–5, 100, 102, 103
al-Khalili, Jim 170, 172
al-Khazneh 208, 209
al-Omari, Dana 312, 322–5, 327, 423
al-Qadhafi, Mu'ammar 86, 87, 88, 90, 91, 93, 95–7, 100, 105–12, 114, 291

- 457 -

Al-Qarafa 178–9
al-Quwatli, Shukri 239
al-Shafi'I 178
altar of Hieron 44
Amman 220, 221, 229
Amorite Hammurabi 247
Amsterdam Declaration (1952) 443
Amun-Ra 118, 119, 166
analytical disputation 359
analytical philosophers 288
Anatolia 216–18, 328, 331, 342,
    348, 355, 390, 396, 421–35
    Christians 361, 365, 367, 369,
        371, 372, 384, 435
    Hittites 248, 373
anchorites 149, 151, 187, 195
Anglo-Egyptian Settlement 169
Ani 401, 413, 415, 417–20
Anscombe, Elizabeth 173–4
Antakya 339, 345–9, 356
Antep 373–4
Anthony of Sourozh 139
Antichrist 24
anti-Lebanon 287, 292, 307, 325, 328
Antioch 315, 339–59
Antiochus cylinder 303
Antiochus IV 355
Antonine Levant 348
Apamea 320-22
Apocalypse 439, 441–5
Apollonius 141
apophatic theology 201–3, 224,
    233, 430, 439
Apostolic Age 70, 192, 196, 212
Aqaba 207–8
Arab Revolt 225, 239, 274
Arab-Israeli conflict 207, 224–8
Arafat, Yasser 221, 226
Aralik 411, 412–15
Aramaic 248, 282, 292, 296, 303,
    375, 384, 386
Ararat 393, 398–420

Ararat, Mount 1, 406, 410, 411, 447
Archaeological Museum of Paolo
    Orsi 47
Archaeological Museum,
    Palermo 58
Archimedes 45–50, 51, 53, 170, 199
Architecture for the Poor 183
Archytas 46
aretaic eudaimonism 256
Aristarchus 141
Aristotle 146, 147, 304
Armanazi, Ghayth 335
Armenian Cathedral of the Forty
    Martyrs 318, 331
Armenian genocide 298, 331, 368,
    404, 410, 434
Arsuz 339, 340–42, 343, 344, 345
Art of Loving, The 30
artificial intelligence 55, 56
Ashurbanipal's Library 58, 304
Asketikon 150
Assyrians 193, 311, 374, 383, 386
astronomy 172, 236, 303, 304, 323,
    355, 386
Atatürk, Kemal 312, 344, 393, 421,
    422, 428, 432, 433, 435
Athanasius 142, 145, 149, 201
atomism 40, 41
Augustus, Emperor 17, 141
Aurelian, Emperor 297
Avignon 1–16, 18, 437
Avignon papacy 7
Avnon, Asaf 205, 206, 286
Axiom of Infinity 93, 180
Ayer, A J 290

Ba'ath Party 240, 254, 255, 335, 337
Babylon 128, 170, 247, 248, 300,
    302–5, 330, 409
Baghdad 148, 170–72, 236, 269,
    283, 384
Baldick, Julian 429

Balfour Declaration 207, 225
Basilica of St Paul's Outside the
    Walls, The 23, 24
Basra 256
Battesti, Vincent 123, 125
Battuta, Ibn 155, 178, 287
Beit Azem 242–4
Benedict XVI, Pope 231
Benedictine College of
    Sant'Anselmo 14
Benghazi 103, 112, 169, 381
Berber tribes 119, 120, 127, 148, 372
Berlin, Treaty of 364
Bernini, Gian Lorenzo 15, 18
Beyond Boredom and Anxiety 8
borrowing 262, 263
Bosra 214, 280–81, 292
bound time 257, 258
Brest–Litovsk, Treaty of 416
Brock, Sebastian 191
Bryce, Viscount 368, 372
Building Crafts of Cairo, The 184
Burns, Ross 319
Byzantine Levant 240, 281
Byzantium 13, 20, 193–4, 212–13,
    234, 236, 252, 292, 378, 386,
    413

Cachia, Frank 96
Cairo 153–85
    carpets 176–8
    Coptic 166–9
    Historic Cairo Restoration
        Project 159, 184
    Islamic 158–62, 175, 183, 184
    mediaeval 155, 158, 159, 175,
        183
Cairo: The City Victorious 155
calculus 22, 41, 53, 179, 245, 257,
    290, 445
caliphs 212, 214, 216, 233, 266,
    413, 434

Camus, Albert 11, 81–2, 235
Cantor, Georg 53, 197, 199
Cantor's Theorem 53, 93
capital accumulation 163, 164,
    241, 275
capital flow 270–73, 276
capital investment 249, 272
capitalism 19, 140, 229–30, 249,
    266, 268, 271, 275–6, 290, 310,
    359
    contemporary 177, 242
    greening 269
    industrial 183, 297, 432
    laissez-faire 265, 444
    post- 358
    state 230, 432
capital-labour substitution 250
Captive Mind, The 190, 345, 355, 356
Carrington, Philip 342
Carson, Rachel 268
Castel Gandolfo 24
Catania 37–8, 56–7
categorical actions 6
categorical activities 6, 9, 27, 30–31
Cavafy Museum 144, 166
Cavafy, Constantine 137, 139, 144,
    349
Cefalù 64
Centre for Egyptian Civilisation
    Studies (CECS) 182, 184
Chahine, Youssef 4
Chalcedon, Council of 142–3, 150,
    167, 191, 193
Chaldiran 405, 406
chance 181
Charles V 19
Chatwin, Bruce 118, 133–5, 194
Chayes, Sarah 274
Chouinard, Yvon 269
Christianity 21, 25, 30, 42–3, 69,
    149, 191, 199–201, 295, 352–3,
    355, 359, 444

Chrysostom, John 192, 202, 352
Church of Santa Maria della
    Vittoria 15
Civilisation 236
civilisational reconciliation 231, 232
Clark, Kenneth 236
Claudius Ptolemy 141, 303
Cleopatra 137, 141, 142
climate change 268
Cloud of Unknowing, The 201
Codex Sinaiticus 188, 190, 440
Colli Albani 23–5
Colosseum, the 17
Committee of Union and
    Progress (CUP) 365, 366, 369,
    370, 435
Common Word, A 231–5
Companions of the Prophet 212,
    213, 233
Conrad, Joseph 265, 277
consciousness 26, 59, 180, 181,
    182, 290, 380
Constantine, Emperor 18, 149,
    192, 213, 216, 297, 346, 351–3
consumption 10, 11, 109, 177,
    241–2, 250, 256, 258, 259, 269
Convent of Our Lady 264
Coptic Cairo 166–9
Coptic Church 138, 142
Copts, the 166, 167, 168, 169, 173,
    193, 215
Corrie, Rachel 7
corruption 109, 112, 134, 276–7,
    295, 335, 384
Cosa Nostra 61
Counter-Reformation, the 21, 71
Crac des Chevaliers 322–4
craftsmanship 152, 184, 185, 189,
    241, 242, 245, 433
Crusaders 208, 234, 320, 321, 354,
    375, 427
Crusades Through Arab Eyes, The 217

Crusades, the 216, 217, 218, 219,
    221, 234, 328
Csíkszentmihályi, Mihály 9, 151
Ctesiphon 212, 214, 386
cuneiform 58, 182, 248, 302, 303,
    316, 329, 374, 403
    tablets 58, 247, 256, 259, 282,
        300, 301, 304, 311, 314, 409
Cunning of Reason, The 245, 246
Cynics 42, 350
Cyrenaica 102–14, 120
Cyrene 104–5, 106, 107
Cyril of Alexandria 191
Cyrrhus 319–20

Daedalus 73
Daesh 297, 298, 336
Dakrour 122–3, 133
dall'Oglio, Paolo 292, 294–6, 423
Dalrymple, William 240
Damascus 215–16, 236–74, 277–8,
    282–8, 291, 295, 300, 310, 334
Damascus Historical Museum 261
*Damascus: Hidden Treasures of the Old
    City* 252
Dar al-Islam 155, 171, 212, 215,
    218, 219
Darius, King 33
Darwin, Charles 3, 181
Darwinism 181, 317
Dawisha, Karen 275
de Bellaigue, Christopher 378
De Rerum Natura 40
de Unamuno, Miguel 6, 181
Dead Sea 219–20
death 289–91
debt 156, 262–3, 266, 363
Decius, Emperor 193, 349, 351
Deir al-Suriani 148
Deir Al-Za'Faraan 381–4
Deir Dar Musa 292–4
Deir Ez-Zor 297–9, 302, 331, 370

Delacroix, Eugène 90, 176
Delphic Oracle, the 48
Delphic principle 194
Demetrius Phalerus 141
Demma, Isaac 209, 210
democide 371
Democritus 40, 46, 47, 351
demography 102, 162–6, 316
Derna 108, 109, 110–13, 114
Descartes, René 288
Description de l'Egypt 184
Destiny 4
dhimmis 212, 216, 218, 219, 233, 434
dialectical materialism 357
dialogues 27, 58–60, 64–5, 70, 157–8, 278–9, 332–4
Diocletian, Emperor 142, 149, 193, 299, 351
Diodorus 56, 60, 64, 73, 118
Dionysius the Areopagite 201, 202, 231
Dionysius the Great 45
Dionysius's Ear 44
Diophantus 141, 170
Dioscorus of Alexandria 167
discrete mathematics 53, 54
distribution 264–6
divine law 224
divine love 16, 33, 42, 43, 151, 166, 199, 429, 430
divine reason 145, 146
Diyarbakir 385–97
Dobrowolska, Agnieszka 184
Doğubeyazit 405–8, 412
Door of Prophecies 148
dream 288–91
Dream, Death and the Self 287, 288
Drifting Cities 143
Dumbrill, Richard 330
Dumlupinar, Battle of 432
Duomo di Siracusa 39
Dura Europos 248, 299, 300

Durrell, Lawrence 82, 83

Early Christian Church, The 342
Easter Sermon, the 352
Eastern Turkey: An Architectural and Archaeological Survey 400
economic
    development 157, 163, 169, 250
    dysfunction 257
    freedom 12, 258, 358
    growth 139, 162, 242, 269
    haecceity 244–7
    history 242
    model 229, 241
    opportunity 335
    output 258, 259
    policy 275
    reform 284
    rent 112, 272, 277, 335
    security 67, 256
    theory 9, 67, 230, 244, 249, 272
economics 89, 134, 169, 258
    academic 244, 276
    borrowing 262, 263
    development 274
    Epicurean 4, 257, 323
    existentialist 67–8
    heterodox 4, 10–11, 242
    narrow banking 89
    utilitarian calculus 10, 41
economy
    cash 88
    false 185, 249, 260, 323
    free 264, 265
    global 244, 265, 269, 358, 388
    international 184, 271
    liberal 11
    modern 30, 63, 249, 259
    political 4, 73, 113, 175, 242, 266, 284, 323, 381, 388, 442
Edessa 360–84

Edom 206, 208
efficiency 11, 12, 165, 177, 258, 260, 264–6, 271
Elements 141
Elina Makropoulos 6
Emesa, Battle of 297
Enlightenment, the 197, 203, 246, 350, 353, 362
environmentalism 268–70
Ephesus, Council of 20, 191, 386
Epic of Gilgamesh, The 58, 155, 324–5, 410
Epicurean economics 4, 257, 323
Epicureanism 40–43, 129, 198, 203–4, 351
Epicurus 9, 38, 40–42, 65, 139, 198, 215, 290, 439, 442
Erasistratus 141
Eratosthenes of Cyrene 141
Erice 72, 73–4
erotic-romantic love 16
Erzurum 423–6
Etna, Mount 35, 36, 37, 38, 56
Euclid 141, 146, 170
Euryalos 45, 47–51
Eusebius 187
Evagrius of Pontus 201
existential freedom 11, 66–8
Existentialism 65

Fall of the Ottomans, The 369
Faoud, King 161
Farah, Seti 219, 220, 229, 230, 236
Farouq, King 161
Fathy, Hassan 169, 182–5, 323
Fatimid dynasty 171
Fertile Crescent, the 247, 268, 287, 375
fidelity 78–80
Fides et Ratio 43
Finkel, Irving 409
First Balkan War 365, 366

First Gulf War 255, 256
First Republic of Armenia 411, 415–17
First World War 7, 120, 207, 225, 236, 274, 360, 367, 370, 372, 388, 415, 421, 422
Fisk, Robert 39, 70
fitna (civil war) 215
flow state activity 151, 182, 204, 241, 256, 257
flow 8–10, 15, 76, 185, 445
Forster, E.M. 135, 137, 139, 345
Fort Saint-André 8
Fouad, King 120
France, Anatole 27
Franciscan Order, the 19
Frederick II, Emperor 57, 58, 216, 234
free time 257, 258, 259, 265
freedom 66–8, 256–61
From the Holy Mountain 240
Fromm, Erich 30, 31, 76, 78
Futuh al-Buldan 213

Galbraith, J K 11, 257
Gaziantep 361
Gaziantep Archaeological Museum 373
Gebel Musa 187–9, 195, 199, 203
Genoa 13-14
Gilgamesh *see also* Epic of Gilgamesh 70, 81, 130, 155, 197, 311, 324–5, 409, 410, 444
global population 100, 162, 163
globalism 12, 95, 96, 334
Goethe 34
Golan Heights 207, 226, 242, 247, 250
Golden Church 188, 281, 346, 347, 348
golden rule, the 227
Gospel of John, the 22, 144, 196, 441

Gothic invasions of Rome 193
Grand Tour, the 3, 35
Great Financial Crisis (2007–8) 262
Great Persecution of Diocletian 149
Great Schism of 1054 24, 194
Greece 302–5
Green Book, The 88, 105, 106, 107–8, 109–10, 112, 291
'green growth' 269
green movement 268–70
Green Revolution, the 163, 164
Green Square, Tripoli 90, 91, 94
Grottaferrata 24, 25
growth theory 165
Guardian Europe, The
Guide of the Perplexed, The 224
Gulf of Aqaba 207
Gülhane, Edict of 362

Ha'aretz 205, 206
hagarism 213
Hagia Sofia 62, 98, 431
Hague Convention (1907) 370
Hajj, the 273, 274
Hall, Edward 12
Hama 320, 321, 324–7
Hama uprising 292
Hamid, Sultan Abdul 104, 364–6, 371, 424, 435, 439
hammams 160, 161, 175, 267, 278, 391
Harran 378–9
Hasankeyf 390–1
Hassan, Dr Nawal 169, 182–5
Hatay 339, 340, 341, 345, 349, 356
Hatay Archaeological Museum 347–9
hedonism 9, 10, 41, 106
Hegel, Georg 48, 49
Heikal, Hassan 266
Heilbroner, Robert 11

Hellenes 349, 351, 444
Hellenic mind, the 141, 350, 439
Hellenic religion 350, 439
Hellenism 33, 38, 39, 42, 48, 64, 77, 129, 135, 349, 355, 359, 444
Henry the Navigator 219
Hepper, Morrat 143
Hepper, William 143
Hera 78, 79, 82
Heraclitus 145, 146
Heraclius 193, 212, 213, 215, 217, 232, 292, 347, 413
Herculaneum 31
Herodotus 106, 236, 438
Herophilus 141
hesychia (sweet repose) 151, 187, 190, 201, 202, 380
heterodoxy 191–6, 340
Hezbollah 207
Hidden Dimension, The 12
Hieron II 50
Hijra 211, 213, 216
Hilmi, Abbas 117, 120, 156, 168, 169, 184
Hippocrates 50, 439
Hira, Mount 213
Historic Cairo Restoration Project 184
History of Arab Peoples 103
History of the Crusades 217
History of Western Philosophy 146
Hittites 248, 303, 311, 329, 373, 403, 431
Hollis, Martin 245, 246
Homage to an Ancient Poet 326–7
homo economicus 10, 245, 257, 284, 445
Horeb *see* Sinai, Mount
Hourani, Albert 103
House of Ananias 254
Hovannisian, Richard 402
How to Live a Happy Life 41

Howard-Johnston, James 213, 215
Hoyland, Robert 214
Höyük 340, 341, 344–5
Hudaybiya, Treaty of 213
Hume, David/Humean 22, 182, 197, 245
Hünkâr İskelesi, Treaty of 362
Hurrian songs 330
Hussein, Saddam 2, 4, 49, 51, 243, 255, 256
Hussein, Sharif 65, 208, 225, 239
Hypatia 142

ibn al-Arabi, Muhyiddin 287, 293
ibn al-Haytham, Al-Hassan 171
ibn al-Khattab, Omar 214, 215, 281, 312
Ibn al-Nafis 171, 283
ibn al-Walid, Khalid 213, 214
ibn Ishaq al-Kindi, Abu Yusuf 170, 171, 313, 314
Ibn Tulun mosque 159, 161, 162
IDF (Israeli Defence Force) 207, 226, 285, 286
Idris, King 111, 112
Iğdır 408–12, 413
ijtihad 172
Incarnation, the 197, 199, 200, 201, 210, 441
Independent, The 1
Innocent III, Pope 18–19
innovation 11, 134, 163–5, 230, 241–2, 249, 260, 269, 272, 380
interfaith 222
International Atomic Energy Agency 4
international business 260, 266, 271
International Herald Tribune 35, 66, 205, 437
International Solidarity Movement 285

Iraq
    ancient 58, 60, 236, 301, 302–5, 329
    invasion of 1, 2, 49, 212
    weapons of mass destruction 2, 5, 35, 59, 255
Irenaeus 20, 192, 202, 441
irrational numbers 52, 54, 146
Ishaq, Hunayn ibn 170
Iskenderun 339–40, 341, 342, 344, 360, 404
Islam
    conquest of the Levant 214, 215
    early 166, 232
    mediaeval 158, 160, 184
    pillars of 211, 212
    political 296, 433
    Sunni 170, 254
Islamic Cairo 158–62, 175, 183, 184
Islamic economic principles 100
Islamic golden age 234, 313, 386
Islamic State group 233, 295, 297
Islamic theology 170, 233
Issus, Battle of 33, 254
Ittihadists 281, 366–8

Jayyous 285, 286
Jdeydeh 286, 318, 331
Jebel Akhdar 104, 108, 109, 111
Jerash 220–21
Jibril 212, 232, 412
Jihad 172, 218, 367
John Paul II, Pope 43, 218, 292, 358, 359
Jordan 205–35, 243
Judaism 212, 222, 223, 224, 300, 346
Jupiter Capitolinus 18, 49, 100
Jupiter-Amun 117, 118–21, 122, 126, 129
Justine 82

Justinian, Emperor 167, 188, 189, 264, 305, 320, 381

Kadesh, Treaty of 248
Kairouan 85, 161
Kant, Immanuel/Kantian 6, 47, 55, 203, 245, 246, 402, 442
kanun 173, 312, 313, 428
Kapuscinski, Ryszard 274
Karlowitz, Treaty of 362
Kars 364, 414–19, 421–3
Kars, Treaty of 411, 417
Keenan, Brigid 252
Kemalism 432–5, 437
Ketman 356, 357
Ketuvim, the 223
Keynesian 257, 259
Khaldun, Ibn 134, 169, 287, 384, 388
Khalid Shoman Foundation 236
Khalid, Tarif 222
Kharma, Atania 243
Khomeini, Ayatollah 255
Kierkegaard, Søren 66
Kirkuk 256, 385
kleptocratic autocracy 267, 271
Klimakos, John 271
Knights of Malta, the 15
Knights of Outremer 217, 218, 219
Konya 291, 370, 427–31, 433, 446
Kos 438–9
Krief, Norah 5
Kronecker, Leopold 53
Kurds, the 59, 256, 336, 364, 367, 370, 383–4, 387–8, 392–3

L'Étranger 81
Ladder of Divine Ascent, The 190
Lake Van 398–9
Lampedusa, Giuseppe Tomasi di 79, 80
Landes, David 362

Lane Fox, Robin 350, 352
Lascaris Palace 13
Latakia 327–9, 330, 331
Lateran Palace 18
Lausanne, Treaty of 383, 423
Lawrence, T.E. 208, 236
Lectures on the Philosophy of World History 48
Leger, Robert 219
Leibnitz, Gottfried 46
Leopard, The 79
Leptis Magna 97–100, 102–3
Lewis, C.S. 197
Libanius 106, 351, 352, 355, 384
liberal democracy 260, 270, 272, 442
liberal economic model 241
liberal economy 11
liberalism 32, 253, 270, 271, 366
libertarians 95, 266, 267, 271
Libya 86, 87–101
Life of St Anthony, The 150, 151
Lindos 436, 437
logic 23, 172, 180, 181, 267
logos 144–7, 172, 192, 199–201, 229, 231, 234, 246, 266, 442–4
Lossky, Vladimir 190, 198
Louth, Andrew 190
love 16, 27–28, 30–31
Lucas, Robert 276
Lucretius 40
Luther 40
Luther, Martin 19

Maalouf, Amin 217, 218
Maaloula 281–2
Mackay, James Hector 1, 339–45, 423
Madaba 228–30
Magnesia, Battle of 49, 129, 345
Mahfouz, Naguib 94, 138, 139, 166
Maimonides (Moses ben Maimon) 5, 222–8
Makropoulos Case, The 6

Maloyan, Bishop Ignazio 394
Malthus, Thomas/Malthusianism 163, 15
Mammon 11, 258, 353, 442, 443
Mandelstam, Osip 377
Manzikert, Battle of 194, 216, 406
Mar Musa al-Habashi monastery 292, 293
Maragno, Severino 14
Marcellinus, Ammianus 351
Marcellus 50, 51
Marcuse, Herbert 36
Mareotis, Lake 135, 136, 137
Mari 299–302
marriage 28, 32, 79, 80, 83, 84, 123, 124
Marsala 68
Marxism 67, 230
Masefield, John 177
Masnavi 428–31
materialism 154, 179–82, 198, 199, 232, 290, 357, 433
mathematics 48, 55, 78, 93, 141, 146, 172, 179, 182, 248, 305, 386
   ancient Iraq 304, 305
   applied 171
   Babylonian 304
   calculus 22, 41, 53, 179, 245, 257, 290, 445
   continuous 55
   cultural transmission of 303, 304
   cuneiform 304
   discrete 53, 54
   Greek 21, 44, 46, 136, 141, 142, 303
   Indian 170
   infinity 46, 47
   irrational numbers 52, 54, 146
   logic 180
   mathematical 'fit' 179, 181, 197, 232, 430
   meta-mathematics 55
   method of exhaustion 45
   models 141, 171, 179, 180
   mystical numbers 304
   Newtonian calculus 53
   philosophy of 304
Mathematics in Ancient Iraq 304
Mathuisieulx, Henri Méhier de 87–8
Matrough 116, 117
Mecca 85, 173, 213, 214, 215, 225, 239, 240, 273
Medina, the 84, 86–8, 90, 91, 94, 96
Mehmed V, Sultan 331, 366, 367
Mergellina 26
Merton, Thomas 151
Messina 34
metaphysical infinity 46
'method of exhaustion' 45, 46, 53, 56
Michelangelo 18, 20
Middle East peace process 205, 221
Midyat 386, 387, 388–90
Milan, Edict of 149, 350
military-industrial complex 260
Milosz, Czeslaw 345, 356–8
miracles 22, 26, 195, 197, 233, 444
Miramar 138, 143, 144
Misr 156, 159
modernism 172, 183, 432–5
monasticism 21, 113, 150
Monreale 61–2, 80–81, 85, 189
Monte Pellegrino 60–61
Monuments arméniens du Vaspurakan 400
Monuments of Syria 319
mortality 6, 25, 31, 70, 81, 154, 155, 197, 429, 444
Moscow, Treaty of 417
Mouseion of Alexandria 140
Mu'tazilites/Mu'tazilism 172, 234
Mubarak, Hosni 95, 158, 166, 168

Muhammad, Prophet 113–14, 188, 209, 211–16, 224, 232, 264, 280, 287, 293, 430
Mukhtar, Omar 109, 111
mummification 154, 167
Murti-Bing 356–9
Musamerchi, Ferdinando 37, 38 56
Music of Rumi, The 430
musical compositions 330
Muslim Brotherhood 169, 254, 292, 325
Muslim conquest, the 208, 217, 218, 328, 352, 354
Muslim expansion 212, 219
Mussolini, Benito 61, 109
Mystical Epicureanism 203–4
Mystical Islam 429
mystical numbers 304
mysticism 16, 69, 198, 199, 200, 201, 295, 430
Myth of Sisyphus, The 81

Nabateans 207, 208, 210, 215
Najaf 256
Naples 26, 29–43, 52, 348
narrow banking 89
Nasser (Nasr), Gamal Abdel 137, 143, 168, 184, 240
National Museum (Naples) 33, 34
National Museum (Tripoli) 91, 93
natural selection 12, 179–81
Nausea 357, 361, 396, 398, 405
Navarino, Battle of 168
Nebo, Mount 228, 229
Nemrut Daği 229, 398, 399
Nero, Emperor 19, 24, 107, 441
Neronian persecution 19, 20
Nestorius 191, 192, 386
Nevi'im, the 223
'New Faith' 357, 358
New Testament and the People of God, The 196

Newton, Isaac 45, 46
Nicaea, Council of 149, 191, 201, 346
Nicene Orthodoxy 142, 145
Nineveh 58, 243, 248, 300, 304, 374, 409
Nisibis 385–8
Nitria 147, 150
Noah's Ark 409, 410, 423
North African campaign 109, 111
Nostromo 265, 277
Noto 51, 52
Numismatico Museum 44
Nuweiba 205–7

Occam's Razor 177
Old Babylon 248, 302, 303, 304, 330
old religions 350, 351
Olmert, Ehud 228
Olson, Mancur 275, 276
One-Dimensional Man 36
Oriental Weavers 176–8, 244
Origen/Origenists 142, 150, 192, 199–201, 203
Origins of Christian Mystical Tradition 190
Orontes, River 297, 320–21, 325–6, 328, 330, 343, 346–7, 349
Orthodox Church, The 191
Orthodox Theology 190
Ortygia 38, 39–43
Osborne, John 40
Oslo Accords 222, 226, 228
Ospitale di San Giovanni di Pré 14
Ottoman Armenians 332, 361–73, 393, 415
Ottoman conquest 13, 171, 218
Ottoman Empire 218, 225, 230, 234, 331, 341, 362–8, 370, 385, 400, 411, 415, 421, 424–5, 432, 434

ownership 12, 204, 206

Pachomius 149, 150
pagans 349–53
Pagans and Christians 350
Palais des Papes 5, 7
Palatine Hill 17
Palermo 57–62, 63, 64, 265
Palestine 7, 206, 207, 214, 218, 221, 225, 227, 228
Palmyra 296–7
Pantheon, the 17, 129, 297
Papacy, the 18, 19
Avignon 7
papal authority 25
Pareto's principles 100, 101
Paris 1, 2, 4, 445
Parnassus, Mount 16
Parousia 441–5
particularity 196–8, 209, 232
Pasha, Muhammad Ali 119, 157, 168, 171, 178
Pathfinders 170, 162
Patmos 439–41
Pax Romana 149
Peacocke, Jermey 90
Peloponnesian War 38
perfect love 8, 27–8, 31
Persians 113, 212, 248, 252, 346
Petra 208–11
Pharos 135–8, 159, 161
phenomenology 67, 81
Philo of Alexandria 145
pi (π) 45
Pietà 18
Planck lengths 40, 47, 54, 55
Plato 146, 147, 199, 200, 201, 353
Platonism 142, 146, 198–202, 203, 234, 439
Pliny 29, 107
Plotinus 142, 199, 200
Polybius 49

Pompeii 29–33, 41
Pompey's Pillar 142
Pontifex Maximus 18
Porte, the 362–7, 383, 393, 424
prayer 25–6
pre-Socratic thought 146
'presumption of regularity' 271
Procession of the Mysteries, Trapani 68, 71, 72
production functions 272
productivity 11, 162, 164, 241, 258, 268, 323
Project Hope 285
Ptolemy I 140
Ptolemy II 141
Ptolemy III 141
Putin's kleptocracy 275
Puzzle of Experience 288
Pythagoras 141, 146, 444
Pythagoras's Theorem 146

Qasioun, Mount 286, 287
quantum physics 54, 55
Quinquireme of Nineveh 177
Quneitra 250–52
Qur'an 127, 167, 172, 212–13, 224, 232, 234, 237, 395

Ramesses II 154, 155
Ramesses III 118
Ramtha 236–8
Raphael 18, 147
Raqqa 295, 305, 306, 336
Ras Hillel 105, 108–9
Rashidun caliphate 234
rational choice theory 245, 246
rationalism 39, 42, 43, 48, 147, 197, 198, 231, 232, 351, 353
Ravenna 23, 281, 347
Readings in St John's Gospel 145
Rebel Land 378
Renaissance, the 13, 16, 17, 242, 244

repression 33, 43, 109, 149, 161, 165, 223, 237, 251, 274–5, 277, 313, 333, 349, 356, 370, 381, 393
Republic 199, 304
Resafa 305–6
Resurrection, the 21–3, 25, 43, 192, 197, 202, 294, 350, 444
Rhodes 436–8
Rhône, the 5, 8
Rhossus 342–4
Rifai mosque 161
Rifai, Najim 308, 309, 310
Robson, Eleanor 304
Rodenbeck, Max 155, 156
Rogan, Eugene 369
Roger II, Emperor 57, 58
Roman Catholicism 18, 21
Roman state religion 350
Rome 14–28
    Benedictine College of Sant'Anselmo 14
    catacombs 19
    Church of Santa Maria della Vittoria 15
    Colosseum, the 17
    Palatine Hill 17
    Pantheon, the 17, 129, 297
    Vatican, the 14, 18, 23, 25, 179, 188
    Via Appia Antica 20
Rome on the Euphrates 133
Rommel, Erwin 117
Roquebrune 10–11
Rumi, Jalal ad-Din 312, 427–31
Rummel, Rudolph 371
Runciman, Steve 217
Ruqayya bint al-Husayn mosque 263
Russell, Bertrand 146

Sa'dabad, Treaty of 411
Saba, Julian 188
Sabratha 96
Sadat, Anwar 168, 216
Said, Edward 176
Saidnaya 263–4
Saladin *see* ad-Din, Salah
Salihiye 286–7
Salle Benoit XII 5
Salonica 340, 365, 366
Sammandağ 353–4
Sant' Apollinare 23
Santa Maria della Consolazione 20, 21
Santa Maria Maggiore 18, 23
Sarris, Peter 219
Sartre, Jean Paul 66, 405
Sasanians 149, 213, 215, 217, 248, 299, 300, 315–16, 350, 413
Savage, Martin Leslie 126, 127, 128
Sayings of the Muslim Jesus 222
Sayyida Zeinab 174–5, 178
Sazonov-Sykes-Picot agreement 225
Scarfe Beckett, Katharine 222
Scetis 147, 150–52, 183, 198
schism 7, 24, 167, 191, 193, 194, 233
School of Athens, The 18, 147
Schwarzkopf, General Norman 255
Second Balkan War 366
Second Crusade, the 322
Seeing Islam as Others Saw It 214
Segesta 63–4, 332
Seleucid 49, 223, 300, 302, 303, 346, 347, 351, 355, 385
Seleucus Nicator 299, 320, 328, 375
Seljuk invasion 216, 217
Sen, Amartya 11
Senoussi Order 109, 111, 112, 120
Serapis 102, 142
Sermon on the Mount, The 291
'seven sigma' event 22
Severus, Septimius 98, 99, 128
Sèvres, Treaty of 424

sexual desire 31, 32, 33
Shah of Iran, the 161
shahada 211
Shakir, Bahaeddin 369, 371
Shali 119–21, 123, 125, 131, 133
Sharon, Ariel 222, 227
Shennib, Mahmoud 108, 110–15, 423
Shi'ite 178
Sicily 23, 45, 52, 60–62
Siege of Syracuse 49
Silent Spring 268
Silphium 106, 107
Simeon Stylites the Younger 353, 354
Sinai 186–204
Sinai, Mount (Horeb) 187, 190, 195
Sinan, Mimar 277, 424, 425, 427
Sinclair, T.A. 400
Sinjar 233
Sirat Rasul Allah 213
Siva 426–7
Siwa 117–30, 131–2, 145, 168
Siwi culture 119–21, 123–5, 127, 128
Smith, Adam 242, 263
Social Darwinism 222
Socratic principle 194
Sollum 113–16
Song of Songs 150, 200
Songlines, The 118, 133
Sostratus 136
Souq Sarouja 237, 238–40, 253, 261
St Anthony 149, 150
St Augustine 32, 33, 170
St Basil of Cappadocia 150
St Catherine's monastery 186, 187–204, 293
St John 145, 146, 147
St John of the Ladder 16
St Mark 145, 148, 166, 168
St Nilo, church of 24

St Paul 23, 24, 31, 32, 39, 40, 444
St Peter 18, 20, 24, 39, 189, 382, 413
St Peter's Basilica 14, 18
St Simeon Stylites 315, 316
St Teresa 10, 15–16, 20, 43, 202
St Thomas 22, 43, 202–3, 385
Stark, Freya 129, 133
stone of Sofis 58
Story of Syria, The 335
subjective experience 5, 47, 151, 182, 200, 288, 289, 290, 380
Sublime Porte 168, 218, 234, 239, 407
Suez 186–7, 206
Suez Crisis 138
Sufi 112, 120, 173, 287, 293, 312, 428–32
Sufism 198, 217, 233, 277, 287, 293, 312, 429, 431
Süleyman the Magnificent 361, 432
Sumer 247, 248, 311, 314, 329, 375
Sumerian 223, 247, 269, 300–303, 323, 426
Sunni 70, 170, 178, 233, 254, 281, 337, 356, 440
Surmali 410, 411
Symposium 199
syncretism 127, 129, 136, 145, 196, 233, 293, 299, 315, 351, 353, 355, 362, 444
Syracuse 37–40, 43, 44–6, 48–52, 56
Syria 212–15, 218, 239, 243, 247–8, 254, 296, 297, 310, 336–7, 341
   civil war 334–8
   Golan Heights 207, 226, 242, 247, 250
   Northern 311, 319–38
   Southern 280–91

Takiyya al-Suleymaniyya 277
Tanakh, the 223
Tanzimat reforms 362, 434, 439

Taormina 34–8
Tapwater 92
taqlid 172
Tatvan 396–7
Temple of Athena 39, 50
Temple of Hera 78, 79, 82
Temple, William 145
Tertullian 20
Thaïs 27, 28
Theoria 199, 200
Thessalonica, Edict of 142
Thierry, Jean-Michael 400, 414
Thieves of State 274–7
Thucydides 39, 50
Tigris, River 236, 299, 310, 361, 390, 391, 393, 410
time 36, 37, 256–7, 263, 268
Todd, Olivier 76, 81
Tomar 219
Torah, the 223, 224, 229
Toynbee, Arnold J 368
Trapani 68, 71–4, 75, 82–3
Treatise on Optics 171
Treatment of Armenians in the Ottoman Empire 1914-1916 368
Trinacria 34, 44–62, 382
Trinitarian doctrine 149
Tripoli 86, 87–97, 100–101, 103, 111
Tripolitania 87–101
Triumphal Arch of Oea 87, 88
Tunisia 83–6, 97, 316
Tur Abdin 381–4, 387
Turkmenchay, Treaty of 411

Ugarit 248, 278, 311, 329–31
Ugaritic alphabet 329
Umayyad
    caliphs/caliphate 216, 240, 266, 281, 309, 378, 413
    dynasty 215, 216
    Mosque 240, 243, 253, 261, 278, 281, 283, 287, 312, 394

United Nations (UN) 4, 60, 221, 225, 270, 295, 318, 336, 337
    Arab Human Development Report 229
    Department of Political Affairs 310
    Food and Agriculture Organisation project 163
    Security Council 49, 336
United States 49, 59, 205, 255–6, 270, 275, 371, 416, 434
universal humanism 4, 231, 232, 235, 359, 372, 443
Ur 247, 375
Urartians 373, 374, 396, 399, 403
Urban II, Pope 172
Urfa 374–81
Uruk 130, 247, 301, 324, 325
utilitarian calculus 10, 41
utilitarian theory 9

Valberg, Jerry 287, 288, 380
Valley of the Temples, Agrigento 77, 78
value creation 157, 249
Van 399–405
Vaspurakan 399–401, 405
Vatican, the 14, 18, 23, 25, 179, 188
Venice 14, 242, 269, 309
Ventimiglia 13
Verba Seniorum 151
Veritatis Splendor 358
Versailles, Treaty of 416
Vesuvius, Mount 29, 31–2
Via Appia Antica 19, 20
Villeneuve 8–10
Vita San Antoni 149

Wadi Natrun 16, 138, 147–9, 173
Ware, Kallistos 191
Warnock, Mary 65

Washington Consensus, the 157, 230
weapons of mass destruction 2, 5, 35, 59, 255
Weiss, Julien (Jalal Eddine Weiss) 312–14, 325, 423
Wenham-Prosser, Alan 430
West Bank, the 221–2, 226–8, 285, 286, 349
Western civilisation 236, 377
Weston, Charles 93
Weston, Maureen 93
White, William 262
Williams, Bernard 6
Wisdom of the Desert, The 151
Witnesses to a World Crisis 213

Wright, N.T. 196, 197

Yarmouk, Battle of 194, 214, 237, 281
Yathrib (Medina) 212, 213
Younes, Muhammad 156, 157
Young Turk Revolution 365, 366

Zein, Riad 291
Zeno's gadget 249–50
Zeno's paradoxes 46, 47
Zeus 77, 78, 79, 119, 129, 132, 142, 197, 355
Zoroastrianism 212, 299, 300, 352, 429
Zuhab, Treaty of 411

More non-fiction from Envelopebooks

A ROAD TO EXTINCTION | JONATHAN LAWLEY
When Britain colonised the Andamans in 1857, the welfare of its African pygmy inhabitants was of no concern. Nine tribes died out. Dr Lawley now assesses survival prospects for the three remaining tribes and weighs up the legacy of his grandfather, who ran the colony in the early 1900s.

ARTIST SPY PRISONER | GEORGE TOMAZIU
Artist George Tomaziu was imprisoned and tortured for monitoring Nazi troop movements through Bucharest during the Second World War but imagined that his heroism would be recognised if Romania ever became free. He was terribly mistaken. Three years after the war ended he was imprisoned again—this time for thirteen years.

POSTMARK AFRICA | MICHAEL HOLMAN
Made an Amnesty Prisoner of Conscience while he was under house arrest as a student in Rhodesia, the author went on to document Africa's emergence from colonialism as Africa Editor of the Financial Times. This book is a must-read introduction to Africa's dreams of independence.

WHY MY WIFE HAD TO DIE | BRIAN VERITY
There is no known cure for Huntington's disease, a wasting condition that sufferers acquire from a parent. In this painful account, the author vents his rage at society, lawmakers, health services and the Church for not grasping the need, as he sees it, to legalise compulsory sterilisation and assisted dying.

THE WEST AND THE REST | IAN ROSS
Having worked in the oil and tobacco industries, Ian Ross argues that trade is objectively more creative than democracy in bridging cultural divisions. Where diplomats are necessarily held back by caution and principle, business executives are incentivised to be forward-looking, adaptable, unprejudiced and trusting. An eye-opener.

More non-fiction from EnvelopeBooks

FROM BEDALES TO THE BOCHE | ROBERT BEST
Bedales, the progressive boarding school founded by J.H. Badley in 1893, instilled values that sustained many of its pupils for the rest of their lives. Robert Best recalls its influence on him as an enthusiastic army recruit in 1914 and, from 1916, in the Royal Flying Corps.

WEMBLEY SPEAKS: A YEAR IN THE LIFE OF A LONDON SUBURB
How do people talk to each other, react to each other, give and ask for advice, conciliate, commiserate and laugh? In a modern reconstruction of Mayhew's landmark 19th-century social study, EnvelopeBooks turns to the *Nextdoor* social networking app to observe a community engaging with itself on day-to-day issues. A priceless archive.

A QUESTION OF PATERNITY | DAVID TERESHCHUK
TV reporter David Tereshchuk has traveled the world questioning the perpetrators of injustice and their victims, but could never prise one answer from his own mother: who his father was. Her evasion set him off on a life of insecurity and alcoholism. And a quest.

THE MARTYRDOM OF AHMAD SHAWKAT | MICHAEL GOLDFARB
When Gulf War II broke out in 2003, Ahmad Shawkat became guide and translator to NPR-reporter Michael Goldfarb. After the fall of Saddam, Ahmad set up a cultural magazine, published eleven issues and was assassinated for publicly decrying Islamic terror. This is his story. A TLS Book of the Year.

Fiction from EnvelopeBooks

THE GREEN MAN | DAN JONES
After humiliating a fellow inquisitor at a trumped-up witch trial in Northern Italy, Brother Jacobus of Vienna is intrigued by rumours of strange events in Northern England. In defiance of the cardinals in Avignon, Jacobus travels to Berwick where he finds a land in disarray, beset by Scottish raiders, eccentric Franciscan friars and talk of demons in the woods. Can he solve the mystery and keep his faith and reason intact?

MRS WOODBINE'S PREJUDICES | MICHAEL LADNER
Prof. Arthur Lash, born Artur Lasch in pre-war Austria, takes his American wife and their three sons back to Vienna, in 1960, to see how well his father is rebuilding the life that was interrupted by Nazi Germany's annexation of Austria in 1938. For Arthur, the journey helps him re-establish his links with the city he was brought up in; for the rest of his family, other emotions are awoken—all watched over by Mrs. Woodbine, the needy, disregarded but loyal family nanny.

BELLE NASH AND THE BATH SOUFFLÉ | WILLIAM KEELING ESQ.
In the first volume of The Gay Street Chronicles, bachelor Belle Nash attempts to navigate bigotry and corruption in 1830s Bath without compromising his boyfriend, the nephew of Immanuel Kant, or his best friend, the widow of Bath's greatest lawyer. Intrigue and whimsy overflow after—horror!—a soufflé fails to rise.

THE TRAIN HOUSE ON LOBENGULA STREET | FATIMA KARA
An anguished, folksy and life-affirming novel, set within the Indian community in Bulawayo, Rhodesia, from the 1940s to the 1960s, about the capacity of women to gain the same advantages as men in the modern world while remaining faithful to traditional Muslim values. Affectionate and passionate.

More fiction from EnvelopeBooks

A SIN OF OMISSION | MARGUERITE POLAND
An emotionally intense novel, set in 1870s South Africa at a time of rising anti-colonial resistance. The book examines the tragedy of a promising black preacher, hand-picked for training in England as a missionary, only to be neglected by the Church he loves. Winner of the 2021 *Sunday Times* CNA 'Book of the Year' Award in South Africa.

MUSTARD SEED ITINERARY | ROBERT MULLEN
When Po Cheng falls into a dream, he finds himself on the road to the imperial Chinese capital. Once there he rises to the heights of the civil service before discovering that in addition to the ladders that helped him ascend, there are snakes facilitating his fall. Carrollian satire at its best.

FRANCES CREIGHTON: FOUND AND LOST | KIRBY PORTER
Love demands trust, but trust is a lot to ask for a victim of abuse. Having been bullied in Belfast as a boy, at his school and at his church, Michael Roberts suppresses his childhood pains until the death of a girlfriend years later forces him to revisit lost memories.

BELLE NASH AND THE BATH CIRCUS | WILLIAM KEELING ESQ.
In Volume Two of *The Gay Street Chronicles*, bachelor Belle Nash returns to Regency Bath from Grenada, inspired by a new love that leads him into various pretences that may compromise the ambitions of black circus impresario Pablo Fanque.

LAGOS, LIFE AND SEXUAL DISTRACTION | TUNDE OSOSANYA
Twelve short stories, mostly focused on the struggle to survive in Lagos, Nigeria's commercial capital, illustrate the tensions that exist between the generations, between the sexes and between the country's different social classes and ethnicities.

More from Envelopebooks

THE ATTRACTION OF CUBA | CHRIS HILTON
Chris Hilton went to Cuba to escape the boredom of everyday life and to make money, only to be entranced by the beauty of the country and of Yamilia, a street girl who brought him love and laughter but who could not help him from falling into an inevitable downward spiral.

PRINCESS BRAINY | STEPHEN GAMES
Raine couldn't help being hated for being clever, but it didn't help that her mother was modern and made her father ban the fairies. So what was she meant to do when disaster came to Rainland and the rivers dried up? Accept her fate or get sacrificed to the revolution?

MY MODERN MOVEMENT | ROBERT BEST
London's Festival of Britain in 1951 marked the belief that Modern design was visually, morally and commercially superior. Robert Best, the UK's leading lighting manufacturer, thinks the dice were loaded. This is his memoir.

THE HOPEFUL TRAVELLER | JANINA DAVID
A collection of short stories about—and told by—single women who have put the past behind them but are still looking for their anchor in the present. It includes bitter-sweet accounts of the freedoms of postwar life, of foreign travel, of the rekindling of old friendships and of the search for new ones.

A GIRL'S OWN WAR | K.J. KELLY
Flt. Lieut. Oliver Carmichael and Baron Julius von Stulpnagel had been living together in Berlin, trying to sell forged paintings. Why are they now in run-down Ballingore, in wartime neutral Ireland in 1940, and how will ex-convent-girl Mary Collins and her devoted red-headed sidekick Niamh Slattery play into their hands? Hilarious Irish farce.

www.ingramcontent.com/pod-product-compliance
Lightning Source LLC
Chambersburg PA
CBHW020348080526
44584CB00014B/932